THE HUMAN
RESOURCES
MANAGEMENT
HANDBOOK

THE HUMAN
RESOURCES
MANAGEMENT
HANDBOOK

Principles and Practice of Employee
Assistance Programs

Edited by

Samuel H. Klarreich
James L. Francek
C. Eugene Moore

PRAEGER

PRAEGER SPECIAL STUDIES • PRAEGER SCIENTIFIC

New York • Philadelphia • Eastbourne, UK
Toronto • Hong Kong • Tokyo • Sydney

Library of Congress Cataloging in Publication Data
Main entry under title:

The human resources management handbook.

    Bibliography: p.
    Includes indexes.
    1. Employee assistance programs—United States—
Addresses, essays, lectures. 2. Employee assistance
programs—Canada—Addresses, essays, lectures.
I. Klarreich, Samuel H. II. Francek, James L.
III. Moore, C. Eugene.
HF5549.5.E42H85   1984   658.3'82   84-13447
ISBN 0-03-070676-9

Published in 1985 by Praeger Publishers
CBS Educational and Professional Publishing
a Division of CBS, Inc.
521 Fifth Avenue, New York, NY 10175 USA

© 1985 by Praeger Publishers

ISBN 0-03-070676-9

56789 052 98765432

Printed in the United States of America
on acid-free paper

Contents

Foreword: Historical Perspective of EAPs   ix
     Lewis F. Presnall

1   Introduction: Toward a Systems Approach to EAPs   1
     James L. Francek, Samuel H. Klarreich, and
     C. Eugene Moore

Section I Introduction: Policy, Procedures, and Marketing   **5**

2   The Rationale and Critical Issues of EAP Development   7
     Otto F. Jones

3   Policy and Procedures: The Essential Elements in an EAP   13
     David A. Wright

4   Marketing an EAP for Success   24
     Thomas D. Francek

5   Strategies of Implementing an EAP   31
     John B. Maynard and Jennifer L. Farmer

Section II   EAP Models   **43**

6   Variations in EAP Design   45
     John C. Erfurt and Andrea Foote

7   EAP Service Center Model   58
     Susan K. Isenberg

8   Assessment/Referral   69
     Sandra Turner

9   Assessment/Treatment Model   80
     Samuel H. Klarreich

10   Union-Based Programs   95
     Madeleine L. Tramm

11   Peer Referral: A Programmatic and Administrative Review   102
     Daniel J. Molloy

Section III   A Coordinated Approach: Roles within an EAP   **111**

12 Occupational Physician–Role in an EAP   115
C. Eugene Moore

13 Contemporary Occupational Psychiatry   129
Alan McLean, William Ellis, Ian Lipsitch, and Leonard Moss

14 The Role of the Occupational Social Worker in EAPs   144
James L. Francek

15 Occupational Clinical Psychologist   155
James J. Manuso

16 The Occupational Health Nurse Role in EAPs   163
Laurel Burns

17 Management's Role in EAPs   171
James T. Wrich

Section IV   Training Issues in an EAP   **181**

18 EAP Training to Integrate Performance Appraisal,
Evaluation Systems, and Problem-Solving Skills   183
Mark Cohen

19 Training Referral Agents for EAPs: Knowledge, Skills, and
Attitudes   189
Sherri R. Torjman

Section V   Research and Evaluation Methods and Issues   **201**
within an EAP

20 Modes and Levels of Data Management Affecting the EAP
Practitioner   203
Paul M. Roman and Terry C. Blum

21 Can Change Be Documented?: Measuring the Impact
of EAPs   222
Bradley Googins

22 An Exploration of the Ability of Broad-Based EAPs to
Generate Alcohol-Related Referrals   232
Martin Shain

23 Evaluation of EAP Programming   243
William G. Durkin

24 Monitoring the Development and Operation of an EAP   260
Edward J. Larkin, Patricia A. French, and Kim Ankers

Section VI   Preventive Approaches in an EAP   **271**

25 Integrating EAPs with Health Education Efforts   275
Jean B. Case

26 Executives, Families, and the Trauma of Relocation   281
Lockie J. McGehee

27 Toward Coordination of Employee Health Promotion and
Assistance Programs   291
Martin Shain and Bernard Boyle

28 Stress: An Intrapersonal Approach   304
Samuel H. Klarreich

29 Educating Employees in the Area of Chemical Dependency   319
Janis L. Levine

30 A Rational-Emotive Approach to Acceptance and its
Relationship to EAPs   325
Albert Ellis

Section VII   Critical Issues Relevant to an EAP   **331**

31 Social Policy Issues and EAPs   335
D. Wayne Corneil

32 Ethical Questions Concerning an EAP: Who Is the Client?
(Company or Individual?)   342
Katharine H. Briar and Michele Vinet

33 TOPEX Study: "Hitting Bottom in High Places"   360
Charles E. Shirley

34 Alcoholism as a Major Focus of EAPs   370
William R. Byers and John C. Quinn

35 EAPs: An Opportunity for Improving Mental Health
Services 381
Jack Santa-Barbara

36 EAPs: Barriers to Effectiveness 393
A. J. Riediger

37 Quality of Work Life Programs and EAPs: The Reorganization
of the Workplace 409
Louis A. Ferman

Postscript 418
The Future of EAPs and New Directions
James L. Francek, Samuel H. Klarreich, and
C. Eugene Moore

Index 423

About the Authors 437

Foreword: Historical Perspective of EAPs
Lewis F. Presnall

It is customary to ask an old-timer to write the foreword for a new book. The request is especially appropriate when the work is an edited volume written by several authors.

In that case, the foreword can add historical perspective to the more specific topics which follow. It may also serve as the glue which helps to join the diverse shapes of the authors' views into a united whole.

At the start, a whole picture viewpoint is essential. "Employee assistance" is a phrase now used to describe a unified approach to intervention and assistance for a wide variety of related human problems in the workplace.

Historically understood, this method is a whole person type of approach. It usually deals primarily, but not exclusively, with alcoholism, emotional disturbances, familial or marital crises, drug dependencies, work stress, and other miscellaneous problems affecting work performance.

However, it does not take remedial and therapeutic action merely on a one-to-one basis. The personal warmth, the confidentiality of information, and the concerned follow-up on the needs of recovering persons are integral parts of a responsibly operated assistance program. But, there is also a deep recognition that human health maintenance is intimately related to everything else that people experience.

For instance, industry, labor unions, and government have all begun to recognize the employee assistance program (EAP) as one method of loss reduction. Also, in this time of increasing work production costs, it is a method upon which they can all agree, and can all take action.

Even as a neophyte in the field, I had been impressed with the way in which everything affected everything. In 1954, after only two and one-half years experience in developing a program within an industrial operation, I was asked to give a paper at a state meeting of mining engineers. In putting together some preliminary evaluative data on the program, I chose to title my presentation, "People, Production, and Personnel Counseling."

I could just as appropriately have entitled it "How Labor and Management Work Together On People Problems," or "How To Save People And Money," or "The Health Network: Labor, Management, and Community Services."

Subsequent papers which I gave during the next four years were even broader. For example, as the program evolved, action got into issues, such as: fringe benefits coverage for stigmatized illnesses, hiring policy regarding recovered persons, and how to evolve disciplinary procedures that were both fair and corrective. We became involved with the problems of work stress, job placement and adjustment, personal conflicts on the job, and the effects of family crises upon safety—both on-the-job, and off-the-job.

When one starts to deal with neglected, or poorly understood, health problems, the remedial trail often leads into unexpected complications. One also bumps into exciting opportunities to remedy problems which, at first, appear to be unrelated or insolvable.

These kinds of broadening perceptions have been experienced through the years by all persons who have worked in the employee assistance field with earnestness, intelligence, and curiosity. The obvious effect of everything upon everything is a feature that attracts talented people to employee assistance work. It is the principal reason why I have commented to many students and other persons entering the field that "In this work, you will be constantly frustrated; but very seldom bored."

Occupational communities, whether large or small, are tightly integrated human systems where one can be an observer/participant. The work place is a world where people spend a major part of their time. They can be involved with others. They can also see the connections between their individual actions and the effects upon others in the workplace. In contrast, it is usually difficult to feel we belong to the larger city where we live.

However, at work we become a part of the complex ways in which groups approve and disapprove of behavior, and the means by which human communications occur. So, when a program is developed to meet human health needs, and when that program is designed to cut across all the usual boundaries of occupational groups, it affects everything!

As background, I shall try to answer two questions.

First, what distinguishes employee assistance programs from the related fields of: 1) occupational health, 2) industrial relations, and 3) labor movement counseling services? What is unique about an EAP, as it is commonly called?

Second, from a historical view, what are the persistent and pervasive work place needs which prompt development of employee assistance programs?

Occupational Health

Classically, the field of occupational health has been concerned primarily with: 1) emergency care for industrial accidents, 2) prevention of illness through inoculation, and 3) secondary prevention through physical examinations and health education.

Except in geographically isolated areas where health services are scarce, industrial health staffs have not provided extensive treatment. They have confined themselves to making preliminary diagnoses and giving emergency care when work performance problems have seemed related to some health condition. Referral, as needed, has then been made to employees' private physicians in the community.

Especially during the 1940s to 1950s period, interest began to increase in the behavioral-medical illnesses. Some of the more imaginative occupational physicians recognized that progress had reached a point of diminishing returns with physical health problems. The "new frontier" was in the area of unmet needs, such as: emotional illness, alcoholism, and what used to be called "people crises."

Medical departments, such as those at DuPont, Eastman Kodak Co., Consolidated Edison of N.Y., and some of the companies in the AT&T system, initiated special efforts to deal with alcoholism during the 1940s. Caterpillar Tractor Co. launched a specific medically-directed program in an attempt to deal more effectively with a broad range of behavioral ailments, particularly emotional disturbances and alcoholism-related problems.

During the same period, and earlier, a few companies began to engage full-time or part-time psychiatrists. The objectives were to advise and assist in better prevention and/or referral of what was broadly defined as mental health problems.

In some instances, these efforts have continued to survive and develop. In others, for a variety of reasons, programs failed to identify significant numbers of cases. In general, those which placed heavy emphasis upon therapeutic approaches to alcoholism and alcoholism stigma tended to survive. In time, they broadened to include a wider range of behavioral-medical diagnoses. Programs which were primarily structured along mental health lines were poorly staffed to understand the therapeutic needs and alibi-concealment mechanisms of stigmatized conditions, such as alcoholism or drug dependencies. So, many of these programs died. One of many examples was the early behavioral-medical program at Caterpillar Tractor.

Surviving programs began to exhibit features which departed from the limitations of the classic occupational health functions. The following emphases evolved to mark the later EAP approaches as uniquely different from the usual mode of industrial medicine:

1. The necessity for workplace programs to become more involved in assurance of qualified diagnostic work, initial counseling support, plus careful follow-up and evaluation of community resources use.
2. Special staff orientation and/or administrative assurance that diagnostic and treatment referrals for alcoholism and other chemical dependencies must embrace more than the basic medical mode; and must give special emphasis to workplace confidentiality of personal information.

Industrial Relations

The origin of industrial relations has been often credited to the in-plant studies conducted in the 1930s at the Hawthorne Plant of Western Electric Co. by Harvard University.

However, that is certainly an over-simplification. The findings from the studies did nonetheless publicize the vast reservoir of personal conflicts, discontents, fears, and stresses which lurk close below the surface and adversely affect worker efficiency.

Publication of the information in 1939 stimulated the growth of industrial staff activities regarding workplace relationships.[1]

One of the first remedial steps taken at the Hawthorne Plant was a move to recruit and train a large number of persons as lay counselors. These individuals reported administratively to the head of an expanding industrial relations department.[2] Subsequently, this innovative experiment was also described in detail.[3]

The World War II period, with its industrial population displacement, provided a nurturing soil for an enormous growth of personnel counseling programs. Like most quickly implemented approaches to complex human problems, the movement had a short life. It also left considerable disillusionment, particularly among those who had perhaps expected too much of the programs.

With hindsight, we can see that the movement at that stage had several inherent weaknesses. One of these was the practice of trying to solve the problems solely through the services of in-plant counselors. In most situations, there was little recognition that many personal problems, which surfaced on the job, were caused by deep and chronic ailments. Referral of employees to outside diagnostic and treatment services was usually not considered to be a necessary option.

During the 1940s some prominent companies developed alcoholism programs under the aegis of industrial relations. Like the programs of that decade which were based in medical departments, they relied heavily upon Alcoholics Anonymous in making employee referrals. They also used some community health agencies, primarily for detoxification, or those in-patient facilities that were specifically designed for the treatment of alcoholism.

Examples were North American Aviation in the Los Angeles area, the Allis-Chalmers Manufacturing Company's large Milwaukee operation, and the Great Northern Railway.[4]

However, it was not until the development of two industrial relations-based programs in the 1950s that elements of the integrated community services-management-labor approach began to evolve.[5]

In the first instance, at the Chino Mines Division of Kennecott Corporation, I was engaged in 1952 to develop a broad personnel counseling service covering any and all behavioral-medical problems. Through both self-referral and referrals from management or labor persons, employees and their families had opportunities to secure confidental assistance through the service.

The responses built quite rapidly to a surprisingly large caseload.

About two years later a development occurred which stimulated further innovative advances in program methods. A corporate decision was made to install industrial relations staff departments in all of the company's Western Mining Divisions. During the next two years, this restructuring of personnel functions directly involved changes in fringe benefits administration, absentee records and controls, corrective disciplinary procedures, internal communications systems, and supervisory training approaches.

The changes at Chino Mines Division provided an unusual opportunity to integrate the counseling-referral services with all the personnel relations systems. In effect, a unique laboratory program experience was created. The unprecedented size and problem breadth of the caseload which then occurred demonstrated the value of new methods which have been useful in program development, even to the present time.

The second example of unified program development occurred at the so-called alcoholism program of the New York City Transit Authority. Again, the events were a combination of the accidental impact of personality and organizational events.

The program developer was a person who had long years of experience in the organization and who knew its structure intimately from top to bottom. He had suffered from alcoholism and had made an excellent recovery through a personal contact with AA. After that, he sold management on the idea of giving him the assignment to develop a program of recovery for other employees.

In itself, this was not an unusual development. What was unique were two circumstances that combined to formulate actions which went far beyond alcoholism recovery steps. First, Gilbert Talbot, the program's manager, not only knew the complex structure of the organization, he also knew its key people in both labor and management. Second, after his personal recovery, it became apparent that Gil Talbot possessed a fantastic native talent for working effectively in the areas of organizational politics and objectives.

Consequently, he put together what amounted to a combination of: 1) an alcoholism program, 2) a fringe benefits loss control program for all sick-leave and accident absences, 3) a system of effective referral for non-alcoholism health problems, 4) a set of consistent corrective disciplinary practices, and 5) good labor-management coordination on work performance crisis situations involving all of the above.

Again, as in the Chino Mines experience, new records were achieved on case identification and loss reduction. To most outsiders, and the majority of insiders, the Transit Authority effort was known as an "alcoholism recovery program." But it was much, much more than that!

The "more" was what made it work so well.

During the ensuing two decades the concepts and methods, pioneered largely from these experiences, were refined, adapted, expanded, and applied by various students and practitioners in the field.

Today, when the concepts of employee assistance programs are fully implemented, they do much more than create a healthier work environment. They open excellent avenues for a wholeness approach to human problem solving within work places.

As a craft, industrial relations has received much criticism as being too stereotyped—a kind of mechanical lock-step approach to a mechanistic industrial society. And yet, mere attempts to change the game by changing the name from industrial relations to human relations have seldom improved either the techniques of the craft, nor its underlying concepts. Complex people problems in our society will not be solved either by panaceas nor cute terminology.

As John Naisbitt has pointed out, the new direction called for by the information society is creating innovative human relationships.[6]

We have left the age of industrialism, and the mechanical, clockwork universe of Newtonian physics. We are into the age of information, and a quantum physics universe!

At a time when all solutions need to be tested, the EAP approach to one segment of the work scene has two corrective checks upon its design and performance:

1. How well does it do in case-finding and in case management?
2. Does it show an objective, ascending record of cost savings in tangibly measurable dollars?

Labor Movement Counseling Services

The CIO Community Service Committee was established in the 1950s under the union's President, Walter Reuther, to concern itself with various health and welfare needs of the membership. The Committee's Director, Leo Perlis, pointed out as early as 1955 that both labor and management were interested in counseling for individual workers.[7] That focus from the labor side continued into ensuing years after the merger of the CIO with the AFL.[8]

Special courses for lay counselors were initiated throughout the country by the Community Service staff members. A heavy emphasis came to be placed upon assisting members who had developed alcoholism.

During the 1960s the U.S. Steelworkers also launched their own national campaign to promote joint labor-management alcoholism programs.[9]

Subsequently, as the designation of EAP came into vogue, local and state union organizations participated in various joint program activities with management. In other instances, union groups pursued their own course in furthering counseling and referral programs.

The union movement has generally influenced workplace counseling programs toward concern for their humanitarian benefits. They have also been influential in the growing recognition under the EAP concept that, within unionized shops, the best and most useful approaches are those which involve labor, management, and the community in their respective roles. In other words, participatory democracy is part of the wholeness concept here.

On the other hand, dividing program activity into unilateral segments is like trying to treat human health problems as though illnesses could somehow be divided into segments of physical, mental, emotional, and spiritual malfunction.

Like the individual person, a work community is a single interrelated entity!

Persistent and Pervasive Needs

From a historical view, what are the persistent and pervasive work place needs which prompt development of employee assistance programs?

"Persistent" and "pervasive" are key words here.

If society does not continue to feel that something important is needed over a period of two or more decades, it is unlikely that apathy and customs will be disturbed enough to make basic changes.

Also, if a need is not felt throughout many social levels, and across all areas of a country, a lasting national movement will not occur.

The forces which are thrusting the EAP movement into the mainstream of the occupational communities have been the following persistent and pervasive needs:

1. The need to do more about the neglected, and often stigmatized, behavioral-medical problems in the work place—primarily alcoholism, emotional disturbances, and drug dependencies, in that order of prevalence.
2. The need to *act* upon the growing awareness that, like any social organization, the workplace is *both* a human problem-breeder, and a problem-resolver.

3. The need for greater humanizing actions within the workplace. (With the decline of personal community caring and sharing in urbanized areas, people seek such relationships at work.)
4. The need for new work place patterns, which would actualize the increased awareness that everything is related to everything, i.e., health wholeness, the value of work, the worth of the individual, communication of ideas, sharing of responsibility, and the cost of production.

To the degree that the EAP methods and craft move toward a sophisticated and effective set of tools for meeting the unified needs, *they will survive and grow*!

If EAPs lapse into parochial thinking, or if they are more concerned with survival *of themselves* than with innovatively meeting the *needs of today and tomorrow*, they will become a passing fad!

References

1. Roethlisberger, F.J., and Dickson, W.J., *Management and the Worker*, Harvard University Press, Cambridge, Mass. 1939.
2. Personal conversation with W.B. Cowan, Medical Administrator, Corporate Offices, Western Electric Co., Nov. 8, 1983.
3. Dickson, W.J., and Roethlisberger, F.J., *Counseling in an Organization: A Sequel to the Hawthorne Researches*, Harvard University Press, Boston, 1966.
4. Presnall, L.F., *Occupational Counseling and Referral Systems*, Utah Alcoholism Foundation, Salt Lake City, 1981, pp. 6, 7, 83.
5. Ibid, pp. 83, 91–95.
6. Naisbitt, John, *Megatrends*, Warner Books, Inc., New York, 1982.
7. "Saving Men and Money," from *Proceedings of the 4th Alcoholism-In-Industry Conference,* Chicago Comm. on Alco., Mar. 11, 1958.
8. Presnall, L.F., *Occupational Counseling and Referral Systems*, Utah Alcoholism Foundation, Salt Lake City, 1981, pp. 9–10.
9. Ibid, pp. 148–149.

1

Introduction:
Toward a Systems Approach to EAPs

James L. Francek
Samuel H. Klarreich
C. Eugene Moore

When we sat down to discuss the purpose of this book, we realized that the field of employee assistance programming had come a long way over the last decade. It was clear that, while a number of fine works had been put together, there was no one book that could be used as a resource text to cover the multiple disciplines working in this field. With that in mind, we have attempted to draw together some eminent practioners and scholars to discuss various aspects of EAP issues. We do not see this work as the last statement on the topic, but rather a discussion of the state of the art at this time.

The development of EAPs over the last ten to fifteen years holds out both opportunity and promise for many workplaces in North America. This movement was initially formulated as an effort to assist employees in the resolution of job performance or behavior problems related to alcohol misuse or alcoholism. As companies became more aware of the multiple applications of this approach, programs expanded from the initial single focus of alcohol problems to eventually encompassing a broad range of personal situations which included alcohol or drug misuse, emotional, familial, marital, and other crises situations.

The introduction of this approach to workplace problems has drawn staff from a broad range of training and disciplines. This has allowed for a rich diversity of approaches to emerge. The editors of this book feel that it is time that a dialogue between these multiple actors be documented. It is with this in mind that we present this collection of thoughts for your perusal.

It is hoped that this collaborative effort will move the field towards a clearer definition of a system's approach to EAP.

Often programs were initiated by a dedicated individual working alone attempting to assist troubled persons in the workplace. These efforts were, for the most part, separate from the normal administrative procedures of the workplace and were often perceived as "external to the work system." As programs have matured, it has become clear to many observers that if an EAP is to remain vibrant and effective it needs to become integrated into the workplace and not perceived simply as an extra appendage.

The focal point of this book is to begin the process of defining a system's approach to EAP. The American Heritage Dictionary defines a *system* as "a group of interacting, interrelated, and interdependent elements forming or regarded as forming a collective entity." Prior to establishing an EAP, companies or unions have developed systems within systems. These systems are living organisms that interface, touch, and affect both individuals and other systems. In doing a "systems" analysis a comprehensive review will include:

- how power is distributed,
- how relationships are structured,
- how roles are defined, and
- how communication is used to convey messages.[1]

Much of the conceptual framework for developing a systems approach flows from the family system's theory developed in the 1970s. In taking the time to formalize this approach for EAPs, it is hoped that the reader will discover the importance of understanding the ecology of the social network within the workplace. To study the relationships between the organism (EAP) and its environment (the work system) is to come to know its ecology.

The work system as we know it in North America is undergoing unprecedented levels of change. Power is being redistributed, the structure of work relationships are shifting dramatically, roles are being redefined, and communication patterns are in total revolution. If EAPs are to survive as vital entities, their stewards need to gather the broadest range of facts and theory and work them towards a disciplined conceptual framework of operation.

In this book, we asked some of the most experienced EAP practitioners and thinkers to write "indepth" on specific topics relevant to their work. Even as this work goes to press, we are aware of the changing nature of our work and the constant need to integrate. We have organized this book using a systems approach, see Figure 1.

It is our hope that these discussions will give both light and heat to our field of endeavor. In addition to our bias about the critical need for a "systems approach" to developing EAPs, we feel it is necessary to identify our other major biases so that the reader of this work will recognize them as they surface.

EAP SYSTEMS

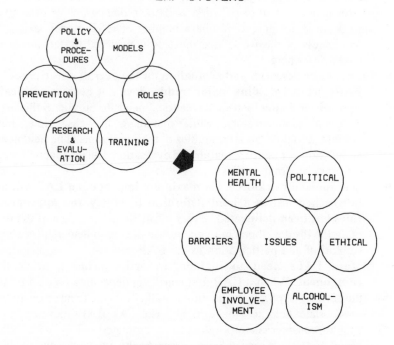

FIGURE 1. EAP Systems.

- **No single discipline, profession, or life experience in itself prepares one to do the comprehensive job of EAP.** The EAP field has developed out of a need to address a number of health matters, behaviors, and situations that exist within the workplace. No matter what our training or life experience has been, we can learn a great deal from cross fertilization with other disciplines and others' experiences.

- **A keystone to the evolution and development of the EAP movement is the recognition of alcoholism as a major health problem that affects the health and productivity of employees.** The occupational alcoholism movement was founded on the premise that individuals suffering from this health problem could be motivated to seek treatment by using a combination of "accountability for job performance" and "an offer of professional help." A comprehensive EAP has as one of its essential elements the evaluation for alcoholism in its defined mission.

- **No one model of program development fits all work situations**. The size, location, nature of work, and socio-demographics of a given work force are unique. While a number of EAP models exist, the uniqueness of the workplace must be considered in deciding what model fits where.
- **Efforts to do research and evaluation on the overall effectiveness of EAPs, while revealing major trends, have not been scientifically rigorous and conclusive**. A great deal needs to be said in this area. Program administrators, while managing the case flow, have attempted to do evaluative studies of their programs. The field needs an infusion of quality research and evaluation designs that will allow for cross program studies.
- **In a unionized workforce, the maximum impact of an EAP will not be reached unless a joint definition of policy and appropriate roles has been delineated**. Every effort should be taken at the time of an EAP's development to encourage the union leadership's active support of and participation in the EAP.
- **Mature EAPs need to include an active primary preventive component**. When a EAP first starts up, depending on its size and the severity of problems identified, staff efforts are focused on getting appropriate help for the critical cases. As EAPs develop, they should consider incorporating a coordinated effort with allied professionals, e.g., physicians, nurses, health educators, and the like. We argue for a primary prevention module that includes a focus on health education and wellness.
- **EAP staff should function at the level of their training and expertise**. Professionals function within defined areas of expertise. Individuals who have not studied and worked with alcoholism should not present themselves as experts in that area. Likewise, those whom have not acquired a suitable level of training in mental health or other disciplines should not present themselves as competent in handling cases with these problems.

These assumptions represent but a few of our more salient biases. As you read our work you may be able to pick out a few more. We encourage you to dig into each chapter with vigor. We have devoted considerable effort to the task of identifying some of the best practitioners and thinkers in the field. We hope you enjoy their work.

Reference

1. Thorman, George. *Helping Troubled Families*, Aldine Publishing Co., N.Y., 1982, p. 174.

SECTION I

Introduction:
Policy, Procedures, and Marketing

Without question, the cornerstones of EAP development include those to be laid in these three areas of policy, procedures, and marketing. "Policy" is a word which brings trepidation to some who would prefer to proceed with more simple approvals for their new EAP, such as a letter of agreement from the chief executive officer or the head of personnel. The simple use of the term *guidelines* may allow matters to proceed, while waiting approval of "policy" might jeopardize or slow the process. "Procedures" are the "what you see" workings of an EAP. "Marketing" is a talent and a necessity; where it is lacking, the EAP staff will need to acquire these skills, perhaps even by drawing from the talents of others, e.g., external consultants or people within the organization.

Jones, in his chapter, discusses in more detail the critical issues of EAP development, including a review of the essential features of internal, external, and school-based programs. He raises concerns about the philosophy of some institutions, whose primary goals are to fill beds, of procuring educational funds by including EAP materials in their curricula, or increasing treatment-generated income from their own EAP diagnostic/referral arm.

Policy and procedure essentials for the well-thought-out EAP are outlined in the chapter by Wright, in which he looks at philosophy, objectives, confidentiality, reporting mechanisms, roles, and responsibilities. The Family Service Association's (FSA) detailed approach is also reflected in the careful delineation of the various types of referrals, and the need to attend to data collection.

In their discussion of implementation strategies, Farmer and Maynard show that ingenuity can mix with the more tried and well-proven methods to demonstrate that "we are here." Implementation procedures begin with finding the key people to whom the EAP must talk and with whom they must seek support at early, middle, and later mature stages of the program. "Fighting fires" is one way to gain exposure where more traditional organization chart scaling has proved unrewarding or rather slow. Supervisor training is one of these indispensable methods by which the principles of the EAP are "learned" by those best in a position to bring help to employees needing it most.

Francek, in his chapter on marketing the EAP, refines the steps and procedures that will help the EAP consultant to survey the needs of the prospective company client, to reach the decision makers, and to tailor the package to match the proper EAP with a client who will make best use of it. Given the many varieties of approaches available, even the EAP newly in operation may have trouble finding the best combination of program features to match both the company's needs and the staff person's personality and particular skills. The outside consultant with marketing skills can help. Once established, the EAP's marketing targets are the employee public and the supervising managers. Here again the consultant to an EAP can be of great help in bringing the lessons of past experience to bear.

2

The Rationale and Critical Issues of EAP Development

Otto F. Jones

The rationale for developing an EAP is diverse, ranging from the need to create a job position for a relative or friend (qualified or not), to well planned programs based upon "needs assessments," inquiry, research, and study.

Most companies sincerely care for the health and welfare of their employees and dependents. The primary reasons are humanitarian, but to some it also makes good business sense to invest in the development of human resources. "People maintenance" contributes to maximizing human potential and resources. Thus, monetary return on investment can be realized. Work attendance is improved, hospital, medical surgical costs are reduced, as are other expensive benefits that are overutilized.

Sometimes recent experiences within an organization will provoke a "decision maker" to establish an EAP. A suicide or the termination of a valuable employee because of alcoholism or drug abuse can precipitate the EAP, or dissatisfaction in production results can also motivate change and contribute to the creation of an EAP.

It is possible that a company or corporate president, CEO, board chairperson, or even the spouse of any of these people, has learned of an EAP and because of their interest and concern they may influence the "powers that be" to institute a program.

Most people in the business of providing EAP services are talented, appropriately trained, well intentioned, and ethical, but there are some who will use the EAP as a means to fill their hospital beds, fill their clinical hours, or misuse the service to meet their own needs. These people and organizations are in conflict of interest and hurt the EAP movement drastically. Their intent seems to be to create a "patient-flow" to fill their clinics and/or hospitals.

The intent of an EAP should be defined clearly to maintain proper focus. Some public agencies use benevolent and charitable funds to unfairly compete with the private sector in providing services. Many see EAPs as a revenue source that can financially save their ailing institution.

Sometimes graduate schools "propose" EAPs to companies for financial benefit. Sometimes these schools create programs without adequate supervision but justify the program because they have a "good" field placement for their students. The EAP becomes questionable in its effectiveness because the program is available only a limited number of hours per week during the school year and, in addition, has a yearly turnover in counselors. The client's needs then become secondary to the questionable primary needs of the school.

The best way for a school to give students a good field experience in this area is to place them within already established programs. If there are none, they should establish demonstration programs for two to three years with a provision for coverage through the summer and accessibility to the program 24-hours per day, seven days per week. This would then create full-time job opportunities for professionals rather than filling these positions with students within organizations that do not wish to fully invest in a permanent program.

Potentially there are 93 million working Americans. At best, fewer than 10 million now have accessibility to a program. With a target population in excess of 90 million American employees there continues to be a need to implement well conceived, and efficiently run programs.

Fortunately most programs are effective. The few that are "self-serving", in conflict of interest, or manipulating in some fashion, usually do not last long. Unfortunately, these failures can retard the opportunity to run a "good" EAP by as much as a generation.

Program Setting: Alcohol and/or Drug Abuse Only

Rationale for a program influences the "type" of program a company decides to use. Historically, many EAPs began with a concern for the employees who had problems with alcohol or drugs. These programs are often administered by "recovering" people, but unless they carry necessary credentials they have a liability risk that threatens the programs. This statement does not mean that "recovering" persons are not good therapists and/or counselors; many are. This statement is intended to underscore the need for insurable counselors who can reduce the liability of an organization.

Hospitals and Clinics

The motivation for hospitals and out-patient psychotherapy clinics to have an EAP is questionable. The most apparent reason is to have opportunity to "channel" potential patients into their treatment facilities, where third party payments would pick up the fee in part or in full for services rendered. If this does in fact happen there is an obvious conflict of interest involved. In some cases these programs are virtually "given away." The remuneration comes through the treatment costs.

Hospitals must have approximately 80% bed occupancy in order to "break even." Sometimes profits are not realized until over 90% of the beds are being used. Survival is contingent upon use. Too frequently people are hospitalized in order to generate revenue rather than to serve a physical need.

Public Agencies

Agencies that receive charitable and/or benevolent funds are in unfair competition with those tax paying organizations that provide the same services. The administrators of some of these agencies feel "threatened" by EAPs; they feel a need to compete and provide similar services. The rationale, by some, for doing this is as follows: Non-profit agencies solicit contributions from business and industry for their approved projects. They erroneously think that if an organization has an EAP they will not need the non-profit organizations. This thinking exposes an ignorance that frankly is surprising. EAPs are pre-treatment/intervention services that concentrate on secondary prevention. United Funded agencies are direct service or treatment providers and, therefore, not in competition with EAPs at all. They do often establish "information and referral" programs that are primarily "hotlines" that counsel callers by telephone and that often use nonprofessional or paraprofessional counselors. From my vantage point, this type of program is irresponsible and depreciates the value of a full-service EAP that is professionally administered.

In-House Programs

There are many good in-house programs to be found. If they are staffed by professional clinicians and supported by an organization, so that they are not just "paper" programs, they can be very effective.

Since liability is always an issue, caution must be given to staffing and program service delivery. Close working relationships should be established and maintained with the medical department, if in fact a medical department exists.

Union Programs

Most union-sponsored programs are well founded and supported. Care again must be given to staffing to assure the professional delivery of service.

Unions often have informal communication channels to and with the workers. These "connections" can be very helpful in reaching those troubled employees that are absent or hard to find.

Volunteer committees are also used upon occasion by union-supported programs. These people are used for support and follow-up. Liability must be addressed and the appropriate insurance coverage arranged for. For the most part, with supervision, these volunteers are very effective, especially with a recovering alcoholic or non-alcoholic drug abuser.

Out-of-House Programs

There are many "vendors" in the EAP business. Some are well established, professionally staffed, and very effective. Others are conceived out of desperation for job security. Some are not legally incorporated. Others have no experience, but brandish statistics that are either contrived or stolen.

Depending upon the program, vendors offer a variety of services with optional pricing modes. This approach often enables the program "purchaser" to design a program tailored for their needs.

Confidentiality is more easily achieved through the out-of-house program. Organizations that are sensitive to career jeopardy seem to lean towards out-of-house programs. Government or military establishments are examples, with public organizations and agencies fitting into the same category.

Out-of-house programs are usually less expensive to operate, therefore, return on investment is greater. Higher utilization rates are experienced with out-of-house programs. Return on investment is also commensurate with utilization.

School-Based Programs

Graduate school field placement programs that are not well supervised are seldom successful unless the student is placed within a well established EAP and a professional clinician oversees the students' work.

Program Model

There are several program models to be aware of. They include:

1. Full-service programs.
   a. comprehensive services
   b. employees and dependents
   c. retirees and dependents
   d. disabled and dependents
   e. any kind of problem
   f. unlimited utilization
   g. no cost to utilizer
   h. 24 hours per day, seven days per week
   i. live answering service/pagers
   j. approximately 40% of the utilizers referred out
   k. approximately 30% who do not need extensive care or who are not ready to make a commitment to do anything about their problem
   l. voluntary
   m. confidential
   n. professional clinicians as counselors
   o. follow-up and aftercare
   p. outreach
   q. supervisory training
   r. employee orientation
2. Limited utilization programs.
   a. provide approximately 5–8 free sessions but charge the individual or third party carrier for anything beyond that
   b. this can be a fee-for-service arrangement
3. Information and referral only programs.
   a. no face-to-face counseling
   b. referrals made by telephone
   c. little or no follow-up

Critical Issues

Program intent must reflect the setting and model chosen. Policy must be constructed to accommodate the program desired. Rationale must take philosophy into account. Objectives are usually designed to reduce problems within the workforce and retain employees. It is recognized that no one is immune to problems. Unfortunately, these problems are hardly ever convenient. Individuals do not have internal "switches" that enable them to turn off problems that originated at home as they walk through the corporate door to work. Likewise, problems that are generated at work are often "carried" home. Unattended problems usually get worse and adversely affect job performance. The prognosis for problem resolution is greatly enhanced with early identification and professional attention.

The Policy Statement

Corporations have personalities that reflect the personalities of the decision makers within them. Through experience, these personalities develop philosophies that affect virtually every aspect of their lives. Policy makers create policy that is influenced by their individual philosophies.

The policy making process usually begins with a needs assessment that generates documentation necessary for justifying policy creation and implementation. Many times an awareness of dissatisfaction becomes the motivator for change. Policy can facilitate the action necessary to accomplish the change. Once need is determined, objectives must be established to design the policy so that achievement of the defined "intent" can be attained.

The policy statement should state that the purpose of the EAP is to provide individualized services that will assist the program utilizer in problem resolution. To achieve this goal it is necessary to provide assistance for such human problems as: familial, marital, alcohol, drugs, financial, legal, emotional, etc. The program must provide problem assessment, counseling (either long-term or short, whichever is appropriate) and/or referral. All costs are incurred by the company or insurance coverage whenever possible.

The policy statement must detail who is covered by it. It should contain managerial endorsement and, when the company includes unions, should have their approval as well.

Confidentiality and the voluntary aspects of the program must be outlined and stressed. Program utilization will not jeopardize job position nor professional career.

Sick leave may be used for EAP purposes as it would be for other health or medical reasons.

The EAP policy should not be in conflict with other already existing policies and if it does, the other policies should be changed.

The policy statement should be general enough to allow flexibility. The statement should not be an inhibitor for utilizer involvement and it should outline recording and evaluation methods as well.

It should be emphasized that a well constructed policy enables successful program administration. A poorly conceived and established policy will cause the EAP to flounder and die. Company support and endorsement should be made through this instrument.

3

Policy and Procedures:
The Essential Elements in an EAP
David A. Wright

Introduction

This chapter will deal with one of the most important fundamentals of an EAP, the creation of the program policy. In the past six years the Family Service Association (FSA) of Metropolitan Toronto has implemented EAPs with twelve companies. Prior to the beginning of the counseling program, FSA officials offered consultation to the management and union (or employee representative groups) in the creation of the policy document. The advice and examples shared here were from a combination of that specific consulting experience and other policy documents and issues that had come to the attention of the author.

Regardless of the form a policy document will take, it is becoming increasingly clear that a successful program will require a coherently written policy statement.

Statement of Program Philosophy

Although this statement is typically one of the shortest, it is of major importance and even perhaps the most often quoted section of the document. This section sets out the overall operating premise of the program and also attempts to integrate the apparently disparate notion of corporate self interest and humanitarian ideals.

Typical clauses in this section might include:
- Every employee faces problems in their personal lives and often do not know where to turn.
- This program deals with a wide range of human problems which include marriage, family difficulties, financial or work related prob-

13

lems, and emotional distress or problems caused by alcohol or drug abuse.

- This program is strictly confidential and is offered as a helping hand, not as an attempt to pry or punish.
- The main reason for this program is to help employees and their families enrich the quality of their lives, whether or not they are experiencing job-related problems. It is recognized, however, that in time, a secondary benefit related to the general level of job performance may accrue to the company.

This section not only sets the tone for the rest of the document but presents a macro purpose statement against which all other statements that follow can be tested for consistency.

The Policy Statement

This section flows naturally from the philosophy section, in that it makes the overall intention of the authors more specific. Again, these statements will set a tone but will also serve as an acid test for the consistency of all that follows. Typical policy statements will need to consider the areas illustrated by these samples.

- This service is primarily designed to assist employees and/or members of their immediate families (spouse or dependent children) who are experiencing personal difficulties and who choose to seek out the assistance of the EAP counselor on a voluntary basis.
- No personal information that is given to the counselor in the process of assisting the client will be shared with any other source, either within the company or the general community, without the written consent of the employee in question.
- Employees may gain access to the program through voluntary, suggested, or mandatory referrals, which will be described below.
- While the suggested and mandatory referrals may be used by the management as an option in dealing with an employee whose performance is in question, it is not an automatic step in the disciplinary procedure.
- The policy maintenance, planning, and evaluation of the EAP is the responsibility of a committee made up of representatives from a cross section of company employees. This effectively assures that the program will work only for the purposes of offering assistance to troubled employees at all levels of the organization.
- The professionals contracted to deliver the service on this project will maintain a clearly neutral role in matters affecting the relationship of

the company, its employee representative groups, and the employee.

- The professionals who deliver the direct service on this project will work within the frame of reference of the EAP Design and are primarily accountable to the providing agency or department. These representatives cannot be required by either the steering committee or any member of that committee or the company to act outside the code of ethics of their profession or the policies of their agency.

It is important to show that the accountability line allows for some degree of safe distance between the company and the professional in the operation of the program. With reference to this last point, this safe distance is more easily created when the line of accountability is to a source outside of the organization such as is the case with a social agency or a consulting firm delivering the service. However, with in-house programs it is even more important to show an accountability line to some internal system that is perceived as non-threatening.

The Objectives of the Program

As we proceed from the general to the specific, this section sets out the objectives in a simple and concise manner. "Management by objective" advocates argue that an objective is not useful unless it can be stated and evaluated in terms of numerical measure. Perhaps surprisingly, this is possible in an EAP, but it requires the authors to distill their hopes for the program down to simple and measureable objectives such as the following:

- To implement a confidential counseling service to assist employees and their families with problems that affect their personal and on-the-job functioning.
- To deliver training and orientation sessions to all company employees.
- To develop a public relations package which will describe the program to employees and assist them to use it appropriately.

If these objectives are amended to include such specifics as implementation dates, number of employees to be trained, and dates of completion, etc., it is very easy to evaluate the extent to which they have been achieved.

A more specific set of annual goals for such things as penetration rate, number of addiction cases seen, etc., can be evaluated and revised regularly. Bearing in mind that we are discussing a policy document that must be written with the longer view in mind, the authors would be wise to state the objectives in a general manner and perhaps leave the specific time-limited statements for goals to be set annually and recorded in some other document.

Roles and Responsibilities

This section describes the operation of all the program elements and their relationship to one another. The functions described in this section will vary depending on the particular program, but should at least include descriptions of the following functions: the Steering Committee, the trainer, the counselor, supervisory/management, the union, the occupational health department, and the employee.

Within the confines of the space allowed we will give a brief overview of what is typically found in these descriptions. In some documents these roles are described in crisp and pointed job or role descriptions. A description of the types of issues typically raised follows in a narrative format.

- **The Steering Committee**. The Steering Committee has planned the program in collaboration with the professionals involved and after implementation is responsible for the overall management of the program. The members of the committee are not party to any case material but do offer input at the level of program policy. This committee will receive input from the professional staff, including statistical reports derived from case data and summarized in such a way that confidentiality is maintained. The committee is also responsible for coordinating the training and orientation program in the firm, in collaboration with whatever professional trainers are involved.
- **The Trainer**. The trainer works in collaboration with the counselor and the committee to deliver programs to employees at all levels of the company—programs which are designed to explain how to use the service as either a recipient or a referral agent. This job is usually completed as soon as possible after the program has been implemented. From time to time the trainer will also offer seminars in other areas of interest, such as addiction, stress management, balancing work and family life. etc.
- **The Counselor**. The specific role of the counselor will vary from program to program. In FSA programs, the counselor offers a broad brush treatment service for the total range of psychosocial problems. The counselor is available at an on-site (in the company) and off-site

(at the agency) office. The counselor must be aware of the company structure and relevant policies. Counseling records and files are not company property and are kept securely separate from the day to day operation of the company. Above all, the counselor must be the guardian of confidentiality of information. The counselor will work in collaboration with the trainer in the delivery of most of the training and orientation programs.

- **Supervisors and Managers**. The supervisory/management team of the company is expected to support the program and provide information where necessary to employees as to the appropriate use of the service. The supervisors' and managers' responsibilities include proper documentation of job performance, such that an employee is made aware of problems as they develop. If the employee is not responding to confidential remedial help, the supervisor should consider whether or not the program would be an appropriate way to help. The supervisor's responsibility to maintain performance and to set appropriate standards do not cease if the employee is seeking counseling assistance.

- **The Union**. Union representatives are, as is management, active at both the senior and plant floor level. Senior union officials will help plan and support the program and encourage members to use it. At the plant floor level, the steward will be present, if the employee requests it, for meetings where a member and a supervisor are discussing any kind of job action, including a mandatory or suggested referral. The steward will make every effort to interpret to employees the policies and procedures of the program in a positive manner.

- **The Occupational Health Department**. The company doctor and nurse will relate to this program in a variety of ways, depending on the particular needs and history of the company. If the medical department has a good reputation in the eyes of employees, especially in the area of the maintenance of confidentiality of information, the relationship between the EAP and medical people will evolve in the direction of a multidisciplinary team. In such a case the medical department will operate within the general policies of the program, which involve observing the rules of confidentiality and professional practices regarding the use of consent forms, etc. Where the medical department has a less than satisfactory reputation among company employees, it is advisable to separate the functioning of the EAP from that of the Occupational Health Department.

- **The Employee**. The employee's responsibility is to acquaint himself or herself with the program and to seek help from the program as needed, hopefully before job performance is affected. If the employee uses the program on a management referral basis, the employee is expected to work hard at acceptance of the service and to cooperate with the counselor.

Although there may be other types of roles in programs (for example, some programs have addiction consultants), those listed here cover the majority of policy documents.

Types of Referrals

A description of the various methods that bring employees into contact with the program is perhaps the most important part of the document. The range of options will vary from program to program, with some addiction programs using only a management (mandatory) referral. The EAP model utilized by the FSA has a range of referral mechanisms that runs from self referrals to various types of mandatory referrals. Whichever referral structure a program uses, it must be thoroughly thought out and written down before the program begins. It should be, as well, explained thoroughly to management, union, and the employees of the company. Even when this thorough planning and training has been accomplished, it is wise to expect some confusion in this area, especially at the beginning of a program. When this confusion arises the written policy becomes invaluable.

In the FSA model, the referral mechanisms are discussed in the planning phase, with collaboration of management and union. Our service model employs three types of referrals: the voluntary or self referral, the suggested referral, and the mandatory referral. To deal with our organization, the company must adopt the voluntary referral, but we offer the suggested and mandatory referrals as a choice to be decided upon by the committee. Some companies will choose to utilize only the voluntary referral while others will adopt the voluntary and suggested referrals, with the majority choosing to use all three referral mechanisms. For example, companies that use the voluntary and suggested referrals only, may choose at a later date to adopt the mandatory referral.

Understanding the policy issues related to the referral mechanisms is extremely important for the service provider as well as for the employer and union. The method chosen to transmit this information in this article is a complete section from a typical "policy and procedures" document currently in use with one of our major firms. We will then briefly amplify certain other issues that arise.

A) The Voluntary Referral

Voluntary assistance is provided to any employee or his immediate family. Contact can be made directly to the counselor or to any branch office of the FSA. Employees may also request their immediate supervisor or union representative to arrange the appointment with the counselor. No entries are made in the employee's record and the strictest confidence is maintained. The counselor exchanges no confidential information with any source, without the consent of the employee concerned, unless required by law.

B) The Suggested Referral

1.　　If, in the normal administration of discipline, a supervisor has reason to believe that the employee has a personal problem that may be contributing to his poor performance, the supervisor may suggest that the employee arrange for an interview with the employee assistance counselor. In such cases the written record of the discipline interview will note that a suggested referral was made by the supervisor, and a copy will be forwarded to the employee assistance counselor.

2.　　If the employee chooses to use the services of the suggested referral and is prepared to sign a release of information form, this procedure allows for limited information sharing between supervisor and counselor. The information sharing between supervisor and counselor will not include detailed discussion of the employee's personal problems.

The intent of this information sharing is to be of assistance to the supervisor in determining appropriate performance expectations of the employee as he proceeds through the early stages of counseling. During this period it is understood that the supervisor may choose to apply some flexibility to performance expectations, providing he/she is assured that the employee is actively participating in the program.

C) The Mandatory Referral

1.　　The mandatory referral procedure is an option available to management to use during the latter stages of the discipline procedure, typically where there is a documented case for termination.

2.　　When deemed appropriate, the manager may refer an employee facing dismissal or seeking reinstatement following dismissal, to a counselor on a mandatory basis as a condition of continued employment. If the employee rejects the option of mandatory referral, or after accepting the option fails, without good reason, to keep the appointment, the normal discipline procedure will be followed.

3.   The mandatory referral will be fully explained to the employee in question, in a face-to-face meeting with the department manager or his designate. If the employee agrees to participate in the mandatory referral procedure, the department manager will make telephone contact with the employee assistance counselor to arrange the first interview. In addition, the department manager will complete the mandatory referral letter and mandatory referral memo. The employee will bring his copy of the mandatory referral memo to the first interview with the counselor.

4.   In the first mandatory referral interview, the employee will be required to sign the release of information form, which gives the counselor permission to share limited amounts of information related to the following areas:

a) Is the referral of this employee to the counseling program considered appropriate by the counselor?

b) Does the employee plan to participate in an ongoing manner in the program?

c) What time away from work, if any, will be required to facilitate the employee's treatment?

As with the suggested referral, the intent of this information sharing is to offer the company sufficient information to determine appropriate performance expectations of the employee during the early stages of treatment. No detailed personal information or diagnostic statements will be shared with the supervisor or any member of the company.

5.   If the employee in question is not prepared to sign the release of information form, the counselor will inform the employee that he/she is not accepted into the program. The counselor will inform the director of personnel, the department head, and the appropriate union officer of this fact.

6.   Employees will be terminated if their performance does not show improvement within a reasonable period of time, in spite of the assistance provided. Such cases are jointly reviewed by the director of personnel, or his/her representative and the appropriate department official and union officer. The employee's counselor is also responsible for informing the director of personnel, department manager, and the appropriate union officer whether counseling should be terminated before treatment is completed.

7.   When an employee has been accepted into the program, the counselor shall, in all cases of mandatory referral, refer the employee to the company medical officer for examination to determine whether there is a contributing medical problem. This will happen whether or not the mandatory referral is because of an addiction problem.

8.   After the initial interview and medical examination, a decision is made by the counselor as to the appropriate form of treatment. Where an addiction is known or suspected, the case is reviewed with the addiction counselor.

9.   The counselor will have regular meetings, no more than two months apart, with all employees under mandatory referral. Documentation of these meetings, on the FSA case recording system, is to be maintained. The counselor is responsible for obtaining information on employee performance prior to such meetings.

10.   Where there is a contributing medical problem, the counselor shall ensure that the employee in question is receiving regular medical care, and if this is not taking place, may arrange for this through the company medical officer or the employee's family doctor.

11.   The director of personnel may from time to time require the counselor to report in a confidential and general manner on the progress of any or all of the active mandatory cases. The director of personnel may choose to discuss this information in a confidential manner with department managers.

12.   In the case of a mandatorily referred employee, the mandatory referral will form part of the employee's disciplinary record.

A few issues about referral policy deserve emphasis, especially with reference to the mandatory referral, which is the most complex of the three forms. The first point to note is that the policy document needs to show the mandatory referral as an *option* (see C, 1) available to management. If this is not made clear, the management will technically be bound to mandatorily refer all employees in the later stages of discipline. Note also that it is very important to have a well-documented performance file that shows termination as a logical possibility in the immediate future for the candidate in question. Without this, the "or else" element in a mandatory referral is very much blurred. Where such a case is not available, company officials may be on safer ground using the suggested referral.

Reference was made (see C, 3) to a mandatory letter and memo. The mandatory letter serves to briefly and formally inform the employee of the mandatory referral. Sometimes the letter will name the counselor and the date of the first meeting, which will have already been arranged by the company with the counselor. The mandatory referral memo lists in brief, but specific terms, the performance problem that led to this job action. Both the mandatory letter and memo are shared, in confidence, with the appropriate union officials, director of personnel, senior management, and the counselor, as well as with the employee. For the sake of continuity, draft versions of both these documents are to be included as appendices in the policy document.

With reference to the release of information form (see C, 4), use an FSA release document amended to include the specific names and titles of those company and union officials with whom information will be shared. Be very careful to explain the limited nature of the information that will be shared with these officials (see C, 4, a,b,c).

Data Collection

Some form of data collection will be required in every EAP. While these systems may vary dramatically from one program to the next, they must all manage to illustrate program statistics in a manner that protects the confidentiality of individual employee clients.

In many programs the statistical information system is addressed in the policy document. This is wise for several reasons. First, the committee involved in planning the program should devote time before the program has begun to ask themselves what data will be required to monitor and evaluate the program. This not only is a fundamental principal of good planning and management but it also will allow the service provider to begin coherent data collection from the first day of the program.

Secondly, if the data collection system is thoroughly discussed in the policy document it will serve to allay the concerns of anyone who may be anxious about the confidentiality issue. In these programs, included are the complete data collection system in the appendices of the project design.

FSA has a system which, with slight amendments, has served many firms. This system has four major sections requiring two pages of data and is produced quarterly. It shows the previous year's statistics for comparison to the quarter in question and has a year-to-date column, with the result that the fourth quarter report is also the annual report. These reports are available by the middle of the month after the end of each quarter, and the regular committee meetings are often scheduled for a date just after distribution of these reports.

The four major sections of the system involve:

1) **Time Capture**. Where the time expended by the counselor(s) in various activities is compared to the time purchased by the company.
2) **Case Activity**. Which shows cases carried over from the previous period; number of new cases; closed cases; number of interviews, etc.
3) **Demographics Of Cases**. Which shows problem categories of referrals; job category (large populations only); years of service; referral mechanism involved; sex of the client, etc.
4) **Evaluation**. A very simple post-hoc notation by the counselor on a four point scale ranging from very helpful to not helpful.

The question of overall program evaluation is rarely addressed directly in the policy document. Periodically, policy documents will clearly state the resolve of the authors to complete a comprehensive evaluation within a specified period of time. Certainly, setting of moderately specific objectives and the regular collection of program statistics will assist in the evaluation process, which more often is a steering committee function that is carried on separately from the activity of creating a project document.

Summary Comments

This chapter has reviewed the essential elements that should be considered as the minimum requirements for an employee assistance policy statement. Before the document goes to final printing, it should be reviewed by company and union officials who are sufficiently experienced with other company policy documents, in order to be assured that no part of the newly created policy conflicts with existing policy. When issues arise after the program is implemented that may have a bearing on the policy of the program, this document should be consulted. The group of company and union officials who created the document will need to review and revise the policy statement from time to time.

4

Marketing an EAP for Success
Thomas D. Francek

Introduction

Success breeds success. How often we use these words as the basis for our association with admired individuals and/or organizations. A great deal has been written in various textbooks, journals, and periodicals on the subject of "Marketing: the how-to approach." If there was one magical way to "do" marketing there would be no desire or need to write this chapter. In truth, the diversity and complexity of the targeted organizations, coupled with the need for versatility and adaptability on the part of the marketing experts suggests a dynamic interplay that makes simple solutions next to impossible.

The central focus of this chapter is on the integration of traditional marketing techniques with human service skills in a way that brings about the sought after success that in turn breeds more success. The common theme repeated throughout concerns the unique characteristics of the individual doing this work. The marketing plan is the single most important criterion in successfully marketing an effective EAP.

Marketing Plan—Traditional Techniques

In many ways a sound marketing plan for an organization is analogous to an effective therapeutic experience for a person with problems. A *differential assessment* of the targeted organization (differential diagnosis of the problem) sets the stage for a sound plan of intervention. An *intervention plan* identifies clear strategies for achieving the priority goals (treatment plan developed with specific measurable outcomes). An ongoing *monitoring and evaluation* activity allows for timely adjustments that lead to the achievement of stated goals (evaluation of the individual treatment plan). The marketing plan is the systematic tool for achieving the desired successes.

There are at least four distinct components to an effective marketing plan. The first is the *mission*. The mission clearly states the group's or organization's overall purpose. Secondly, *goals* are generated and are usually stated in long range, "ideal" terms. Goals may be either general or specific in nature. Thirdly, *objectives* are specified in measurable terms that outline the practical methods for reaching the goals. Finally, *strategies* are employed in the form of tasks or specific work programs whose end result is the accomplishment of the objectives.

Operationalizing the Marketing Plan

Management techniques that maximize participation by the organization are used to operationalize the marketing plan. Use of broad input leads to consensus and establishes clear priorities and ownership by the management team. Investigating, exploring, and evaluating an organization's *strengths, weaknesses*, the *opportunities* in the marketing place, along with the *threats* and *strategies* (SWOTS analysis) will provide a detailed path for most likely success. Group consensus arrived at through a participative management style produces the motivation, uniformity of direction, and specific designation of responsibility necessary for a workable plan. The key element of this plan is follow-up. Dates are set for quarterly evaluation of the plan. Modifying the strategies is critical if goal attainment is to be a possibility.

Having developed the important elements for establishing a solid marketing plan, one must then consider how these techniques can be used in the implementation and maintenance of EAPs. Clearly, the application of these techniques needs to be discussed from both external and internal perspectives.

External Marketing

External marketing is the process that defines the target population, leads to direct access to the decision makers, and ultimately results in a "closing of the sale" or contract. This activity occurs before an EAP is established within a workplace.

Target Population

The analysis of the target population using traditional marketing techniques often surfaces many opportunities. Organizations differ in dynamics and personality, just as consultants differ. For example, small organizations are more informal in structure and composition, while large organizations are usually committed to a more formal organizational hierarchy that presents different and sometimes difficult hurdles to jump. Large organizations may often need many meetings to establish a position with the decision makers. It may take up to 18 months to convince the management of a multi-layered organization to establish an EAP, while small organizations may move to have a program in a matter of days. In addition to the issues of large vs. small companies, a comprehensive plan must also consider its approach based upon the type of industry, i.e., manufacturing, service, etc., and whether the organization is an "open shop" or unionized. Each variable requires different doors to be opened before one can proceed.

Decision Makers

The strategy for gaining access to the decision makers of an organization is critical in the achievement of the consultant's goal of implementing an EAP. Access to the decision makers allows for the development of the needed support that results in establishing an EAP. The consultant positions himself/herself using several widely accepted strategies, such as being active in community action groups, becoming a leader in local professional associations, and providing speaking engagements on several topics, so that the decision makers perceive the consultant as someone who whom they would want their organization associated. The professional consultant must enjoy a reputation for credibility, ethics, and competency in the eyes of the decision makers.

Opening, qualifying, presenting, demonstrating, negotiating, and closing are all components of the selling process. In successful EAP development, the professional consultant will focus his/her attention on specific details in each of the above-mentioned parameters. The selling process requires a systematic approach to successfully conclude the "sale." The most neglected part of this process is "closing the sale."

Closing the Sale

Once the interest has been created, decision makers usually choose to have a program based on one of three motivations of the organization: economic, humanitarian, or pragmatic. It is important for the consultant to "read" the "players" in the formal meetings, so that the primary motivation of that particular organization can be identified and addressed in the formal proposal. Timing becomes the most critical factor in successful consultation. A great deal of time and energy will be invested in developing the relationships necessary to achieve program implementation. It is quite easy for a consultant to proceed with too much haste and, in the process, "blow" the whole deal. The bottom line in all contracts is that the employer organization will be the ultimate source of financial support. It is important that they "own" the decision to implement an EAP. Some guidelines to "closing the deal" are:

- Expect the unexpected
- Expect resistance
- Anticipate the objections
- Know the market
- Recall earlier meetings
- Be knowledgeable about the organization's history, structure, and procedures
- Understand human nature and the basic reluctance to buy
- Be prepared to offer alternatives to the provision of a full contract. Any part of a contract offers a foot in the door
- Be professional

After scrutinizing and evaluating the plan carefully, the consultant reaches one of the final steps in all marketing activities—that of establishing the cost of the program. What are these services going to cost? Will the market or economy support the cost? These are just some of the considerations for arriving at the price for the services being proposed. The bottom line in a successful program sale is to establish that delicate balance between what the program will cost and the expected outcomes that justify the expenditures. The consultant must be ready to show which reasonable costs can be recovered and also what humanitarian and pragmatic benefits support the program's development.

Finally, a few words concerning the importance of "packaging the product." The most important attribute of this stage is flexibility. Designing a package that maximizes the flexibility of the product (service) will result in the greatest success. Employee organizations are diverse in their product line, management style, philosophy, and approach to employees. A consultant who thinks there is only one way to package an EAP will have few contracts. Marketing packages need to include the following elements:

- Corporate client list currently being served
- Description of staff to serve the corporation or union, and a statement of the history and philosophy of the service organization

Once a program has been approved, the process of implementation or internal marketing begins.

Internal Marketing

Internal marketing is the systematic promotion of an EAP to a specified employee population. The promotion is carefully tailored to meet the unique needs of the workforce. A program is not successfully implemented until it has been satisfactorily marketed inside the organization. The primary goal of an ongoing marketing approach within an EAP is to make sure that employees and their dependents know when and how to use the program. This marketing approach will also include a specific orientation for management and union representatives that focuses on their specific roles and responsibilities.

The key elements of an internal marketing strategy include:

- A *systematic evaluation* which includes demographic descriptions of the client population that identify from where clients originate and do not originate. These efforts will allow for timely and target-specific promotional activities for low use areas.
- A high level of *program awareness* by both management and union leaders regarding their specific roles and responsibilities. The survival of the EAP over time will depend in a large part on this ongoing awareness.
- A high level of *program visibility* needs to be established and maintained over the life of the EAP through both program promotion efforts and organizational networking. These efforts are described in more detail below.

Program Promotion

Keeping current and meaningful information readily available to all employees is one of the mainstays of successful program utilization. One method used at the onset of most EAP programs is the mailing of brochures and "topic related" materials to all employees' homes to establish a level of awareness for the employee and his/her family members. This establishes that confidential information and help are available through the employee assistance service. Another effective method in program promotion is the systematic provision of a series of convenient onsite presentations of psycho-social-emotional or health issues.

Organizational Networking

Organizational networking is that activity which assists in the development of relationships with all levels of management, union, divisions, and departments within a particular organization. The ability to foster and participate in informal relationships will often encourage cooperation toward the overall goals of the EAP. Organizational networking offers a horizontal link within organizations that conventional rigid bureaucracies, with their vertical lines of authority, cannot deliver. The multidimensional nature of networking presents a highly complex yet very effective form of organizational structure. Establishing a network within an organization allows for the appropriate involvement of personnel from different levels, strengthening the EAP in every respect. The value gained from networking within an organization is multi-faceted for both the organization and the EAP.

The Marketing Consultant

The profile of a successful EAP marketing consultant will include skills, experience, and education. Often the mixture of human service and business interests creates grist for the mill that produces the stereotypes each holds for the other. If the consultant is to be successful, he or she will need to be able to translate the product (human service) into the language of business (finance). Both groups will need to come to a broadened understanding of words such as *profit, bottom line, help, assistance, efficiency, cost containment*, and *communication*.

A successful consultant will need specific skills in making both written and oral presentations, negotiation, market analysis, organizational analysis, and networking.

Their knowledge base needs to include a good understanding of both clinical and organizational issues, crisis intervention techniques, and a systems approach to problem solving. The educational level of EAP marketing consultants may range from a high school diploma to a doctoral degree. Experience seems to be most crucial for the marketing consultant.

In the final analysis, those individuals who are concerned with the details of program promotion, meticulous in their follow through, and committed to evaluating their program, have the highest probability of being affiliated with a successful EAP. The marketing efforts are intertwined with the numerous components that comprise the EAP. The complex nature of networking, the successful training events, the appropriate assessment, referral and intervention, consistent and timely evaluation of how the program is working, and the development of written brochures, articles, and topic-related information series are just a few of the diverse yet necessary tasks for a viable program. The mine fields that are always present in the world of work constantly remind EAP personnel to find their way carefully and to expect the unexpected. Reviewing and adapting the strategies to the systematic plan requires constant and diligent work.

In summary, the EAP will have high utilization by employees and their family members because a great deal of valuable information has been transmitted in all directions within the organization. Organizations, on the other hand, reap benefits in economic and humanitarian terms. Improved morale and a happier, healthier work force are some of the humanitarian reasons, while lower rates of absenteeism, fewer on-the-job accidents, and reduced grievances can be equated in economic terms.

5

Strategies of Implementing an EAP
John B. Maynard
Jennifer L. Farmer

Introduction

Too often, EAP practitioners have overlooked the importance of the initial implementation steps in establishing an EAP. The activities performed and the approach taken during the start up phase of a program set the tone for a long time to come—first impressions are lasting. It is these initial activities that will, in large part, determine who supports the program, how many employees will use its services and for what types of problems, how many supervisors and managers will allow themselves to benefit from the expertise and assistance of EAP staff, and what contribution the program will make to the company's goals.

The strategies advocated in this chapter are applicable both to in-house programs and to programs operated by external consultants. They are important in small local firms and in huge multi-national corporations, in unionized and non-unionized companies, in organizations with predominantly white collar professionals, and in organizations with predominantly blue collar laborers.

Background Research and Planning

The bedrock in which all other implementation and operational activities are anchored is the initial research about the company and its motives and goals for the EAP. The essential question is: "What do we have to know in order to decide 1) what the company wants from its program, 2) who should be involved in the planning stages of the program, 3) how and where the program should be integrated into other company functions and systems, and 4) what specific implementation activities should be conducted and in what order?"

It is sometimes, but not always, true that cost reduction or productivity improvement is a motivating factor in the decision to establish a program. Numerous other factors, both internal and external to the organization, typically contribute to the decision to implement a program, and any of them may be the predominant motivator for a given company (Maynard, 1983).

The set of motivators for establishing the program should be considered to be a statement of program goals as seen by key decision makers in the company. To survive and remain viable over the long haul, the program must be designed, implemented, and operated in ways consistent with this particular set of goals.

Of course, the various key people in a company may well have different sets of goals, both open and hidden, for the program. The first step in determining these goals, then, is to determine who the key people are. Some of this information can be obtained from an organizational chart or a look at the formal structure of the company. Often, even more important is the informal power and influence network within the company.

The people in this network may be more difficult to locate, but it is critical to the later success of the program to identify them. They may be supervisors, union representatives, or secretaries. But in any case they are the people to whom others turn when they have a question about some aspect of company operation or policy. They will be the ones to whom people will turn when they are questioning whether or not the EAP might be helpful to themselves or their employees or fellow workers.

It is particularly important to identify the person or group who initiated the idea of establishing an EAP, as well as those who helped push the idea through to a successful implementation decision. It is also important to identify those who resisted the idea.

Once the key people have been identified, the next step is to meet with them individually, if possible, to learn how they feel about the program, what they are hoping it can do for them and the company, and what they do not want it to do. This meeting process also allows the EAP coordinator to educate them about possible benefits the program can offer that they may not have considered and to evaluate their responses to those benefits.

These meetings take time, but they are an important step in the data gathering process. When they are completed, the EAP coordinator will have a good understanding of who supports the program, who doesn't, and why.

The EAP coordinator should make it a point to quickly develop a working knowledge of company personnel policies and procedures, and should find out all he or she can about how alcohol, emotional, and other personal problems have been handled by the company in the past. Other more general information should also be gathered during the researching phase. The history of the company, its future plans, its reputation in the community, the emotional climate at the work site (including labor-management relations), and the status of human resource management in the company hierarchy are all important to know when planning a program that will be effective and long-lasting in that particular company environment.

Involving the Right People

An EAP cannot be effectively planned or successfully operated without the personal involvement of many people throughout the company. Developing personal involvement requires more than formal orientations or meetings, it requires careful listening and the fostering of mutual respect and understanding between the EAP coordinator and the other individuals.

The involvement process begins during the initial research phase already discussed. The importance of the involvement of the chief executive officer (CEO) or chief operating officer (COO) and of top union representatives is widely acknowledged among EAP professionals. The visible endorsement of these officials opens many doors that may otherwise remain closed to the EAP coordinator. Less frequently discussed, but of equal importance, is the cooperation and involvement of many others in the organizational system. By virtue of their positions in the formal structure, those who are primarily responsible for production or operations activities are usually key individuals, as is the controller or chief financial staff person. Certainly the executive responsible for human resource management or employee relations is key.

There are any number of others in the informal power and influence system in whom it is important to instill a sense of ownership of the program. These people have the ability to subtly (or not so subtly) encourage appropriate use of the program or to sabotage it. Particularly critical in this respect are those people who have informally acted as helpers in the past.

Informal helping sytems exist in every organization, and they represent a tremendous support network for the EAP if the coordinator is sensitive to them. Often this function has been performed by human resource or medical personnel, but it may be anyone in the company, especially those who have suffered from problems in the past and have overcome them. If they sense that the EAP will take this rewarding work from them or discount them, the EAP will have lost an important and effective ally. If they feel supported and acknowledged by the EAP, they can provide great insight into how the company works and can help generate many program referrals, often at an early stage of problem development.

The various key people with whom the EAP coordinator meets and develops relationships will have differing views about what is important and what should be done. Therefore, it is important that the coordinator balance these various opinions and keep them in perspective. The coordinator should keep all the key people informed of the steps being taken and the reasons that the program is being implemented in the particular way that it is.

Almost as important to program success as maintaining the involvement of the right people is avoiding too much involvement of the wrong people. There are times when individuals or groups in the company will see the EAP as a means to achieve their own political or other ends. If the EAP becomes overidentified in peoples minds with someone who is viewed negatively in the organization, the EAP will absorb part of the stigma. If some employees, managers, or factions believe they can manipulate the EAP to enhance their own needs, they will try to do so. The best way to avoid these dangers is to stay constantly in touch with as many key people in the company as possible and to avoid becoming too identified with any single person, group, or department.

Integrating the Program into Other Company Systems

Obviously, the relationship-building discussed in the preceding section is the single most important aspect of integrating the EAP into other company systems. But many other aspects need to be considered if the program is truly to become an integral part of the way the company does business.

When newly hired employees are oriented to the company, the EAP should be mentioned and its literature provided in the same way as are other employee benefits. If the company uses group orientations during which a number of specific resource people make presentations, then perhaps the EAP coordinator should make one also; otherwise, the EAP should be described by the person who normally does the orientation. A description of the EAP should be included in any employee handbooks or other literature and should be written in the same style and format as other descriptions.

EAP-related policy statements should always be presented as one of the basic company personnel policies. The format and style in which they are written should conform to the format and style in which other company policies are written. Company corrective, disciplinary, and grievance procedures should be revised to incorporate the EAP into them; EAP-related practices should not be described separately as if they were simply grafted on to the basic procedures as an afterthought.

Similarly, any supervisory or management training must be integrated into regular company training practices. If all management training is done by a training department except that EAP-related training is done by the EAP coordinator, the company is clearly communicating that appropriate use of the EAP is not really part of mainstream management expectations. To integrate the program fully requires that the EAP coordinator work with the regular trainers to have EAP principles incorporated at all relevant points into their courses (Wilkinson, 1980).

If, as is often the case, no regular supervisory or management training occurs in the company, it may not be appropriate to conduct formal EAP training either. A better approach would be to find out how supervisors and managers learn what is expected of them in their roles, then tap the same mechanism to communicate EAP-related expectations.

In other words, the EAP should always operate as consistently as possible with other company practices and goals. The EAP coordinator, while scrupulously avoiding intra-organizational political or power struggles, should remain as visible to as many people as possible and should make sure that his or her role is clearly understood—what it is and what it is not.

Specific Implementation Activities

A number of specific activities are necessary to the successful implementation of an effective EAP. The activities themselves are described in this section, and programmatic implications of the order in which they are done are described in the next section. In all the activities described, the EAP coordinator's goals include: communicating the benefits of the EAP to various company groups (e.g., executives, supervisors, union representatives, employees, personnel staff) in terms relevant to each group, developing an understanding of the needs and concerns of each group, identifying influence networks and potential program supporters or resisters, and becoming personally visible and known.

Meet with Company Contact Person or Supervisor

Whether the EAP coordinator is hired in-house or represents an outside consultant, he or she will have one primary person with whom to communicate with on a regular basis. Meeting and developing a relationship of mutual trust with this person is the first major step in implementing the program. At these meetings the coordinator can supplement or begin research about the company (described in a previous section of the chapter) and plan what other key people need to be drawn into the planning process. Arrangements for meeting with key executives and union leaders can also be made.

Meet with CEO/COO/Union Leaders

To be effective, the EAP must be seen as an important and basic part of the management system within the company. This attitude can only be conveyed from the top. By meeting with the chief executive or chief operating officers, the EAP coordinator can solicit their visible support and active assistance in setting up meetings with vice-presidents, department heads, or other key executives. The goal here as in other meetings should not be simply a brief introduction, but rather the development of a sense of personal confidence and trust in the coordinator. If the company is unionized, the coordinator should also meet individually with top union leaders. The goal for these meetings is the same: to develop a relationship of trust and confidence that will facilitate use of the program by troubled people from any level or part of the company. The essential ideas to be included in EAP-related company policy statements should be discussed and developed during these initial meetings.

Brief Managers, Supervisors, and Union Representatives

It is often helpful, immediately after the meetings with top management and union leadership, to conduct quick briefings for middle managers, supervisors, and union representatives if forums exist for doing so. (In some companies, memos from the leadership can serve much the same purpose when opportunities for personal briefings don't exist.) At these briefings, the chief executive or union leader should introduce the coordinator and request the audience's cooperation in setting up meetings and otherwise supporting the EAP. The coordinator or other company officials can explain the EAP concept and the company's rationale for establishing such a program.

Meet Individually with Other Key Personnel

The term *key personnel* is used here to include people with a number of roles in the organization. They may be executives or department heads, personnel or medical staff members, union representatives, or employees who are influential among their peers for various reasons. The meetings with executives and department heads are used to plan the department-by-department implementation of the program. This includes arranging for group employee orientations and needs assessments, planning and arranging for the orientation and training of supervisors, and enlisting the visible support of the executives.

During the meetings with personnel and medical staff members and with union representatives, the process of developing "nuts and bolts" procedures for integrating the EAP into various personnel policies begins. By virtue of their positions, these individuals are likely to have assisted troubled employees on an ad hoc basis prior to the decision to implement a formal EAP. Therefore, it is important to avoid the appearance of "stepping on their toes" or discounting their previous work in any way. Their active support and advice should be solicited and appreciated. This is also true of the informal influence leaders in the company. Obtaining their support and cooperation during these meetings can significantly accelerate the pace of effectively integrating the program into the informal organizational system.

Conduct Employee Orientation Meetings

Each of these meetings requires only about 20 minutes and can include as many employees as can be gathered in one place at a time. They should, of course, be conducted on all shifts. At these meetings, the coordinator should be introduced by an appropriate company official known to the employees. The coordinator should then briefly explain what the EAP is, how employees can use it, what they should expect after they make an appointment, how confidentiality is protected, and to what statistical information the company has access regarding program use. A brief explanation of the supervisory or other non-self referral process should be given. Examples of typical problems with which EAP can assist should be mentioned in a way designed to normalize and de-stigmatize the use of the program by employees and their families. Opportunity for employees to ask questions should be provided. If none are asked, it is often useful for the coordinator to emphasize certain points by specifically mentioning and answering questions that have come up in other orientation groups.

Although the content of the information presented at these meetings is certainly important, it is the process itself that is the critical variable in program implementation. First, it is quickly clear to employees and their supervisors that the EAP is seen as important by the company when they are pulled from their jobs for even a few minutes to participate in the meetings. Second, the personal exposure to the coordinator and the opportunity to ask questions serves to make the program much less threatening to employees. The visibility and personal connection helps to defuse much of the anxiety about potentially using program services. Third, the coordinator has the opportunity to hear the kinds of concerns employees have about the program, and can address major issues, either on the spot or in later promotional literature.

Assess Needs of Employees

It has been found helpful to include a brief needs assessment questionnaire as part of the orientation meetings described above. The questionnaire is anonymous and is designed to be answered in about five minutes, simply by checking off various response alternatives. Essentially, it asks employees what types of problems they, their families, and their coworkers may have experienced. All indications are that employees answer the questionnaires truthfully.

Although it is helpful to have the data from the questionnaire, the real value again lies in the process. Answering the questions helps define for employees the scope of problems with which the EAP might be helpful. The individual feeling of participation in the design and implementation of the program that filling out the questionnaire provides, increases the employee's own investment in the program's success. When summary results of the needs assessment are made available (e.g. 14% of employees report being currently affected by marriage or family problems), employees who themselves are suffering from such problems feel less deviant and are, therefore, more likely to come to the EAP for assistance.

Distribute Materials

Descriptive brochures explaining to employees what the program is, why it has been established, and how to seek assistance from it should be distributed as widely as possible. Mailing brochures to employee's homes makes it more likely that spouses or other family members will learn of the program. Brochures and other literature (e.g., business-size cards with the EAP number) should be available throughout the worksite in places where employees will see them and have a chance to pick one up without necessarily being observed by others. Personnel and medical staff, managers, supervisors, and union representatives should all have several brochures that they can hand out to specific employees as appropriate. All EAP-related literature should stress the strict confidentiality and lack of stigma associated with using the program.

Orient and Train Supervisors and Managers

In a previous section of the chapter, the importance of integrating EAP training for supervisors and managers into the regular company training process was emphasized. This integration is essential to communicate to managers and supervisors that identifying and constructively confronting problem employees is a relevant and central supervisory function and that appropriate referral of problem employees to the EAP is a key aspect of their supervisory duties.

When first implementing a program in a company, it is helpful to supplement the ongoing integrated training with an orientation session for all supervisors and managers. The goals of this session are to familiarize participants with the newly developed EAP-related policies and procedures and to make them aware of the benefits of using the EAP as a tool to assist in supervising troubled or problem employees.

Ideally, each orientation session should include 20 to 50 supervisors or managers, with roughly the same degree of supervisory responsibility. Sessions should be conducted in a format that promotes active participation by the supervisors and allows them to ask any questions or state any resistance to the program that they may feel. Examples used to demonstrate identification, confrontation, and referral techniques should be totally consistent with the organizational style and structure of the participants' own departments.

Put Out Fires

During any of the implementation activities discussed, someone may bring to the attention of the EAP coordinator one or more situations with which the EAP can be helpful. It is important to capitalize on these early opportunities to demonstrate the effectiveness of the program. A single example of a long standing problem situation being corrected by the new program will do more to ensure its acceptance in the company than weeks of more routine implementation activities. This is not to suggest that the activities can be abandoned; it means that supplementing them with real world examples of program usefulness multiplies their impact and helps guarantee a successful program implementation process.

Strategic Considerations

The order in which the implementation activities described above are done can affect the way the program is perceived by its various constituents. In general, to avoid labor-management difficulties in a unionized company, it is important to conduct parallel activities throughout the entire process for management on one hand and union representatives on the other. This begins with the researching phase and continues for the life of the program.

If the first word of the program in the company comes when employees receive materials at home or attend orientation meetings, the program will tend to be viewed as primarily an employee benefit. On the other hand, if the initial effort is to orient and train supervisors and managers, and word directly to employees comes later, the program will tend to be viewed more as a management tool. Clearly, these are only differences in degree, and they can be overcome in time to achieve a different balance, but the order will have some initial impact.

Both general approaches are equally valid, depending on the company's goals for its program. Emphasizing the employee self-referral services first will usually produce a higher first year use rate. Emphasizing the management aspects first will usually produce more supervisory referrals in the first year. In either case, if the program provides excellent help to its clients, no matter how referred, the EAP will be effectively implemented.

As a general guideline, the authors recommend conducting the activities in roughly the same order as they are presented in this chapter. Many, of course, can be done essentially simultaneously. The individual meetings tend to come first because they involve a large program design and planning component. Then, the services are introduced to employees personally during the orientation meetings before the written materials are distributed. Experience has shown that this order of presenting the program tends to increase the number of employees and families who read the literature and put it away for future reference.

The orientation and training of managers and supervisors comes after the program has become generally known throughout the company. Often, this helps produce orientation sessions that are more efficient and useful than they might otherwise be because the participants come with specific questions and concerns about their roles that have been generated during the program announcement process.

A concern in the EAP field has been the relatively low rate of program use by executives. Especially with in-house programs, the placement of the EAP in the organizational structure may have an impact on the executive use rate. However, a more important dynamic in both in-house and contract programs is the personal credibility and approach of the program coordinator.

As discussed earlier in the chapter, the goal of the coordinator in the individual meetings with executives and other key personnel is the development of a relationship of mutual trust and concern. The time should not be spent talking entirely about the needs of "those employees out there." As much as possible, the coordinator should provide an atmosphere of "active listening," letting the executive express his or her own feelings and concerns and making it clear that EAP services are open to them also.

A Last Note

The rapid growth and increasing competition in the EAP field has led many would-be EAP providers to propose to companies what are essentially "boilerplate" assessment and referral services. Such services, in their attempt to be as inexpensive as possible, sacrifice many of the implementation activities described in this chapter, as well as other ongoing organizational coordination components of an effective program. This is a dangerous trend in the EAP field because it misses the point that the real strength of an EAP lies in its becoming an integral part of the company's internal operations. EAP professionals have learned over the years that remaining a real part of the organizational system requires constant personal interaction and visibility with others in the company. We hope that the trend in the future is a return to an emphasis on educating companies about the benefits of a quality program rather than on the negligible costs of a minimal one.

References

Maynard, J.B. (1983). *Factors that influence executive decision makers in medium size private companies to establish company counseling or employee assistance programs*. Doctoral dissertation, University of Colorado, Boulder.

Wilkinson, L.L. (1980). *Supervisory training principles and research: Implications for employee assistance and occupational alcoholism programs* (Report 80-1). Boulder, CO: Employee Assistance Research Institute.

SECTION II

EAP Models

Introduction

As will be noted in the chapter by researchers Foote and Erfurt, EAPs come in many shapes and models. To intelligently decide among them, one may ask at least three questions: What is to be covered by the program? Who is to accomplish each function? and How is each to be done? For instance, it is generally accepted that supervisor referrals are an essential component, but the energies required to accomplish them (i.e., supervisor training, etc.) are considerably greater than those needed to promote voluntary referrals among employees. Attention is also devoted to the variant types of EAPs, and how they relate to preliminary and "in progress" objectives visualized by the EAP itself. Organizational factors are reviewed in detail.

As will be discussed by Isenberg, the service center, consortium, and other external models have their proponents and real place in the EAP world, particularly for smaller companies whose number of employees could not justify the larger expenditure of an in-house program. Among their advantages are the employees' perceptions of increased confidentiality of their sensitive information.

Turner will look at the issues of assessment and referral, providing information that should prove of interest both for the experienced EAP professional and the relative novice. Attention is paid also to methods for in-depth evaluations of referral resources. Internally housed programs are unquestionably better able to understand the inner workings of the company to maneuver to take advantage of openings and opportunities and to network. Such skills must be carefully considered by the company in its hiring of just the right persons for the EAP. Otherwise, programs may progress more through "flying by the seats of their pants," and on-the-job training than by careful planning. Skills in the diagnosis and referral of alcoholism are always

43

mandatory in EAP staff credentials and the operation of responsible programs.

Klarreich will discuss the design of an EAP which includes staff that are fully licensed, and who deliver not only assessment, but also the treatment of employees within the workplace. This model allows a direct stewardship of treatment costs, since the majority of treatment is done internally. The individual's professional training and skills may have coinage in terms of allied activities as well, such as in stress management, health education, and the like.

Union-based programs are the subject of the chapter by Tramm. Such programs, or non-union EAPs within represented companies, present added challenges and perhaps greater opportunities. Generally, it will be prudent and desirable for management to consider the inclusion of existing unions in development of the EAP at all levels. Well trained union representatives on the shop floor can readily detect early problems among fellow workers, perhaps long in advance of behavioral or work problems on the job. Union service programs, ordinarily structured to provide other liaison activities for members, may also be the source of referrals to the EAP, if their key members are apprised of the role they may rightly play.

The peer referral model, described in a chapter by Molloy, proves most interesting, as it may signal the next tide change in the dogma of how EAPs can best reach their "hard to reach" clients. Patterned after the family intervention models of Vernon Johnson, and first regularly used in the airline industry, it can be valuably applied in work situations where tight supervision is not easily "do-able," or where employees are of high achievement, high independence categories—or both. Can new subgroups of employees be reached by this method? Are senior level executives—a difficult group to reach—among these subgroups? The peer committee concept proposed may be usefully aligned with the function of quality circles. Are there other lessons to be learned here?

6

Variations in EAP Design
John C. Erfurt and Andrea Foote

Introduction

A casual look at the employee assistance field will show that there are many different models or methods for operating EAPs. The remaining chapters in this section describe a number of those models in detail. In this chapter we will examine the functions of EAPs, and explore some sources of variation in how these functions are performed.

EAP Functions

Figure 6-1 organizes the various EAP functions graphically into three systems of activity (labeled A, B and C). System A deals with case finding or identification of employees who may benefit from program services, encouraging or inducing those employees to seek help from the EAP, and referring them to System B. System B handles initial problem assessment, some short-term counseling, referral for treatment if required, follow-up and assistance with return to work, and sometimes additional monitoring of work performance. In addition, System B is usually responsible for the system maintenance activities shown on the right in Fig. 6-1, although some of these activities may be shared with others. System C involves the treatment services and other forms of assistance to which employees may be referred. (See Erfurt and Foote, 1977, for a more detailed discussion of these program functions.)

Variations in EAP design may be grouped into three major categories: 1) variations in decisions regarding which functions in Fig. 6-1 will be emphasized by the program, 2) variations regarding who handles each function, and 3) variations in how each function is carried out. We will discuss these variations separately for each system.

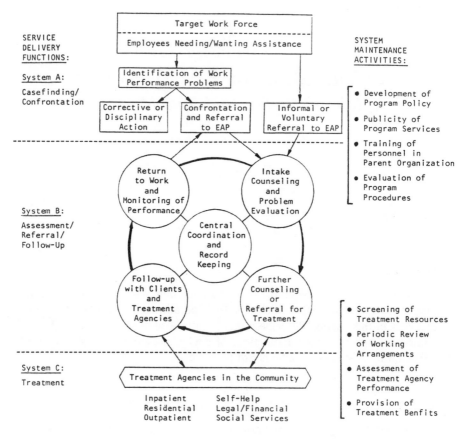

FIGURE 6-1. Reproduced with permission from Erfurt and Foote, 1977. Copyright 1977 by the Institute of Labor and Industrial Relations, The University of Michigan.

Variations in System A

Virtually all EAPs conduct some type of case finding activity. Similarly, confronting and encouraging or inducing employees to seek assistance for their problem and referring them to the EAP are also emphasized by most programs, and these activities—case finding, confronting, and encouraging/inducing/referring—tend to go together. The variations across programs in these activities are not so much in the degree of emphasis placed on the activities, as in who conducts the activity and how it is handled (Archambault, et al., 1982).

Fig. 6-1 identifies the major differentiation in case finding activities; some clients are identified through work performance problems and others voluntarily seek out the EAP (though usually with informal pressure from others). Programs that focus on case finding through deterioration in work performance devote a considerable amount of time to the training of personnel within the organization to evaluate work performance and to take appropriate action with employees showing difficulties. Training may be given to supervisory staff (Trice and Belasco, 1968; Kurtz, 1982), union representatives (Trice and Belasco, 1966), and other groups that are in a position to review various aspects of work performance, such as medical departments, safety officials, and labor relations personnel.

The effectiveness of this method of case finding clearly rests on the ability and willingness of a large number of people to carry out specified activities. Many programs have de-emphasized this method of case finding, whether due to inability to find an adequate training mechanism, uncertainty about the ability or willingness of this large number of people to carry out the case finding and confrontation/referral activities (Googins and Kurtz, 1981; Beyer and Trice, 1978), or a philosophical preference for inducing employees to seek program assistance without a formal referral (Shain and Groeneveld, 1980). These programs use quite different methods for case finding, focused on frequent publicity about the program and its services, attempts to de-stigmatize the kinds of problems for which people need assistance, and provision of information about the positive effects of treatment.

While case finding through work performance review normally induces people to seek assistance through a confrontation focused on the potential threat to job security if performance is not improved, case finding through publicity attempts to induce people to seek assistance through promises of improved quality of life. The latter is clearly a weaker strategy, particularly for people who are accustomed to denying that they have any problems. On the face of it, therefore, it would appear that the two case finding/inducement strategies should attract a somewhat different set of people to the program, and there is some evidence that they do (Foote, et al., 1978, pp. 47–50). Advocates of the work performance review and confrontation strategies focus attention on the EAP's objective to assist people with deteriorating performance to take action before their job is in jeopardy. Advocates of the publicity/self-referral strategy focus attention on reaching and assisting employees before their work performance has declined seriously. These are clearly different program objectives, and whether intentionally or not, many programs have constructed their activities so as to emphasize one objective over the other.

To summarize the variations in System A, there is general consistency across EAPs in the functions included in this system—all include case finding, confrontation, and inducement to seek assistance. There is considerable variation, however, in how these activities are conducted, and similarly in who conducts them. Programs aimed at improvement of deteriorating work performance will develop methods for identifying poor work performance, and must rely on a range of people within the workforce to conduct the identification, confrontation, and inducement activities. Programs aimed at early identification through self-referrals will conduct a considerable amount of publicity (using posters, newsletters, newspaper articles, direct mailings, and informational meetings) over which the EAP staff (in System B) generally has control. These activities lead to self-referral (or informal referrals by co-workers, etc.), and confrontation is normally conducted by the EAP staff.

The activities of System A are generally embedded within the parent organization (i.e., the organization sponsoring the EAP). While there is variation in whom within the parent organization will conduct System A activities, they are seldom conducted by a group outside of the parent organization. Various types of resources—e.g., publicity materials—may be provided by outside groups, but the responsibility for publicity is generally internal.

Variations in System B

The activities of System B (shown in Fig. 6-1) generally involve linking employees at the work site (System A) with treatment or helping resources in the community (System C). This system can be thought of as the EAP proper, with System A delivering clients to the program, and System C receiving patients from the program. System B is usually the organizational component charged with the responsibility for insuring that the program is operated according to organizational policy. Thus, in addition to the client-focused activities described in Fig. 6-1 for System B (intake counseling and assessment, referral for treatment, follow-up, and assistance with return to work), this system is normally also responsible for central coordination and record-keeping, and for conducting or coordinating the system maintenance activities.

There is great variation across EAPs regarding a) which activities are included in or emphasized by System B, b) who handles these activities in general, and each function specifically, and c) how each function is conducted. In some programs the client-specific functions of System B almost disappear, with personnel who handle the case finding making direct referrals to treatment (Schramm, Mandell and Archer, 1978). Even in this case, however, someone must handle the system maintenance activities, or the program will gradually disintegrate.

Most EAPs include a program intake and assessment function, and referral for treatment as required. However, some provide no additional counseling with program clients after the referral to treatment is made, and some conduct no follow-up with program clients (Reichman and Young, 1982). These programs focus their attention on the process of getting clients to appropriate treatment resources, and rely on those resources to provide all subsequent services. The degree to which programs maintain adequate records is also variable, with some programs keeping virtually no records beyond a count of clients seen, and others maintaining careful records of client progress and outcomes, as well as documenting other program activities (Weiss, 1978). Thus, there is substantial variation across EAPs in the components included in System B.

In looking at EAPs, the most obvious design difference is in the location of the System B activities. Many programs, especially those in larger work sites, hire or appoint staff to manage the program and to handle System B and system maintenance tasks. Others arrange for these services to be provided by external agencies, on a contractual basis. The following are common models for handling System B functions, but by no means a total listing of possible models:

1) System B activities are conducted by internal staff with professional training relevant to EAP activities (e.g., psychologist, social worker, certified alcoholism counselor).

2) System B activities are conducted by internal staff, with primary responsibility carried by personnel with some training and a personal interest or background relevant to EAP activities (e.g., recovering alcoholic, medical department staff member). These staff members are frequently part-time, with other responsibilities within the organization.

3) System B activities are handled externally, through a consortium of firms that have jointly sponsored an EAP to provide services for employees from all of the firms.

4) System B activities are handled externally, through a central diagnostic and referral agency (CDR) that receives clients from the firm and makes appropriate referrals to treatment facilities in the community.

5) System B activities are handled externally, by a treatment agency (or a consortium of agencies) that receives clients and either provides treatment or makes appropriate referrals to other agencies.

The selection of a given model has clear implications for EAP activities. An external program does not have access to work records and cannot easily conduct follow-up activities at the work site. An external program may also find it more difficult to work with System A in its case finding functions, and these system maintenance activities may in fact be assigned to personnel within the parent organization rather than to the external program. Finally, an external program that also provides treatment may be inclined to keep patients who might better be referred elsewhere, or who may not require treatment at all. On the other hand, external programs may be better able to deal with System C (the treatment community), and may be more readily trusted by employees who are already in trouble at their place of work.

Another variation in the design of System B is frequently overlooked but very important in its effects, and that is the staffing of System B (Foote, Erfurt, and Austin, 1980). Programs which rely on part-time, relatively untrained staff tend to show a lower level of penetration (i.e., see fewer clients), and make referrals to more expensive types of treatment (inpatient rather than outpatient). These factors may be related, i.e., programs seeing fewer clients may be seeing only the more serious cases. On the other hand, nonprofessional staff are more comfortable in referring clients to the highest level of care than in making a differential diagnosis about the appropriate level of care.

There is also some evidence that the training and background of program staff affect the type of clients identified (Archambault, et al., 1982, p. 49; Intveldt-Work, 1983). This is a somewhat ominous finding. It may mean that people in the target population come to know that Staff Member X works well with alcoholics while Staff Member Y works well with people having marital difficulties, and thus gravitate to the appropriate person. On the other hand, program clients seldom choose the staff member they will see. One large association of treatment facilities reported that after they provided intensive inservice training in alcoholism for their counselors, the number of cases of alcoholism identified rose substantially (private communication). Since the patient population itself did not change, it appears that counselors diagnose the types of problems with which they are most familiar. The training of EAP staff thus becomes very important in insuring that appropriate assessments and referrals are made. (It may be argued that a professional assessment will be made by the receiving treatment facility, but it is rarely the case that a facility will diagnose a problem for which it does not provide treatment.)

The size of the EAP staff is often overlooked as a source of variation in EAP design. Programs with a small amount of staff time available are simply not able to see large numbers of clients, not able to conduct follow-up with clients they do see, not able to monitor adequately the resources in the community, etc. Programs with substantial staff time, on the other hand, may be able to handle all of the activities normally considered to be part of an EAP, and also to devote some time to primary prevention activities or other functions that will enhance the effectiveness of the program. Some programs, for example, maintain close linkages with other departments within the worksite that have related objectives (e.g., quality of work life programs, health and safety departments).

In summary, the variations in the design of System B across EAPs are numerous, beginning with variations in functions included or emphasized. Some programs emphasize intake, problem assessment, and referral for treatment, and de-emphasize or do not provide other System B components. Some provide short-term counseling for many clients, while other programs discourage any in-house counseling. Some EAP staff members spend a substantial amount of time working with System A (e.g., supervisory training, maintenance of relationships with other key departments) and with System C (e.g., reviewing treatment resources, developing plans for improving treatment), while other EAPs devote little time to these activities. The choice of components included in System B is closely related to the amount of staff time available for EAP activities, and to the organizational placement of staff.

Finally, there are also variations in how System B functions are carried out, although these are more difficult to specify, as each program differs in some degree from all others in how it operates. In general, it may be said that there are differences in intake, problem assessment, and referral procedures, depending on the training and background of the staff members handling these functions. There are differences in adequacy of record-keeping, depending on how much accountability is required for EAP activities. And there are differences in the amount of follow-up and monitoring of work performance, depending on how closely the EAP's objectives are tied into work performance criteria.

Variations in System C

System C includes the hands-on treatment or assistance provided to employees for the problems they are having. There are two primary sources of variation in System C. The first is the range of available resources within a community, which varies considerably from place to place, especially from rural or small town locations to large urban areas. The EAP usually has little influence over this, certainly at the initial program design stage, although programs sometimes choose to devote more of their resources to encouraging the development of missing treatment modalities.

The second variation, more interesting from a program design point of view, is the inclusion of System C functions within the parent organization (i.e., provision of treatment by program staff). For most EAPs, in-house treatment cannot be conducted to the exclusion of referral, since the program is unlikely to be able to treat all of the various types of problems that employees present. However, programs that see large numbers of people who have the same type of problem may find it both cheaper and more effective to provide treatment on-site. The advantages are evident: employees cannot play the treatment agency against the worksite; the program may be able to monitor work attendance or work performance to evaluate the success of the treatment intervention; there may be less lost time from work with on-site treatment.

Finally, while EAPs may not have much influence on the range of treatment resources in the community, or the treatment methods used by those resources, they do control the choice of resources they will use. As previously noted, there is variation across programs in the degree to which they use inpatient or residential treatment for alcoholism, as opposed to outpatient or self-help only. There is likewise variation in the degree to which people with emotional difficulties are referred to psychiatrists, psychologists, or family service type agencies. For many programs these decisions are highly influenced by the third-party payment structure of their organization's health benefit plan. They may feel compelled to refer people to a higher-priced service while believing that a lower-priced one would be equally effective, because the lower-priced resource is not a covered benefit. Some programs have found ways around this, e.g., by developing a direct payment mechanism rather than going through the third party payer. Others expect that employees should pay for all or part of their treatment. In any case, the structure of the benefit plan remains an important source of design variation across EAPs.

However, the selection of treatment resources rests with the EAP staff who make the referrals. Since community treatment facilities have a considerable financial interest in receiving referrals, they can be expected to do their best to convince EAP staff to refer to them. Program designs vary regarding guidelines for deciding when treatment is necessary, and for selecting among available facilities. Unfortunately, there is insufficient research available from which programs may draw to develop such guidelines, and program staff no doubt will wish to err on the side of more rather than less treatment. Staff without professional training are particularly vulnerable here, and may have to make more referrals as a form of self-protection against possible legal consequences. Professional staff should be better able to justify their recommendations based on accepted professional practice. Thus the training and qualifications of the EAP staff often affect the program design in terms of treatment resources most often utilized.

Causes of Variation in EAP Design

.   It is evident that there are many ways in which EAPs differ in their design; the field developed around varying traditions, programs were developed with varying purposes in mind, and there is no accepted standard for what constitutes an EAP. It is possible to make some sense out of these variations, however, by looking at some of the reasons behind this diversity. There are two major causes of diversity: differences in program objectives and differences in the size and structure of the parent organization.

Differences in Program Objectives

EAPs were developed for many different reasons, and the origins of EAPs vary significantly from one program to another. Many of the early programs developed as a means for dealing with employee drinking problems. These programs were specifically focused on alcoholism and alcohol abuse, and since there was no professional group generally acknowledged as the most qualified for dealing with these problems, the programs tended to be handled by lay staff with interest and experience in dealing with alcoholism (Trice and Schonbrunn, 1981).

Other programs developed along quite different lines, and were focused on counseling of employees for the whole range of problems that might trouble them and affect their work (Dickson and Roethlisberger, 1966). As these programs became established, they tended to rely on trained professionals (psychiatrists, clinical psychologists) who were acknowledged as being skilled in counseling (Presnall, 1981).

These early programs were generally developed as a result of the keen interest of someone in the company. However, there were also external influences supporting the development of alcoholism programs, perhaps beginning with the "Yale Plan for Business and Industry" (Henderson and Bacon, 1953). Such activities were greatly expanded in 1972, with the establishment of occupational program consultants in every state, funded through the federal government, whose task it was to foster the development of programs in every work location. By this time the program focus was expanded to offer service to employees with any kind of problem which was interfering with work performance. While the objective was still to reach alcoholic employees, it had become clear that the methods used to reach this objective were attracting employees with many other problems, and the program would have to deal with them. Futhermore, it was felt that a broader program focus would reduce employee reluctance to use the program because of the stigma attached to alcoholism (Wrich, 1980).

The initial program design was thus a function of who established the program. Informal programs, operated by recovering alcoholics, took on the flavor of self-help and were often loosely and informally structured.

Counseling programs operated by professionally trained personnel were often more formally structured, requiring at least a slot in the organization chart occupied by the professional.

These historical differences in the development of EAPs produced programs of considerably varied purpose and structure. While programs have not remained static over the years—and in many cases have developed new methods and beliefs—historical effects often persist. Many programs find themselves frustrated in attaining their present objectives due to a program structure that will not allow them to do so. Of particular concern are staffing patterns that are no longer appropriate for present objectives, but that cannot easily be changed because of organizational interests in retaining the present arrangements and because it might be unfair to incumbent staff.

Thus it is often necessary to take account of historical differences to explain differences in EAP design. However, it should be equally illuminating to examine present program objectives, either stated or implied.

Program objectives are of greatest significance in explaining program design, if the program is held accountable by its parent organization for reaching those objectives. If an EAP is expected to help reduce absenteeism, then the program design can be expected to move toward a) a method for identifying employees with excessive absenteeism and providing the appropriate confrontation and referral, and b) follow-up and monitoring of the absenteeism of EAP clients. Or if the program is expected to provide service to a maximum number of employees each year, then case finding activities will be emphasized, and follow-up activities will be de-emphasized or discontinued.

Many times the program objectives are not stated clearly, but must be inferred from the types of questions being asked about the program by those in authority. The program can be expected to gear its activities toward providing satisfactory answers to those questions.

Thus far we have not discussed differences in program objectives related to disease or problem focus. There is growing agreement that EAPs must be prepared to deal with all types of employee problems, and some evidence that there are no substantial differences between alcohol-focused and comprehensive programs in terms of program functioning (Roman, 1980; Foote and Erfurt, 1981). However, programs with a specific disease focus can be expected to differ somewhat in their design, if only through the greater emphasis on that disease in publicity and training activities.

Differences in Organizational Size and Structure

The second major factor explaining the diversity of EAPs is the size and structure of the parent organization. The presence of an EAP is highly related to organizational size. Large companies have been faster to adopt programs than smaller ones (Intveldt-Work, 1983). Furthermore the structure of the program is also related to company size, primarily with regard to the placement of System B. Large companies generally favor the hiring of on-site staff to handle System B activities, while smaller companies are more likely to utilize external resources, such as consortia, central diagnostic and referral agencies, or treatment facilities to handle these activities. In fact, as smaller firms have become more interested in providing employee assistance services for their work force, the variety of services available in the community has increased dramatically, increasing the variability of program designs.

The structure of the parent organization also affects how EAP services are provided. Organizations with large populations within a limited geographical area tend to hire on-site staff to operate the program, but organizations with similarly large populations that are dispersed across a wide geographical area have a more difficult problem. Some of these firms hire "circuit riders" who provide services to the various locations on a rotating basis, or as the need arises. This model is more common for populations within a reasonably small area (e.g., a state). For populations scattered across the country, firms are more likely to contract with local resources to provide System B functions. However, the need to coordinate the program across multiple sites normally dictates another type of staff function which is managerial in nature. Thus large multi-site corporations will include in their EAP design the provision of staff to train, coordinate, and oversee the activities of the EAP.

Finally, the presence or absence within the parent organization of related activities can affect the design of the EAP. Firms with medical departments will frequently tie the EAP into that department, while firms without such departments must rely on other resources for any medical expertise. These observations may appear obvious, but should not be overlooked in explaining the variations in EAP design.

Conclusion

We have examined variations in EAP design, and some of the implications of the more common variations. We have also looked at some systematic causes of variation in program design. Differences in program objectives affect which program components are emphasized, and also affect the type and number of staff selected to operate the program. Differences in the size and structure of the parent organization are highly related to where the responsibility for each program function is assigned, with larger and less dispersed firms keeping more functions internal, and smaller and geographically dispersed firms more frequently contracting externally for certain activities.

It should be clear from this discussion that there is not a discrete set of program designs, but rather a variety of decision points in developing a program. There are two major decision points; the first involves establishing specific program objectives. From these will flow decisions about which activities or functions are to be included in the program design, and what kind of staffing arrangement will be able to handle these activities. Second, the constraints posed by the size and structure of the parent organization will affect decisions about the distribution of these tasks or functions within the organization and/or among external agencies.

References

Archambault, R., Doran, R., Matlas, T., Nadolski, J., and Sutton-Wright, D. *Reaching Out: A Guide to EAP Case finding.* Troy, MI: Performance Resource Press, Inc., 1982.

Beyer, J.M., and Trice, H.M. *Implementing Change: Alcoholism Policies in Work Organizations.* New York: The Free Press, 1978.

Dickson, W.J., and Roethlisberger, F.J. *Counseling in an Organization: A Sequel to the Hawthorne Researches.* Boston: Harvard University Press, 1966.

Erfurt, J.C. and Foote, A. *Occupational Employee Assistance Programs for Substance Abuse and Mental Health Problems.* Ann Arbor, MI: The University of Michigan Institute of Labor and Industrial Relations, 1977.

Foote, A. and Erfurt, J.C. "Effectiveness of Comprehensive Employee Assistance Programs at Reaching Alcoholics." *Journal of Drug Issues* (Spring 1981), II:217–232.

Foote, A., Erfurt, J.C., and Austin, R. "Staffing Occupational Employee Assistance Programs: The General Motors Experience." *Alcohol Health and Research World* (Spring 1980), 4:22–31.

Foote, A., Erfurt, J.C., Strauch, P.A., and Guzzardo, T.L. *Cost-Effectiveness of Occupational Employee Assistance Programs.* Ann Arbor, MI: The University of Michigan Institute of Labor and Industrial Relations, 1978.

Googins, B., and Kurtz, N.R. "Discriminating Participating and Nonparticipating Supervisors in Occupational Alcoholism Programs." *Journal of Drug Issues* (Spring 1981), II:199–217.

Henderson, R.M. and Bacon, S.E. "Problem Drinking: The Yale Plan for Business and Industry." *Quarterly Journal of Studies on Alcohol* (June 1953), XIV: 247–262.

Intveldt-Work, S. "Staffing Patterns, Relationships Profiled in Nationwide EAP Survey." *The ALMACAN* (June, July & August, 1983), 13:6ff.

Kurtz, N.R. "Dynamics of the Identification and Referral Process in Work Organizations." Chapter in *Occupational Alcoholism: A Review of Research Issues.* Washington, D.C.: DHHS Publication No. (ADM)82-1184, 1982, 273–314.

Presnall, L.F. *Occupational Counseling and Referral Systems*. Salt Lake City: Utah Alcoholism Foundation, 1981.

Reichman, W. and Young, D.W. "Psychodynamics of the Return and Follow-up Process in the Work Organization." Chapter in *Occupational Alcoholism: A Review of Research Issues*. Washington, D.C.: DHHS Publication No. (ADM)82-1184, 1982, 331–349.

Roman, P.M. "Employee Assistance and Employee Alcoholism Programs in Major American Corporations: Similarities and Differences in 1979." *Labor-Management Alcohol Journal* (1980), 9:211–222.

Schramm, C.J., Mandell, W., and Archer, J. *Workers Who Drink*. Lexington, MA: Lexington Books, 1978.

Shain, M. and Groeneveld, J. *Employee-Assistance Programs*. Lexington, MA: Lexington Books, 1980.

Trice, H.M. and Belasco, J.A. "Supervisory Training about Alcoholics and Other Problem Employees: A Controlled Evaluation." *Quarterly Journal of Studies on Alcohol* (1968), 29:382–99.

Trice, H.M. and Belasco, J.A. "The Alcoholic and His Steward: A Union Problem." *Journal of Occupational Medicine* (1966), 8:481–487.

Trice, H.M. and Schonbrunn, M. "A History of Job-Based Alcoholism Programs: 1900–1955." *Journal of Drug Issues* (Spring 1981), II:171–198.

Weiss, R.M. "Report on the Third Conference Board Study." Presentation to the Seventh Annual Meeting of ALMACA, San Francisco, October 5, 1978.

Wrich, J.T. *The Employee Assistance Program: Updated for the 1980's*. Center City, MN: Hazelden, 1980.

7

EAP Service Center Model
Susan K. Isenberg

Introduction

Historically, EAPs have been established in large work organizations where one or more individuals operate the program on a part or full time basis. However, more than 60% of the workforce in the United States and Australia are employed by organizations having less than 500 people. The Service Center (SC) model has been developed as a means of providing EAP services to small or medium size employers ranging in size from 5 to 5000 workers, which do not have the resources of an internal program or which prefer to utilize an outside EAP service provider.

The SC model emerged in the United States in the early 1970s. The National Institute of Alcohol Abuse and Alcoholism (NIAAA) funded various host organizations to test their suitability for providing EAP services to small and medium size businesses.

The staff, volunteer board members, and member companies of the Lincoln EAP in Lincoln, Nebraska, which was a recipient of NIAAA funding from 1974–81, have been recognized for their efforts in breaking new ground and refining the SC model. Many of the issues discussed in this article are now identifiable because of the pioneering efforts of those involved with the Lincoln EAP.

This article describes the structure and services provided by an EAP Service Center and highlights in a fairly pragmatic way major administrative and programmatic issues to be resolved in operating a SC. Implications of being "on the outside" are also discussed.

The author has assimilated information for this article from her experience as Executive Director of the Lincoln EAP in Lincoln, Nebraska, from 1977–83, and from her observations and consultation work with other EAP Service Centers throughout the United States and Australia.

Service Center Structure

Independent of Direct Service Providers

Don Phillips and Harry Older, Ph.D. (1981), classified EAP service delivery systems into four basic models: internal program, service center program, treatment or social service agency-based, and union-based. They distinguished between EAP services provided to different workplaces by a free standing, independent SC, and those provided by a community resource which was affiliated with an agency providing direct services, such as a hospital, mental health center, or alcoholism treatment center. Reference to the SC model in this article refers only to those centers which are either free standing or independent of agencies or hospitals providing direct services. The SC model is diagrammed in Figure 7-1.

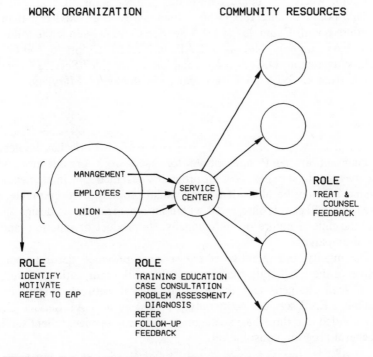

SERVICE CENTER MODEL

WORK ORGANIZATION   COMMUNITY RESOURCES

MANAGEMENT
EMPLOYEES
UNION

SERVICE CENTER

ROLE
TREAT &
COUNSEL
FEEDBACK

ROLE
IDENTIFY
MOTIVATE
REFER TO EAP

ROLE
TRAINING EDUCATION
CASE CONSULTATION
PROBLEM ASSESSMENT/
   DIAGNOSIS
REFER
FOLLOW-UP
FEEDBACK

FIGURE 7-1. Service Center model reprinted with the permission of the authors and *EAP Digest*. Phillips, Donald A. and Older, PH.D., Harry J., "Models of Service Delivery", *EAP Digest*, May/June 1981, p. 14.

Consortium or Service Center

Paul Roman (1980) makes a distinction between an EAP Service Center and an EAP consortium. An EAP consortium is generally initiated and developed by common consent of those work organizations interested in receiving EAP services or benefits available through association with the consortium. The consortium is governed by its member organizations, which collectively own the system of service delivery. An example of a non-profit EAP consortium is Employee Assistance of Central Virginia, Inc., in Lynchburg, Virginia.

In contrast, the EAP Service Center is initiated and developed by an outside group of EAP specialists who are interested in providing EAP services to employees, supervisors, and union representatives in different work organizations. Each work organization or member has a contract for a specified time period, which lists the services available from the SC and other terms of agreement. Since the members pay for services through a contractual arrangement, they do not "own" the SC as is the case in an EAP consortium. SC policy is determined more by professionals than in the consortium, where the board determines policy. Some SCs may have a voluntary board of directors, whose function is more advisory than the consortium board. Examples of EAP Service Centers include the following: Lincoln EAP, Lincoln, Nebraska; EAPs in Boulder, Colorado; and COPE, Inc., in Washington, D.C. A more complete list of EAP Service Centers is available from the NIAAA Clearinghouse in Rockville, Maryland.

Services

The primary role of the EAP Service Center is to design, implement, and maintain an EAP appropriate for each work organization which subscribes for its services. Not all programs designed and implemented by the same SC may be alike. If the individual program is to be viable, well utilized, and effectively integrated within an organization, its design should reflect the unique nature of the company, its product or function, and the types of employees.

The quality and quantity of the services provided depend upon the expertise of the EAP staff, the nature of the work organizations served, the type of fees charged, and the existing referral network system in the community. EAP services commonly provided by an EAP Service Center can be divided into three basic categories: company services, client services, and general program consultation.

Company Services

The steps taken by a small or medium size company in establishing an EAP are similar to those taken by a large corporation in implementing an internal program. The SC provides consultation services to the company to design the program and develop the policy statement and procedures for handling troubled employees in line with the company's existing policies and procedures. The administrative location of the program is designated by the company, an internal coordinator is appointed, and a plan for actual program implementation is jointly developed. Sometimes a joint labor/management steering committee is also appointed to monitor the program's effectiveness. Usually the SC, in consultation with the company's personnel or training department, provides the actual training to supervisory and union personnel on how to handle an employee with a job performance problem and when to refer them to the SC. The SC is responsible for consulting with the internal company coordinator for ongoing program maintenance and evaluation. Educational and orientation programs for employees are jointly planned to keep the services visible and utilized. Some SCs also provide ongoing training and education to the internal company coordinator to enhance his/her effectiveness.

Counseling Services

The EAP Service Center is intended to function as a link between the employee or family member and qualified, affordable referral resources in the community. The SC generally does not provide the ongoing care or treatment which is available elsewhere in the community. One exception may be short term counseling whereby the individual resolves his/her problem in less than six sessions and does not require additional assistance in the community.

Professional staff of the EAP Service Center provide the initial assessment, motivational counseling and referral to community resources to employees, their immediate family members, and to others as noted in the contract. Consultation is made with company and union personnel as appropriate. The case is managed or coordinated by SC staff and ongoing follow-up with the employee, the supervisor, the steward, and the community referral resource for as long as necessary.

EAP Consultation

EAP Service Centers may also be called upon to provide other EAP consultation services. For example, a SC may contract with a large corporation to provide back-up counseling and company services to its internal program, or to help design, implement, and train the staff for a new internal program. Direct service agencies interested in offering EAP services to employers may request EAP consultation and staff training from experienced staff of an EAP Service Center.

Administrative Issues to be Resolved by a Service Center

Staffing an EAP Service Center

It is important that an EAP Service Center practice what it preaches and establish its own system of personnel administration with appropriate personnel policies, performance appraisals, an administrative disciplinary system, and an outside resource to provide EAP services to the SC. Staff of an EAP Service Center are not immune to job performance issues and personal problems common to other work settings.

In light of the variety of the work organizations and employees served, flexibility and diversity are key ingredients for staffing an EAP Service Center. Staffing patterns may include hiring specialists, generalists, or a combination of both.

An EAP generalist is a "jack of all trades," able to do the marketing, counseling, training, education, and ongoing maintenance functions to specific accounts. Smaller SCs may find the generalist approach to be a useful staffing pattern because of enhanced communication and credibility with each account. Member companies like having just one person handle all their EAP needs. The obvious difficulty of the generalist approach is staff selection. EAP "jacks of all trades" are hard to find and train.

Larger SCs may employ a number of EAP specialists who limit their responsibilities to only one or two of the primary EAP functions and may work with all member accounts. The advantages of the specialist approach include enhanced quality control and consistency in the delivery of services, and greater flexibility in staff selection.

The professional expertise needed for a successful EAP Service Center makes it important to have a staff development program whereby new staff members have ample opportunity to learn the operations of the SC, as well as how to provide high quality EAP services. Until recently, "flying by the seat of one's pants" and on-the-job training were the primary means of EAP staff training.

The Lincoln EAP, in existence since 1974 in Lincoln, Nebraska, estimates that it can take one full year to train an experienced counselor or therapist to make the adjustments necessary in their counseling approach to EAP clients. During the first year, new counseling staff at the Lincoln EAP concentrated on perfecting their skills in providing EAP counseling services. It was not until their second year with the Lincoln EAP that they were given additional company responsibilities, such as providing supervisory training and program consultation with individual accounts.

The academic degrees of staff of EAP Service Centers vary considerably, from no academic degree but a great deal of "experience," to Ph.D.'s. Ideally, it is wise to recruit individuals with a variety of skills, training, interests, and experience. Experience in alcoholism, particularly the identification and intervention of early alcoholism, is commonly regarded as an essential requirement for counseling staff of an EAP Service Center.

Funding

The funding source for most EAP Service Centers is the employer, rather than the union or the employees served. Some SCs have had additional government subsidy; affiliates of the National Council on Alcoholism and the Chamber of Commerce have also provided funding for independent SCs.

The most common types of fee structure used by EAP Service Centers include fees by the hour, by the specific service performed, or by the number of employees in the organization. Per hour charges for EAP services range from $25–$75. Per capita rates, whereby an employer's annual fee is determined by the number of its employees, vary from a low of $5 per employee per year in a non-profit SC, to a high of $35–$50 per employee per year in a for-profit SC.

The fee structure and funding source directly impact the quantity and quality of services rendered, and the internal operations of an EAP Service Center. For example, hourly fees for specific counseling services and supervisory and union training sessions may affect how often EAP services are utilized. An employer may be selective in which employees are referred to a SC which charges by the hour for counseling and consultation. Or, an employer may be resistant to update training for supervisors or educational programs for employees if additional fees are charged.

SCs charging a per capita fee may find it too costly to service a business with less than 150 employees. Unless the per capita rate is sufficiently high to absorb its indirect costs, the SC runs the risk of actually losing money with a small account. A SC may lose money with any account if the referral rate is higher than anticipated or it takes more staff time to service the account than originally planned.

Because the employer is usually the funding source, the SC must be responsive to the employer's needs and expectations to insure continuation of the program and the contract each year. The success or failure of an individual client referred to the SC may indeed impact the company's view of the value of maintaining its EAP and its contract for services with the SC. The programmatic implications of this financial reality pose interesting challenges for SC staff in their efforts to serve the employee, the union, and the employer in a manner which does not involve taking sides or favoring one or the other.

Management Information System

The type of management information system an EAP Service Center establishes is directly influenced by the agreements in the contract with each employer. For example, the SC may be obligated to prepare annual reports for each account, summarizing the type of services provided throughout the year and the number of people served. Some accounts may want additional cost effectiveness information. It is important that the SC anticipate these needs and establish a paperwork system which is efficient and will produce the reports promised in the service contract. Increased use of computerized EAP data systems is expected in the future by EAP Service Centers.

Programmatic Issues to be Faced by a Service Center

Quality or Quantity

Marketing strategies of EAP services often reflect the SC's preference for quality or quantity programs. Is it more important to market many new contracts each year and devote energies into start-up services? Or, is it more important to channel energies into program maintenance and thereby enhance the quality and depth of existing individual programs? Financial realities are pivotal and influence how an EAP Service Center responds to the quality or quantity issue and develops its marketing strategies.

However, in the long run, it appears that successful programs which are well established and competently maintained are the most effective marketing tool for an EAP Service Center. Prospective employers will become seriously interested in implementing an EAP and contracting for service with an EAP Service Center with an established track record (Isenberg, 1983).

Piecemeal or Complete Service Delivery Contracts

A second programmatic question to be faced by a SC is whether to provide EAP services on a piecemeal basis to any interested employer or employee, or to market a complete program service delivery system to employers with a service contract. A complete EAP system would include written policies and procedures, supervisory and union training and orientation, employee education, assessment and referral services, program evaluation, and a plan for ongoing program maintenance and follow-up.

The piecemeal approach, whereby any EAP service is provided to any interested employer, is sometimes used by new SCs as a way of getting established and developing a track record. Though this may prove successful in the short run, it often proves to be unmanageable over time and may result in reduced quality services, cancelled contracts, and an unfavorable reputation among employers.

There are distinct advantages of offering a complete EAP service delivery system. By offering employers a complete package of EAP services, the SC is distinguished from other social service agencies in the community which also may be interested in providing training, counseling, and educational services to employers. Second, a complete EAP system, once established in a company and carefully maintained by the company and the SC, increases the likelihood of success cases among employee referrals which, in turn, results in enhanced union and management commitment to the program. In contrast, by offering assessment and referral services to an employee whose employer has not established a formal program, the SC may be at a disadvantage of trying to build a "house without having first laid the foundation."

Program Maintenance

Without proper nourishment, programs will die on the vine. To insure continuation of programs and employer contracts, it is important that an EAP Service Center develop options of program maintenance with individual employers which are appropriate to the type of work setting and the expectations of the employer and the employees. Creative new programming ideas in supervisory/union training and employee education have been explored as SCs devise ways to keep their services in demand and the programs properly maintained at individual work sites.

Parameters of EAP Services Offered

An EAP Service Center may be asked to expand the scope of its services to employers to include organizational and management consultation. For example, a small business may be interested in improving its personnel practices or starting an organizational development program. Because the staff of the SC are known and trusted by the employer, they may be the first ones approached. The SC may elect to serve as a broker for employers in locating a suitable consultant or may choose to offer the services directly. Other areas of involvement for EAP Service Centers in the future may include occupational health and safety efforts and industry wellness programs.

Implications of Being on the Outside

There are distinct advantages and disadvantages of being on the outside and trying to service an "out-house program" as compared to managing an "in-house program." Following are the advantages which the SC model has in delivering EAP services to employers, along with a list of disadvantages or challenges to be overcome.

Advantages

- Contracting for services with an EAP Service Center is likely to be less expensive for employers with less than 5000 employees.

- The confidentiality of the program is more easily perceived and maintained, since the SC is outside the structure of the work organization and the counseling sessions may be held away from the worksite.

- An EAP Service Center may establish valuable clout among the community referral resources and thereby insure that its clients receive priority treatment. Referral resources are quick to learn that unsatisfactory care of an EAP client or lack of cooperation in handling the client may result in less referrals.

- Because EAP may be "their business, their only business," an EAP Service Center an advantage over other social service agencies in responding to the particular needs of employers and employees in the workplace.

Disadvantages or Challenges to Be Overcome

Being on the outside does pose some problems. Phillips and Older (1981) list five disadvantages:

- No on-site counseling
- No ownership of the program by the work organization
- Reluctance by supervisors to deal with "outsiders"
- Lack of knowledge about the internal workings of the organization
- Difficulties in communication between the SC and the work organization

Each of these very real problems identified by Phillips and Older can be overcome by an EAP Service Center by developing a well thought out plan of ongoing program maintenance.

For example, on-site counseling services are now being offered by some EAP Service Centers as part of their ongoing effort of program maintenance. Regular visits to the company for in-plant counseling are excellent ways of maintaining program visibility and increasing utilization.

The SC can encourage program ownership by the employer in a number of ways. The company can be responsible for printing program publicity materials and featuring stories about the program in its in-house newsletter. The company coordinator can assume all the program coordination functions that an in-house program coordinator would have, except that they refer the employees to the SC for counseling, rather than attempt to assess and refer directly. Encouraging a company to provide testimony about its program to other employers is another effective way of facilitating program ownership by an account.

The company may be the most important client of the SC. The qualities in an effective relationship between the SC and the work organization are similar to those in an effective relationship between a counselor and a client. The SC must try and get to know the organization by taking a tour of the facilities, and becoming familiar with its products and management practices. Staff of the SC should take a personal interest in the company, actually care what happens to it and how it survives hard economic times. Demonstration of genuine interest and concern can take place by regularly scheduled visits to the worksite, and attendance at special company events, such as a 50th anniversary celebration or a company open house. Reliable, consistent communication is essential in maintaining an effective relationship with an account, just as with a client. To the extent that a solid working relationship is established between the company and the SC, to that extent the disadvantages of being on the outside are reduced.

Perhaps the most important way to strengthen the SC's relationship between individual accounts and supervisors is through the effective management of employee referrals. Pockets of support for the SC are established within the workplace as employees use the program. Over time there may be a powerful rippling effect as the program and the credibility of the EAP Service Center become firmly rooted within the organization. This process may take two to four years depending upon the number of employees referred.

Summary

The SC model is proving to be a practical, effective way for expanding EAP coverage to the total workforce, and for incorporating EAP systems into standard operating procedures of small and medium size organizations.

This article has attempted to describe the structure of an EAP Service Center, to list the services typically provided, and to highlight the major administrative and programmatic issues to be resolved in managing a SC. It has demonstrated that the SC model is an attractive, efficient vehicle for small and medium size work organizations to utilize and provide EAP services to their employees and their family members. The disadvantages of being on the outside can be overcome with a properly designed plan for ongoing program maintenance.

Glossary of Terms

EAP consortium: a free standing or independent resource initiated and developed by common consent by those work organizations interested in receiving EAP services or benefits through association with the consortium.

EAP Service Center: a free standing or independent resource, initiated and developed by outside EAP specialists not affiliated with a direct service provider, which provides EAP services to different work organizations.

Generalist: an EAP professional who is a "jack of all trades," able to do the marketing, counseling, training, education, and ongoing maintenance functions for specific accounts within an EAP Service Center.

Specialist: an EAP professional who limits responsibilities to only one or two of the primary EAP functions performed by an EAP Service Center.

References

Phillips, Donald A., and Older, Ph.D., Harry J., "Models of Service Delivery", *EAP Digest*, May/June 1981, pp. 12–15.

Isenberg, Susan K., "Report on Australian Industry Programs", Australian Foundation on Alcoholism and Drug Dependence (AFADD), Canberra A.C.T., Australia, September-December 1983 (Unpublished Paper).

Roman, Paul M., "Adapting to Success: A Study of Organizational Transition in an Employee Assistance Program Service Center", Tulane University, October 1982 (Unpublished Paper).

"Service Centers for Employee Alcoholism Programs: Observations from a Field Case Study", Tulane University, October 1980 (Unpublished Paper).

8

Assessment/Referral
Sandra Turner

Introduction

The previous chapters in this section developed the notion of variety that exists in this field of employee assistance programming. A diversity of program models, auspice, scope, and method of implementation is tolerated in achieving the program's major objectives. Whether the program is directed only toward alcohol/drug dependency or all manner of personal, emotional, family, health, legal and financial problems; whether the program is sponsored by management, the union(s), or both jointly; whether the program is internal or contracted by an external consultant; the assessment and referral function is common to all programs. It is the primary activity performed by EAP counselors.

In this chapter, assessment and referral will be defined. Guidelines for conducting the assessment and referral interview as well as qualifications of staff performing in this role will be presented. Case examples will illustrate the critical role of the assessment/referral activity. These examples consider the problem of alcoholism. It remains the single greatest human problem in the workplace, one for which an accurate assessment is essential to a successful treatment outcome.

The ability to accurately describe employee problems and refer those persons to effective treatment modalities is increasingly valued by the workplace. The era of accountability envelops us all. As health care costs escalate, state-of-the-art assessment procedures gain greater attention. Enhancing one's knowledge and skill in the areas of both assessment techniques and treatment modalities will produce cost-effective outcomes in the workplace. This is essential to maintaining programs in the 1980s.

Working Definitions

The discussion of assessment and referral is suited to the workplace where the setting always has an influence upon the manner in which assessment and referral is conducted. The workplace is a contained setting which affords easy access to employees and to information about their behavior in productive, task-oriented activities. The culture of the workplace expects diversion from productive activity to be kept to a minimum. Assessment, referral, and follow-up contacts with employees by the program must be efficient.

Assessment is the definition of a problem being experienced by an individual employee or dependent(s). Job site factors relating to the employee's problem are considered. However, assessment of the job site for organizational change is not within the purview of this definition. Referral is the interpretation of the problem by the EAP counselor to the employee/dependent which results in acceptance of the preliminary treatment plan. Referral depends upon the availability of good treatment modalities in the community. The decision to counsel within the program or refer out depends upon the program model, the skills, knowledge, and availability of program counselors, the variety of community resources, and the nature and severity of the employee's or dependent's problem(s).

The Assessment and Referral Resource

The assessment and referral resource links persons in need with appropriate assistance. It is an independent, neutral site. Whether internal to the organization or an external, contracted service, this resource should be independent of all treatment modalities. There exists in the community a great variety of specialists: alcoholism counselors, marital/family therapists, hypnotherapists, cognitive-behavioral psychologists, financial consultants, nutrition counselors, etc., who perceive problems through their filters of bias. The EAP counselor is a generalist who determines which of the above-mentioned specialists is most appropriate for any given employee. The only bias evident by the EAP counselor is in achieving a suitable match between employee and treatment.

The Assessment Interview

There are numerous ways by which an employee comes into the program. Self, supervisory, union, and family referrals are most common. In addition, former clients, co-workers, medical department, personnel department, literature mailed to employees' homes, posters, newsletter articles, and training sessions for key employees generate referrals. Whatever the source of referral, the employee is normally anxious and frightened during that initial interview. Some time should be taken by the counselor to describe the guidelines for participation and highlighting the program's key elements: It is a confidential, professional service for employees and their dependents; health insurance benefits can be applied toward the cost of treatment; and no evidence of participation enters the medical or personnel files.

Data to be obtained during the assessment interview include: medical history and results of any recent physical examinations, family and marital history, psychological and social interaction patterns, and drinking and drug use experience. The focus is upon current functioning in the arenas of job, marriage and family life, social networking, and legal and financial circumstances. Historical data that further explains current functioning usually is elicited at the counselor's discretion.

The first source of information in the assessment process is the employee. Additional sources of information are desireable to corroborate the initial, presenting problem. The employee's manager, supervisor, union coordinator, family, and company medical department can be excellent sources. In many such circumstances, it may be appropriate to obtain written permission to obtain specific information in advance from the employee. In the counselor's judgement, if the request for permission to obtain additional data would jeopardize the rapport being established with the employee and negatively affect the employee's motivation to accept help to achieve problem resolution, then the request is withheld. In these instances, further assessment through psychological testing and evaluation can be utilized to achieve corroboration of the presenting problem.

The assessment interview should conclude with:

- Statement of the problem(s) using empirical data provided by the employee and his/her manager, supervisor, union coordinator, family, and company medical department
- Prioritization of the problems: primary, secondary, tertiary
- Recommendations for resolving the problem(s), including referral for treatment
- Reassurance that accepting the offer of help is the first step toward symptom amelioration
- Schedule of follow-up sessions with the program to support progress being achieved or to revise the recommended plan of action

The assessment may not be completed before treatment begins. It is appropriate to motivate the employee to begin working on the primary problem in order to relieve emotional pressure. However, the assessment process should be completed within the first two weeks of treatment.

Referral

Following immediately upon the conclusion of the assessment comes the entry of the employee into treatment. Treatment providers can be psychiatrists, other physicians, psychologists, other mental health counselors, social workers, alcoholism counselors, educational specialists, attorneys, nurses, dietitians, physical therapists, etc., who are expert with the problems of marriage and family, mental health, alcoholism and drug abuse, physical illness, day care, housing, child custody and visitation rights, consumer fraud, bankruptcy, wage garnishment, etc. Services can be provided in various settings: inpatient, outpatient, intermediate group homes, etc.

There are many questions to ask of treatment providers. Is there Joint Commission for the Accreditation of Hospitals accreditation or other licensure accessibility? What are the admission and pre-admission policies? Are the surroundings clean and comfortable? Is detoxification provided (alcohol and drug dependency)? What is the expected duration of inpatient confinement? What are the diagnostic and evaluative services available? What is the philosophy of human development and treatment of its problems? With which clients, by age, race, sex, marital status, intelligence, social status, verbal acuity, etc. is the provider most successful? What is the staffing pattern? What are the credentials of the staff—educational disciplines and experience? Is there a waiting list? What is the cost? Is health insurance coverage applicable? Are Medicare, Medicaid, SSI accepted? Are extended payments permitted? What is the nature of the relationship with the referral resource? How are records kept, are there admission and discharge summaries, psychological testing, counselor notes? What is the continuity of care? Each treatment resource should be visited before employees or dependents are referred for service. In doing this exhaustive review of treatment options, one can effect the availability of a variety of modes of professional care at a reasonable cost.

Follow-up

It is essential to maintain contact with the treatment provider to determine the employee's progress, and with the employee to determine progress and to elicit feedback concerning the treatment resource. When suitable permissions by the employee are in effect, follow-up with management regarding job performance, with the union coordinator regarding relationships with peers, and with family regarding behavior and relationships at home, is desireable. The nature and severity of the employee's problem will determine the frequency and duration of follow-up.

Assessment and Referral Staff Qualifications

There is a variety of human service professional disciplines represented in the workplace. Each brings a unique orientation to the process of assessment and referral because of its philosophy about both human development and problem resolution. Where there is opportunity to employ several counselors in the program, an inter-disciplinary team is desireable.

The criteria that provide a positive indication of one's ability to perform well in the assessment and referral role have been described by Jim Wrich (1980).

1. Educational level can be an indicator of one's knowledge of the problems with which an EAP must deal. Degrees in psychology, social work, psychiatry, and other human services fields can be valuable. Whatever the degree, however, the person in this position must also have training in alcoholism and other forms of chemical dependency. The effectiveness of the assessment and referral resource will be severely diminished if he or she does not have formal training in alcoholism and other forms of chemical dependency and its etiology. In fact, those employees suffering from an addictive disorder may actually be worse off for the encounter because misdiagnosis will feed the denial process.

2. Clinical experience, especially in the counseling of human problems, is valuable. We emphasize that the assessment and referral resource is not a counselor per se, but one who assesses the nature and severity of problems and then refers the employee to appropriate care. However, the experiences and skills acquired as a counselor can be a considerable asset in fulfilling these two functions. Again, we want to emphasize that such experiences are less significant if gained working with only one type of problem. Experience should have brought the applicant in contact with a variety of problems matching the scope of the EAP. The program cannot handle a greater range of problems than the assessment and referral resource is capable of accurately identifying.

3. Personal recovery from human problems can be a valuable asset in this position. The essence of its value, however, may not lie in the personal recovery itself, but rather in the empathy and understanding it generates in the recovering person towards other people with problems. The quality rather than the fact of recovery is the critical issue. In general, the person serving as the assessment and referral resource must be stable or the program's credibility will suffer.

A recovering alcoholic in this position who relapses, has very short-term sobriety, or is struggling to work out his/her own program will have a difficult time in this position. A person with chronic marital, emotional, or other problems will also have difficulties. While it may be possible for people with such problems to function acceptably in other jobs, EAPs cannot afford the risk.

4. Previous successful experience as an assessment and referral resource for an EAP is one of the best qualifications for the position. Five years ago it was almost impossible to find someone with this type of experience. However, the availability of experienced assessment and resource people has increased greatly. We expect that the numbers of qualified assessment and referral resource people will continue to increase in the years ahead, based on the numbers of people who are interested in the EAP field and that are inquiring how to obtain qualifications.

5. Experience in developing an EAP does not assure competence as an assessment and referral resource, but it can add a valuable dimension to the person carrying out that function. This is especially true if there has been experience in policy development, key employee orientation, and development of communications methods between the program and other key groups such as employees' families, senior management, and the unions. Such experience can be particularly helpful to a program that is just getting started. But such experience should not be regarded as a substitute for the professional occupational program consultant who may be needed to design, develop, and implement the EAP. The essential skills of the assessment and referral resource are not the same as the essential skills of a consultant who develops and establishes EAPs. It is unusual to find someone who is highly qualified in both areas.

6. Overall work experience should be recognized when reviewing the qualifications of a prospective assessment and referral resource person. One problem that frequently arises is that while a person trained and experienced in human services is able to empathize with the employee having problems, that person cannot comprehend and empathize with corporate or union objectives. A candidate who has experience working for a company of comparable size and structure in the same or a related industry can bring a valuable dimension to the position. This is particularly true if the candidate has had supervisory experience or has been an active member of a labor union (Wrich, 1980).

Professionalism

Becoming a professional is an evolving process. It is not a resting place, but rather a constant attainment. The process combines academic training with an apprenticeship in the field.

A professional knows his/her boundaries: areas of expertise as well as limitations. He/she knows the major methodologies of their area of practice, and knows where to go for knowledge that he or she doesn't possess. The professional continues to study, to expand skills, and to consider new solutions for old problems.

Future Directions

The assessment of the individual, his/her problems and unique circumstances, and the subsequent referral to a particular treatment modality is more critical to treatment outcome than might be realized. In the case of alcoholism, not everyone is suitable for a 28-day residential alcoholism treatment facility. Almost all, but not everyone, can be involved in AA to retain sobriety. How does one decide which treatment modality is best for a given employee or dependent?

The way that each of us selects a treatment resource is through our filter of bias based on our experience. In addition to our own biases and intuition, there is another method for selecting appropriate treatment. Differential diagnosis is a concept developed by Frederick Glaser of the Addiction Research Foundation in Ontario, Canada. The first studies that he completed on this subject were written in 1979, although research has been collected over the past thirty years. The concept has been developed in relationship to alcoholism treatment, but has application to other human conditions as well.

Differential Diagnosis

Differential diagnosis assumes that every man is in certain respects like a) all other men, b) some other men, and c) no other man. For example, I am like all humans in having basic needs; like some other humans, a woman; and like no one else because I am me. Similarities and differences exist among individuals. There are distinct types of alcoholic clients differing widely in personality and psychopathology. It is dangerous—very dangerous—to assume that all individuals presenting a certain set of symptoms can be treated in the same way. This matching concept, as it is called, depends upon the recognition that individual clients or subgroups of clients are more different than they are alike. The population with alcohol problems is diverse, so treatment services should be diverse.

Controlled experimentation suggests that the results of uniform intervention applied to an undifferentiated group of clients is no better than minimal interventions, such as merely giving advice. In theory, it is very logical that matching a discrete remedy to a particular problem is a sound idea. However, in practice, the convenience of possessing a single remedy for a set of problems proves to be too tempting to avoid. Treatment centers often boast about their individualized treatment plans. In reality, all clients pass through their routinized programs.

Matching is the deliberate and consistent attempt to select a specific candidate for a specific method of intervention in order to achieve specific goals. For it to work, there must be an adequate evaluation of clients, of methods of intervention, of goals, and a rational method for aligning candidates, interventions, therapists and goals. The ability to determine the outcome of treatment by means of follow-up is critical.

Each of these components: clients, interventions, and goals will be looked at separately.

Specification of clients

One must know a great deal about an individual client prior to referral for treatment. A careful assessment must be conducted. Demographic factors such as present situation, family system, work record, legal entanglements, as well as psychometric variables such as verbal ability and abstract reasoning ability should be noted. The content of assessment includes medical, historical, social, attitudinal, psychological, vocational and recreational information. Strengths, abilities, needs, and life style must be specified. This will provide ideas about the most appropriate match with treatment and will provide a baseline against which future change can be measured. The process need not be elaborate. Simple demographic data gathered carefully can form a good basis for matching.

Specification of interventions

The evaluation of treatment methods is not well developed. Forty years ago, Dr. Jellinek observed that the only possibility of improving treatment for alcoholism was to bring greater order into psychotherapeutic procedures. By this he meant that a definite effort had to be made to establish criteria for the suitability of any given method for a particular client. Consider the special attributes of the therapist and the special attributes of the client. Is there a match? Consider the geographical proximity of treatment to client and family? Is it convenient? Is there a good variety of treatment programs from which to choose?

Specification of goals

Examples of goals include abstinence from alcohol, learning better ways of talking with others, learning how to enjoy free time, and satisfactory job functioning. Goals must be clearly stated and related to the specific method of intervention for outcome evaluation. The salient aspects of various treatment preferences should be presented to the client, along with the goals of these treatment methods. Clients should be involved in selecting the treatment method and establishing goals. As EAP counselors who do have some control, some are tempted to impose their brilliance and authority upon the alcoholic, telling him/her what to do, and ultimately losing them to seething compliance.

Knowledge of outcome is the only way of deciding whether a match has been achieved, that is, whether there is a positive outcome with regard to one or more explicitly stated goals.

- Follow-up with the employee on a regular basis for six months to one year. These interviews are the best method for determining outcome.
- Determine the rate of referrals completed. Have employees successfully engaged in treatment?
- Determine the attrition rate. What is the percentage of employees who have completed treatment?
- What is the status at the conclusion of treatment? Status considers job, mental, emotional, psychological, and physical functioning.

All methods of determining outcome depend upon systematic recording in the program file.

Some of the conclusions that can be drawn from this hypothesis of matching are:

- Greater analysis of "treatment" is necessary to specifically describe its components.
- A thorough assessment of clients is desirable in order to make better referrals to appropriate treatment.
- Follow-up must be conducted regularly to ascertain client outcomes over a lengthy period of time. One of the greatest problems in alcoholism treatment research is the lack of longitudinal studies. Most clients are only followed for two years.

There are some obstacles to matching experimentation:

- Clinical settings may show reluctance to submit to such close scrutiny.
- Often multiple interventions are applied, so it is not possible to determine which is responsible for the observed results. For example, Antabuse, AA, group therapy might all be recommended for a client.

- Therapists are usually strongly committed to their particular method of intervention and are unwilling to consider other options.
- Programs competing for health insurance reimbursement dollars are reluctant to refer clients to another method of treatment, even if those clients are not suitable for their setting.

Ideally, treatment resources would coordinate services and cooperate with one another. Each could provide a special modality of treatment, and serve a specialized population rather than compete against one another with similar, generalized treatment. An independent setting, like the hub of a wheel, can differentially diagnose and refer to the spokes. A successful example of this is being developed by the General Motors Substance Abuse Program in Doraville, Georgia.

The more effective the match, the better the likelihood of follow through and successful recovery. That is the goal. There is never a guarantee of another recovery after a relapse, so it is important to attempt to make the correct match the first time. In the Sheldon and Eleanor Glueck prospective study, *Delinquents and Nondelinquents in Perspective* (1968), 110 of the 400 juveniles studied developed alcoholism at some point in their lives. Each was followed for 5 to 8 years after treatment. At the end of that time only 24 were still abusing alcohol. All the rest had died or become abstinent!

All of us have seen colleagues, or even ourselves burn out with pessimism and frustration after several years of EAP practice, disillusioned by the insignificant changes in some of the persons with whom they worked. As helpers, we must acknowledge that recovery from any human problem is the employee's own responsibility ultimately, and that we are powerless over another's alcoholism, drug abuse, depression, or schizophrenia. The EAP counselor does not render himself/herself useless by this acknowledgement. The statement expresses an appreciation for the process that must occur between the EAP counselor and employee to effect change.

Conclusion

There is a functional relationship between assessment and treatment. An accurate match assures the greatest likelihood of symptom amelioration in the most reasonable period of time. As the EAP expands into areas of prevention, the basic function of skillful assessment and referral of individual problems must be maintained.

References

Barlow, David H. (ed.). *Behavioral Assessment of Adult Disorders*. New York: The Guilford Press, 1981.

Erfurt, John, and Foote, Andrea. *Occupational Employee Assistance Programs for Substance Abuse and Mental Health Problems*. Ann Arbor: Institute of Labor and Industrial Relations, The University of Michigan—Wayne State University, 1977.

Glaser, Frederick B. "Anybody Got A Match? Treatment Research and the Matching Hypothesis," *Alcoholism Treatment in Transition*, ed. Griffith Edwards and Marcus Grant, Chapter II, 178–196. London: Croom Helm, 1980.

Glueck, Sheldon, and Glueck, Eleanor. *Delinquents and Nondelinquents in Perspective*. Cambridge, Mass.: Harvard University Press, 1968.

Presnall, Lewis F. *Occupational Counseling and Referral Systems*. Salt Lake City: Utah Alcoholism Foundation, 1981.

Solomon, Susan. *Tailoring Alcoholism Therapy to Client Needs*. Rockville, Md.: U.S. Department of Health and Human Services, 1981.

Wrich, James T. *The Employee Assistance Program Updated for the 1980's*. Center City, Minnesota: Hazelden Educational Foundation, 1980.

9

Assessment/Treatment Model
Samuel H. Klarreich

How the Program Evolved

Over a decade ago, the company's employee relations department became somewhat concerned about certain problems of an emotional, psychological nature which employees were expressing. Therefore, an employee relations staff member took it upon himself to explore this further. What became evident was that a program was required to meet these emotional/psychological concerns. The staff member, in turn, prepared a number of documents highlighting the necessity for the establishment of a counseling service.

The details of these documents stirred considerable interest. Several years later, the regional medical services director and the industrial psychologist explored the possibility of establishing an EAP. The medical services director, in particular, when conducting periodic medical examinations, discovered that there were a considerable number of emotional problems being expressed by the employees, which in turn required clinical intervention. Registering his concern to the industrial psychologist, they both proceeded to expand upon the earlier efforts of the employee relations staff member.

For approximately the next one and a half years, the medical services director and the industrial psychologist researched the possibility of establishing an EAP. Their efforts took them to a variety of EAP programs in the community. They spoke to psychologists, social workers, psychiatrists, administrators, union officials, and other related staff members. After considerable time and energy, the two clearly realized the benefits of an EAP. Their efforts also brought them to the conclusion that an in-house assessment/treatment approach to the counseling of the company's troubled employees would be the most appropriate. This program, they decided, would be managed by a clinical psychologist. Once their ideas were drawn up in the form of a proposal with a detailed budget, they presented this to a senior management committee of the company. The committee fully endorsed the proposal.

Rationale For Its Development

There were a number of key reasons which prompted the development of this particular type of program.

A very important consideration was **service availability**. It was critical that the service be available when the employee required assistance and/or counseling. As such, the hours of operation of the program were consistent with the hours of work for the employees. Additionally, the service was designed to accommodate appointments after the normal workday, as needed.

The next consideration was **service accessibility**. It was important that the service be easily reached by any employee who required help. As such, considerable effort was expended in deciding upon the appropriate office location and the appropriate office environment. As well, planning was carried out to determine how employees could contact the service and arrange for appointments without long delays or disruption of their job activities. An office, therefore, was established close to the elevators, and the employee, once he/she phoned for an appointment, could simply get off on the appropriate floor, turn a corner, and conveniently enter the office.

The next consideration was **service credibility**. It was felt quite strongly that the program could gain immense credibility if it were established, not only inside the company, but also within the medical department. In fact, many in-house programs are established within medical services (Presnall, 1981). The medical department has enjoyed a very respectable, credible, and high-regarded reputation for approximately 35 years. It was felt that the EAP, by association with the medical department, could establish and maintain its credibility more easily. In fact, this has proven to be the case.

The next important consideration was **service accountability**. It was felt that the program had a greater chance of succeeding if it was properly managed and held accountable like other programs within the company. It was essential that medical management understand the nature and activities of the program, as well as its utilization and effectiveness. This could be accomplished more readily and more regularly with an in-house program, simply because greater cooperation and closer supervision could take place, especially in the initial stages of the program.

The next important consideration was **organizational knowledge**. It was felt that it would be important for the psychologist to have a clear understanding of the nature of the organization and its needs. The organization is a complex matrix of departments with various levels of management, and for the EAP to become well established it was necessary to have a full appreciation of these. If the psychologist were in close proximity to the daily workings of the organization, then the service being provided would be more reality-based, more relevant, and probably more effective.

The next consideration was **service visibility**. It was felt very strongly that the psychologist should remain visible within the organization, by conducting EAP-related activities, such as seminars and lectures. The most important benefit would be acceptance of the program by the employees of the organization. Visibility would reduce the mystique and the reservations about a psychologist and the EAP services associated with this "mental health professional." In essence, if the person running the EAP made his presence known, then any reservations about the EAP would be reduced.

The next consideration was **service adaptability and flexibility**. It was essential that the service be designed to readily deal with a wide variety of emotional/psychological problems, including severe crises which would require immediate attention. An in-house EAP managed by a clinical psychologist could efficiently accommodate the range of presenting difficulties.

The final consideration was **confidentiality of the service**. It was realized that confidentiality is the cornerstone of a counseling service. Because the medical department within the company had always adhered to strict standards of confidentiality, assurance was required that the EAP would adhere to the same.

How To Prepare For Its Implementation

Following are a variety of activities to be conducted which are important to carry out prior to the implementation of the program. Some activities were carried out during the operation of the service, and probably needed to have taken place prior to the beginning of the program. The reader need not feel that there is a logical progression of steps which must necessarily be followed in a precise fashion. However, certain activities need to be considered and pursued in order to properly prepare for the introduction and ultimate realization of this EAP.

The first activity involves **meetings with key people in the organization**. Meetings with the senior managers from the various departments in the organization are important to pursue (Crawford and Adamson, 1980). Basically, they are an opportunity to introduce yourself. In the exchange, the manager will form certain impressions about you, will correct certain misconceptions, and will come to an understanding about what you bring to the company as well as what you can offer to his/her specific department. Also, this will establish the groundwork for later involvement with this particular department.

Another important series of meetings would be with the senior employee relations/personnel staff (Presnall, 1981). They have a full appreciation of the dynamics of the organization, and are daily exposed to the concerns of employees. Basically, the meetings with the senior employee relations staff will follow the same directions as the meetings with the senior management staff. An exchange of ideas, a discussion of philosophies, an elaboration of your capabilities will occur, and enhance a trusting relationship between you and these key individuals.

Finally, the meetings with the medical staff are critical (Graham, 1983). Working very closely with them, it is essential that they understand your role in the medical department. It is important to describe the nature of your skills and this description will give the medical staff a clearer indication of what you regularly plan to do. The more enlightened the staff is, the more helpful they become, and a better working relationship can thus be established. In addition to meetings, conduct a number of "mini-workshops," outlining the counseling/treatment methods to be employed. When the medical staff made referrals to the EAP, they were able to provide the employees with an understanding of "what might occur once they entered my office." Employee hesitation was reduced, which greatly increased the likelihood that they would follow through with the referral.

The next activity to consider is **the development of basic objectives and the establishment of program policies and procedures** (Shain and Groeneveld, 1980). This creates your standards and criteria for success. Furthermore, this can be employed as a tool to educate the organization about the nature and operation of the EAP. The following items are important to describe: basic purpose or mission statement of the EAP; specific goals; eligibility; types of problems handled through the EAP; confidentiality; the role of the employee; the role of the EAP director; the roles of other significant people such as supervisor/manager, union steward where appropriate, medical services director; and referral procedures to the EAP. This information can be prepared in the form of a booklet and distributed to senior management in the various departments throughout the company.

Another important activity is **the development of a data-collection and record-keeping system** (Foote and Erfurt, 1981). This establishes a monitoring system which will ultimately serve to evaluate the effectiveness of the EAP. It is necessary to decide upon the demographics of the population that you wish to record. These may include: name of the employee and attached code number; age; sex; date of birth; number of years with the company; nature of the presenting problem; department; the referral source;

and date of the initial interview. To maintain ongoing records/notes, it may involve the creation of an intake form; a history form; a form for progress notes and a form for closing the case. What is also valuable to develop is an evaluation form which could be sent to and completed by the employees after the termination of their counseling (30 to 60 days after), to determine how useful they found the service. This form would be completed anonymously to maximize honest feedback. The data collection system should be arranged so that the information at the end of the year could be readily compiled and prepared in the form of an annual report. Since data would be regularly recorded on the employees utilizing the EAP, it would be worthwhile to devise a monthly reporting system that would indicate the level of program activity. This lays the groundwork for a regular process of accountability.

A critical decision is to **determine what assessment and treatment procedures you plan to do in-house** (Manuso, 1983). This will determine the nature of the counseling practice. What is essential is to fully appreciate what you are and are not capable of providing. Where there are gaps in service, it is then important to move out into the community and meet with those specialists who can provide the missing service components which would ultimately allow you to offer a more comprehensive service. As such, meet with alcoholism treatment agencies, Alcoholics Anonymous, long-term treatment specialists, and therapists who practice family therapy. Additionally, meet with diagnostic specialists, particularly in the area of neuropsychology and vocational assessment.

The next important activity to consider is **the training program that you plan to offer** (Presnall, 1981). This is an essential way of educating supervisors about the EAP and how it may be utilized when the need arises. In developing a training package, focus on four main areas: "the troubled employee," "the EAP," "the supervisor," and "the corrective interview." This is a three-hour training session which utilizes a variety of activities including lectures, role-playing, small group discussions, viewing of a film, case studies, and question-and-answer periods. This vehicle increases visibility and helps to reduce the mystery that is associated with any EAP director, especially one who is "a psychologist."

Another activity is the formulation of **orientation material for employees** (Wrich, 1980). This might simply be the creation of a handout, a brochure, or an orientation workshop which newly hired employees receive when they are oriented into the organization. When an employee is hired or transferred to work in the Toronto area, he/she is given a handout which briefly describes the nature of the service, and how to access it. The purpose here is to continue to maintain the visibility and the profile of the EAP, especially for new employees who come into the organization and are looking to gain knowledge about the various resources which are available.

Another significant activity relates to **health education efforts** (Shain and Groeneveld, 1980). This is a critical component, because it not only creates visibility and profile for the EAP, but also links the EAP to prevention and the preventive aspects of health education. A health education committee was formed in my organization and it has proven to be extremely successful in providing employees with lectures about such health-related topics as stress, fitness, cancer, etc. EAPs, especially assessment and treatment programs, are obviously associated with the intervention aspects of health care. Equally as important are the preventive aspects of health care.

A final item to consider is **program evaluation** (Scanlon, 1983). It is important to have a system in place which will allow assess to the usefulness and the effectiveness of the EAP. For my program, I prepared an annual report with two distinct components. The first component was program evaluation. Program evaluation is the extent to which the EAP accomplished what it set out to do. The second component was cost-benefit analysis. Cost-benefit analysis compares the costs and results attributed to the EAP in monetary units which accrue to the company. This method of reporting indicates a concern about accountability, and about the costs and benefits of the program.

Consideration should be given to the **announcement of the program** (Schmitz, 1983). This formally introduces the EAP to the employee population and a number of routes may be taken. In my company, a letter endorsed by the executive director of the medical services was sent to the homes of all the employees in the Toronto area announcing the establishment and the availability of the EAP. The announcement included a brief description of my background and, most importantly, emphasized the confidential nature of the service. Subsequently, a feature article in the company newsletter described in greater detail my background, skills, orientation, etc. It further highlighted the nature of the EAP and what was hoped to be accomplished.

The Practice of an In-House Assessment/Treatment Program

In the Toronto area, there are approximately 2800 employees whom I service. These are mainly white-collar, non-union employees. They are located in approximately eleven sites, four being considered main sites which house a considerable number of employees. My office is located on the medical floor in the main office building of the company. It is a private, spacious, comfortable environment, easily accessible and very conducive to the counseling process.

Approximately 60% of my time is spent in clinical service. This includes assessment, treatment, referral to outside agencies, and follow-up. In regards to assessment, the clinical interview is used to gain the necessary information to diagnose the problem (Anastasi, 1982). An elaborate intake and history form is used to record important details in the formulation of the diagnosis. On occasion, more standardized paper and pencil questionnaires and tests are used, but these measures are used infrequently. Where a specialized form of assessment is required, such as neuropsychological appraisal, vocational testing, or the assessment of a child or an adolescent behavioral disorder or learning difficulty, a referral is made to an outside agency which can offer this specific assessment procedure.

With respect to counseling, I employ a brief yet intensive, structured, problem-oriented, and educationally-oriented approach. It may be labeled cognitive-behavior therapy, or more specifically, rational-emotive therapy. It is a pragmatic, persuasive, directive, and action-oriented approach to counseling (Ellis, 1973). It is also short-term in nature. The employee is strongly encouraged throughout the counseling process to first confront his/her problem at the thought or cognitive level and, secondly, at the behavioral or action level. This method of therapy has been very well researched and documented (Ellis and Grieger, 1977), and has proven to be most successful—certainly with my employee population. In fact, it may be interesting to point out that employees were counseled an average of four sessions. Seventy-five percent of the employees indicated that their problems were satisfactorily resolved, and they found the service most helpful.

The utilization rate of the service, which has been in operation for three and a half years, is approximately 24% of the population. What also may be interesting to note is the rate of recidivism. One might suspect that because of the low number of counseling sessions, the rate of recidivism would be very high. This is not the case. Approximately 10% of the employees return with the same outstanding problem. In the provision of in-house counseling, particular attention needs to be paid to the type of counseling/therapy methods utilized. I do not believe that one can afford to offer long-term, analytical, or non-directive methods of counseling. It is not cost effective (Cumming, 1977); and the employee gradually becomes disillusioned with the whole process, because it is so slow, plodding, and not necessarily efficacious. Utilizing rational-emotive therapy certainly inspires changes in the employee and also dictates that the counselor/therapist remain actively involved in the therapeutic process until the therapy is completed. This approach ensures more meaningful results (Ellis, 1973).

An interesting aside is the fact that employees seem to be utilizing the service at a much earlier stage in their problems. In the initial months of the program, I was intervening in a wide variety of problems, many of which were more chronic and long-standing in nature. However, more recently, since the program has established its credibility, employees contact me much earlier. They are not waiting until their problems become more serious disorders. They seem to be taking greater responsibility for their health and, as such, want to tackle their difficulties more readily.

A breakdown of the types of problems that are presented follows: approximately 55% of the problems are personal and emotional in nature; approximately 20% are job-related; an additional 20% are marital and family in nature; and the final 5% consists mainly of alcohol and drug-related problems. With respect to the referral patterns, the majority of the referrals, about 65%, are self-referrals. The remaining 35% are from medical and/or management. Finally, 95% of the employees are seen by me and the remaining 5% are referred to outside resources.

Approximately 10% of my time is spent in training activities. The majority of the training involves conducting workshops for managers and supervisors on "the troubled employee and the EAP." This workshop is a very intensive 3-hour program and has been well received because it is intensive, yet concise. It is important to note here that training and education within many organizations are not at this time priority items (Phillips et al., 1980). Many organizations adopt the philosophy of "being mean and lean," which translates into a de-emphasis on training. However, if training is to be conducted, it must also be somewhat "lean and mean." This implies that the training be limited in terms of time, yet remain intensive and content-oriented. Particular effort is needed to decide upon the most effective training techniques which can accommodate these requirements.

An additional 10% of my time is spent in employee education. This typically involves delivering "stress" lectures, talks on other health-related matters, and some presentations about the nature of the program and my role in the company. These are very important for the obvious reason that I am visible and people begin to "put a face to" the director of the program. A most significant ingredient of education is the inherent message that "you, the employee" are to take greater responsibility for early recognition of your problems, then act on this awareness by seeking help. In fact, after these educational lectures there is often a surge of self-referrals to the program.

Another 15% is spent on program administration and program evaluation. This would include the preparation of various analyses and reports. It would involve data gathering, preparation of statistics, and reporting of such. These activities allow me to monitor my rate of progress and success. They help decide whether any meaningful program changes need to occur and what directions will be taken. The information may suggest health trends among employees. Corrective measures may then be implemented to address these.

Finally, the remaining 5% is spent in consultation and liaison activities. This includes consulting with internal organizational staff regarding a variety of issues or as liaison with outside agencies regarding specialized services and programs which may have some relevance for the troubled employees of my organization.

Programming For Success

The most important ingredient for success, an ingredient which has often been referred to in this paper, is **the policy of confidentiality**, especially given this type of program (Fisher, 1983). This must be clearly stated in any document about the EAP. In fact, make a point of informing each employee whom you counsel of the confidential nature of the service. Point out the location of your records; the security features in storing the records; and the fact that no one has access to the records. Additionally, indicate that you are bound by the psychologist's code of ethics to ensure that these rigorous standards are maintained. Discuss the issue of "informed consent" with each employee, pointing out very clearly that should he/she choose to release information to anyone, he/she must sign a release of information form which specifically identifies what information is to be released and the individual who is to receive it. Make certain that the employee understands this before engaging in any form of counseling. Whenever I give a presentation or lecture regarding the EAP, the element that is most emphasized is the policy of confidentiality. A good indicator that the EAP is viewed as a confidential service is a large percentage of self-referrals.

The next important ingredient to ensure success is **the location of the office** (Schmitz, 1983). It is wise to establish the office on the same floor as the health services. My office is situated beside the regional health center. When an employee arrives on the appropriate floor to see me, it can be assumed by other employees riding the same elevator that this employee is simply going to the medical services, thus the stigma that may still be associated with being seen going to the "psychologist's office" is minimized.

Another way of ensuring success is **servicing the employees' needs**, both junior-level employees and senior-level employees. This simply implies that the program must be prepared to handle concerns from employees at all levels. Programs of this type often fail because junior staff view it as a service for the senior staff, or vice versa. What is often reflected in that perception is the inability to adequately relate to and help that sector of employees.

Another way to ensure success is to make certain that you clearly indicate your policy regarding **requests for confidential information** (Minter, 1983). Certain people in the organization occasionally need to be reminded that the service is a confidential one, and more importantly that information about any employee will not be discussed unless the employee has voluntarily signed a release of information authorizing the exchange of information. Often this message needs to be repeated, especially in the early stages of the program, until it is firmly embedded in the minds of "curious" employees who need to test the strength of your policies.

Another measure to ensure success is related to **program evaluation and cost-benefit analysis** (Weaver, 1979). A program is successful if it is utilized by the employees, and if it brings about significant changes which can be costed out. It will be imperative to decide upon measures which will be used to evaluate and to cost out this effectiveness. It will also be critical to properly educate your management group about the limitations of any cost-benefit analysis, that is, not all of the benefits which accrue to the EAP can be computed in monetary units.

Need For A "Professional"

To effectively manage an in-house assessment/treatment program, a "professional" is needed. It is not my intent to suggest that a "professional" is equivalent to a psychologist. What I hope will become eminently evident is that knowledge, skills, and experience in certain core areas embody the characteristics of a professional and are necessary requirements in order to manage a program of this nature.

It is essential and basic to have an appreciation of **the nature of man**, an understanding of human behavior and the elements that influence it. Furthermore, it is critical to have an understanding of "the nature of human disorder" (Guidano and Liotti, 1983) and how emotional/psychological problems develop and evolve, and how these can be assessed and ultimately treated.

Knowlege and skills in the area of **assessment and psychodiagnostics** are important (Most and Glazer, 1983), particularly as they relate to chemical dependency and emotional disturbance. This further entails expertise in the use of assessment procedures, tests, and interviews. Tests may include personality measures, tests relating to alcohol misuse, questionnaires relating to interpersonal functioning and tests relating to skill deficits. Assessment will include experience in conducting the clinical interview, where through an effective history-taking process important clinical data may be derived to assist in the formulation of the problem and the direction to take in therapy.

Knowledge and skills in the field of *counseling and psychotherapy* are requirements. This essentially entails a broad understanding of the field of psychotherapy. Included would be a thorough appreciation of the basic methods of therapy and an understanding of their differences (Garfield and Bergin, 1978). Once a general understanding of the field is gained, it would be necessary to decide upon the particular brand of therapy to be used in this EAP. This would require knowledge and understanding of research as it relates to the effectiveness of various counseling methods and practices. Although very little has been written about the effectiveness of various forms of counseling in organizational environments, much has been written about the positive therapeutic outcomes of specific forms of therapy. There are certain types of treatment, namely cognitive-behavioral approaches, which are well-researched and would be well-suited to a corporate environment (Meichenbaum and Jaremko, 1983).

Another critical ingredient is **the experience level** of the program director, particularly in handling emotional disturbances and chemical dependency disorders. It would be essential to have a very strong clinical/counseling background, including experience with alcohol-related problems. Hospital and/or community clinic experience would be mandatory. Exposure to and involvement with business organizations would be valuable.

Another important ingredient would be the knowledge and practice of an **ethical code**. When dealing with the employees' most intimate feelings and thoughts, it is essential to have a clear understanding of what behavior constitutes ethical practice, and the liabilities which are incurred if this practice is not followed. For the practice of psychology, there exist very clear guidelines in terms of professional ethics and professional conduct (OBEP, 1980). It is made very clear what behavior is expected of the psychologist, and if there is failure to abide by the principles, the psychologist's license may be temporarily suspended or permanently removed.

It behooves the practitioner who provides this type of service to adhere to a code of ethical practice, keeping in mind the potential drawbacks which can occur for failure to do so.

The next important dimension is the ability to **evaluate community agencies**. In any community, there are many agencies which offer a wide variety of clinical services. It is essential to have the knowledge and the basic skills to be able to systematically evaluate those programs that are useful and effective from those which do not have much utility.

Knowledge and skills in the area of **research** are most important when considering evaluation and cost-benefit analysis. It would be important to have a basic understanding of research design and evaluation research (Schulberg and Baker, 1979), especially if regularly called upon to provide analytical reports, and to remain accountable to your management group.

Another area is effective **public speaking**. Experience and skills in this area are needed especially if planning to engage in training and education. EAP staff who have had a number of previous opportunities to teach courses are at a distinct advantage. On occasion, in-house coordinators may seek outside resources to provide training and education to the employees. I would caution against this, simply because the training and education components of an in-house assessment/treatment program are critical ingredients in maintaining one's visibility as earlier indicated.

Other skills needed are related to the broad area of **consultation and communication**. These skills are often assumed to be present. Consultation and communication refer to the ability to listen and the ability to problem-solve. Added to these is the ability to express ideas well, whether verbally or written. It is worth noting that the way one would consult and prepare proposals and letters of communication in a clinical environment, is somewhat different from the way one would do in an organization/business environment. There is a greater demand for precision and clarity in a business setting. In a clinical setting, the individual has the luxury to ponder, to reflect, and to pontificate for a period of time. However, these same opportunities are not always available in organizations, where there is a need for precise advice and counsel. To complicate matters, however, one must not lose sight of the limitations of our helping professions, and these limitations may be voiced during a consultation meeting.

The final dimension, which is not often written about, is **the personality of the individual managing the program** (Nahrwold, 1983). There are some people who come to an organization with the belief that they will "eliminate all the ills present in that working environment." Some people may further believe that they will change the organization so that it becomes an environment that is "stress-free and anxiety-free." Others may take themselves "far too seriously." They may assume that because they are "professional," anything which they articulate is virtually "the gospel truth and worthy of being carved in stone." "Clinical jargon" may frequently be the language of choice for some, which may in turn deter the development of meaningful relationships with key people in the organization. Others may be so capable at selling, that they oversell their capabilities and the effectiveness of their counseling. This may lead to false expectations which later damage the credibility of the program. Some people may remove themselves from the organization and simply set up an "in-house private practice," basically offering a specialized service removed from and out of touch with the rest of the organization. If this particular position is taken, it will once again seriously damage the image and the credibility of the program.

What am I suggesting? Flexibility is a critical ingredient in the personality of the coordinator who is attempting to manage an in-house assessment/treatment program. In addition to that, humor is a very important ingredient. It has been cited in research related to treatment and counseling that the humor of a therapist is often an important variable in the therapeutic process (Walen, Di Giusseppe, Wessler, 1980). This also holds true especially for the coordinator of this EAP. If seen as too serious, you may often be avoided, and judged as being "much better than the rest of the individuals in the organization." Not relying upon jargon and scientific terminology is an aid in communicating. It is very easy for people to fall back upon their specialties when engaging in discussion with others. However, if you can go beyond that and simply present yourself "naturally," it will aid in establishing credibility and trust, and an open line of communication. In promoting your program, it is also critical to outline its limitations. Often as practitioners we are so enamored with our services that we tend to oversell. Should you do this in an organization, the increased expectations may not be met, which will greatly hamper the impact of the EAP.

Summary

I have provided you with a case study of an in-house assessment/ treatment program. If you are a professional considering placing yourself in a central EAP role, before considering such a program it is important that you introspect. Understand your strengths and know your weaknesses; determine your capabilities and recognize your limitations. Assess your knowledge, your skills, and your experience; and if you have decided that you are ready, hopefully the organization will be ready as well. If you have the support of the organization to develop and implement a program of this nature, "go for it!"

References

Anastasi, A. *Psychological Testing*, New York, MacMillan, 1982.

Crawford, R.L., and Adamson, H. "Managerial Responses to Mental Disorders Among Employees," *Journal of Occupational Medicine*; 1980, Volume 22, Number 5, pp. 309–315.

Cumming, N. "Prolonged (Ideal) Versus Short-Term (Realistic) Psychotherapy," *Professional Psychology*; 1977, Volume 8, Number 4, pp. 491–501.

Ellis, A. *Humanistic Psychotherapy, The Rational-Emotive Approach*, New York, Julian Press, 1973.

Ellis, A., and Grieger, R. *RET, Handbook of Rational-Emotive Therapy*, New York, Springer Publishing, 1977.

Fisher, G.L. "Employee Counseling Programs and Related Services in the Public Sector," in *Occupational Clinical Psychology*, edited by J.S.J. Manuso, New York, Praeger Publishers, 1983.

Foote, A., and Erfurt, J. "Evaluating an Employee Assistance Program," *Employee Assistance Program Digest*; 1981, October, pp. 14–25.

Garfield, S.L., and Bergin, A.E. *Handbook of Psychotherapy and Behavior Change: An Empirical Analysis*, New York, John Wiley and Sons, 1978.

Graham, R.S. "The Corporate Medical Department: History of the Development of Occupational Health Programs and an Overview of the Future," in *Occupa-*

tional Clinical Psychology, edited by J.S.J. Manuso, New York, Praeger Publishers, 1983.

Guidano, V.F., and Liotti, G. *Cognitive Processes and Emotional Disorders*, New York, Guilford Press, 1983.

Manuso, J.S.J. "The Metamorphosis of a Corporate Emotional Health Program," in *Occupational Clinical Psychology*, edited by J.S.J. Manuso, New York, Praeger Publishers, 1983.

Meichenbaum, D. and Jaremko, M.E. *Stress Reduction and Prevention*, New York, Plenum Press, 1983.

Minter, J. "A Contracted or In-House EAP", *Employee Assistance Program Digest*, 1983, May/June, pp. 20–22.

Most, R.B., and Glazer, H.I. "Contemporary Psychological Assessment in Organizational Settings" in *Occupational Clinical Psychology*, edited by J.S.J. Manuso, New York, Praeger Press, 1983.

Nahrwold, S.C. "Why Programs Fail" in *Occupational Clinical Psychology*, edited by J.S.J. Manuso, New York, Praeger Press, 1983.

Ontario Board of Examiners in Psychology (OBEP). *Standards of Professional Conduct*, Toronto, Ontario Board of Examiners in Psychology, 1980.

Phillips, D.A., Purvis, A.J., and Older, H.J. *Turning Supervisors On to Employee Counseling Programs*, New York, Hazelden Press, 1980.

Presnall, L.F. *Occupational Counseling and Referral Systems*, Salt Lake City, Utah Alcoholism Foundation, 1981.

Scanlon, W. "Trends in EAPs: Then and Now," *Employee Assistance Program Digest*, 1983, May/June, pp. 38–41.

Schmitz, H.V. "Executive and Employee Counseling Program Models and their Uses," in *Occupational Clinical Psychology*, edited by J.S.J. Manuso, New York, Praeger Publishers, 1983.

Schulberg, H.C., and Baker, F. *Program Evaluation In The Health Fields*, New York, Human Sciences Press, 1979.

Shain, M., and Groeneveld, J. *Employee Assistance Programs*, Lexington, D.C. Heath and Company, 1980.

Walen, S.R., DiGiuseppe, R., and Wessler, R.L. *A Practitioner's Guide to Rational-Emotive Therapy*, New York, Oxford University Press, 1980.

Weaver, C.A. "EAPs—How They Improve the Bottom Line," *Risk Management*, 1979, July, pp. 22–26.

Wrich, J.T. *The Employee Assistance Program*, Centre City, Minneapolis, Hazelden, 1980.

Glossary of Terms

Behavior therapy: a form of psychotherapy, based on learning theory, which attempts to modify problematic behavior.

Cognitive-behavior therapy: a form of psychotherapy which attempts to modify internal mental processes such as knowing, perceiving, judging, and imagining, etc. and to change problematic behavior.

Humanistic-existential therapy: a form of therapy, based on acceptance and understanding of the client's present level of functioning, which encourages client change.

Neuropsychology: the study of the relationship between brain function and behavior.

Non-directive counseling: a form of therapy, based on unconditional acceptance of the client, which facilitates the client's decision to change.

Psychoanalytically-oriented therapy: a modified form of Freudian psycho-analysis, which is more brief, more directive, and more focused.

Recidivism: a recurrence of the same problem by the same individual.

Utilization rate: the percentage of employees who make use of the EAP.

10

Union-Based Programs
Madeleine L. Tramm

Introduction

Occupational alcoholism programs, and to a lesser extent EAPs, are predicated on a model of human behavior at work by which, it is argued, 1) employees afflicted with alcoholism or other chemical dependency manifest the disorder through deteriorating job performance, and 2) management, on the basis of that behavior, confronts the employee, motivating him or her to seek professional assistance.

In an organized work setting, where does the union fit into this paradigm? Is the union's primary function to protect the chemically dependent, including the alcoholic, from disciplinary action by management? Is it to act as watchdog for the chemically dependent's job while the sick individual participates in treatment? Or is it to sanction the "human contract" of labor-management relations—the possibilities for a relationship of total human concern—while management is more interested in issues of economy and production? These stereotypes concerning the union's role are partially accurate, yet none sufficiently characterizes labor's responsibilities in occupational alcoholism and EAPs. It is the purpose of this paper to explore these roles and thus to accurately define union-based programs.

Occupational Alcoholism Programs vs. EAPs

To analyze labor's role in EAPs assumes a consistent model, as well as its application. In fact, these programs are highly variable in their history, reason for being, and focus. For this reason, some definitions are in order.

Historically, occupational alcoholism programs (OAPs) arose primarily from the efforts of recovered alcoholics, acting with organizational support, to establish a mechanism in industry to treat employees afflicted by a drinking problem. Plant leaders on both labor and management sides were alerted to the deleterious consequences at work of chemical dependency, were trained to confront on the basis of deteriorating job performance, and were encouraged to refer to the in-house program. Program personnel were actively involved in "treatment"—frequent counseling sessions, typically based on the philosophy of Alcoholics Anonymous (AA). Other activities consisted of referral to facilities for detoxification and rehabilitation, and referral to a local AA group. The facilities used also tended to be based on the twelve-step program of AA.

EAPs have had a different genesis, rationale, and mode of operation. Some arose from OAPs to address the many problems of living with a chemical dependency. Others evolved into "broad brush" programs primarily to de-stigmatize the disease, and the program. Still others were developed as a response to industry's perceived need for a catch-all service to address non-industrial issues, such as equal employment opportunity, affirmative action, and employee counseling.

The distinction between OAP and EAP is not academic, for the nature of the particular program affects its capability, strength, and significance to industry. Importantly, and regretably, many of those programs which evolved from OAP to EAP lost their ability to attract the chemically dependent, or to attract them in as great numbers.

Moreover, a general counseling service does not necessarily require a strategy of intervention at the worksite. As the need for education and training at the worksite has diminished, so too has involvement of those there. What was once a focus on industry, with the chemically dependent seen in this context, became a focus on the individual. A decreased emphasis on industry also often meant a decreased interest by it, for the program's importance may not have been as immediately perceived.

The emphasis on AA and on facilities based on techniques of the Fellowship in some cases diminished. As EAP staff were hired to fill a broader role, the tendency to refer out increased. De-stigmatization of alcoholism and other chemical dependency in society, and the strengthening of the disease concept, which legitimizes medicine's role in treatment, has sanctioned this trend. Where AA and recovery homes based on AA were once the norm for recovery, increasingly hospitals, JCAH-accredited residential facilities, and outpatient services by doctors from a variety of backgrounds became popular.

Ideally, union or management based EAPs should be capable of managing a range of employee needs, without losing their capability either to address the chemically dependent or to marshal industrial support. This capability requires flexibility of program staff, and internal support and visibility for the program.

The Union Programs

Appreciating the complexity and variability of industrial programs, we can proceed to characterize these as they have been developed by unions.

One prerequisite for a successful union-based program is the development of a joint labor-management policy statement. This is a contract signed by both parties which recognizes alcoholism or chemical dependency as a disease; the desirability of encouraging people to seek assistance and of providing appropriate insurance coverage; and the continued application of the collective bargaining agreement.

Joint programs have been shown to be more effective than union-only, or management-only programs, for the following reasons: the program obtains greater visibility; individuals utilizing it avoid possible job discrimination or other punishment; education and appreciation of the problem and consequences for industry are maximized; and management and labor, by presenting a unified posture with respect to the afflicted individual, enable a greater probability of successful treatment.

At the workplace, a chemically dependent employee experiences more than deteriorating job performance—the hallmark of management's reason to intervene. Since alcoholism is a complex disease which pervades the victim's psychological, physical, emotional and social functioning, there are many manifestations. These may be so subtle that only persons in close association with the chemically dependent, such as coworkers or shop stewards, will be aware of them. Since the union's role is to support and assist, a member alerted to another's difficulties may be able to intervene in a nonthreatening, effective manner. Moreover, since physical and behavioral changes are an earlier indicator of chemical dependency than is deteriorating job performance, labor is in a unique position to intervene early in the disease, before it has taken a heavy toll on the victim and family.

Deteriorating job performance, a later sign of chemical dependency, is also labor's concern. Work performance is a contractual issue. Union representatives both manage the contract in factories (by handling difficult labor-management problems such as decisions to arbitrate) and work as liaison between labor and management. They also are actively involved in the definition of the contract and facilitate employer-union relations. Thus, it is clear that deteriorating work performance provides an opportunity for labor as well as management to intervene. The argument can be even more strongly stated: although only management has the right to terminate an employee for unacceptable work performance, the union can most often affect that decision.

To begin with, the union interprets the contract to members, educating them about all issues, including the limits beyond which labor cannot protect them. For example, stealing and fighting on the job transgress those limits. In the context of chemical dependency manifested at the worksite, this translates into the business agent (union representative with special management skills) warning the member about the possibility of disciplinary action by management because of poor work performance, and the provision of an alternative, professional assistance. In this manner, the business agent, as intervener, is helping the person to begin the process of recovery. Secondly, in its relationship to management the union acts as advocate for the affected member. In industries where labor-management relationships are good due to a long association and the existence of small factories, the labor representative can be involved with the employer in interpreting whether or not a member's performance has deteriorated. Once the person is in treatment, it is labor's role to become vigilant in protecting full job rights.

Thus, the worksite represents an important arena for labor to intervene, both at the late stages of disease where management also exercises its privileges, and at an early stage, based on the first and subtle signs of chemical dependency. The union has other potential channels for early intervention. These include member or social services departments, union health centers, credit unions, and affiliated insurance carriers.

Member services department handle employee concerns not addressed by the collective bargaining agreement. Information on taxpayer programs such as Social Security, educational counseling, and strike assistance are examples. These departments typically operate through a network of member services committees, established in plants around the country by members volunteering to act as the liaison between the union and community services. Members receive training either from department staff hired by the union's national headquarters, or by the AFL-CIO community services agency representatives from the area. Problems presented to these programs can camouflage alcoholism and other chemical dependency conditions. Therefore, union-based EAPs normally provide training about the disease and techniques of intervention to services staff, and they, in turn, refer to the program. This is an example of labor's potential for early intervention.

Union health centers also facilitate early intervention and contribute to the union's ability to monitor the progress of the afflicted member. Many labor-management contracts provide for ambulatory health centers to which members can go free of charge. A range of medical, diagnostic, and psychiatric services by specialists are available. Where an EAP exists and is visible, these medical centers refer members who display some of the clinical signs of chemical dependency, or other problems suspected of being disease-related. The program encourages this by educating health center personnel. They, in turn, clinically evaluate individuals through liver function tests and blood analyses, and provide them with related medical services as needed.

Credit unions also constitute a mechanism of early intervention for the unions, as well as providing a method for monitoring the progress of afflicted members. Through training and education, credit unions can be effective in alerting the program to those who suddenly go into debt, or whose saving and spending habits become erratic. These patterns may indicate a dependency problem. After recovery, the credit unions can continue to maintain contact with the union program, alerting staff to changes which might signal relapse.

A final channel available to labor for early intervention is the opportunity provided by its relationship with insurance carriers. Unions which are self-insured or insured by an affiliated carrier are in a position to access insurance records. Disability claims which appear alcohol-related can be targeted for further attention. Intervention may not involve breaches of confidentiality because of the legal relationship between the union and carrier. Two intervention strategies may be profitable to pursue. One is to send a letter, including a brief questionnaire about the program to all who have recently filed a disability claim. Responses may provide information about: 1) the prevalence of chemical dependency, and 2) its relationship to other medical disorders.

A second option is to preselect claims which may appear chemical dependency related (e.g., certain intestinal disorders), and to alert these claimants about health assistance services available through the union. Again, self-referrals are assessed for chemical dependency, and patterns of medical disorder, if any, are noted. At the Amalgamated Clothing and Textile Workers Union, utilizing records of a management-funded affiliated carrier, the Amalgamated Life Insurance Company, response rates to a mailing of all disability claim recipients in the New York City area averaged 27% over a thirteen-month period. Such mailings have significant research as well as programmatic potential. They can contribute to early intervention since chemical dependency may not be the apparent presenting problem, and may not be advanced.

Multiple sources of referral available to union-based programs maximize the possibilities for effective follow-up, because a great deal of information about given cases can be marshalled. For example, with the individual's signed consent, information about the individual's physical condition can come from union health centers and from physicians elsewhere involved as a result of the search of insurance records. Information may be further available from the business agent, shop steward, local or joint board manager, Social Services Committee member, or headquarters staff person.

Even for persons referred by management, the program can enlist union involvement, since contractual issues may bear on the problem, and job performance issues are labor's as well as management's concern. The union, in effect, surrounds the affected member.

Education

To activate all potential referral channels, union-based programs must spend considerable time and effort in educational activities. The many channels of referral available, the reluctance of union leaders to become involved in job performance issues which they may perceive initially as punitive, and the many ramifications of job protection concerning an affected member once out sick and initially back on the job, necessitate ongoing education. Such education needs to address the disease, manifestations of chemical dependency at work and its relationship to job performance, effects on the family, and the perception of the program within industry.

Education can be formal, such as training seminars conducted by the program in joint sessions for labor and management. Alternatively, sessions can be informal, as exemplified by the program, Outreach Coordinator, visiting factories with a representing business agent for the purposes of building program visibility and obtaining referrals.

Wherever there is a joint labor-management program, both sides need to be educated to see their mutual concerns in a new way—a way that emphasizes the possibility of a medical and behavioral disorder and a hopeful solution, rather than one which places labor and management at loggerheads over a troubled, and troublesome, employee.

Research and Evaluation

The subject of union-based programs cannot be closed without mention of research and evaluation. The potential gains from research as a data gathering and analyzing activity are enormous. If the labor-based programs of even a few of the major AFL-CIO unions obtained and categorized rudimentary demographic and medical history information about their target populations, tremendous insights regarding the health of working people could be gathered.

Evaluation of program development, including the histories of those referred, has been a key activity of many union-based programs, because many of these have been government grant funded. As such, they were required to develop and analyze data. Evaluation was encouraged because, with grant funds, union-based programs could afford large staff. Unlike management programs which often have only one or two staff, labor-based programs commonly have four or five, including one whose primary responsibility is program evaluation. The union-based programs, in cooperation with academicians, have contributed tremendously to research results in the field of industrial programs.

Conclusion

Description of union-based programs demonstrates that these provide numerous and often unique contributions to the decrease of active chemical dependency among employees, and to the development of insight for the field. The bond which exists between member and union legitimizes union officials' involvement in the intervention, motivation, and treatment process. The potential for participation by a variety of union representatives, observation occurring on several fronts simultaneously, maximizes the chances for recovery. Although labor does not fire—the ultimate weapon available to encourage those affected to seek help—labor is involved in the definition of job performance and its deterioration. Utilizing its many bonds to the membership, labor is in a unique position to intervene early in the disease process. Working with management in joint labor-management programs, surely the problems of chemical dependency can be effectively addressed.

11

Peer Referral: A Programmatic and Administrative Review
Daniel J. Molloy

Introduction

Through the 1970s, a decade of enormous growth for occupational and industrial programs, a single case finding strategy clearly dominated the landscape of this field. It centered around job performance and a job site supervisor who could detect and document a decline in such performance and who could then initiate a constructive confrontation with the worker about his/her diminishing productivity. If performance continued to slip, a job jeopardy situation developed. This involved escalating, coercive motivation leading to the alternative of seeking help, or facing disciplinary action and ultimately loss of job (Trice and Roman, 1978).

It soon became clear that with the job impairment model the field was expanding well beyond its base in assisting workers with problems of alcoholism and chemical dependency. While the strategy was designed primarily for the chemically dependent person and carefully constructed to avoid problems associated with stigma, labeling, and witch hunt, it clearly opened the door for an expanded assignment for occupational programs. Obviously, many human problems can interfere with work, the recognition of which has been surrounded by confusion, conflict, and opportunity for this emerging field. This expansion beyond chemical dependency has been greeted by some with enthusiasm and by others with reluctant acquiescence.

As the employee assistance field grew beyond an industrial-manufacturing base, the job impairment model itself began to show signs that it could not be the total universe of this field (McClellan, 1982). It was not suitable for work environments with inconsistent or loose supervision. Evaluations showed it was uneven in its application, the lower the worker was in the line the better his/her chance of being confronted. Because of its heavy reliance on the supervisor, it was not always convergent with the values of labor organizations and professional associations. Confrontation, which is often necessary with alcohol and drug dependency problems, was not seen as the appropriate strategy for human service needs, where denial was less of an issue, or no issue at all. Even with alcohol and drugs, there was an issue as to whether the supervisor was the first to know (Trice, Hunt & Beyer, *Alcoholism Programs in Unionized Settings*).

A major new model emerging in the industrial field, that of peer detection and intervention, will be discussed in this paper. Can peers and colleagues make successful interventions? Can they be as effective in problems of chemical dependency as supervisory interventions? Or, will their usefulness be in other areas? Is concern as potent a motivating force as coercion? Has there been any program development and activity utilizing this model?

The Central Issue

The crucial test for the peer model is in whether it can function as well as the supervisory model as a motivator to seek help in conditions characterized by rationalization and denial. While many models can be successful with workers who have the motivation and capacity to seek help, the supervisory-based job impairment model has demonstrated effectiveness in reaching and assisting those who are unwilling and unable to seek assistance. Can the peer model achieve the same measure of success in this core area of concern?

Initial Breakthrough in Airline Industry

The airline industry has been the first to use the peer intervention model extensively in their program design. Two programs, in particular, have played a key leadership role in this area and have been noted both for conceptual soundness and considerable success. Reference is to the EAP of the Airline Pilots Association (Hoover et al., 1982) and the Association of Flight Attendants (Feuer, 1982). While these programs have educational as well as motivational strategies, concentration is on the central issue of the unmotivated worker, suffering from a condition he/she both denies and of which has no appreciation of a steady progression.

Anatomy of an Intervention

To describe the actual anatomy of an intervention, the Airline Pilots Association's program utilizes the principles of intervention developed by

Dr. V.E. Johnson (Hoover, 1980). Johnson's principles result from years of work with alcoholics and have been applied in family, community, and industrial settings. Johnson defines an intervention as presenting reality (specific data) in a receivable form (with concern). *Concern* is the major motivating force, and factual data from both *on* and *off the job* are the substantive materials fueling the intervention. The goal of the intervention is to present reality to the troubled individual in a way he/she can accept, while simultaneously requesting that corrective action be taken. For Johnson, there are five distinct and essential principles of intervention:

1) The intervention must be by people meaningful to the person in question.
2) They must present specific, documented data.
3) They must consistently strike a theme and tone of concern.
4) They must offer alternatives and choice.
5) They must develop a follow-up plan.

Johnson sees the intervention as a moment of reality for the chemically dependent person. Intervention is based on the acceptance and recognition of three factors; chemical dependency is a progressive disease involving increasing physical, emotional, and mental deterioration. It is chronic in nature, thus not cured but capable of arrestment. It is primary, at least from a practical viewpoint. It blocks the lasting effect of any other care, while the addiction itself is still active. While delusion and impaired judgment characterize the disease and lock dependent people into self-destructive patterns, Johnson believes that even the sickest are capable of accepting some useful portion of reality, if that reality is presented in forms they can receive (Johnson, 1980).

Self Identified Conditions

As with the supervisory model, peer interventions are designed primarily for illness characterized by denial. Its applicability for conditions which can be self-identified is much less complex. The peer committee can also be the arms and legs of an occupational program, getting the word out about the program's ability to offer a whole host of concrete and advocacy services. In such instances, the peer is an information agent acquainting the workforce with the variety of needs for which the industrial program is capable of being responsive. The peer also has a mediating role, bringing back to the industrial program information about a particular problem constellation to which the program is not yet responding or may not yet even perceive as a need for service. A major aim of peer training then, is to stimulate and cultivate self-referrals by disseminating information about the industrial program throughout the organization and bringing back to the program information about the service needs of the population it serves. While this is an important variable and supports the program's ability to reach beyond problems of chemical dependency, it is by far the easier and less complicated goal to achieve. As has always been the case in the industrial field, the ultimate test is with the illness characterized by denial. In such instances, the suffering person cannot and will not act. It remains for others to observe behavior, to identify a co-worker in trouble, and to take action.

Issues in Selection

The selection of the individuals who will serve on the peer committee is itself an issue crucial to the program's outcome and is actually an essential ingredient in the program's design. The peer, individually and collectively, must have characteristics which will help them gain the confidence of their fellow workers, as well as the organizational and occupational sanction necessary to fulfill their roles. A peer intervention strategy depends on an organization taking seriously the way the giving and receiving of help is exchanged, and its being willing to study and formalize the informal. This requires an organization and/or relevant occupational groupings with a high degree of equilibrium and consensus. Peer selection and training procedures must carefully cultivate and exploit these natural helping arrangements in organizations. If they are not sufficiently present in both quality and quantity in a given occupation or working group, the strategy is probably not workable.

Selection, then, must reach for the very best and most willing individuals capable of offering peer assistance. Poor selection would undermine the entire effort. Not only would the peers have difficulty in fulfilling their function, but the occupational unit would also reject such a group as an expression of its helping identity.

The Airline Pilots Association has developed several sound criteria for peer selection (Hoover, 1980). While no individual could meet all these specifications, selection aims at finding individuals who best match this profile. The qualifications are:

1) capacity for being empathetic
2) ability to be non-judgmental about and sensitive to human needs
3) honest about limitations
4) knowledgeable about industry and occupation
5) non-controversial figure

6) leadership ability
7) capable of keeping confidence
8) respected by fellow workers
9) solid recovery in cases of chemical dependency

The Peer Model and Organizational-Managerial Theory

Organizational and management theories have not addressed the employee assistance field per se to this point in time, but some interesting associations and parallels can be drawn. Certainly, the emphasis on the supervisor, constructive confrontation, and job impairment fits well into the bureaucratic-hierarchical conception of organizational structure. As has been mentioned, that is both its strength and its weakness. It fits neatly and works well in organizations which are structured as such. On the other hand, research has demonstrated that application is uneven; the lower the worker in the line the better his/her chance of being confronted. Still another liability is that not all job environments have either tight or consistent supervision. However, there is clearly a comfortable administrative fit between the supervisory model and the most common view about how organizations function, assign and delegate tasks, and how they hold their workers accountable.

The peer model would seem to fit better with some less traditional notions of organizational theory. It is much closer to the thoughts, concerns, and findings of organizational theorists like Argyris and McGregor (Theory Y) and Ouchi and Jaeger (Theory Z) (Leavitt, Pondy and Boje, 1980). The peer model assumes workers themselves are capable of assuming responsibility for determining what behavior on the part of co-workers elicits personal concern; what behavior conflicts with organizational and occupational goals; and what behavior calls for a corrective intervention. Theory Y postulates a management which has confidence in human capacities and which itself is directed more towards its own objective than to employee control. The peer model would seem to fit better into this type of organizational philosophy.

The safeness of accepting help is another important issue. It is no accident that the peer model has emerged first in the airline industry. How could there be anything but avoidance and denial for any human problem that hinted at job impairment, when an admission would almost certainly mean a revocation or suspension of a license? It had to become safe to discuss problems and to seek appropriate help. Peer interventions and policy assurances that pilots could safety admit to a need for assistance were the right chemistry for this highly sensitive industry.

The peer intervention model also addresses a major administrative and policy concern in the developing field of industrial social work. To date, most occupational programs have addressed the needs, problems, and impairments of workers while paying little attention to work organizations. The need for industrial programs to attend to the culture of the work organization and to clearly differentiate between client and organizational need has been discussed in social work literature (Akabas and Kurzman, 1982). The peer model helps mitigate some of these difficulties, because the peers will in large measure set the tone of their work and create their role in the occupational program. Certainly, they will be taking a careful look at their organization or occupation to determine what are its human service needs. Such an examination will have implications not just for present service needs, but will also suggest areas where preventive strategies might be devised. The peer model presents an opportunity for a whole organization to look at what problems workers are having, how to identify workers with such problems and offer assistance, and how to educate those not yet affected to make personal or organizational adjustments which might prevent such problems from occurring. In short, it would seem to provide a clear blend of cause and function.

Some of this was recognized by Bertha Reynolds, who noted that workers conduct was held in bounds by informal rules, known by almost everyone, as to what was acceptable and unacceptable. In reflecting on her experience at the National Maritime Union, it was her feeling that the organization and the social worker should work together in identifying unacceptable behavior which threatened both the individual and the organization. Interestingly enough, Reynolds illustrated this point in a discussion of the disease of alcoholism (Reynolds, 1941).

Another important reason for emphasizing concern is that, in the end, it must take the place of coercion anyway. No one stays afraid forever and daring returns. Fear is ultimately an unsatisfactory foundation. Unless there is psycho-social and spiritual progress in recovery, there is still a hurting person, although he/she may be dry. The peer community, fueled by concern, offers continuity between intervention and the sustaining of recovery. The peers are available to continue to support and assist after intervention and treatment. Since it can be assumed that many of the peers would themselves be recovering people (some of whom might actually have been helped by the industrial program), their own recoveries are a precious organizational commodity. While industrial programs must respect confidentiality, many people believe they serve their own recoveries best by sharing them with others. Troubled workers suffering from behavioral-medical problems look at those who were once obviously ill and now recovered as hope to be clung to. The recovered demonstrate that one need not be locked into his present circumstance. While the peers would need to be trained not to cast everyone into their own recovery mold, many of their recoveries are outstanding individual and organizational achievements, which belong to, and can assist, the whole occupational community.

In review, the author would base his contention of the administrative soundness of a peer intervention program and the training of a peer committee on the following points. As the supervisory model draws support from some of the more traditional, vertical notions of organizational and managerial theory, the peer model strikes a resonant chord with the more horizontal, participatory notions. In highly sensitive, but loosely supervised occupations (airlines, maritime industry, the professions), where certification and/or licensing is involved, the peer model is perceived as safe. The model is very much in line with the direction and values of the self-help movement, which has both influenced and contributed enormously to the employee counseling field. Peer training offers an opportunity to focus as much on the organization as on the individual, thus coming closer to values and concerns raised by the social work profession. Peers do hold each other to a standard of behavior, especially in membership organizations and professions. A peer committee sanctioned by an organization is in touch with the culture of that organization's work environment. The peer committee can come to know the hazards of that work setting more fully, as well as the personal and collective adjustments which are called for. Finally, the peer model allows a workforce to capitalize on its recovering people, a precious occupational commodity.

Conclusion

In summary, the author contends in this programmatic and administrative review that the peer model addresses the major past and present concerns as well as the future needs of the occupational/industrial human service field. Camaraderie, mutual concern, and care are as much a part of the world of work as supervision, performance, and accountability. Both can work toward assisting the troubled worker. Constructive confrontation, job impairment, and coercive motivation are the conceptual tools, which were developed through the 1970s to make the supervisory model operative. Intervention, deepening concern, and ongoing support are new tools which can make the peer model operational and carry it from lofty human aspiration to an effective and administratable program.

Finally, most of the attempts to stimulate program growth in the EAP field have been aimed at top labor-management leadership and administration. It is workers whom these programs serve, and they ultimately will judge whether such programs address their needs or not. When EAPs are perceived as benefits intimately connected with an occupational identity and the right to work itself, these programs will rest on a firm and lasting foundation. The peer model gives workers a role in program design and activity. It can also help cultivate a sense that such programs, their protections and service, are part of the very fabric of work.

References

Akabas, Sheila, and Kurzman, Paul. *Work, Workers and Work Organizations*, (Prentice Hall, Englewood Cliffs, New Jersey, 1982).

Argyris, Chris, in ed. by Leavitt, Pondy, and Boje, *Reading in Managerial Psychology*, (University of Chicago Press, 1980) pp. 223–239.

Feuer, Barbara, *Program Description—Peer Referral Model, Association of Flight Attendants*, Employee Assistance Program.

Fine, Michelle, Akabas, Sheila, and Bellinger, Susan. "Cultures of Drinking, A Workplace Perspective" *Social Work* Vol. 27, No. 5, 1982.

Hoover, E. Paul, "EAP Concepts as Applied to Non-Supervised Professional Work Groups". Proceedings: Ninth Annual ALMACA Meeting and Exhibits, Oct. 7–10, 1980 (Washington D.C., Association of Labor-Management Administrators on Alcoholism, 1981).

Hoover, E. Paul, Kowalsky, Nestor, and Masters, Richard. *An Employee Assistance Program for Professional Pilots (An Eight Year Review)*. (Human Intervention and Motivation Study, Airline Pilots Association, Denver, Colorado, 1982).

Johnson, V.E. *I'll Quit Tomorrow* (revised edition), New York, N.Y., Harper and Row Publishers, Inc. 1980.

McClellan, Keith. "Changing EAP Services" *EAP Digest* Vol. 2, (No. 6), 1982.

McClellan, Keith. "How EAPs are Changing", National Council on Alcoholism Annual Forum, 1982.

McGregor, Douglas M., in ed, by Leavitt, Pondy, and Boje. *Readings in Managerial Psychology*, pp. 310–321.

Ouchi, William, and Jacgwe, Alfred, in ed. by Leavitt, Pondy, and Boje, *Readings in Managerial Psychology*, pp. 679–692.

Reynolds, Bertha, *Social Work and Social Living*, (NASW Classics, 1941).

Trice, Harrison, and Roman, Paul, *Spirits and Demons at Work: Alcohol and Other Drugs on the Job*, (New York, Cornell University—New York State School of Industrial and Labor Relations, 1978).

Trice, Harrison, Hunt, Richard, and Beyer, Janice, "Alcoholism Programs in Unionized Work Settings: Problems and Prospects in Union-Management Cooperation," *Journal of Drug Issues*, Vol. 7, No. 2.

SECTION III

A Coordinated Approach:
Roles within an EAP

Introduction

It is fascinating to watch the evolution of EAPs from the early programs to the present. In the past, the choice of a person to head the EAP was a devoted, often broadly experienced, although not necessarily well trained individual. His/her background and education for the post were often no more than the fact of their recovered alcoholism; or having been simply a loyal and interested company employee who saw a need, and convinced management of it.

Today it is clear that two trends are developing, each of which celebrates and maximizes the uses of diverse talents in the EAP. First, it is accepted that the EAP deserves more highly trained people with more certification. Talented people from a number of disciplines now operate an exciting variety of programs. Indeed, occupational social workers, psychologists, certified alcoholism counselors, and others are managing successful EAPs.

A second trend is somewhat more apparent in in-house than externally-based programs. This is the trend toward integration of EAP activities into the workings of other parts of the organization, simultaneously creating new working relationships with other units of the organization. For example, programs conducted in concert with employee relations may deal with the stresses of downsizing in a company; programs with the organizational development group can analyze and seek steps to improve the "health of the organization" at the macro and micro levels. Today's EAP requires staff open to these ideas.

This section looks individually at several such key specialties which may play roles within the new EAPs.

The occupational physician and occupational health nurse are pivotal in full service EAPs. As will be discussed by Moore, medical departments are felt by many to be the ideal home for EAPs, reflecting the belief that both physical and psychosocial health are a continuum. The medical aspects of various "EAP diseases" may be slighted in their handling without devoted medical personnel; alcohol and drug cases may be misdirected or missed entirely. Nevertheless, veterans of EAPs and alcohol programs are rightly suspicious of many in the medical profession. "Old school" doctors, including many now in practice, know very little about the early and middle stages of alcoholism, and not a great deal more about stress and other psychosocial conditions. Nevertheless, there is good news, in that growing numbers of enlightened doctors and nurses work in industry today and are taking on larger roles in preventive medicine and the stewardship of EAPs.

Seeming newcomers in the EAP arena are members of the psychiatric profession. In a section which served as a report on occupational psychiatry for the American Psychiatric Association, McLean, Ellis, Lipsitch, and Moss relate how psychiatrists have moved forward in recent years, from their traditional role as outside consultants to a more pro-active role within company health and EAP-type programs. Among the examples are activities regarding the effects of "loss," and stress factors in the job and workplace as they affect mental health.

More and more, psychiatric consultants will be found near the boardroom and in management circles, discussing mental health problems and trends as they see them, even conducting training to non-psychiatrist managers in crisis management and intervention.

In the section by Manuso, the history of occupational psychologists' involvement in industry is described in detail. He follows their evolution from simple workplace placement and psychological testing to such current activities as the surveying of the prevalence of workplace conditions and psychological consequences in the workforce. They are not only actively involved in training activities, but also in conducting programs in biofeedback and stress reduction. Within EAPs they are playing ever larger roles, including actual EAP operation in some companies.

The expanding role of the occupational social worker is described in detail by Francek, beginning with a discussion of the changing paradigms of organizations viz-a-vis their employees. A new model for EAP students to study is the systems approach outlined here, an approach generic to the social work field, but which has broader applicability than may first be apparent to the EAP and psychosocial/mental health fields.

Burns' section illustrates the "front lines" position of the occupational health nurse (OHN) in industry, where he or she may be the sole representative of health and wellness issues in many plants or companies not wishing to pay for medical departments or even fully-complemented EAPs. The nurse may be the first contact for decompensating employees becoming ill, whether from EAP-style conditions or more routine medical problems. Thus, it is vital that OHN's become familiar with EAP principles, particularly if the EAP itself is one of their assigned or adopted functions.

Another critical issue is management support for EAPs. The section by Wrich notes his group's experience, i.e., that support at CEO or similarly high levels leads to improved data analysis and tight program controls, which in turn usually lead to improved "benefit to cost" results. Such considerations first require, of course, great care in the selection of staff. Criteria and queries to be answered in the staff selection process are presented in detail.

On the clinical side, it is well recognized that higher management support leads in turn to improved supervisory referrals. A sign of even more effective programs, however, will be such referrals at stages pre-dating performance problems, at the "aware of something wrong" level.

And finally, Wrich points out the need to clarify EAP roles, as separate from the roles of management, with particular regard to disciplinary actions. It would seem that management, the EAP, and the employee most benefit when each follows their appropriate roles in the workplace.

12

Occupational Physician—
Role in an EAP
C. Eugene Moore

Introduction

The issues dealt with by an EAP, whether limited to alcoholism and drugs or more broadly inclusive of such conditions as stress and family problems, all represent adverse impacts on the human mind or body. By that extended definition, they are "medical" in nature. The medical field used to consider alcoholism and drug abuse as largely moral issues in their inception, while psychological problems and family concerns were most often referred out to other specialists. Especially in the workplace, these concerns are now becoming accepted as extensions or causes of illnesses and diseases. For example, as noted in a published study on risk factors in heart disease, stress and type-A behavior have now been acknowledged to be as significant a risk factor for (heart) disease as any other known entity (Review panel on coronary-prone behaviour and heart disease, 1981). Stress "represents a rallying point for those interested in the varied aspects of the mind-body relationship, and it is this area which offers the greatest promise for the prevention of heart attacks and other diseases of civilization." (Rosch, 1983).

The medical model thus suggests itself as a key approach to follow in developing and maintaining an EAP. The occupational physician or the overall coordinator of medical policies and services is in an excellent position to integrate EAP services into the overall health delivery system.

The approach will be to look first at some of the biases and perceptions which may initially hinder the medical professional's understanding of "EAP diseases" and prevent his/her utility of an EAP. Following will be a discussion of roles in the EAP and the overall guiding principle of "management skills," which the medical professional should seek to gain and improve on.

Medical Biases—How They Can Affect an EAP

Beginning with the common biases inherent in traditional medical thinking on the conditions addressed by EAPs, most occupational physicians will need some degree of retraining, so that they will be better equipped to play a major role in the development, promulgation, and dispersal of the EAP concept. As a consequence, he/she can become more than "just the doctor" who reviews physical findings and lab tests for EAP patients. If honed and applied, their managerial skills and position of respect in the company hierarchy can become major factors in the eventual credibility and success of an EAP.

The model "occupational" physician in the 1980s is better trained than was the case even a very few years ago. At that time most small and large companies simply delved into the ranks of private practice to create or add to their physician staff. In many cases the chosen candidate was the same individual previously used by them on a private basis, now to be placed on payroll to do the annual physicals.

The Education (and Need for it) of the Occupational Physician

Today's company physician is likely to be a broader-based person, with credentials or training in some aspect of occupational medicine, e.g., in such diverse fields as toxicology, epidemiology, and industrial hygiene. He/she is as much administrator, salesperson, and manager of people as is an old-fashioned doctor. He/she is likely also to be more of a humanist, a product of the liberal, ecology/environment-oriented college years of the 60s and 70s, looking to the human and social values as well as the traditional medical ones.

It is a sad truism of the trend, however, that medical school itself gave short shift to the issues of the era. Nor did such schools know much about or contribute to the medical students' understanding of occupational medicine, to alcohol programs in industry, or to any of the other predecessors of our EAPs.

Non-medical persons involved in EAP efforts, whether maintaining the operation of a program or establishing one, may find that they have the special task of assessing and educating the medical personnel with whom they expect to deal with. This is especially true if the EAP is not already associated with a medical department. In smaller companies using part-time physicians to serve the medical needs of an EAP, one will often find private doctors relatively or totally inexperienced in alcoholism and EAPs.

The well-trained doctor in the EAP field reaches his/her understanding of the need for and role of EAPs by several routes. He/she may have seen several problem cases in private practice, the military, or after joining the company. Perhaps one has had personal or family experience with alcoholism. Not uncommonly, he/she may have simply been asked by the company medical director to take on the EAP project or act as the "medical contact" for a program established elsewhere by the company or by an outside group, and has educated himself/herself accordingly. It is equally possible that the unions in a company or the employee relations department have enlisted him/her in the EAP's development stages, having tired of tallying, coddling, firing, or otherwise dealing ineffectively with employees openly known to have job performance problems with alcohol, drugs, or psychosocial stresses.

A change of attitude and/or approach is often the result of having seen one or two cases handled successfully, and realizing the handsome payoffs for the patient, the employer, and the family.

Frequent Biases and Prejudices to be Overcome

Though doctors are trained as helping and caring professionals, they tend to carry with them into occupational medicine several misconceptions about the diseases and conditions to which EAPs devote themselves. These misconceptions may also lead to actually mishandling cases. Alcoholism ranks high as the candidate for such misconceptions.

Still apparent is the often held perception by doctors of alcoholism in its narrow medical/pathological model, which is not far removed from the view held by the general public. This may be highlighted with dramatic memories of decaying and sodden livers, brought on by presumed willful (or, paradoxically, uncontrollable) inebriation. The major diagnostic signs to such doctors will be the flushed red face, tremors, and abnormal liver function tests. Compounding this is the faulty remembrance of how hopeless and bothersome these cases are. They did, after all, awaken the doctor too often in the middle of the night long ago in his/her internship and residency training.

As expressed by Millman (1979) in discussing traditional doctors' attitudes:

> A major obstacle to the effective treatment of this group of behaviors has been the attitudes of physicians and other health professionals, e.g., of "They did it to themselves." As in all other branches of medicine, an inquiring, compassionate attitude is essential to the treatment of these patients. A related serious problem is a conceptual one: Physicians regard alcohol and drug abuse as an acute illness, liable to complete cure. When people relapse, there is a tendency to consider them incurable and dismiss them.

And as described by Robert Straus (1977):

It is probable that the persistent reluctance of physicians to recognize or come to terms with drinking problems in their patients is related in part to a sense of inadequacy in dealing with the behavioral and attitudinal aspects of illness generally. This underlines an urgent need for more attention in medical education . . . (directed) both to the problems of alcohol abuse and to the application of behavioral science principles in patient interviewing. . . .

Clearly, there is an obligation to re-orient doctors and all medical staff in the psychosocial and—yes—early physical signs of beginning and middle stage diseases. While alcoholism is used as a classic example, such early changes of other substance abuse (e.g., cocaine or Valium) may also stand ready for refreshing of the doctor's knowledge. How many doctors have kept in mind the diagnostic features of early depression or borderline personality dysfunctions and schizophrenia?

Among the many nontextual resources available for teaching the doctor, nurse, and other health professional about alcoholism itself are selections in the videotape library of the AMA and an excellent series of films, readings, and discussion materials produced expressly for that purpose by Project Cork of Duke University.

Often, however, even the doctor refreshed in his/her awareness of the complexities of alcoholism is like an intern or resident again, feeling unsure about a list of newly-learned behavior patterns and symptoms (including those elusive psychosocial changes). In early cases, even with adequate or unequivocal lab work, many doctors will be loath to consider the diagnosis of sensitive diseases such as drug misuse or alcoholism. With training, though, he/she may succeed in accepting the non-stigmatic nature of the conditions.

EAP workers may face another subtle barrier from the less sophisticated occupational physician—an unwillingness to give up his/her patient to the EAP. Just as had been dealt in start to finish fashion with other illnesses over the years, he/she may feel they know how to handle these alcohol or "not strictly medical" cases. They will be reluctant to turn over the patient, whose trust he/she may have so assiduously garnered, to an EAP person whose disposition of the case he/she may not know of, approve of, or understand. It can be disillusioning also if he/she finds the EAP staff person to be a non-professional who has handled more such cases than can be easily counted. Paradoxically, our average doctor would surely turn over such cases to a psychiatrist.

An even more important bias to be overcome among doctors is one very like that found among supervisors and managers—the reluctance to confront a client in question with the "facts." Each should be able to observe and collect his/her respective "data" and use it in his/her chosen role and profession.

Supervisors are expected to manage by measuring job performance; doctors manage their patients with the measures of a well-documented history, physical exam, and laboratory tests (and, in the workplace, with any information provided by the supervisor on declining work performance).

It is not that doctors lack courage; they are not strangers to confrontation of a sort, as many an overweight heavy smoker will testify to. But such common conditions as cigarette smoking and obesity are ones for which the information is neither very new (in most cases), nor very threatening. No anger is aroused; the doctor has no fear of losing the patient. Perhaps most of all, the doctor is on solid medical ground, ground well-trodden over years of experience and familiarity.

On the other hand, in most societies and even for an experienced doctor, confrontation about such things as alcoholism or drug misuse is tantamount to an accusation, and implies all those legal, moral, religious, and personal fortitude issues long imbedded in our psyches. The physician is uncomfortable. He/she can easily fear losing such a patient, and will often shy away from suggesting more than "cutting back a little," unless he/she has achieved a certitude regarding the diagnosis.

The modern doctor also prides himself/herself on practicing preventive medicine. But without fuller knowledge on this set of diseases and problems, the opportunity to educate "at risk" patients about alcoholism, drug, and stress problems will be missed.

Reassurance and re-education of the "new" doctor by the EAP professionals may be necessary, and may be assisted most readily by sensitive and professional cooperation in the early stages of their mutual cases. Nothing will succeed like success; more than this, nothing will improve the doctor's confidence and boost enthusiasm so readily as will a track record of recoveries. A positive outcome leading to recovery often is the one breakthrough that makes believers out of unbelievers.

One should not forget, of course, the role for which doctors have been initially trained, that of treating patients and referring when appropriate. An important consequence to a successful EAP will be the referral by this doctor and the medical department of their "regular" employee patients to the EAP when such referrals are warranted by the conditions found. Though accurate figures are difficult to locate, one could be reassured of "penetration" of the medical department if a third of the EAP's clients come from that source (and one third each from self-referrals and supervisors).

Development Phase

The occupational physician present at the early stages of developing an EAP has an opportunity to influence its direction, particularly in regard to decisions on choices about several key issues. Among these are:

- primary lead by a particular department
- records management and confidentiality issues
- extent of problems covered (broad-based or limited to certain conditions, such as alcohol and drugs)
- involvement of medical in promoting program to management, prior to and after approval of EAP
- staff qualifications and selection
- relationship of EAP to other medical programs
- liaison to other company affiliate EAPs

Primary Lead by Department

The author proposes that, whenever appropriate, an EAP should fall under the direction of the company medical department.

As discussed above, the conditions addressed in EAPs fit the medical model, i.e., the care of physical and medical disease includes the effects on the patient of psychological problems, family troubles, alcohol, and drugs. Mind and body comprise the "jurisdiction" of the doctor who cares to consider the *total* health of the employee. Within industry, it is the medical department's responsibility, in its dealings with management, to ensure that its own skills are of a caliber to handle the expanded range of these medical issues. EAPs can assist this effort.

There is usually no disputing the need for medical input in EAPs. However, the reality of the situation in any given company may be that there is a rather small medical presence, or that the interest and commitment of medical personnel to take on the duties of an EAP are minimal. In such circumstances, or by virtue of a different history of the program, employee relations or personnel departments frequently become the operators of the EAP.

EAP development rarely is, and should not be a "tour de force" by any single department alone. Preferred is the development of an EAP as a combined, well-planned effort of medical, employee relations, the unions and, if possible, the organizational development function in a company. The interaction among them synergistically profits each of them, benefits the EAP, and tends to reduce the number of mistakes which might arise from a narrower focus of EAP management.

Many fine programs are indeed operated under the aegis of personnel or employee relations departments; medical departments themselves frequently are under the jurisdiction of these same units. However, the traditional role of these nonhealth-related departments generally includes the stewardship of performance records, counseling, and disciplinary actions against the employees. For this reason, employees may have initial difficulty accepting that there is no crossover of information from the EAP records to their personnel records, or that the EAP is not simply another arm of the disciplinary process.

Locating the program within the medical department clearly identifies the framework of professional, unbiased, confidential care that underlies successful penetrance of the EAP to the greatest number of employees.

Management may need to be led to an appreciation of these issues. In turn, active efforts on their part should be made to clarify to employees these principles, as well as the distinctions between EAP procedures and those of any department associated with the EAP.

Records Handling and Confidentiality Issues

When the early stage EAP is moving toward or is already under the direction of employee relations, an outside agency or another administrative unit, the occupational physician should assure that sound medical practices are an integral part of the program. This applies particularly to issues of patient and record handling. The need to preserve sensitive and confidential data in a professional fashion must be clearly understood by all those directly involved. If employees needing help fear that their personal sensitive data may be revealed or kept in personnel files, their participation will be significantly less. Often the importance of this issue is not intuitively well recognized by management, and efforts to clarify it are very important.

Management is usually interested in its employees' welfare. The issue, however, for the EAP and health professional is where to draw the boundaries for information exchange with management, and how then to defend them.

Fortunately, guidelines do exist. A particularly useful one is the code that follows. As specified by the Code of Ethical Conduct for Physicians Providing Occupational Medical Services (1976), management's rights to information about an employee's medical status are limited; the medical professional will:

> ... treat as confidential whatever is learned about individuals served, releasing information only when required by law or by overriding public health considerations or to other physicians at the request of the individual according to traditional medical ethical practice; and should

recognize that employers are entitled to counsel about the medical fitness of individuals in relation to work, but are not entitled to diagnoses or details of a specific nature.

Within the framework of an EAP, these communications with management ordinarily should be limited to advice about "return to work" dates and limitations, if any, in the ability to continue normal assigned job duties. Also appropriate is advice to them on the participation or non-participation status of the employee in the EAP recommendations. The other primary exception to these information release guidelines would be in those instances where there is a clear threat of harm to others or to the patient themselves. In certain other circumstances, the EAP staff may encourage a client to release other information, but these efforts should be carefully evaluated as to need.

It is suggested that the following policies be considered for adoption:

- accept the above-discussed and the guidelines
- specify that diagnosis and treatment files be kept separately by the EAP from any existing employee relations and medical records. This precaution may also specifically exempt the EAP records from examination by certain governmental bodies which may otherwise have access to occupational medical records.
- actively educate employees as to the policy on confidentiality and the sanctity of this information, especially if the EAP is operated by an in-house program, whether within medical or elsewhere

Hopefully, the existing reputation of the company's medical department on confidentiality issues will be of considerable help.

Extent of Problems Covered

Management's directive in the talking stages of an EAP's development is often to "do something" about a perceived problem. This may be alcohol or drugs, or perhaps stress associated with a spell of terminations or other reorganizations. The job jeopardy approach to an EAP, which management eventually accepts as an issue of productivity, will by its very nature, not yield just a predetermined selection of specific problems. Rather, it should yield a wide range of causes of declining job performance. Consequences will vary, depending on which of two common approaches is finally approved.

An EAP with a wide focus of problems handled is obliged to have in place the skilled personnel to properly evaluate such conditions. To remain credible, the EAP must then be able to refer any identified client problem to an appropriate community resource. As discussed in detail elsewhere, the broad-based program should successfully uncover many important problems, including alcoholism at early stages, since that condition will often have come into the EAP under the cover of "family" or other problems.

An EAP limited to a subset of problems (such as alcohol) can quickly produce unfortunate results. Supervisors know the program only handles "certain" problems. They soon recognize that they are obliged to pre-diagnose what they suspect to be the cause of their subordinate's declining performance. If they refer poor performers who do not have one of these "problems," the EAP most likely sends such employees back to the supervisor without the problems resolved. The supervisor, the employee, and the EAP have been placed in awkward positions. But in any case, the supervisor will probably think twice from then on before referring to the EAP, waiting until he/she is quite clear the employee has the "clearly defined" problem before doing so. Clearly the most likely consequence is that referrals will only be made for the most obvious—probably late stage—problems.

Involvement of Medical in Promoting Program

Prior to higher management's approval of an EAP, the occupational physician can play a major role in using the trust developed between management and medical to clarify the objectives of a planned EAP. Management's usual reluctance relates to their fear of becoming involved in the private lives of their employees. The properly defined EAP will, however (as described above), be but an extension or reaffirmation of the medical department's existing care of physical problems, psychological/emotional stresses, and chemical dependencies. Of course, the EAP usually strengthens the success of these efforts. In some circumstances, management may be mollified further if the EAP is structured to require that only evaluation and referral of all such problems be allowed without the actual treating of cases in-house.

Once the EAP has received the blessing to proceed, the occupational physician managing an EAP could, of course, choose to limit his/her role to that of a supervisor. However, he/she can serve more productively by continuing to promote the EAP among company management circles to which he/she belongs—in the executive dining rooms and in the course of medical interactions with his/her peers and superiors.

Not surprisingly, upper level management tends to think of EAPs as lower level or blue collar missions; the doctor's inclusion of the EAP's services as a routine option for personal or stress problems found in an executive, e.g., in relation to medical examinations, both reinforces its existence as a resource and reminds the senior level patient that he/she may also suffer from such problems.

Of the many options available to enlist management support after approval is another very successful method used by the employee assistance program at J.C. Penny in New York City. The doctor and EAP manager (and employee relations representative as appropriate) solicit time from department heads to sit individually with them. The arranging of this "foot in the door" of these often busy people is perhaps best left to the most senior management person related to the EAP, e.g., the medical or employee relations director, via an introductory letter requesting time for these guests to pay a call.

The stated objectives of these meetings are to acquaint the executives with the features and rationale of the new EAP, while also gaining approval to perform supervisor training within their departments. The secondary objectives, however, are perhaps the more important. The senior executives are placed face to face with the personnel of the EAP in a comfortable situation; they are queried as to how best to tailor the EAP to their departments, and will hopefully also agree to support and endorse its principles at the start of the supervisor training for their department. And, as noted above, they are apprised that the EAP is for use in the client sense by people of their level as well. In that regard, they should also be asked what, if anything, would prevent them from using the program themselves.

Plans should then proceed to implement supervisor orientations. The degree of success of this effort is, in many evaluators' eyes, the true measure of the EAP's mettle. The doctor's or nurse's participation in these sessions is highly recommended, preferably with a suitable employee relations person present as well. Such three person-presentations (including the EAP manager or staff) serve very effectively to show the attending supervisors that the EAP has impact and utility in both a medical and management sense.

Staff Selection

The choice of internal staffing versus the use of an outside service is beyond the scope of this chapter. However, the "medical model" promoted here suggests strongly that several features be considered for criteria in the selection of an internal person to run the program. If one accepts that the charter of an EAP is to professionally manage the evaluation, referral, and treatment of these complex psychosocial conditions and substance dependency problems, then the selection process should seek a suitable professional. In this new field no particular medical or social science discipline has the clear lead in offering a choice to head an EAP. However, an increasing number of people are becoming well trained and qualified.

Suggested criteria do ideally include certification in a health, psychological, or social service field. Managerial skills are essential, especially if a larger staff is planned, but also for the normal management liaison work intrinsic to the job. The constant need to promote the EAP imples the need also for experience in the business field, skills in public speaking and networking, and the ability to handle a variety of complex mixtures of business, health, and administrative problems.

In many companies, EAPs have been started or operated under the jurisdiction of the occupational health nurse. This talented and often more available resource should not be overlooked in the search for a suitable EAP manager or coordinator. The OHN "is frequently the only medical professional who is available on a full-time basis and is, therefore, responsible for providing a wide variety of health-related functions ... [and] ... is in a position to help educate employees in the various implications of alcohol and drug abuse." (Guida, 1978).

Where then does this leave us: is the EAP manager to be an experienced social worker, psychologist, or nurse, or can he/she be simply a recovered and interested employee? Only a skillful screening process appropriate to the needs of the particular workplace will determine the final choice.

Relationship to Other Medical Programs

Whether located within or external to a company, the EAP and other medical department programs can benefit from each other's presence if imaginative links are drawn between and amongst them.

A most useful liaison is with any health education efforts. This is discussed in more detail in a separate chapter. The rationale for this link exists at several levels. Within the larger framework of a full occupational medicine department, health education can be viewed as a logical implementation of the preventive medicine concept for both physical and mental health. Likewise, the EAP is an extension of the evaluation and treatment arm of clinical occupational medicine into the same physical and mental health problems.

Visibility is a key "side effect" of such health education efforts. More than one promising EAP has languished for reasons of unsuccessful advertising and promotion of its usefulness and very existence. Virtually by definition, a health education program uses public-oriented media (speeches, presentations, displays, literature, etc.) to accomplish its aims. Since one of its primary messages is the prevention of stresses and strains which might lead to problems handled by an EAP—especially a broad-based one—it is most appropriate to include in such presentation materials reference to the existence of the EAP, and its ability to handle such problems needing care (i.e., where health education efforts have not yet been entirely successful). Inclusion of the EAP manager or staff as presentors or discussors can be particularly valuable. This illustrates again the usefulness of looking for communications skills in the EAP manager as a criterion in the hiring process.

Elsewhere, useful ties may be made with stress management and ongoing employee relations-sponsored management training programs. The goal, indeed, is to incorporate EAP principles of performance monitoring and appropriate referral into management's common list of strategies.

Liaison to Other Company Affiliate EAPs

Organizations having multiple geographically dispersed units or affiliates are more often decentralized in their approach. The goal in this situation for the occupational physician is likely to be the promulgation of a variety of EAP models to each of the other affiliates. Here the occupational physician can often play a very useful role, for the occupational medical department is generally a common established link among the affiliates. By promoting the EAP as a legitimate extension of the medical department activities in each location, its acceptance by new managements is more likely.

This process of creating a demand may be desirable from the EAP's point of view, but will usually require considerable efforts at convincing local managements. Quite helpful will be the availability of the EAP manager to consult with and visit the burgeoning prospective customers. The occupational physician's influence, where proper at the time, will be able to accomplish this. This will, of course, create the potential for staffing problems at the home office, where routine client and organizational support for the program must continue while the EAP manager is conducting his/her other roles as promoter of the program and consultant. Obviously, priority setting and planning are essential for appropriate time management.

Summary—The Occupational Physician as Manager

The foregoing discussion raises the central issue of appropriate managerial skills for the occupational physician, where they can best serve the goals and needs of an EAP by becoming an effective manager. Where management skills serve well elsewhere in the medical department, they are crucial to the success of an EAP.

Perhaps the occupational physician is manager or overseer of an EAP situated within the medical department; perhaps he/she acts as contact for an outside EAP, or perhaps he/she is more simply the "medical" piece of a program managed by others. In any of these situations, the goals and principles of the EAP may be advanced by the occupational physician's participation in its developmental, operational, and expanding phases. His/

her influence as a respected member of management lends authority to and can smooth the path for acceptance of the EAP, the success of supervisor training, and the associations with other quasi-medical and traditional management training functions. The need to thus proactively "manage" such activities, rather than allow others to carry the lead alone, is emphasized by McDonagh:

> If the occupational physician takes refuge in technical expertise and ignores the managerial challenge, lay managers increasingly will control the destiny of occupational health programs ... A number of our colleagues are not interested specifically in management and have no great desire to acquire additional skills in this area. [While it may be] logical to assume that such programs are the responsibility of health professionals, [the] days when this assumption was accepted passively and unquestionably are past. ... They require effective leadership (McDonagh, 1982).

Where the OHN is the counterpart or colleague of the occupational physician in an EAP, the principles are the same, to the extent that she/he gains these management skills and breaks older models of "what a nurse should do", she/he too can be a powerful implementer for the EAP.

In summary, the occupational physician or OHN is an essential player in the development and appropriate implementation of an EAP. Their clinical and managerial skills can be most effective when cooperation is sought all along the way, through a networking with management, other health professionals, other employee-oriented groups within the organization—such as the employee relations, communications, and organizational development functions. Together they can be nearly insurmountable in their energy and ability to move corporate mountains.

References

1. Review panel on coronary-prone behaviour and heart disease. *Coronary prone behaviour and coronary heart disease: A critical review*. 1981, 63:1119–215.
2. Rosch, PJ. Letters to the editors. *Stress, cholesterol, and coronary heart disease*. Lancet 1983, 2:851–85.
3. Millman, RG, and Solomon, J. *Alcohol and substance abuse in the occupational setting*. In Clinical Medicine for the Occupational Physician, edited by Alderman, MH and Hanley, MJ. Marcel Dekker Inc., N.Y., 1979.
4. Straus, R. *Alcohol abuse and physician's responsibility*. Arch Intern Med 137: Nov. 1977, 1513–514.

5. Code of ethical conduct for physicians providing occupational medical services. J Occ Med., August 1976 (cover). Originally issued by the American Occupational Medical Association on July 23, 1976.
6. Guida, MA. *OHNs are in the best position to help workers fight alcoholism.* Occupational Health and Safety. Sept/Oct, 1978, 48–52.
7. McDonagh, TJ. *The physician as manager.* J Occ Med., Feb 1982, Vol. 24, No. 2. 99–103.

13

Contemporary Occupational Psychiatry
Alan McLean
William Ellis
Ian Lipsitch
Leonard Moss

Introduction

There is a risk to psychiatry of not attending to the world of work. There is an equal risk to industry if psychiatrists are not involved. And if one element could characterize the work setting of the 1980s, that element is change. Change, even change for the better, brings with it fear, stress, and misunderstanding. Because psychiatrists understand the psychic processes and dynamics of growth, interpersonal interaction, and the influences of external forces on the individual, they have a unique opportunity to work with management and labor alike to assure that the change in the work environment which is inevitable is a positive process.

However, there is presently a moat of misinformation and miscommunication beween psychiatry and industry which frequently limits psychiatry's role as a change agent and facilitator in the work setting and which extends both ways. Many in the labor force, from executives to union leaders to blue-collar workers, see psychiatrists as nondirective passive listeners who charge too much, prefer to work in isolation, will not share the information they receive, and who either prefer long-term analytic treatment or use medication too freely. On the other hand, psychiatrists may be vulnerable to the stereotyped perception of the corporate executive as a member of the "old boys' network" whose primary concern is personal profit and who is callous to the needs of his/her workers and the stresses accompanying change in the work environment.

This report will examine these barriers and make recommendations for surmounting them. To do so, however, it is first important to have some understanding of psychiatry's history of involvement in the world of work.

Background

What has become a rather rich literature in the field of occupational psychiatry had its beginning during World War I. The field assumed considerable stature in the 1920s, regressed during the Great Depression, and saw a similar advance and post-war cutback with World War II. However, occupational psychiatry's real surge of steady growth and variety has occurred during the past 25 years, as the role of the psychiatrist in the workplace has grown, evolved, and become increasingly significant. This growth, however, has not been without its bursts of activity and its retrenchments.

Industrial medicine, emphasizing care of medical emergencies occurring in the industrial plant, did not develop as a separate specialty until the early 1900s; and it was only gradually that this field generated a subspecialty of prevention and positive health maintenance which came to be called "occupational psychiatry." The first actual review of the literature in occupational psychiatry was done by Sherman in 1927[1]. He suggested then that the psychiatrist's rightful area of concern was "the individual's adjustment to the situation as a whole." It has not been more aptly put since. Other hallmarks of the history of "industrial psychiatry," as it was then known, include the first full-time employment of a psychiatrist in American business in 1922 at Metropolitan Life Insurance Company[2] and Elton Mayo's decade of study of working conditions in the Hawthorne plant of the Western Electric Company in Chicago. Starting his work in 1924, Mayo, (not a psychiatrist) defined the functions of the work organization and the situations that lead to worker stress[3].

V.V. Anderson, M.D., was first able to put many of these newly emerging ideas into practice in the later 1920s in the personnel department of Macy's department store in New York City. He was mainly concerned with personnel interviewing techniques and with using psychological tests during placement procedures. He also studied accident prevention and effected a remarkable reduction in the accident rate of the store's delivery truck drivers. He developed the team approach to mental health problems by directing a group of psychologists and social workers in using their particular skills in dealing with a broad array of industrial mental health problems. From Anderson's experiences at Macy's came America's first book on occupational psychiatry in 1928, *Psychiatry and Industry*[4].

Concepts of emotional first-aid were developed at the Oak Ridge, Tennessee, atom bomb community in the mid-1940s; and the first post-residency training program for occupational psychiatrists was begun in 1948 at Cornell University's School of Industrial and Labor Relations with an endowment from the Carnegie Corporation[5].

The involvement of the American Psychiatric Association (APA) in the practice of psychiatry in the work setting got off the ground in 1959 when the Association's Committee on Occupational Psychiatry published a pamphlet entitled "Troubled People on the Job," which, in its various forms, sold several million copies. In 1965 the committee, which had served as a clearinghouse in the field since the 1940s, published the book *The Mentally Ill Employee*, which sold more than 25,000 copies. From 1960 to 1965, the committee published a newsletter with a circulation of nearly 1,000.

In 1965, however, the National Institute of Mental Health (NIMH) created the National Clearinghouse for Mental Health Information and named occupational psychiatry as one of the 20 key topics to be researched, abstracted, and followed. The newsletter of APA's Committee on Occupational Psychiatry was absorbed by NIMH's new "Occupational Mental Health Notes," which carried both news and abstracts of the literature until 1970, when several forces converged to create change and new directions for this growing area. First, the National Institute of Alcohol Abuse and Alcoholism (NIAAA) established a new branch to develop occupational alcoholism programs (two per state). These programs, the precursors of today's EAPs, grew from an initial involvement with ten companies to work with some 5,000 businesses. In addition, the National Council on Alcoholism, while NIAAA was making its major industrial outreach effort, provided a parallel private sector initiative through its labor-management division.

Some institutions that had begun to show an interest in occupational psychiatry would continue their efforts to foster it. In 1971, for example, the Center for Occupational Mental Health of Cornell College Medical Center began quarterly publication of the journal *Occupational Mental Health*, which achieved a circulation of 6,000 before it was forced to discontinue in 1973 due to lack of funding.

One sector within the world of work—organized labor—was more conspicuous by its absence than by its involvement in occupational psychiatry. While some psychiatrists did, and still do, provide the usual types of psychiatric evaluation and treatment within union-sponsored clinics, psychiatrists simply do not have a history of serving as consultants to unions, other than in a strict clinical context; and organized labor has, by and large, tended to view psychiatric consultants hired by the parent companies more as agents and extensions of management than as people brought into the organization to work on behalf of labor. What work has been done in union health centers and union-sponsored research and demonstration projects has been done mostly by social workers[6].

Shortly after the APA Committee on Occupational Psychiatry published *The Mentally Ill Employee* in 1965, the committee was disbanded, and APA did not focus direct attention on this issue again until 1981, when the timing seemed right for several reasons. The community mental health movement, while not without its successes, had also had its share of disappointments, not the least of which was the disaster of deinstitution-alization of state hospital patients without adequate community resources to meet their needs. The economic recession that plagued the nation also belied the democracy of the entitlement of all citizens to basic rights in certain areas, among them the right to health care and the right to a job.

Why Involvement with Industry is Relevant to Psychiatry

The reasons for the growing relevance of the work setting to the psychiatric profession are numerous.

First, the absolute number of people who spend a large proportion of their lives in salaried employment has grown enormously. Not only has the population grown but the family constellation has shifted so that the proportions of both dual career and single parent families are much higher today than they have ever been. As is noted in a recent report from the Group for the Advancement of Psychiatry (GAP)[7], "For the first time in the history of the United States, most households are classified as having double incomes, with both husband and wife working out of the home. . . . Increased participation of women in the labor market seems to be leading to a corresponding change in the power structure of many families" toward mutuality of power between the parents.

The woman's growing place in the work force—and today women constitute half of it—is also affecting the work environment, as men have to learn to accept women as equal colleagues in roles that traditionally have been the purview of men.

Second, employed people, when hired, are functional individuals with personal and occupational assets. Even if they experience mental illness, they are more likely than others to have a favorable prognosis for returning to their previous normal level of functioning. Interventions in the world of work have great promise in the context of primary and secondary prevention. Nowhere else in our society do the mental health professions have such remarkable access to a setting in which they can implement preventive techniques that will affect such a large part of the adult population.

Third, it is most often the employer who pays for the health care of his workers as well as any other benefits that might be perquisites of the job. To be able to provide any services to a company's employees, a psychiatrist must be able to convince the employer of the need and be able to fill that need with treatment that is relevant to the situation. And unless the psychiatrist understands the dynamics of the work environment, his/her chances of opening the industrial door are slight.

Fourth, our colleagues in other mental health professions have resourcefully and successfully looked to industry to advance their professions and their professional impact. As a result, new models of mental health intervention, such as EAPs, have evolved and have assumed growing importance in terms of the number of individuals affected. While such programs have been based on good intentions, they have not always been able to provide the level of medical care and advice which is required. Yet, unless psychiatrists show the same level of initiative in approaching industry as their nonmedically trained mental health colleagues, they will continue to be misunderstood and underused in the work setting.

At the top of the list are the large employers in our society, be they in the public or private sector, that have recently shown that they have a major role in the economics of medical care and in care for mental illness by being the purchasers of that care on behalf of their employees. A significant concern to many employers is the rise in health care costs under various benefit plans for which they pay. Benefits covering treatment for psychiatric disorders seem the least concrete and least manageable and, for many, represent the most rapidly growing cost. For example, in the IBM Company in the United States (which in 1981 had 208,000 employees and 442,000 dependents for a total covered population of 650,000) mental health benefits in 1980 were $26.6 million ($14.9 million for inpatient care representing 15.4 percent of total hospital plan costs, and $11.7 million for outpatient care, which was 21.2 percent of total major medical plan costs). In 1967, costs for inpatient care represented only 6.4 percent of IBM's total hospital benefits.

Since most working men and women rely on their employers to provide health insurance as a benefit of employment, it is the company, not the individual, which makes the crucial decisions about type and scope of health care coverage. And in many instances, such as when the employer selects coverage through a health maintenance organization (HMO) or preferred provider organization (PPO), the employer also dictates, at least in part, either the locus of care or the specific provider. The employer may even go further by offering cash rebates to those employees who keep their health care utilization at a minimum. Unless the employer understands how good employee mental health can affect workers and, therefore, the company's output, psychiatry's efforts in this area will have gone for naught. The psychiatrist, then, must generate understanding at the top of the chain of command.

For these reasons and others, it is important that the psychiatric profession examine carefully its role in occupational settings and encourage its members to involve themselves in this important realm.

Business and Other Work Organizations: Roles & Motives

The usual relationship that a psychiatrist has with an industrial employer is that of a consultant rather than that of a permanent, full-time employee. It is crucial in a consultative relationship that the consultee have the feeling that the consultant can enhance the objectives of the organization. Thus, it is important that the psychiatric consultant understand the expectations of his "employer" in order to place his/her endeavors in a meaningful context for mutual understanding.

Executives and managers in industry are motivated by a desire to see their enterprises thrive. This goal clearly involves profits—the proverbial "bottom line." The factors that affect this goal are multiple and range from the weather to the price of raw materials, the state of the economy in general, to the state of mind of the employees, to the competition, the cost of health and life insurance for the employees, and to numerous other factors. However, in every enterprise, a fundamental factor in the equation is the people who work there. They, in turn, are affected by myriad factors such as remuneration, work environment, type of work, equipment, amount of job security, and others. All of these elements, in various ways, influence what economists have termed "productivity," an issue that has received enormous attention in recent years.

Productivity is a concept that has many facets. Not only is productivity at any given time important, but so is future productivity in light of changing technology and conditions. Thus, *change* is an ongoing factor that has implications for the bottom line as well as for the people who work in industry. For the individual, change tends to influence effectiveness and efficiency in a variety of ways. In order to be handled well, employees need to be prepared carefully to deal with change.

Change has been called the "common denominator" of the American worker, be he/she in a white collar position or on the assembly line[6]. The rapid change in the meaning of labor to the individual is a factor of major importance. For example, blue collar workers increasingly expect work to provide not only decent wages but also satisfaction; professionals, in addition, are challenged to be relevant, to make their work mean something in the world around them.

Much of the change stems from the fact that the workforce in Western society is today better educated and more affluent than in prior generations. Other aspects of change have to do with technological advances that restructure the operation and almost always make workers uneasy about their own status quo and, sometimes, actually make them extraneous to the operation. And while money and meaning are important, perhaps the bottom line for the worker is security—if a job cannot offer security, then what can it offer? As recent history has borne out, job loss may be the most significant stressor in the world of work. According to the recent GAP report on job loss[7], "Job loss and the threat of job loss are excruciatingly threatening to many and seriously disruptive, at the least, to others. . . . Job loss contributes to higher levels of ill health; it is also associated with development of severe mental disorders . . . For those who already have chronic mental disorders, it may cause an exacerbation of symptoms."

Schon[8] has clearly shown how established institutions respond to change. "Faced with challenges they cannot meet," he says, "they respond with 'dynamic conservatism'—they fight to remain the same." He maintains that work organizations must become learning systems—maintaining the flexibility to adapt to situations as they arise, decentralizing control, and organizing themselves not around products but around functions.

Another factor, in addition to change, which is linked to productivity— or its opposite—is staff turnover. A worker who is experienced and functional is a valuable asset. The amount of time and expense involved in developing a worker to such a point has a direct bearing on productivity and profit; this is especially true in an economy and a culture that are increasingly based on sophisticated technology.

Still another factor that affects productivity is *motivation*, which depends largely on an individual's identification with and expectations of the employer. How hard an individual works and how strong his/her allegiance is to the goals of the organization dirctly affect his/her productivity. Among the factors that affect motivation is the manner in which communication takes place between worker and manager. Such communication involves information about the organization, evaluations of the worker's endeavors, prospects for the individual's future, and potential rewards, all in addition to the fundamental expectations of the employee.

These are among the factors about which the executives and managers in industry *must* be concerned. Those that affect the people at every level are of particular relevance to the psychiatrist in the occupational setting, for people are his/her major area of expertise.

The Psychiatrist's Function in Occupational Settings

The most common role for psychiatrists in the work world is in what has been termed "case management." Frequently the psychiatrist's "place" within the organization is in the medical department, and the task consists of evaluating employees who are obviously dysfunctional, unable to work, and in treatment for medical reasons. The task is analogous to that performed by other medical consultants—namely to evaluate the employee, to ensure that he/she is receiving appropriate treatment, and to ensure that the necessary information about the employee's work status is being conveyed to those who need to plan. For example, with an employee who is experiencing a major depressive episode and is hospitalized, the psychiatrist's task would involve communicating with the treating physician about the type and severity of the illness, the type of treatment being administered, and the prognosis for recovery, both in terms of extent and time. The psychiatrist would then inform the manager about when he/she can expect the employee to return to work and what limitations, if any, will affect the employee's ability to perform. This feedback enables the manager to make provisions for seeing that the necessary work is done while the employee is away and assures a smooth transition and a feeling of being welcome back when the employee returns.

The purposes of such "case management" are to maintain communication between the employee and employer, to assure appropriate treatment, and to enhance efficiency at the job site by providing practical information with which management can make appropriate plans. Not all cases are as straightforward as this example; but in even more complicated ones, the goal is to bring about a practical resolution that accommodates the needs of employee and employer. Thus, an employee who is inefficient because of growing senility can be spared constant frustration and helped to retire at his/her own pace. Or the alcoholic can be moved toward treatment rather than simply losing his/her job. Each of these examples would fall into the broad category of "case management."

Beyond this role lie multiple tasks the psychiatrist can perform in occupational settings. For example, he/she can advise managers and supervisors about how to recognize changing performance and to deal with specific types of employee problems. He/she can train non-psychiatrists in such areas as crisis intervention, group dynamics, stress symptomatology and genesis, or the effects of drugs and alcohol on behavior. The consultant may be called on for comments concerning a variety of specific problems, such as the human factor in accident prevention or factors in the work environment which support healthy behavior; or he/she may be asked to gather demographic data on the incidence of mental illness in the company's work force. He/she can give advice on health insurance coverage for psychiatric illness or on the implications of a liberal versus a frugal benefits package. And he/she can offer opinions to management about the implications for employee behavior of various types of change within the organization.

This latter role, however, occurs only over a significant period of time after the psychiatrist has earned the trust and respect of his/her employer. Perhaps this position as adviser/confidante is established not so much with direct patient contact as through behind-the-scenes work with other occupational physicians and members of the management hierarchy. As the psychiatrist helps these significant others to understand and cope with deviant behavior, the teaching process spreads his/her productivity enormously.

Moving beyond the fundamental clinical role, the psychiatrist is responsible for teaching the management of work organizations at all levels. Mental health education can easily include informal periodic discussions with small groups of key executives to help members of management understand the role that feelings play in decision making and to further the understanding of group members of their own reactions to stressors at home and work. The sessions often increase management's sensitivity to inter- and intrapersonal issues involved in the operation of a work organization. During this process, the psychiatrist acquires an increasingly sophisticated sense of how the organization operates and the implications of this management style for the productivity and well-being of the employee. For example, in the face of making a difficult decision that will have an unfortunate impact on one or more employees, executives often respond just as many of us do—with guilt, anxiety, withdrawal, and other defenses that can lead them "to confuse their own feelings and needs with the feelings and needs of other people within the organization" or of the organization itself[7]. As the recent GAP report on job loss notes[7], psychiatrists "can look for the hidden suffering in organizations and management teams just as they do with patients, families, or members of a therapeutic milieu team." The report goes on to note that "executives operate in a world of diminished structure and the greater stress of making significant decisions. . . . Most executives have the capacity to ask for and use help if it makes sense to them. . . . Executives also need support in the form of reliable information, objective and honest confrontation, emphatic listening, an opportunity to ventilate and accept their vulnerability, and help with personal and family stress. They should not have to get sick to receive such support."

Once a psychiatrist consultant has gained such acceptance, an employer may look to him to provide advice on broader issues of company policy, procedure, and practice. Such an influence can be extremely constructive for an entire employee group. For example, convincing administrators to move away from policies that tend to foster dependency and paternalistic behavior goes a long way toward making the work environment a healthier one. However, there is also a "seductive" and potentially destructive aspect to the role of the psychiatrist who has earned his/her way into the corporate *sanctum sanctorum*. Some psychiatrists invited as consultants to industry find it to be a heady experience to have the power of potential influence at the highest level and may offer counsel and advice that their background does not reasonably allow. Psychiatrists consulting with industry should at all times take great care to limit their recommendations to those appropriate for their own circumscribed areas of expertise.

Another caution is that while it is appropriate for a psychiatrist to be on the staff of an organization's medical department as the liaison agent between an employee's physician and his/her workplace, as described earlier, it is *not* appropriate for a consultant psychiatrist to serve as a therapist to members of that organizational community, for example, to treat the wife of a vice-president.

Finally, in many respects, the work organization itself may be regarded as the subject of scrutiny or "identified patient" in the sense that any organization becomes a small and dynamic micro-society within the larger one. By studying the corporate personality and using the traditional techniques of clinical study, assessment, diagnosis, and treatment, the psychiatrist can do much to enhance the health and reduce the disability of the people within that subculture.

The Psychiatrist's Background and Its Relevance to Occupational Settings

More than almost any other practitioners in medicine, psychiatrists have been taught to consider multiple environmental factors as they examine and contemplate the "patient" and his/her symptomatology. The realm of basic psychophysiologic medicine is but one example of this multivariate expertise.

In the occupational setting, a psychiatrist's perception is particularly valuable in view of the importance of the welfare of the organization as a whole. However, this utility extends only so far as these abilities are recognized as valuble and used appropriately. Those in authority in occupational settings vary widely in their inclination to use the services of psychiatrists. Some work organizations have a long tradition of psychiatric involvement, in many others such a tradition has never been established or seriously contemplated, and some shroud psychiatry in the same stigma of misunderstanding as does much of the public at large.

Based on the experience of involved psychiatrists, some conclusions can be drawn about the ways in which psychiatric involvement can be an accepted and effective tool for employers. Most of these suggestions require the psychiatrist to be flexible and to adapt his skills to the unique corporate environment rather than to assume that the customary physician-patient relationship will be effective with his industrial client.

   a) Psychiatrists must first realize that when working with industry, they are in someone else's environment; in order to be effective there, they will need the same type of management skills that are required of the company's leaders. While they will be used toward different ends, the tools needed are the same. A useful approach for the psychiatrist to use with his/her industrial client is, "I have skills that may help you, but I also have things to learn."

b) Psychiatrists must be able to alter their traditional psychotherapeutic orientation in significant ways. First, they must acknowledge that one reason they are involved is to further the overall mission of the enterprise. To do so, they must understand the organization: its expectations, the nature of the work, and the realities of the employer's environment. Further, in working with employees, they must be able to accept that their own allegiance must in part be to the overall well-being of the organization and that in certain instances this objective will bring them into conflict with the immediate needs of specific employees.

c) The psychiatrist must be able to adapt to the customs and styles of the organization. For instance, in a chain of command, he/she must respect this management system in the same way that others do unless explicit permission is granted to bypass the usual channels. If certain types of personal attire are encouraged, not to adhere to such standards may be self-defeating in terms of one's effectiveness.

d) Access to health information about employees is a complex and thorny issue. The question is, "Who has access to what medical information concerning employees and prospective employees?" A number of individuals within and outside an organization may claim legitimate access to such data: the employees or the prospective employees themselves, insurance carriers, various levels of management, the occupational physician, the employee's personal physician, the occupational health nurse, the corporate personnel staff, the equal opportunity staff in major corporations, the National Institute for Occupational Safety and Health (NIOSH), and other agencies. The issues to be determined are what type of employee permission is necessary before releasing such information and in what form should it be released? The requirements of handling medical data in the field of occupational health can be defined in terms of operational needs and the protection of employee privacy. Before patients give their consent to disclosures, they should know what information they are disclosing, the exact use that will be made of it, and the consequences of the release. While informed consent is desirable, it rarely occurs in a totally voluntary way. For example, what applicant will refuse authorization to contact a hospital or physician when not signing such a release clearly precludes employment? And, it is rare that managers and personnel directors will really "need" such information as an employee's specific diagnosis; rather, information about "recommended work restrictions" should suffice. The rank ordering of medical information into various levels or tiers of accessibility to different individuals with legitimate need may be the best way to handle this dilemma.

e) The psychiatrist must be able to accept and define his/her role in the organization in terms of being a consultant, advisor, or provider of information. This is frequently an uncomfortable position at first, given the reality that in the treatment realm, psychiatrists are accustomed to being "in charge" and having almost unchallenged authority. Frequently, decisions are made which are not in harmony with the consultant's recommendation. The consultant must be able to accept these decisions and to observe the outcome and continue to offer appropriate recommendations as the results unfold.

Special Issues—Stress Management

The area of stress management has received a great deal of attention in recent years, both in industry and among our nonpsychiatrist colleagues in medicine and other mental health professions. There is little question that "stress" results in psychophysiologic and psychological changes that are uncomfortable and, in the extreme, deleterious. Furthermore, certain work conditions are conducive to extraordinary levels of stress. For example, Levi[9] at the Karolinska Institute in Stockholm, assessed responses to stressful situations with respect to psychological self-ratings, performance, and biochemical parameters reflecting subjectively perceived stress in the subjects. He clearly showed that psychological stimuli can actually affect physiological and biochemical reactions in a potentially pathogenic manner. Smith et al.,[10] of the Behavioral Factors Branch of NIOSH, examined specific occupations of patients admitted to mental institutions. Their results indicated that general and construction laborers, secretaries, inspectors, clinical laboratory technicians, office managers, manager-administrators, foremen, waitresses/waiters, operatives, mine operatives, farm workers, and painters all showed an incidence of stress-related disease significantly greater than expected. They also found that occupational stress status had no relationship to the incidence of stress-related disease. Despite these and other rather careful studies, however, much of the research on occupational stress is encumbered with methodological problems: Few studies relate working conditions to physical or psychiatric disorder, most rely heavily on the use of correlations for their conclusions, and some are frankly anecdotal.

Stress is neither inherently good nor bad. It is part of life, both at work and elsewhere. A tolerable amount of stress is analogous to a challenge. Too much is deleterious both to self-esteem and to good health, in obvious ways. It is, thus, the responsibility of the psychiatric consultant to be an observer who provides relevant information and data to appropriate individuals. To management, the useful data range from how levels of stress and employee expectations are affecting individual and group productivity and efficiency and the extent to which "casualties" are resulting, to suggestions about modifications in the work setting which can help keep the lid on "distressful stress." In addition, education of management about the causes of stress and the reactions of people to change and uncertainty is also useful.

For the individual, advice as to how to identify and understand the source of one's own discomfort is relevant and helpful. If this is not sufficient, referrals to appropriate resources are indicated, and the psychiatrist should be prepared to make them. Beyond the clarification of the issues and needs, however, the psychiatrist is likely to enter into conflict of interest if he/she attempts to provide direct treatment while also serving as a consultant to management.

Special Issues—EAPs

The last decade has witnessed the evolution of highly significant new models of mental health interventions in occupational settings. Among these are EAPs. EAPs have grown so rapidly in the last few years that they cannot be given adequate consideration within the scope of this report. A brief description, however, of EAPs will be provided here.

EAPs have their origins in alcoholism treatment and have enlarged their scope to encompass the "broad brush" approach, i.e., they address a variety of personal problems that adversely affect performance on the job. The basic model of EAPs is that a "coordinator " is available to employees to provide a triage function of defining the nature of the employee's problems and making recommendations about where the employee can seek assistance. The coordinator then acts as a liaison person between employee and community resource and between employee and management. Throughout the process, confidentiality of the communication with the coordinator should be maintained as described in an earlier section of this report. The employees are either self-referred to the program on the basis of subjective concern or are referred by management on the basis of impaired work performance.

The question of the psychiatrist's optimal role in these programs has been questioned. Recognizing that no two programs or settings are identical; there is no single role for the psychiatrist. However, certain important facts about EAPs must be considered.

First, the model identifies people who have a broad mixture of problems, some of which are serious or even life-threatening. This can be because of suicidal or homicidal potential or because of masked medical illness. Second, the process of confronting an individual with serious questions about job performance or job security is one that must be approached with great sensitivity to both the individual and the situation. Finally, treatment in any community can range from being highly competent to minimally adequate to actually dangerous. Thus, decisions about where to refer clients from these programs must be considered carefully. Other disciplines play a vital role in this growing area, and psychiatrists should become familiar with the skills and capabilities of these other mental health professionals. However, sometimes well-meaning individuals, who are not medically qualified and who are working in the EAP setting, are making major medical and treatment decisions for which they lack adequate background—with possibly serious consequences.

For these reasons, there are crucial roles for the psychiatrist in EAPs which should address the problem of how to make them as effective and soundly conceived as possible.

While most of the time it will not be appropriate for a psychiatrist to be in charge of the daily operations of an EAP, it is appropriate and advised that psychiatrists be involved in the planning of the program to assure that it has the necessary medical back-up. At a minimum, every EAP needs a consultant with psychiatric skills whose supervisory involvement is sufficient to assure that clients' needs are being served optimally.

Psychiatrists should be involved in the design of the program to assure that the confidentiality policies pertaining to program users are clear and explicit.

Psychiatrists can serve a useful role in the selection and orientation of the program coordinator. They can, and should, go even further and develop educational materials for the training, skills development, and support of occupational health professionals.

The psychiatrist should be available on an ongoing basis to assist the coordinator in the assessment of difficult cases and to assure that clients are referred to resources where they will receive optimal help or treatment for their problems.

References

1. Sherman, M. *A review of industrial psychiatry.* Am J Psychiatry 83:701, 1927.
2. Giberson, LG. *Psychiatry in industry.* Personnel J 15:90, 1936.
3. Roethlisberger, FJ and Dickson, WJ. *Management and the worker.* Cambridge, Massachusetts, Harvard University Press, 1939.
4. Burling, T and Longaker, W. *Training for industrial psychiatry.* Am J Psychiatry 111:493, 1955.

5. McLean, A.A. "Occupational psychiatry", in *Comprehensive Textbook of Psychiatry*. Edited by Freedman, AM, Kaplan, HI, and Sadock, BJ. Baltimore, Williams & Wilkins, 1980.
6. Weiner, HJ, Akabas, SH, Sommer, JJ. *Mental health care in the world of work*. New York, Association Press, 1973.
7. GAP. *Job Loss: A Psychiatric Perspective*. New York, Mental Health Materials Center, 1982.
8. Schon, DA. *Beyond the Stable State*. New York, Random House, 1972.
9. Levi, L (ed). *Stress and Distress in Response to Psychosocial Stimuli*. New York, Pergamon Press, 1972.
10. Smith, M et al. *Occupational comparison of stress-related disease incidence*. Cincinnati, Ohio, National Institute for Occupational Safety and Health, 1978.

14

The Role of the Occupational Social Worker in EAPs
James L. Francek

Introduction

> "A new civilization is emerging in our lives . . . This new civilization brings with it new family styles; changed ways of working, loving, and living; a new economy; new political conflicts; and beyond all this, an altered consciousness as well."
>
> —A. Toffler, *The Third Wave*

At no other time in the history of civilization has man known the rates of change that he experiences today; the speed of travel, communication and economic upheaval is unmatched, old paradigms for managing the world and its workings are no longer adequate. A simple contrasting of organization design factors, see Table 14-1, for the workplace highlights how far we have come.

The values and decision factors that generated and maintained the industrial age simply do not fit the evolving post-industrial information society. Over the last century social work has fulfilled significant roles within both society and the workplace. Ever since men and women left their farms and went to the factories, social workers have been addressing a wide range of family and work issues. A good deal of this century's experiences of industrial social work developed in Europe. With the coming of four major efforts, industrial social work, occupational alcoholism, EAPs, and occupational medicine (a new conceptual framework referred to as occupational social work) appears to be evolving. See Figure 14-1.

The refocusing of social work into an occupational framework allows for a gentle move forward and begins to build broader alignments to other human service professionals within the workplace.

As social workers deepen their professional position within the workplace through a consistent application of their body of knowledge and experience, it becomes apparent that one of their strongest assets is their "systems approach" to problems. At a time when many professional disciplines have developed excellent specialties, the generic education of social work, focused on "the person in the situation," prepares mature individuals for a unique contribution to the workplace. A systems approach to the workplace could best be illustrated by Figure 14-2.

This approach allows for a maximum analysis of factors impacting both the individual and the organization. It is a dynamic model that draws the actors into a process of analysis, an identification of issues, and plans for action. It typically has as its objectives (all of which are part of the social work profession's agenda):

- the enhancement of personal growth for individuals
- team building for groups
- organizational development
- the development of stronger commitments to human values in society

The purpose of this section will be to highlight the role that occupational social workers can play in the development of EAPs and also to show how this endeavor can lead to an enhanced model of functioning for the occupational social worker. It is hoped that this section will also show how periods of radical change are optimal periods for application of the occupational social worker's perspective.

TABLE 14-1. Organization Design Factors[1].

1890s–1920s	*1960s–1980s*
Uneducated, unskilled	Educated, sophisticated
Temporary workers	Career employees
Simple and physical tasks	Complex and intellectual tasks
Mechanical technology	Electronic and biological technologies
Mechanistic views, direct cause and effect	Organic views, multiple causes and effects
Stable markets and supplies	Fluid markets and supplies
Sharp distinction between workers and managers	Overlap between workers and managers

[1](From *The Change Masters* by Rose Beth Kanter)

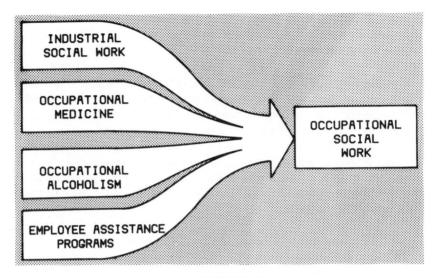

FIGURE 14-1

Employee Assistance Programs

The development of EAPs is a relatively young endeavor that has its roots in the occupational alcoholism field first initiated in the workplace in the 1940s. Alcoholism was seen as a problem that affected a person's ability to perform. Supervisors were trained to identify employees with these problems. Employees were then sent to the relatively few treatment programs that existed, or to Alcoholics Anonymous.

The 1960s brought a more sophisticated approach to alcoholism. The American Medical Association (AMA) had accepted alcoholism as a major health problem.

The National Council on Alcoholism (NCA) was very instrumental in spreading the word that alcoholism was a disease. During the same period, NCA, in its labor and management division, put forth the concept that in order to identify earlier cases of alcoholism, supervisors should be trained to refer employees with declining job performance problems for a confidential assessment of the situation. The hypothesis was that alcoholism affected one's job performance, and that a competent motivated interviewer could detect alcoholism if it surfaced. The passage of the Hughes Act in the early 70s strengthened the occupational alcoholism movement considerably, for it put in place two occupational program consultants in each state to foster such programs. While these supervisor-initiated referrals actually did bring in increasingly more cases of alcoholism at earlier stages, they also brought in a

A SYSTEMS PERSPECTIVE ON OCCUPATIONAL SOCIAL WORK

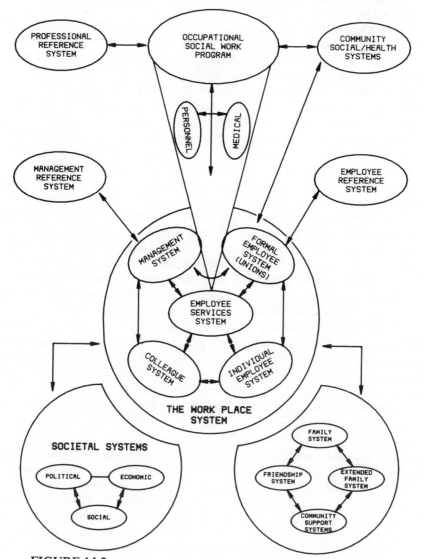

FIGURE 14-2.
WITH THE PERMISSION OF R.J. THOMLISON *PERSPECTIVES ON INDUSTRIAL SOCIAL WORK PRACTICE.*

full-range of human problems, including marital, family, financial, emotional, drug misuse and chronic health problems.

Because of the high numbers of employees identified with alcohol problems, it is crucial that those operating in a direct service mode in the workplace have an extensive amount of training and experience in dealing with alcoholism and other chemical dependencies. This is one area in which social workers, not unlike most other mental health practitioners, have very little focused training, in fact, their belief that alcoholism is merely a symptom of an underlying psychological maladaptation actively blocks them from giving appropriate treatment. Within the last couple of years, headway has been made, but a great deal still needs to be done. I personally received most of my alcoholism training from one who had "walked the road." Many of the pioneers in the occupational alcoholism or employee assistance movement come from similar paths. They "worked hard and long in the vineyard" while most professionals wrote the alcoholic off as a hopeless case. The truth of the matter is that traditional psychoanalysis and psychotherapy alone have a very poor record of recovery with the alcoholic. Today, those mental health practitioners that work well with alcoholics have opened themselves up to the wisdom of those who have "traveled the road" and have incorporated the active participation of their patients with self-help groups such as AA and Alanon along with their treatment plan.

The shift of occupational alcoholism to the broader programs handling a full-range of personal problems, now known as EAPs, was gradual. Most program counselors found that, because they had identified a full-range of services for the alcoholic and his dependents, they could adjust to the broader range of psycho-social-emotional or health problems. As these programs developed, it became clear to both the leaders within management and unions that staffs coordinating these programs needed comprehensive sets of skills in order to deliver quality services.

These developments set the stage for an increased level of interest to be generated by a number of disciplines, including psychologists, nurses, guidance or vocational counselors, psychiatrists and social workers. The joining of these human resource professionals with the recovered occupational alcoholism counselors in the workplace generated a great deal of creativity in EAP development. These multi-disciplinary staffs also developed considerable cross-fertilization. In this context, the occupational social worker, properly trained in chemical dependency and knowledgeable in the areas of labor, management and organizational issues, has with his/her given training much to bring to the overall effort.

EAPs are traditionally set up to address the needs of employees who are experiencing job, behavior, or health problems related to alcoholism, drug misuse, family, marital, or emotional problems. They offer a full range of services for the individual that include:

- crisis intervention
- assessment and differential diagnosis
- interviewing and counseling
- motivation for treatment
- identification and referral to treatment resources
- case management
- orchestration of the crisis
- short term treatment

In all of these services the occupational social worker hopefully extends a non-judgmental service that enhances the individuals ability to take personal responsibility for his/her health, thus leading to psychological independence.

In addition, an EAP may extend the following administrative functions into the workplace:

- supervisor, union, and management training on the EAP
- health education seminars
- the development of related company policies or procedures
- program evaluation modules

Currently, these EAP efforts are continuing to be integrated into the work system. These programs appear to be most commonly identified with the developing framework of preventative health. Again, the application of a systems approach to an individual's set of problems allows for a comprehensive analysis of all the dynamics impacting that individual. How an individual perceives the dynamics of his/her personal system (see Figure 14-3) has a lot to do with his/her psycho-social-emotional well-being and directly impacts his/her overall health.

As more and more companies and unions become concerned about their spiraling health care costs, their attention is moving to preventative, proactive approaches that seek lifestyle change. Occupational social workers, with their generic training, can find particularly good application of their skills in this area. A solid presentation of occupational social work skills in an EAP setting can often open other doors for even further application of their skills and experience in the workplace.

The Environment

The integration of an EAP approach into a given work organization involves networking with various parts of the work and community environment. These contacts internally may include employee or labor

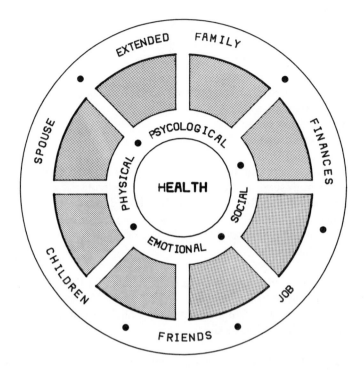

FIGURE 14-3

relations, medical, union, organization and training activities, public affairs, legal, security, benefits, and many others. In the external arena, contacts may be maintained with treatment professionals, agencies, colleagues, and consultants.

It is important at the initial stages of program development that an occupational social worker gather the facts, the history, and the culture of the particular workplace. Using a combination of group and community organization skills, the social worker needs to develop a comprehensive assessment of the host system or community. Using the involvement of a broad range of input from many parts of the system allows for a maximum flow of information and ownership of the identified problems. The engagement of members of the system in a conscious review of the blockages that the system places for maintaining a healthy environment, often moves the organization to positive action. *The process is crucial.* The process itself helps to build a team approach. It identifies the power points of an organization and it assists in identifying allies who can tackle common concerns. Facilitation of group process and communication of ideas builds linkages. These linkages empower the host organization to move towards a healthier state.

As the occupational social worker gains credibility within the organization, he/she can be drawn into discussions around policy development, equal employment opportunity practices, philanthropic endeavors, management training, public affairs issues, quality of work life endeavors, manpower planning, benefit structures, etc. All of these efforts appropriately involve the occupational social worker in opportunities to address the organizational environment itself.

Just as the occupational physician is expected to gather the data regarding the health problems generated by the work environment, and is then expected to address these issues to management, the occupational social worker is also expected to observe the patterns that negatively impact one's social and emotional functioning and then address the organization's leadership directly regarding alternate healthier ways of functioning.

While an increasing number of occupational social workers are finding entry into the workplace through positions that address the organization directly, there is no lack of competition from others equally well trained in the human resource-management field. This is not said to discourage those seeking such entry, but is meant only to add a level of realism.

The Occupational Social Worker—A Broker of Services

Historically, social workers have been called upon in society to create linkages between a given client and a service provider. Whether in hospital or agency settings, the social worker has often been the last professional to see the client/patient before they are discharged. In every real sense, an occupational social worker is often asked to give specific directions to a specific service, thus fulfilling a broker's role. The social worker's knowledge of the resource system in the community enables the client to choose an appropriate:

- child care facility
- nursing home for an aged parent
- inpatient or outpatient treatment center
- career counselor
- financial or legal counselor
- outplacement retirement counselor

This same working knowledge of the external service system is quite applicable in designing many of the benefits within a company. With cost containment such a critical issue these days, a skilled occupational social worker can readily offer excellent consultation and new perspectives that can enhance the administration of cost-effective benefits.

As a broker of services, some social workers have developed educational programs that focus on health consumerism. These programs enhance the employee's knowledge of resources, broaden the employee's choice of treatment options, and empower the individual to take control of how their benefits are used. All of these functions further the acceptance of occupational social work services in the workplace.

The Occupational Social Worker—A Change Agent

At the onset of this section, I attended to the radical levels of change that our world is experiencing. We are fast moving into a post-industrial/information society that is generating unprecedented levels of change within our homes, our families, our workplace, our cities, our nation and the world. The very nature of work itself will be transformed as new modes of electronic technology allow for faster feedback and communication. As I write, computer networks are functioning that link interested parties across the world in ongoing dialogue on any number of issues. The development of homework stations and shorter work weeks is on the horizon.

The river we call life is flowing with an energy all its own. Those who cannot adapt to change and use it to their benefit will be left at the sides of the river: life will simply pass them by. In all of this change, stress has become the badge of honor. The mere mention of the word draws participants from many directions.

Stress can be defined as the "perceived need to change." An occupational social worker armed with a solid systems approach to life and a love for facilitating the process of change will thrive in the present milieu. Areas needing attention abound:

- reduction in work force
- relocation
- reorganization of the work force
- restructuring the nature of work
- introducing new technology
- coping with loss
- early retirement
- manpower planning

In all of the above items, the challenge for the occupational social worker is:

- to raise the awareness of change's impact
- to broaden the ownership of concern
- to synthesize and present the facts
- to clarify the roles
- to facilitate the process
- to establish a focus
- to create new synergy (cooperative interaction)
- to move his/her clients to another level of integration

Change is at the same time exhilarating and threatening. It is the very sustenance of life for some and the bane of living for others. For the right occupational social worker, the current level of change offers the opportunity of a lifetime to be a source of healthy influence on others. To be a conscious agent for positive change is to ride the crest of the breaking waves.

Occupational Social Work—A Call to Conscience

A social worker functioning in an occupational setting is called upon to function according to the highest level of his/her professional ethics. Like his/her colleague in any other setting, one needs to have a clear idea of boundaries. One needs to be in constant balance between the individual client who seeks direction for his/her personal problems or the organizational client seeking consultation on its policies or procedures.

An occupational social worker needs to be constantly vigilant about the way sensitive personal information is kept and managed. Confidentiality and privileged communication have an increasing importance in an age of electronic information systems. Release of personal information needs to be within acceptable informed consent procedures defined by professional codes of ethics or legal statute.

Integrity involves the freedom to be faithful. Faithful to an inner sense of commitment. Commitment to enhancing the lives of others in a way that respects their desire for self determination and maturity.

Summary

Occupational social work is a developing field of practice that focuses on the individual in relationship to his work system. It calls for a generalist who has an excellent knowledge of chemical dependency, organizational theory, history of labor-management issues, health and safety laws, a solid understanding of individual and group intervention, and a systems approach to problems.

Most of all, occupational social workers need to be responsible for their practice in the workplace. They should not present themselves for work for which they are not prepared. For those choosing this line of work, do not expect any two days to be the same. Be flexible. Be ready to engage life itself.

15

Occupational Clinical Psychologist
James J. Manuso

Introduction

The first psychologists were curious pathfinders, academic researchers concerned with the "how's" and "why's" of observed behavior. Psychology has diversified, and the 1960s scientist-researcher model of psychologists' roles has been challenged by the 1970s practitioner model.

In the 1980s, with the calling of industry, the occupational clinical psychologist has emerged from a fusion of academic, research, clinical, organizational, health education and pecuniary interests. The occupational clinical psychologist is concerned with "the application of clinical psychological skills in organizational settings with the aim of facilitating individual and group change processes in order to enhance individual and organizational effectiveness and efficiency" (Manuso, 1983). The growth of this embryonic field has followed a route structurally similar to the earlier development of psychology itself. This section will review the development of occupational clinical psychology (OCP) as seen through its historically unfolding roles, each of which has built on what has come before. The roles examined are those of researcher, tester, educator, clinician, corporate employee, and manager.

Researcher

Traditional doctoral programs in psychology have always prepared their graduates for a feverish pace of research before reaction. Research, and its tool, testing, ultimately brought psychologists into clinical practice. This is as it should be, for without a guide or history, the unknowns reign and we are doomed to wallow in ignorance—within individuals, organizations, and societies.

Harry Levinson, one of the first practitioners of OCP, writes of his introduction into the field: "In 1954 when I joined the staff of the Menninger Foundation, I was asked. . . . to undertake a study of the extent and expression of emotional stress in business and industry" (Levinson, 1983). Indeed, without a solid capacity for vigorous research, how would the contemporary occupational clinical psychologist know how to best design and executive an in-house outplacement program, an EAP, or a stress management training program?

Although the technology, focus, and relative importance of research are different in OCP than in, say, experimental psychophysiology, the occupational clinical psychologist must retain a powerful research orientation or readiness in order to help define the problems and potential solutions in a new field. And since OCP is, by its very definition, an applied branch of psychology, problem-finding and problem-solving are encountered regularly. Without a research orientation, OCP cannot be practiced.

In an era of increasingly limited resources, with more corporate players vying for them, research must be designed and presented to define, clarify, and verify clinical interventions, their effectiveness and cost-benefits within organizations. For example, one of the most basic questions facing the corporate decision maker concerns the nature of the health risks unique to the employee population under consideration. A flip answer is that the larger the population, the more its health profile will tend toward national standards. However, an organization with a commitment to employee health and with limited resources is justifiably concerned with the efficacy and efficiency of different interventions for different employee groups.

An illustration of this point is the recent observation that professionally mediated, individualized stress management treatment is necessary and cost-effective for employees already suffering a stress-related disorder such as headache (Manuso, 1979), whereas a group-administered, audio-visual program is extremely well-suited for employees "at risk" and experiencing unmanageable stress (Sherwood, 1983). Further, for those whose personalities predispose them to heart attack (i.e., the "type A"), group-administered programs are preferable, whereas for the opposite personality type (the "type B"), an individualized regimen is more productive. On a molecular level, these observations are not particularly earth-shattering, and may even verge on common sense. However, when taken in the context of resource allocation within organizations, these observations are significant and may determine the funding of programs.

Research will be more important in the decades to come—with unions, more working women and minorities, government agencies, and the new employee populist movement on the scene. The research role in OCP is critical, and entails a six-step process (Smith and Schleifer, 1983):

1) Set specific objectives that can be met, and specify the questions that are to be answered by the research.
2) Establish a committee of "key persons" (i.e., representatives of the subjects, audiences, and facilitators of the research) to review and make more realistic the objectives and questions.
3) Select the optimally effective *and* cost-efficient methodology that best answers the questions posed (remember the experience of IBM and its first efforts at wellness—the proposed, in-depth research of the program itself would have cost more than the funds necessary to deliver the program).
4) Select and motivate potential participants, with the necessary aid of management support for the research.
5) Have data collection undertaken by neutral parties so as to avoid bias (e.g., early union-sponsored "research" on the grave health effects of small business computers was as ludicrous as corporate ignorance of a problem).
6) Finally, research results should be disseminated to all interested parties, in written form at least, with each specific report aimed at a particular audience in terms of that audience's interests and sophistication.

Tester

Closely allied to the role of research is that of assessment. The practitioner of OCP must be an adept assessor, evaluator, and tester. Psychological testing in the United States came into its own during World War II, when the military was faced with an enormous assessment problem—who should do what best? Societies and their organizations have wrestled with variations on this question for the millennia. In 2200 B.C. the Chinese empire shocked applicants by employing the first known civil service exams for psychological screening (DuBois, 1966). The world has not been the same since.

Americans take particular delight in testing themselves and then comparing results for intelligence, personality, lifestyle-health behaviors, stamina, suitability for jobs, performance capacities and the like. And testing has finally matured, having proven itself as an able assist in predicting, and therefore, controlling behavior. The ease and low cost with which extensive testing may now be offered have favorably affected the use of testing, as have the increased reliability and validity of specific tests. Ultimately faced with more numerous and complex employee selection tasks, corporations will come to rely more on various forms of testing.

All clinical psychologists are testers before they become clinicians. This is reasonable, for a valid assessment must precede appropriate treatment. As they say in business strategy courses, "If you don't know where you're going, any road will do!" For a practitioner of OCP actively engaged in EAP or health risk assessment work, pre-treatment testing is an extremely cost-effective expense.

Human resources or personnel departments in organizations have embraced psychological testing on and off for years. Many employee selection systems rely on some form of psychological screening to discriminate among potential and existing employees. Although pre-packaged selection test batteries are available, the occupational clinical psychologist must be able to formulate a battery unique to the demands of the situation. Because a small proportion of employees accounts for the majority of problem behaviors (such as absenteeism, grievances, infractions, alcoholism, etc.), personality tests may effectively predict and select out these individuals.

From a pre-employment screening perspective, useful testing instruments can predict individuals who could become costly to the corporation through disability and/or litigation. For example, a Type A, coronary-prone employee, although useful to the organization in the short-run, may be a costly expense and lost resource if left untreated. And, some individuals may later bring suit against the employing organization, claiming that the undue work stress brought about their disability.

This latter point brings us back to the classical psychologist's role vis-a-vis testing—to predict psychological and physical liabilities in order to prevent larger-scale breakdowns. Indeed, any wellness program begins with a screening process in order to determine individual vulnerabilities.

There are other significant uses of testing: screening for potentially dangerous and/or unstable personality types in industries where public safety is involved (the prototype here is the nuclear energy plant); executive selection (especially where particular traits, such as leadership, creativity, or research capacity are being selected for); placement and/or career development, which will be increasingly important in the coming era of executive-managerial job scarcity; and, for human resource development, in order that staff may learn to know themselves better and function more efficiently. Psychological testing will always be a part of OCP.

Educator

The original purpose of the Philosophiae Doctoris (Ph.D.) degree was to produce learned professors to teach others. The first "doctors" were teachers, and thus the tradition of being an educator runs deep in the waters of psychology. Until the 1970s, most doctoral programs in clinical psychology had a heavy research and teaching orientation.

The educator role is critically important for contemporary OCP, for the practitioner must train, educate, and teach the managerial class in the behavioral methods of self-improvement, and in the management of employees and of organizations, both large and small. The occupational clinical psychologist, as change agent, is an educator-turned-consultant. As such, this brand of psychologist must be an excellent communicator, a translator of otherwise idle research observations and "techniques" into action principles for application by others.

As health problems become more amenable to behavioral interventions, occupational clinical psychologists also find themselves in the role of health educator, helping employees discover and ameliorate their health risk factors (such as cigarette smoking, poor stress management, etc.).

Clinician

From the beginning, psychologists have been enchanted with, and attracted to the clinical psychotherapeutic role. However, it has only been since the 1940's that psychologists began flooding the mainstream of American psychotherapy. This advent was due, in large part, to the interactions among psychologists' previous roles, the shortages wrought by World War II, and the growing sophistication of an anxiety-ridden public. Also, psychology had matured—its technologies became short-term, more behavioral in orientation and more competitive with respect to traditional health care. Finally, the diseases of adaptation (such as stress-related disorders) began to be implicated in poor overall health profiles; and changes in lifestyle, through behavioral re-education, was the domain of the psychologist.

It was during the 1960s, when the first wave of an urban drug epidemic hit, that more psychologists got involved in treating substance abuse and, therefore, alcoholism. And it was alcoholism which had long been the visible bane of corporate America. Thus, many psychologists broke into OCP through employee assistance programming, which initially involved the treatment of substance abusers. Others came from industrial psychology and consulting.

Once psychologists arrived in organizations, their metamorphosis into occupational clinical psychologists was a speedy one. They became involved in diagnosing and treating alcoholism and drug abuse, depression and anxiety, and traditional psychiatric disorders; they cooperated with medical professionals in the treatment of physical disorders (e.g., heart attack) through behavioral techniques (such as self-monitoring and relaxation training); they worked with groups as well as with individuals; and, they learned to take a preventive as well as curative approach.

Today, the occupational clinical psychologist performs clinical functions similar to those of the occupational psychiatrist excepting the solo treatment of more severe, often organically based, medical disorders and writing prescriptions for medication. In OCP there may be more expertise in clinical research, psychological testing and teaching. However, the demarcation lines between occupational psychiatrists, psychologists, and social workers are fading at the organizational front.

OCP does overlap with contemporary industrial organizational psychology in a number of practitioner-oriented arenas: psychological evaluations, developmental (job-focused) counseling, group counseling, interview training, outplacement counseling, retirement planning, life skills programming, management and supervisory training, and psychological consulting (Morgan, 1983). There is also overlap in the areas of office automation introduction, organization development and productivity enhancement. The leveling influence of enduring corporate employee problems continues to bring together the otherwise separate professional focuses of occupational mental health people, industrial/organizational psychologists, personnel managers, occupational physicians, and others on the scene.

Corporate Employee and Manager

The in-house practitioner of OCP becomes, before all else, an employee of the organization. As such, he/she becomes both subject to and a party for the execution of organizational objectives. And any employee, line or staff, is in the management sandwich, being targeted for exposure to a variety of corporate stressors (Manuso, 1981). The employee must be socialized in the ways of the organization—the corporate code must be adhered to, the corporation's myths publicly accepted, and its members and hierarchy learned. There is no such thing as an observer in the organization, only actors in an ongoing organizational process (this is true of consultants also).

In a large enough setting, and given a significant organization commitment to employee health, the practitioner of OCP becomes a manager. The practical managerial roles of strategist, architect, and politician must be mastered.

The strategist role involves the choice of key services or products the unit (the program) will offer and its distinctive competence to do so. The purpose is to assure a continuing flow of necessary resources to the unit. Thus, the occupational clinical psychologist is cast among other managers seeking a greater chunk of funding for preferred projects.

The role of architect involves the development of an organization structure to execute the chosen strategy. More choices must be made with respect to degree of centralization, staff, time devoted to supervision, repetitiveness of tasks, etc. An organization is designed which matches the strategy developed.

Finally, the occupational clinical psychologist-as-manager must adopt the role of corporate politician. Employees must be motivated, led and controlled in the execution of the mission. Senior managers' approval must be obtained. Outside forces must be addressed—the government and other stakeholders, such as the press and community groups. Those more comfortable as back-room maneuverers or solo clinicians need not apply for the job of organizational manager which entails being a political juggler in a dynamic structure.

Conclusion

Psychology has come a long way since its founding as an academic discipline, in the late nineteenth century. OCP is now in its embryonic phase, and relies on its roots in clinical psychology. These roots, or roles, are those of researcher, tester, educator, and clinician. For the practitioner, the roles of organization employee and manager must be added to the list.

In the next decade, now that attention has been directed to this new field of OCP, psychologists will contribute to the development of the occupational clinical professions, where professional education will determine actual applications much less than in other, more established branches of professions. This early phase of development is perhaps the most exciting and challenging in OCP, where much work needs to be done.

References

DuBois, P.H., 1966. "A Test Dominated Society: China 1115 B.C.–1905 A.D." In *Testing Problems in Perspective*, edited by A. Anastasi, pp. 29–36. Washington, D.C.: American Council on Education.

Levinson, H., 1983. Clinical Psychology in Organizational Practice, Chapter 1 in *Occupational Clinical Psychology*, ibid. p. 7.

Manuso, J., 1983. *Occupational Clinical Psychology*. New York: Praeger Publishers.

———, 1981. Psychological Services and Health Enhancement: A Corporate Model. Chapter in Broskowski, A. et al (Eds.), *Linking Health and Mental Health: Coordinating Care in the Community* (Vol. 2, Sage Annual Reviews of Community Mental Health). Beverly Hills: Sage Publications.

———, 1979. Executive Stress Management. *The Personnel Administrator*, November, pp. 23–26.

Morgan, H., 1983. Clinical Aspects of Industrial/Organizational Psychology. Chapter in Manuso, J., *Occupational Clinical Psychology*, pp. 33–41. New York: Praeger Press.

Sherwood, M., 1983. "Preventive Health Care in the Work Setting." Unpublished manuscript.

Smith, M., and Schleifer, L., 1983. A Guide for Conducting Mental Health Research in Occupational Settings. Chapter in Manuso, J., *Occupational Clinical Psychology*, pp. 275–292. New York: Praeger Publishers.

16

The Occupational Health Nurse Role in EAPs

Laurel Burns

Introduction

The role of nurses in an occupational setting has always been unique. The nurse is often the only medical professional in a plant. Medical decisions on immediate care of illnesses/injuries are often left in nurses' hands, based on their background in the biologic, physical, and social sciences. Each brings to the job his/her unique experiences from acute care and academia.

Depending on the company, the job scope might be as narrow as emergency care only, or so open and varied as to encompass the total physical and mental health of the plant population. The former is typical of days gone by; the latter is the new trend in occupational health. Being on the firing line of health optimization is exciting, challenging, and beneficial, both individually for the nurse as well as for the company, especially in these days of economy and cost containment.

For years the medical departments of industry have been viewed as "necessary" drains on the company's profits. Because of health regulations put on industry across the country, nurses were brought in to meet requirements. They were seen as non-contributory as far as profits were concerned, non-contributing to the manufacturing process; just part of the overhead. Again, times are changing, and the role of the occupational nurse is expanding.

The American Association of Occupational Health Nurses (AAOHN) describes occupational health nursing as the application of nursing principles in conserving the health of workers in all occupations. It involves prevention, recognition, and treatment of illness and injury, and requires special skills and knowledge in the fields of health education, counseling, environmental health, rehabilitation and human relations. This can be quite a formidable task if taken all at once, but let us examine each area a little more closely.

Conserving the Health of Workers in All Occupations

For a good many years now occupational health nurses have been involved in physical screening programs at the worksite. The main objectives were assessing the health of individuals in their pre-employment state, and screening for possible work exposures which would be a detriment to the individual and possibly result in a worker's compensation case for the company. It was a double-edged sword—concern about the individual but with a payout for the company as well. These programs have ranged from rather basic requirements (such as audiometric screening for hearing conservation, pulmonary function testing as with the cotton dust standard, and "management only" physicals to detect early heart disease) to full annual screening of all employees for all body functions.

If you are lucky enough to be involved with a company having a more comprehensive medical program, then screening takes on a new meaning. When blood work shows a gradual change over a number of years, adverse lifestyle changes can be instigated to reverse many such cases. If a pulmonary function test continues to decrease, it can graphically demonstrate why an individual needs to quit smoking. We all get older while we are in the workforce. Our bodily functions deteriorate over a period of time as part of the natural aging process. So does not this goal of conserving our optimum health seem like a losing battle? "No." Many individuals in the workforce really do not understand what they are doing to their bodies. Through annual screening they become more aware of their bodily functions, make educated decisions about their health, and may even become healthier ten years after employment than they were at the time they were hired. Though one can not turn back the clock, a proactive screening program can move employees toward positive health, not just the absence of illness.

Prevention

Many nurses are part of the health team which does employee physicals on a regular basis, with the purpose of early detection of risk factors and disease, thus providing a better chance of prolonged health. In addition to teaching employees about good health and safe practices on the job, the occupational nurse also provides motivation for more safe and healthful lifestyles off the job. By identifying employee needs through the physical examinations, the occupational nurse can easily achieve medical objectives and implementation of health promotion since the target groups have already been identified. Education of these target groups makes this type of program more meaningful. If the intended group is not the audience which responds, often peer pressure from those who do attend such sessions is enough to effect a healthy change in the needy individuals.

Prevention is also where nurses make their most vital impact on cost savings. The areas impacted are sick leave, disability, benefit usage, premature death, surgeries, and extended hospitalizations. If healthier lifestyles are taught and reinforced, sick leave pay should decrease due to lower utilization. If someone does become ill, their recovery time will be less if they have been consciously maintaining their body, and disability claims will be less frequent. If people are healthier, benefit usage will decrease and the workforce will be more productive while on the job. If a company is self-insured, this will be a direct savings. If not, it gives them leverage for negotiating a more cost-effective manner of providing benefits to employees than the traditional indemnity plan. Premature death from heart disease, auto accidents, and other uncontrolled disease processes will become more of a rarity if healthy lifestyles are the norm in the workplace. Understanding alcoholism, distress, substance abuse, nutrition, hypertension, what causes these conditions, and what can be done for them, can prolong the length as well as quality of life. Not only are savings made by avoiding premature death benefits, but one also gains a higher payout on the time and money invested in individuals, their skills, and knowledge.

Many surgeries are the result of diseased organs, secondary to unhealthy lifestyles over an extended period of time. Educating the workforce on how their bodies work and the impact of their habits on their bodies, may prevent unnecessary operations. A good preventive wellness program can return money to the company at a solid rate of return for minimum expenditure. Then, no longer is the medical department a drain on assets, but a contributor to profits.

Recognition/Treatment of Illness and Injury

This is the area most people see as the stereotype of the occupational health nurse—patching people up and filling out workers' compensation and disability forms for the state. Thank goodness for most of us, injury treatment is rare. Because of the skyrocketing costs of work-incurred injuries, most firms now have specialized safety sections, and working safely has become an employment expectation. However, recognition brings us back to the preventive area of medicine again. Recognition of potential hazards to health, as well as the ergonomic aspects of a task, fall into this arena. A nurse's background in assessment makes the subtle changes in the workers noticeable from both a physical and a mental point of view. Any first-aider can patch an injured worker adequately and get them to an emergency care facility. But it takes the added skills in the recognition field to make a medical person worthwhile in industry. Recognition of potentials in the early stages is the key to saving money for the company.

Health Education

Every medical person who assesses an individual, either while doing a physical, or when he/she shows up at the office complaining of a headache, has the opportunity to provide health education. Many times that headache has underlying causes, such as hypertension, stress (from on-the-job or off), poor vision, or a myriad of other sources. This individual has been done a real disservice if just given an aspirin and the real "cause" has not been addressed.

Health education can take many forms. It can be on a one-to-one basis as in the case of the headache, or in a group situation when an unhealthy lifestyle has been identified for a large membership of the organization, such as smoking, cancer, nutrition, weight reduction, etc. Either way it is approached, depending on available space and time, health education can only have a positive effect on a workforce, since people who feel good are more productive.

Counseling

As mentioned, nurses have always done one-to-one health counseling, but they have also been given the role of counseling individuals who are having problems outside of the work environment. Unless special training in this area was sought after obtaining the RN degree, the nurse is really on shaky ground, and should opt to refer people to individuals out of plant who will be able to help them. Again, recognizing that something is wrong or out of balance is a strong nursing function. Diagnosing the problem is not.

Environmental Health

Assessing the work environment's effect on individuals is a responsibility the occupational health nurse shares with the industrial hygienist. Together, data collection and biological or mental impacts are studied and recommendations made to management. Whether it's hearing conversation due to noise pollution, pulmonary function testing because of asbestos or cotton dust, or quality of water going out of a facility, adequate testing and record keeping and review are necessary parts of any successful program.

Fumes from a change in the manufacturing process may not be biologically harmful, but because of the smell, perceived harm is often the issue. Individual exposure records are an integral part of any complete medical file.

Rehabilitation

How often has an individual had a heart attack or bypass surgery and become an emotional cripple? That is a waste of a valuable human being. Reentry into the workplace is a vital component to full recovery. Almost a third of workers' lives are probably spent at work—in some cases more—and their support group is often in this environment. It does not have to be something as severe as a heart attack for the job to be an important aspect in recovery. A broken leg, or even a finger, will heal with less pain, and the morale of the individual will increase if he/she can continue as close to a normal work pattern as possible. This is especially true if the injury occurred at work and some depression about the incident still exists. If they can be useful and still do a full job, loyalty becomes an issue for employees and they feel obligated to return to full duty as soon as possible.

Human Relations

Many medical departments are sandwiched somewhere into the industrial relations/personnel departments. At first this may seem a detriment to the full use of the nurse's abilities in the aforementioned areas. However, by being a part of this group, the occupational health nurse is able to understand policies and procedures and have input into possible updates and changes, as well as being current on benefits available for employees and having an inside track for accomplishing coverage and a successful return to work.

Often the nurse is asked to attend meetings concerning projects or individuals who are problems or potential problems to management or other personnel. While others deal with the cost effectiveness and risk analysis of following through with a plan, it is the nurse who balances the scale with the human aspects of the job and potential physical and mental points which need to be considered.

Employee Assistance Programs

EAPs are one of industry's answers to on the job performance problems. Where in the past employees were fired when they showed up for work under the influence of a substance, now they are offered help as an alternative. Companies see the value in retaining personnel in whom they have invested time and money in training and experience. If the individual is experiencing personal problems to the extent that the job performance is being affected and general well-being is being impaired, it is also affecting those in the workforce around him/her. Companies are now seeing their employees as valuable assets and are attempting to conserve them.

How does this fit into the occupational health nurse role? An EAP is usually a counseling and referral program done at the worksite or off the premises, or both. It is accessed by company or self-referrals, with the cost absorbed by the company or picked up under benefits already carried. As already discussed, the general working principle all occupational health nurses work under is the conservation of the health of workers in all occupations. Therefore, these principles cover management as well as hourly workers. Where else in the work environment can either go and be treated on an equal footing, in a confidential professional manner, and still have their needs met, if it is not in a "non-threatening" medical department?

Confidentiality is a key issue in employee assistance. Because of the nature of the medical department and laws already governing the confidentiality of medical records, this becomes the ideal coordinating point in industry. Personal problems are never discussed, the only information going to management is how long a person will be absent from the workplace and when he/she is expected to return.

Medicine has been doing research for years on the interaction of mind and body. Here industry has that same opportunity to capitalize on it. The nurse already has access to all of the individual's medical data; history, physical, workers' compensation, or state disability insurance injury/illness. When approaching health counseling, the nurse has to ask about probable causes which may have led to the present condition. An example is the same individual who came in for an aspirin complaining of a headache. With further questioning he reveals he woke up with it and has been having frequent headaches lately. This indicates the possibility of an underlying cause. When taking his blood pressure you find that it is elevated, where your records have shown normal readings before. When asking him if anything has been going on which might be bothering him and causing the elevation, he suggests it could be the problem he has been having at home with his teenagers. Here is an indication that the headaches and hypertension could be related to the stress and anxiety of dealing with a family problem. Here exists the perfect opportunity to hook this individual up to the EAP, to get guidance and help with the problem that surfaced as a result of the minor symptom of a headache, and the not so minor one of high blood pressure. Because he will have to return for further evaluation of his blood pressure, followup can be made at that time on the family situation as well. Again, this interface must maintain the same confidentiality all medical records are given.

The same example could play out differently. Maybe the headache is a direct result of a hangover from the night before. How comfortable are you at confronting this individual about the cause? You know he/she drinks heavily, you have the medical data showing liver damage, and you know he/she will be unsafe on the production line without their wits about them. What are you going to do? Hopefully you will have the skill and confidence to confront this individual. If you do not, feeding the data to the company doctor when the individual goes for a physical gives the physician the opportunity. However, this should be avoided unless your confrontation is unsuccessful. Besides, in the meantime, the individual could be injured out on the line. Often a person will deny any problem when first confronted and require a second confrontation from someone in a white coat to make an impact. Our society has abdicated to the "authority of the white coat," and there are times such as these that it can be used to your as well as the individual's best interest. Again, getting them into a treatment program of some sort is the goal, to get them help, and return them as a productive employee.

The principles of employee assistance parallel those of occupational health. Prevention, whether in the physical sense (e.g., acute symptoms from biologic instability) or mental, resulting from perception of stressful situations, falls in the nurse's realm. When an employee presents to the nurse the diagnosis of an ulcer from his/her private physician, several concerns are immediately raised. What caused it? Diet? Stress? The nurse has the ability to counsel the individual on the nutritional concerns, but also to question what the individual perceives as the source of the stress, and refer them to the EAP counselor for professional help. There are many physical symptoms which are the result of underlying mental anxiety and stress. Knowing the inner workings of the work environment gives the occupational nurse an advantage over the private physician in the community in effecting a positive change for this individual. The nurse is more accessible than the private physician, has daily contact possibilities with the individual, and the individual can easily get questions answered and get immediate support.

Rehabilitation, as it relates to the reentry into the workplace of individuals from physical restrictions, has always been an occupational nursing function. But there is also a responsibility for psychological restrictions. Hospitalization for treatment programs, whether for a psychosis or an addiction, requires close work with the medical department during treatment, as well as when the individual returns to work. Precedence has already been set that employees with physical illnesses/injuries have to return through the medical department. It is a natural extension of this policy to follow through on psychological illnesses/injuries in the same consistent manner. With the individual's permission, the manager, the medical department, counselor, and patient should meet together to make sure followup is maintained, expectations are clear, and there is a willingness by all to enhance the chances of a successful recovery.

Human relations is at the foundation of employee assistance; the treating of the "whole" person, not just physical symptoms. Dealing with people is the essence of nursing, whether it is in curative treatment, prevention, providing an ear to listen, consulting on a new job description, or assessing the emotional climate of the workplace. The holistic approach to health is directly tied to occupational health nursing. It is apparent that the occupational health nurse has a special opportunity to contribute to the mental as well as the physical well-being of his/her employees. The nurse has access to information that no one else in a company has, due to confidentiality laws, which make it advantageous both to the individual and to the company to be the in-house site of employee assistance. But no nurse will have a successful program by working alone. The nurse is only one member of a team of professionals who together work toward success. However, as an individual, more opportunities for intervention will come the nurse's (and medical department's) way than to anyone else in the workforce because of the nature of the job. Hopefully, with more companies becoming involved with EAPS the days of passing out pills to mask symptoms and patching up injuries that occur because employees can't keep their minds on their jobs are gone. Hopefully also, the future means that a concept of total optimum wellness is here, with the occupational health nurse being at its core.

17

Management's Role in EAPs
James T. Wrich

"The support of all those people may be important, Jim, but how long do you think the employee assistance program would last without management's support? About ten minutes?"

That is a direct quotation of a comment made to me in a meeting with a group of senior managers at a major corporation. While I don't believe an established EAP would disintegrate in ten minutes without management support, the fact is that many attempts to establish an EAP never really get off the ground specifically for lack of active management support from the very top of the organization on down. In addition, there are many EAPs that have been well established which ultimately declined in function and importance for lack of ongoing management support.

The purpose of this section is to address some of the major issues associated with management support. But first, let's discuss the nature of support itself. Support is not merely the absence of opposition. Support often means to endure bravely; to promote the interest or cause of something; to uphold and defend an issue or a program or another human being as valid or right. It involves active advocacy, even to the point of arguing casting a positive vote. It means a willingness to pay a price and to provide a substantial contribution to assure the existence or continuation of something. It may even mean serving as the foundation, and certainly it means sufficient effort to keep something going. It almost always, at some point, entails active favoring in the face of opposition.

This may seem like a tall order and, in truth, it is. Unfortunately, management support of EAPs is frequently absent even though companies hire staff to design, develop, implement, and operate a program. Few people seem to understand the absolute necessity of support, as illustrated in the terms above. This underestimation of vital EAP support is as likely to be found among the professionals hired to run the programs as in the management that hires them. Professionals frequently are so thrilled at the prospect of having a job in the EAP field and working for a reputable company that they do not even raise the support issue during the interview process. And, it is with the professionals, of course, where the issue of support must first be raised. After all, it is not the personnel interviewer, nor even the organization head doing the hiring who has the training and expertise in what EAPs need to survive and flourish. When professionals themselves seeking employment in this field do not have the experience, and therefore the insights as to what managerial support must really consist of, the issue may be lost before the program even starts.

To begin with, understanding the nature of support necessitates understanding how a program must work to be viable and effective. Other sections of this handbook address those issues so they won't be covered here. But suffice it to say that we have not seen a single EAP fail because of a clinical issue. Failures we've seen have been due to issues of administration, politics, a lack of sufficient evaluation, or inadequate communication of evaluative material. Invariably, the problem causing the failure could be traced to the initial program implementation process. And, a persuasive lack of support, sometime almost imperceptible, was at the core of the cause. All of these issues, of course, are of such magnitude that we cannot adequately address them in this section. We will focus on some of the support components essential to the success of an EAP which when present, lead either to failure or significantly reduced effectiveness.

If an employee assistance program is to flourish and function at an optimum level, it needs the active support of the chief executive officer. This isn't to say that there are not programs that function with less than full and complete support of the chairman. However, in our experience, nothing in an organization—no department, no benefits package, no program of management practices, and certainly no individual—has the positive impact that is generated by the active support of the chief executive officer. It is not a coincidence that the truly outstanding EAPs in this country are in organizations where the chairman has been active, straightforward, and open in his/her support of the program. General Motors, under Thomas A. Murphy; Control Data Corporation, under William Norris; and United Airlines under Richard J. Ferris, are but three examples. In addition to writing articles and giving speeches which squarely put their support on record, they actively supported the program, especially in the early phases, by providing guidance to the EAP staff and promoting the program in dozens of informal ways. In addition, when necessary and appropriate they defended it. Other officers and the employees in general knew that the head of the organization was steadfastly in favor of the program. Managers and supervisors knew that they had a responsibility to refer employees with problems to the EAP and that they too could use it for their own personal or family problems. Employees knew that they could use the program without adverse consequences to their job or future. It is interesting to note, that these three EAPs are among the few which have statistical data demonstrating their effectiveness in both human and financial terms. It is even more noteworthy when comparing General Motors benefit-to-cost ratio (BCR) with United Airlines. The two companies express the BCR differently but a close look shows that the results are extremely similar. General Motors claims a two-to-one BCR after three years, or a $ .67 benefit per year for an initial one dollar investment. United Airlines has demonstrated a 16-to-one BCR projected over a period of 23 years, or $ .70 per year benefit for each dollar initially invested. When the chief executive officer is solidly in support of the program, the likelihood is that he/she is also going to want to know a lot about the program's results. It follows that evaluation is likely to become an integral part of the operation.

Adequate financial support is also essential. Companies claim to want an EAP but not willing to provide adequate financial support are simply unrealistic. What is "adequate" may vary somewhat from one organization to the next, but generally EAPs' operational expenses are going to cost, in 1983 dollars, between $1.50 and $2.00 per employee per month to do the job correctly. Organizations employing fewer than 2,000 people are likely to find it more economical to contract with an outside resource for the EAP services. Organizations over 3,000 employees will generally find it more economical to hire someone in-house. Such general guidelines do not seem to apply to organizations employing between 2,000–3,000 people. Interestingly, the cost per employee per month for programs that are well designed and properly implemented are quite similar when economies of scale and industry pay differential are taken into account. In the months and years ahead these dollar estimates may become obsolete and the reader will have to make adjustments for inflation. But the major point is not so much what an EAP does or should cost; the issue is that there are very few worthwhile programs an organization can undertake which do not require an investment of some kind. EAPs are no exception. If an organization wants a good EAP, financial support is imperative. Moreover, this cost should be accounted for as an identifiable item, not buried in the budget of a large department.

Selection of appropriate staff is one of the most important management decisions. Knowing who to select and why has tremendous impact in a program's success. Not everyone with a masters or Ph.D., or a personal recovery experience is suitable for EAP work. The hiring process requires management support and sometimes the help of an outside EAP consultant. We have broken the staff selection process into three parts: recruitment, interviewee selection, and the interview/final selection. Advertisements in the *ALMACAN*, the *EAP Digest*, and other professional journals have proven to be very helpful. Moreover, the EAP field is rather close-knit and word of mouth recruitment process within the professional organizations almost always yields applicants. We have usually had an objective of interviewing six to ten prospective candidates for each position opening. While there are a number of functions and positions in the EAP field, the most common is that of the employee assistance representative or the assessment and referral resource. In hiring for this position, it has proven to be helpful to review resumes and other application information against the following criteria:

1. EAP assessment and referral experience
2. Experience in counseling chemically dependent people
3. Counseling experience in emotional and family problems
4. Applicable formal education and training background
5. Experience in identifying and developing into a service network a continuum of community based therapeutic resources
6. Any recovery experiences, personal or with family members that the applicant feels could have a positive bearing in their ability to do the job

Numbers 2 and 3 are mandatory and the others are optional. Our experience has been that no one with fewer than the two mandatory and two additional optional requirements have really been suitable candidates. At this point the interviews can be set up with the candidates ranking highest against the above criteria. It should be noted that the above criteria simply get the candidate an interview, not the job. The interview process is much more detailed. While it is not possible to fully capture the essence of the actual interview or to go into all the details, the following lists some of the issues covered:

- What types of problems have the applicants dealt with in their work experience to date?
- What is their basic philosophy regarding controlled drinking vs. Alcoholics Anonymous?
- What was the emphasis in their academic training?
- What is their interest in how an organization works, politically, and otherwise?
- Why would they be interested in working an EAP when they could be working in a treatment center or in private practice?
- What is their basic philosophy of therapy?
- Questions which indicate whether or not the applicant is a self-starter.

- Observation on whether the person is warm, outgoing, and friendly.
- Questions relating to the person's ability to attend to detail.
- What is the applicant's experience and comfort level in making presentations to groups?
- Questions relating to the applicant's ability to be flexible in terms of time spent on the job.
- What has been the applicant's use of sick leave during the past two years?
- Questions relating to the applicant's attitude toward transference and counter transference and how they would handle such issues?
- Any recovery experiences which they feel could bear positively on their ability to do the job.
- Their trust level toward unions and corporations respectively.
- Their experience in working as part of a team.
- The level of chauvinism with regard to women and bias toward minorities.
- Their availability if the position was offered.

This portion of the interview should be conducted by someone knowledgeable in the field of employee assistance programming. Regular personnel department interviewing staff can cover other issues such as the applicant's overall work experience, any gaps that may appear in their employment record, verification of all application and resume information, and a thorough overview of the organization as a whole, the department in which they will be working, and the benefit package. Moreover, personnel staff should make an appraisal of the overall employability in turns of attitude, poise, and temperament.

After money is budgeted and staff is selected, adequate office space is the next major managerial support issue. We have seen excellent staff shunted into inadequate or inappropriate office locations to the detriment of the program. Regulation size office space with extra chairs for both the employee assistance representative and the secretarial support person are usually adequate. After adequate size has been established, location, which is an equally important issue, must be determined. Confidentiality is the primary issue in EAP office location and following immediately behind confidentiality is the issue of accessibility. While recognizing that appropriate office space is not always readily available, especially in expanding organizations, the fact is that serious consideration must be given to the type and location of EAP office space, or the effectiveness of the program can be seriously impaired.

Interdepartmental support contributes heavily to the effectiveness of the better EAPs we have seen. EAPs need the professional assistance of the personnel department, the legal department, the insurance department, data processing, industrial relations, and frequently, the training department within a corporation. If support from any of these departments is lacking, program effectiveness is diminished sometimes significantly.

Participation in the implementation process by key management personnel is imperative to the success of the program. Many organizations formed an implementation committee or committee of concern at the time the program was designed and developed. Labor and management in organized companies participated jointly but in companies having no union, management alone had to provide the membership. People tend to support that which they have had a hand in creating. Because EAPs depend upon strong support from all parties involved, even passive resistance by key individuals is usually sufficient to subvert it.

While the joint implementation committee or committee of concern is really a steering committee which helps to get the program underway and then monitors progress after it has been implemented, its establishment and the participation needed to make it work needs support. It is equally important that managers participate in the key employee orientation sessions which are integral to the implementation and functioning of an EAP. Not only should all managerial personnel sit through the sessions, but should frequently participate in the delivery of the sessions. When senior officers are involved, all other management levels participate far more willingly. Management may also be involved in the development and distribution of correspondence to employees about the EAP. Such correspondence is frequently essential to the EAP implementation program.

Feedback to EAP staff is an important manifestation of managerial support. EAP staff need to know how the program is going and how it is perceived by employees and their supervisors. In our experience among programs that failed, lack of communication of problems, whether factual or perceptual, was nearly always a contributing factor. Managements active support in keeping lines of communication open between their departmental organizations and the EAP is essential.

Up to this point, our discussion has centered on management support for the administrative component of the EAP. Of equal importance is management's support of the clinical side of the program, to which we will now shift.

Referral of employees with personal problems to the EAP is the single most important management support item in the clinical realm. Basically there are three sets of circumstances under which a manager would refer an employee:

1. Job performance problem is in evidence.
2. There is no job performance problem but the employee shares a personal problem with his/her supervisor.
3. There is neither a job performance problem nor does the employee share a personal problem, but on the basis of supervisory observation, something seems amiss.

The more refined programs have significant numbers of supervisory referrals of the Type 2 and 3 variety. Referring employees for help with problems before job performance is affected is the hallmark of nearly every good EAP we have seen. In my experience, managers and supervisors who are sensitive to employees, their needs and their problems, are in a far better position to make the Type 2 or Type 3 referral than the manager or supervisor who consistently takes a hard line approach in dealing with subordinates. Regardless of managerial style, however, there will be a certain percentage of employees who have job performance problems. In my experience, EAPs work best when the manager, whose employee has a performance problem, uses the following five-step approach:

1. Outline the problem in detail, using documentation where possible.
2. Clearly set forth the expectations for the employee.
3. Establish a time duration during which the performance problem must be corrected.
4. Advise the employee what the consequences will be if the problem must be corrected.
5. If at any point during Steps 1 through 4 the supervisor has reason to believe that the employee has a personal problem, he/she should recommend that the employee use the program.

It should be noted that the disciplinary procedure and the EAP are on separate tracks. An employee does not have to comply with the referral for assistance and should not be the subject of retribution if refusing to use the program. Any disciplinary action taken should be based on "bonafide" occupational qualifications, or violation of work rules or regulations. On the other hand, the EAP should not be used as a substitute for appropriate use of discipline. EAP staff should not be expected to make decisions regarding the disciplinary process. In short, the manager should do his/her job and utilize appropriate resources, including the EAP as an integral part of any managerial position. Inappropriate threats usually make matters worse. In instances where an employee shares a personal problem, the manager or supervisor needs to be a good listener, refrain from offering clinical advice or off-the-cuff diagnoses or interpretation of what the problem may be, and should not make any moralistic or judgmental statements. Moreover, the supervisor or manager, in the process of trying to help the employee feel good, should not minimize the seriousness of the problem. They should simply listen and then describe the EAP function and purpose and recommend that the employee avail themself of the service. They may also want to assist the employee in accessing the program by making the appointment. Some managers have even accompanied the employee to the program staff, with the employee's concurrence, of course. Referrals to the program on the basis of personal managerial observation is a bit more difficult, but is becoming more frequent as programs are refined. What usually happens is that the supervisor or manager observes behavior that is either unusual or out of character for the employee. They call the employee assistance staff to discuss the situation and to determine whether or not a conversation with the employee and possible referral to the program would be appropriate. Increasingly, EAP staff spend time in consultation with managers and supervisors about such issues. Frequently, the supervisor or manager desires suggestions as to approach and manner of conversation. Experience shows that when a managerial referral can be made on the basis of a Type 2 or 3 situation, the employee is much more receptive and the manager or supervisor is perceived in a much more positive light. However, there are times when performance has been impaired and, regardless of what the employee's initial perception might be of their supervisor, the supervisor or manager may be the only one in a position to help the employee to access the program. However, it is our experience that when employees understand that such a referral will be made by their supervisor in the event of a job performance problem, they frequently access the program on a voluntary basis to avoid both potential job performance problems and the potential supervisory confrontation.

In union organized work forces, experience shows that referrals based on job performance are best accomplished when management involves the labor representative, and the earlier the better.

The return to work or "the reentry process" can be a very critical time to the employee who has been away from work for treatment for a personal problem. The supervisor's or manager's participation along with the union representative's participation in an organized company, and EAP staff can go a long way toward smoothing out the rough spots that frequently attend return to work. Again, the employee needs reassurance that their problem will not in any way adversely affect their job or their future with the company. In addition, the supervisor will become aware of any particular concerns or worries that the employee has when returning to work and assist in helping the employee with such matters wherever appropriate or possible. The supervisor or manager will again outline the expectations they have of the employee, while assuring the employee that they will be given neither special treatment nor special surveillance. This is not to say that an employee's expressed desire for special support will be ignored, but that generally, where work performance is concerned, the supervisor will have neither higher nor lower expectations of the returning employee than for any other employee.

It is extremely helpful to EAP's staff to have supervisors or managers who have referred employees to the program communicate periodically on the employee's progress on the job. There have been instances where employees have done a much better than average job upon returning to work, and if the EAP staff is aware of it, acknowledgment can be made and the recovery process enhanced. On the other hand, there have been instances where an employee did not perform to standard and the employee assistance representative was aware that the employee was not following the agreed upon program of recovery, but could not relate that to the supervisor or manager because of confidentiality regulations. In such instances, if the supervisor or manager had contacted the EAP they could have provided valuable information that may have supported the EAP staff in their attempts to encourage the employee to follow the recovery program. While EAP participants should not be singled out for special surveillance upon return to work, they shouldn't be ignored either; and good communication between management and the program within the confines of the employee's right to confidentiality is always helpful.

In some organizations an unfavorable relationship may exist between management and the labor unions. In others, labor and management may merely tolerate each other with no real effort to cooperate or recognize each others legitimate perogatives. The EAP staff simply cannot take sides in any labor-management dispute. Their objective is to help people with personal problems so human and financial loss is kept at a minimum. One very critical support item on management's part is to scrupulously avoid dragging EAP staff into the industrial relations arena, particularly if that environment is strongly adversarial. In organized companies, unions have the same ethical responsibilities. Whenever an EAP is used by either labor or management as a tool to advance a hidden agenda, the program suffers and so do the employees who need its services.

An essential prerequisite to any active support, particularly those items listed above, is time. Management must be willing to spend time on the program—time meeting with EAP staff to familiarize them with the operation; time in key employee orientation sessions to learn about the program; time on an individual basis with employees when they have problems; time with employee groups describing the program and encouraging its use; and time reading whatever regulations or policy statements and procedural outlines, as well as other written information, that may be available to increase understanding and awareness. In organizations where management hires professional staff and then expects them to simply handle everything by themselves with very little managerial time spent in communication or other activities, the program will generally limp along for a period of time and ultimately fail.

Obviously, no EAP is perfectly designed, implemented, or managed. We have been involved in the development of over 50 such programs and have had first-hand observational experience with over 100 others; everyone of them had problems. But in the organizations where management was willing to take time to look at what their EAP was doing, to demand excellence, and then to actively fulfill its support role, both administratively and clinically, the programs flourished. When an EAP functions well, everyone wins. But no EAP, no matter how well designed, staffed, or managed can function well over an extended period of time without active management support on all levels.

SECTION IV

Training Issues in an EAP

Introduction

To the EAP staff person, the word "training" brings an image of activities dealing with supervisors and management. However, training, as an issue, has implications also for the appropriate training of EAP staff personnel.

Cohen's section will review current thinking on the EAP role in the training and orientation of supervisors/management, clarifying particularly the constructive confrontation and the performance-related referral. Supervisors do readily accept that job performance is an indicator for an employee's prospects for future advancement and opportunity. But they become distinctly edgy when forced to discover that the same job performance measure can be used to direct the same employee (when in work difficulty) to the EAP, and thus correct some of most serious "health" problems facing an individual in our society. We infer alcoholism problems here, of course, but there are others of similar serious impact.

Supervisors, in this liberal, forgiving age, may have inadvertently become less able to stand apart from their subordinates when performance becomes a problem. But more timely and appropriate referrals of identified employees can be made to occur through comprehensive EAP orientation and training efforts, alleviating significant costs for the individual, his/her family, and the company.

Torjman will relate the training details of a rather unique Canadian program, which is sponsored by the government. In this program, candidates and students training to be a part of EAP programs are guided through formal schooling, emphasizing four areas of study: the description of EAP models, individual behavior as exemplified by normal life stages and crises, organizational functioning (including a look at General Systems and

Contingency theories, day to day issues, and the place of unions in the corporate fabric), and "key problems." Among the key problems are those falling under the rubrics of health (alcoholism and others), psychological, interpersonal, and social. In the skills area, the study program looks systematically at situation analysis, the importance of proper referral mechanisms and, finally, adequate followup. Naturally, the section gives suitable attention to the EAP's intensive participation in the planning and delivery of supervisor orientations.

18

EAP Training to Integrate Performance Appraisal, Evaluation Systems, and Problem-Solving Skills
Mark Cohen

Introduction

The EAP should be viewed as an organizational asset which can play an important role in helping those in positions of authority to resolve complex work performance problems. Once the EAP's policy has been delineated and the roles of those within the organization have been defined, a means of promoting managerial and supervisory expertise in operationalizing the process is required. The most effective means of achieving this is through an orientation to the EAP for all employees who have workers directly reporting to them. Although some prefer to call this "supervisory training," a more generic and less threatening description which we would opt to utilize is "supervisory orientation to the EAP."

A main objective of the supervisory orientation is to help those who manage others to fully appreciate that a wide range of factors can adversely impact job performance and that it is not the supervisor's responsibility to change and/or fix all of these situations. Rather, it is part of the supervisor's role to monitor performance and help employees secure the assistance which they need to perform satisfactorily at work, since meeting the expectations of the job is the employee's responsibility. The supervisor needs to be sensitive to changes in performance and work-related conduct and behavior; only then can he/she differentiate between problems whose origins are cleary connected to the job itself and those that may be related to factors outside of the organization. And in order to best address this task, the supervisor must focus considerable attention on the employee's performance while documenting achievements as well as deficiencies.

Performance Appraisal

The policies and practices of a well thought out EAP must be consistent with those of the organization as a whole. Since all companies need a system for assessing the performance of each of their employees and for intervening in situations where that performance is less than acceptable, the EAP can utilize this set of procedures to identify and help troubled employees. In the course of the supervisory orientation, supervisors can be aided in assessing patterns of declining performance. By such sessions they can also become more familiar with stategies both for coaching troubled employees and for grappling with their own uncomfortable feelings which may arise in confronting these same workers. In essence, performance on the job serves as a barometer for future career opportunities, salary increases, continued employment, and can help in dealing with promotions, stagnation, demotions, or termination as well as being an excellent indicator for ferreting out health and personal problems which may be present.

The supervisory orientation helps those in positions of authority to view the EAP as a managerial tool in assisting the employee whose performance is sub-par. It presumes that supervisors possess the expertise to evaluate job performance and to determine appropriate standards for satisfactory functioning; further, it supports their "positive reactions" when performance is good and requires that they react through the already existing supervisory coaching and counseling process in addressing performance which is inadequate. Supervisors then must be able to communicate expectations, dissect problems, listen to employees' comments, suggestions, complaints, etc. The supervisory orientation process furthers their understanding of typical patterns of deteriorating performance in employees with previously satisfactory work records. These typical patterns include, but are not limited to:

- increased absenteeism
- unexpected vacation requests
- sporadic productivity and erratic performance
- missed deadlines
- increased tardiness
- increased strife with co-workers
- loss of enthusiasm for work
- unpredictable behavior
- increased conflicts with the boss
- increased complaining and moodiness
- an above average rate of accidents at work
- costly errors
- difficulty remembering and following instructions
- outright defiance

Work-related problems such as these are issues that supervisors and managers can easily relate to since they will be prevalent to some extent in any given work group. Supervisory orientation seminars reinforce the supervisor's responsibility for intervening when a worker's performance has declined. He/she can assist the employee to resolve the problem, while simultaneously hold him/her accountable for their performance. In its most simplistic sense, supervisory coaching and/or counseling is the process by which that assistance, coupled with accountability, initially takes place.

Supervisory personnel often require encouragement, guidance, and reinforcement to integrate an ongoing process of performance evaluation into their work routine. They can become preoccupied with "getting the job done" and can lose sight of the fact that evaluating the performance of employees who report to them is an integral component of doing their job. Furthermore, some supervisors will prefer to avoid meeting with employees because they are uncomfortable with the prospect of a confrontation, they have difficulty being "critical," they need to be liked, they want to try it "their way," and so on. This results in the supervisor's postponement of dealing with the issue at hand and the ongoing decline in the worker's performance. Consequently, the troubled employee's performance is tolerated, while the real problem simultaneously worsens.

The supervisory orientation seminar is designed to help reduce the resistance of managerial personnel to assessing the performance of employees and to meeting with them in the course of reviewing and attempting to alter less-than-satisfactory performance. It further serves to reinforce the supervisor's responsibility for intervening when a worker's performance has clearly declined, by pointing out that the intervention process is an integral part of the supervisor's job.

Although most companies do formal performance appraisals on a yearly basis (the format for the review may vary, but the intent is the same), one of the objectives of the orientation seminar is to more fully integrate the evaluation process into the ongoing realm of functioning as a supervisor. It sensitizes supervisor personnel to the notion that perceiving changes in performance, attitude, behavior, and conduct are part and parcel of their role. Being a good supervisor includes maximizing the contribution of those who report to him/her and observing as well as responding to change.

Once a supervisor has observed a change in an employee or a pattern of declining performance, the supervisory orientation seminar reinforces the importance of the supervisor's documentation of the facts relevant to the situation on an ongoing basis. Here again, the principles of "good management" are being reinforced through EAP training. It also highlights the principle that the only means of resolving the work problem is through discussing it with the employee; during that occasion the supervisor can clarify expectations, set up a time frame for anticipated improvement, and schedule a future date for another performance review and discussion. It is important to note that the supervisory orientation seminar helps supervisory personnel avoid a course of action which exacerbates the difficulties. These "supervisory traps" include getting side-tracked or manipulated, making an attempt to diagnose the employee's "real" problem, becoming paternalistic, and getting away from the on-the-job documented facts.

The supervisory orientation seminar also serves as a reminder to managerial personnel of how the company's progressive disciplinary process works, and how use of the EAP is a potential part of intervention with a troubled employee who is subject to progressive discipline. Supervisors are asked to understand that they are not expected to alter company policy and practice; rather, they now have an additional resource which they can use to address complex work performance problems. Thus, the use of progressive disciplines in combination with the EAP can be a problem solving mechanism.

An EAP can be perceived by those in positions of authority to be a means of coddling unproductive workers. The seminar helps supervisors understand that they are providing a troubled employee with a professional resource for problem resolution, while they, the supervisors, maintain control of the employee's ongoing status as an employee within the organization.

The Seminar

In some companies, supervisory orientation seminars are an ongoing component of the EAP, while in others, they can be a onetime occurrence. We recommend that they be viewed as a program component due to the impact of supervisory turnover within a company and its effect upon potential EAP utilization. Separate EAP seminars also serve to reinforce the EAP message, as outlined earlier in this chapter.

Most supervisory orientation seminars are comprised of several sections, providing: 1) information on what the EAP is and who it is for, 2) an explanation of why the company has the program, 3) an outline of how the EAP works, 4) an illustration of the EAP's role and contribution as a managerial tool, and 5) help for supervisors in becoming more comfortable in meeting with troubled employees and in utilizing the EAP. Slide presentations, movies, and role playing are commonly employed as training aids. Although all of these devices have proven to be assets in achieving the objectives of the seminar, the role playing of a supervisor/subordinate discussion of performance problems is particularly noteworthy in view of the importance of integrating the performance appraisal system and the EAP.

Role playing necessitates taking on a risk of some embarrassment by one or more of the seminar participants; however, in many ways, so does confronting an employee whose job performance has been deteriorating. The major advantage of role playing in a group seminar is that it makes a situation "come alive" by giving supervisors a reference point for future use, based on an "actual" experience. Furthermore, the role playing exercise, which usually takes place in the latter part of the seminar, helps "pull together" the concepts and information which have been put forth in the earlier stages of the training sessions. Since much of this role playing simulates troubled employees with deteriorating performances and the strategies for intervention, it serves to summarize and highlight the seminar's objectives. Of perhaps greater significance, it might remind the supervisor of a past or present employee whose performance is or was sub-par, and encourage him/her to formulate a strategy for intervention which includes the use of the EAP.

Finally, the role play experience helps supervisory personnel to become more cognizant of their own feelings, which may otherwise serve as a barrier to discussing performance with their employees. Supervisors can consciously struggle with the issue of why they have avoided such meetings in the past and what was the impact in prior situations of not having a discussion with a troubled employee. Thus, the seminar lessens some of the inherent resistance to engaging in performance appraisal discussions.

The dissemination of information concerning common symptoms of deteriorating work performance is extremely useful in promoting the evaluation skills of supervisory personnel. It clarifies "what to look for" and sensitizes those who manage others to go beyond the recognition of isolated unacceptable work performance as well. The seminar reinforces the concept that supervisors do possess the expertise to determine what is satisfactory performance for a given job, yet it simultaneously emphasizes that they are not expected to have the expertise necessary to diagnose or resolve the health and personal problems of workers which lie behind poor job performance. In essence, when a supervisor needs a specialist, his/her job is to get one, and the EAP can help to do that. This notion is reiterated throughout the orientation seminar.

Finally, the seminar encourages the supervisor's use of practical problem-solving skills by viewing intervention as a process. For example, if an employee has a problem with tardiness, the supervisor may initially explore the problem with the worker and then recommend getting an earlier bus, purchasing an alarm clock, or commuting to work via a different route. However, when these practical and logical management courses of action do not bring about the desired change, and a second or third meeting with the employee becomes necessary for the same problem, the supervisor is then led to understand that something else (beyond the supervisor's skills to evaluate) may be getting in the way of this employee meeting the expectations of the job. The seminar focuses the supervisor's problem-solving skills on the need for intervention in the absence of positive change, and the continuation of the work problem. The advisability of seeking professional help is emphasized, which may lead to a referral to the EAP.

Serving the Supervisor

An essential message conveyed to and reinforced to the seminar participants is that the EAP is a resource which they can consult and use in early preparation for a meeting with an employee whose performance is sub-par. They can also use it to discuss and review a subordinate's conduct, behavior, or change in attitude or enthusiasm about work. The EAP is there for them; not just for the troubled employee. The message of "let me help you to help them get their performance back up to par" is repeatedly espoused in the seminar so that the supervisors do not see the EAP just as a highly specialized service geared solely for "ill employees." In short, the EAP is a consulting service whose use can lead to a more effective intervention. The training supports the notion that it is all right to ask for help and that no one is expected to have all the answers to all of the employee's problems.

Summary

Orientation seminars for the EAP are a very effective means of enhancing supervisory understanding and utilization of the EAP. The seminar also serves to strengthen supervisory problem solving and evaluation skills by integrating the performance appraisal process with the use of the EAP, where the program is employed as an additional managerial resource for complex work performance problems. Common patterns of declining job performance are reviewed in the seminar, as the supervisor's awareness and ability to intervene is fostered and further developed. Those in positions of authority are helped to recognize problems of subordinates, discuss declining performance with their employees, engage in a course of corrective action, and use professional help where it is indicated. More importantly, the relationship between supervisor and subordinate, as one based on a system of accountability, is explored as the best mechanism for aiding a troubled employee, while it also helps the company as a whole.

19

Training Referral Agents for EAPs: Knowledge, Skills, and Attitudes

Sherri Resin Torjman

The Need for Training

There is good news and bad news in the field of EAPs. First . . . the good news. EAPs have spread rapidly throughout North America, especially over the past ten years. Hundreds of private, governmental, and voluntary organizations have established EAPs.

So much for the good news. Now . . . the bad. Specialized training for the individuals staffing these programs—the referral agents—has not kept pace with the growth of the programs themselves. Few individuals have had formal training in the EAP helping process before assuming the role of referral agent.

Until recently, there was no commonly accepted statement of the activities to be carried out by an EAP referral agent. No set of standards for practice in this field had been clearly articulated. There was no overall training program in Canada which spelled out the key competencies of the referral agent role.

In 1979, the Canadian Federal Government responded to this lack by commissioning the preparation of a training program for EAP referral agents (The training program was developed and written by this author). The training program which was developed identifies and describes the major knowledge and skill components of the referral agent role as well as the attitudes considered desirable to this helping process. This section presents a summary of the knowledge, skills, and attitudes discussed in that training program.

Key Components of a Training Program

Knowledge

It is sometimes difficult to separate the content considered to be primarily knowledge from the areas that are purely skills. Indeed, there is a knowledge component to all skills in the EAP field, and usually a skills component to the knowledge areas.

For the purposes of training, however, it is useful to divide the two. The content that is considered to be primarily knowledge is better taught in certain ways, while skills are best taught by other methods. In this training program, knowledge is presented through lecture, readings, brainstorming, written exercises, and small group discussions. Skills, on the other hand, are imparted mainly through demonstration, role-play, audiovisual taping, and feedback.

There are four major areas of knowledge covered in this EAP training program: EAPs, individual behavior, organizational functioning, and key problems. Each of these is discussed briefly below.

1. **Employee Assistance Programs**

The first major knowledge area describes the evolution of EAPs, explains their rationale, and outlines the role of the referral agent. An EAP is defined as a work-based service whose purpose is to assist the individual who is experiencing a personal problem by assessing the nature of the difficulty and by making a referral to the appropriate helping resource. The role of the referral agent, then is, to assess the nature of the problematic situation presented by the employee; to determine in conjunction with the employee possible solutions to the problematic situation; to make a referral to an appropriate helping resource; to follow-up in order to ensure that the action agreed upon has been carried out, and to act as a liaison with helping resources when required.

The role of the EAP referral agent does not include such activities as evaluating job performance; arranging job placements; hiring and firing; collective bargaining; initiating grievance procedures; administering employee benefits; assessing medical status; providing therapy.

2. **Individual Behavior**

Because of the nature of the EAP service, referral agents must have a general understanding of human behavior. The training program provides information about individuals from the perspective of normal life crises (Sheehy, 1976). That is, people pass through stages in their lives, each of which is marked by a number of significant events. A variety of problems may arise around these events. Individuals may or may not be able to cope with these problems with their inner resources and external supports. Keeping the perspective within the normal life context prevents referral agents from delving into pathological states of behavior and from trying to interpret situations from a psychoanalytic orientation.

The material on this subject also considers the factors in individuals' environments which may affect and influence their behavior. Behavior and feelings are seen largely as responses to environmental demands, pressures and influences of the family, the workplace, and society at large.

3. The Work Organization

The third major knowledge area focuses upon the work organization. It is important for referral agents to understand this system in order to "situate" themselves and their service. The referral agent should be aware of how organizational policies, procedures, communication channels, and resources may affect their program. For example, there may be internal resources which would be of assistance to employees. The work organization is also the environment within which employees function on a day-to-day basis. Understanding this environment facilitates the process of "tuning in" to the nature of individual problems.

Two major theories of organization are presented and used as frameworks for organizational analysis. These are general systems theory, and contingency theory. Participants complete exercises on organizational assessment in which they are asked to consider how various aspects of internal functioning might affect the EAP.

The content of this knowledge also includes a discussion of the various aspects of the labor organization. These include the purpose and role of a union in a work setting; the process of collective bargaining; the relationship of the union vis-à-vis the EAP. This information is presented through written materials as well as through a panel of guest speakers who are invited to address these subjects and to engage participants in discussion of these issues.

4. Problem Areas

The final major content area deals with the personal and work-related problems which arise at or manifested in the work setting. Personal problems are classified into four major areas: health, psychological, interpersonal, and social.

Work-related problems are categorized as environmental, interpersonal, or job-related. Attention is focused, however, upon personal problems as these are deemed to be within the competence of the EAP referral agent. While personal and work-related problems are not mutually exclusive, a problem that is primarily related to the work environment should be handled by a supervisor or other appropriate person.

The problem of alcohol dependence, in particular, is explored in some depth. This exploration includes a discussion of attitudes toward alcoholics; the course of alcohol dependence and its physical, psychological, and social effects; the range of treatment facilities available. This problem is singled out for special attention because of its prevalence and because intervention in this problem is particularly difficult.

Another subject considered within the content of problem areas are the procedures by which an individual who has a problem becomes linked with the EAP. Three major types of referral are discussed. These are: self-referrals, informal referrals, and formal referrals. Formal referrals, in particular, are made on the basis of deteriorating work performance. In general, performance can be said to be deteriorating if there is a negative change in one or more of the following areas: quality of work, quantity of work, dependability (use of good judgment, attendance), and compatibility (employee attitudes and morale).

When a formal referral has been made, pressure may be placed upon the referral agent to provide feedback to supervisors. The training program emphasizes that feedback to supervisors should consist only of information about the status of the employee and not about the nature of the problem. Status refers to whether an individual has been seen and whether a referral to a helping resource has been made. The name of the resource itself should not be disclosed.

Skills

There are three major types of skills employed by EAP referral agents. These are: situation analysis, referral, and follow-up. Each of these major areas of skill, in turn, represents a complex set of behaviors.

Situation Analysis

Situation analysis refers to the process of assessing the nature of the situation which has brought an individual to the EAP. Accurate analysis of the situation is essential as it is on the basis of this assessment that a referral to a helping resource is made. Because of its importance, a significant amount of time is allocated to the unit on situation analysis. In fact, a total of 42 hours is spent teaching this skill in the training program, comprising a total of 105 hours.

The first step involved in situation analysis is to obtain a clear description of the situation troubling the employee. Specific events or behaviors should be identified, elaborated upon, and clarified. The second step in this process is to determine who considers the situation to be of concern. Third, referral agents should try to determine why a particular situation has become problematic. Fourth, it is important to find out how often this situation occurs and how long it has been happening, in order to get an idea of its severity. The fifth step is the identifying of efforts that have already been made to deal with the problem at hand.

After determining the nature of the problematic situation, the next step in situation analysis is to identify what solutions would be possible and which helping resources may be required. This step is considered more fully in the "referral" skill area.

Situation analysis refers primarily to the content of the helping interview—that is, what information should be sought. However, the "what" of the interview is only one essential component of the helping process; the "how" of the interview is just as important. The manner and method of communication determine the extent to which referral agents are able to establish rapport with the employee and encourage open discussion and sharing of concerns. There are a variety of behaviors and skills which should be employed in any helping interview.

One of the most important ways that referral agents can make optimal use of themselves in a helping relationship is by means of effective attending behavior. The components of attending include an atmosphere free from noise and interruption, good postural position, appropriate use of eye contact, and communication of respect.

There are, as well, a variety of verbal skills which referral agents must incorporate within the helping process. These skills are the use of reinforcers, paraphrasing, reflection of feeling, seeking information, summarizing, and the effective use of confrontation.

Participants have an opportunity to practice learning these behaviors and verbal skills in small groups. They are given a situation in which they are to act as referral agents. Feedback with respect to their performance is provided on the basis of behavioral checklists. These are a series of lists which spell out the components of the skill. For example, the verbal skills behavioral checklist (see Appendix 1) outlines three specific dimensions of five major verbal skills. Participants are observed along these dimensions and can then focus upon the areas where improvement may be required.

A final but essential component in situation analysis is crisis intervention. During the course of their work, referral agents may be called upon to deal with an emergency situation.

An important point about crisis situations is that any crisis may be comprised of a number of factors that are stressful to the individual. It is not helpful to try to deal with every aspect of a complex situation when a person is in emotional turmoil. The general rule of thumb is to identify the key problem area which requires immediate attention. Other aspects of the problem can then be tackled at a later date.

Referral

Once the nature of a problem has been assessed, a referral to an appropriate helping resource may be necessary. Referral agents require substantial knowledge before they can make appropriate referrals. First, they must be aware of the resources that exist within the employing organization. These resources may be in the form of direct services, such as medical treatment or retirement counseling. They may also be in the form of indirect services which refer to the subsidization of goods and services provided outside the work organization. Information about such resources can be obtained through orientation sessions, examination of policies, reports, collective agreements, and visits to various departments.

Referral agents must be knowledgeable about the helping services available in the local community. They must understand the roles of various helping professionals. They should be able to distinguish between public and private community services and know why such a distinction is important. Finally, they should be able to identify the specific resources available within twelve major areas of community service: financial assistance, health, mental health, alcohol and drug dependence, legal services, education and re-training, recreation, emergency services, resources for children, resources for senior citizens, self-help groups, and planning, coordinating and funding bodies.

The key skill taught here is the process of engaging the employee in identifying the variety of possible solutions to a problem and in considering the resources that would be most appropriate to the situation. This skill also involves helping employees make contact or "link" with those resources.

An important aspect of making referrals is knowing what resources are appropriate to various problem situations. This skill can be taught by providing a list of guidelines for making referrals. Among the guidelines is the referral agent's determination of whether the individual is already linked with a helping resource. This existing network should be reinforced only if the source of help is appropriate and the employee agrees that this helping resource has been of assistance in the past.

Finally, one of the most important principles upon which the helping relationship is based is that of confidentiality, that personal and private information which the employee shares with the referral agent remains in confidence. During this training, information should be presented about the specific actions which can be taken to maintain confidentiality. Such actions include selectively recording personal information; restricting access to files; obtaining written permission before any information is released to a third-party referral agent, or to a helping resource in the community. Written permission should be in the form of a consent letter which indicates what information is being shared; when this information is being released; the need for such disclosure; the period of time during which the information to be disclosed is valid.

Follow-Up

Follow-up constitutes the third major skill area to be mastered by the referral agent. Follow-up is a short-term contact made by phone or in person for the specific purpose of determining whether the action decided upon has been carried out. There are three types of possible outcomes in the helping process: the agreed-upon plan was carried out; the agreed-upon plan was not carried out for a variety of possible reasons; or the employee has decided that he/she is no longer interested in receiving outside assistance.

Participants are provided with an opportunity to practice a follow-up interview involving each of the three outcomes. The role that referral agents may play in acting as a liaison with community services is also considered.

Attitudes

There are certain attitudes which contribute to the effectiveness of a helping relationship. It is essential for referral agents to have a genuine interest in and a positive attitude toward people. A willingness to listen carefully to employees and to involve them in all phases of the helping process is important. Referral agents should also be receptive to the ideas of employees, managers, and union personnel who may make recommendations with respect to improving specific aspects of the program. Every individual should be seen as a potential resource who has something worthwhile to offer. Despite the fact that referral agents may have a good deal of knowledge about the employee assistance process, their knowledge stands to be enhanced by the contributions of others.

All individuals must be treated with dignity and with respect. Any problem presented should be considered as a serious concern. Negative attitudes held by referral agents toward certain types of persons will seriously jeopardize the helping process. For example, referral agents may consider alcoholics and drug users to be weak individuals who must try harder in order to overcome their immoral habit. Referral agents may react angrily when they discover that such persons are not "snapping out of it." Such attitudes interfere with referral agents' ability to act fairly and to treat those individuals with the respect to which all employees engaged in the helping process are entitled.

Finally, certain attitudes toward work are helpful. Flexibility is essential. Referral agents must be both optimistic and realistic. That is, every situation should be seen as having the potential for improvement. Realistically, however, referral agents must realize that in certain cases only a minimal amount of change may be possible.

Teaching referral agents about helpful attitudes is best accomplished through self-awareness exercises in which they are asked to identify their likes and dislikes and the things in life that are important to them. Information should be presented with respect to the attitudes that are considered desirable to a helping relationship. Individuals can compare their present attitudes with the "ideal" attitudes. They can then make a conscious effort to strive toward the ideal throughout the course of their work.

Key Elements of a Training Program

The training program upon which this section is based is now being taught throughout Canada to prospective and practising EAP referral agents. The program has been well received by participants and by instructors. It appears that there are several reasons for this positive evaluation.

First, the content focuses specifically upon the key knowledge areas that are of particular relevance to referral agents: EAPs, individual behavior, work organizations, and problem areas. It also spends considerable time exploring the essential skills inherent in EAPs: situation analysis, referral, and follow-up. Each of these key areas of knowledge and skill is filled out with material that is of a "how-to" nature: how to assess a problem; how to find out information about community services; how to make a referral; how to maintain confidentiality.

The training program is highly experiential in nature—that is, it provides participants with opportunities to practice the skills demonstrated in the program and to simulate in the classroom the situations in which they have been or may be involved. This experiential training method is complemented by a built-in feedback process in which participants are provided with immediate information as to the effectiveness of their performance.

Finally, time is allocated for discussion of practical issues of concern to referral agents. It appears that a combination of relevant and practice-based content taught in an inductive and highly experiential manner is essential to any successful EAP training program.

Good News?

In Canada, the situation with respect to the training of EAP referral agents has improved significantly over the past few years. There is now a commonly accepted statement of the knowledge and skills required by referral agents and of the attitudes deemed helpful to this work. There is a clear articulation of ethical considerations, such as the protection of confidentiality and the involvement of employees in decisions concerning the help they may require.

In fact, if the present trend toward improved training continues, it may be necessary to change the "good news, bad news" story about EAPs. Perhaps, a few years down the road, it will be possible to say: "There's good news and bad news with respect to EAPs. First . . . the good news. Training programs for EAP referral agents have spread rapidly throughout North America. Now . . . the bad news. These programs are so popular that it is practically impossible to get in to one of them." On second thought, that may not be such bad news after all.

APPENDIX I

Verbal Skills Behavioral Checklist

The following verbal skills are required for the helping interview:

Paraphrasing

Did the referral agent:

YES   NO

1. respond to the basic content of the client's statements?
2. check out the accuracy of the paraphrase?
3. sharpen the client's meaning, thereby encouraging him/her to continue discussing that subject?

Refection of Feeling

Did the referral agent:

YES   NO

1. respond to the feelings the client was expressing?
2. verify the accuracy of the reflection?
3. respond to nonverbal expressions of feeling as well as to the direct verbal messages?

Seeking Information

Did the referral agent:

YES   NO

1. appropriately identify the areas which required further exploration?
2. employ open questions when seeking information?
3. employ indirect questions when seeking information?

Summarizing

Did the referral agent:

YES   NO

1. demonstrate an ability to select the key points discussed?

2. demonstrate an ability to tie these points together? _____ _____
3. feed these back to the client in a clear and
   concise way? _____ _____

Confrontation

Did the referral agent:

	YES	NO
1. demonstrate an ability to point out discrepancies in the individual's behavior?	_____	_____
2. use confrontation after he/she had already developed a relationship with the client?	_____	_____
3. make the confrontation in a caring way rather than as an angry accusation?	_____	_____

References

Benjamin, A. *The Helping Interview*. Boston: Houghton Mifflin Co., 1969.

Carkhuff, R. *Helping and Human Relations: A Primer for Lay and Professional Helpers*. Volumes 1 and 2. New York: Holt, Rinehart and Winston, Inc., 1969.

Clarke, T.E. "The Work Environment and Mental Health." *Studies in Personnel Psychology*. October 1971. Volume 3: 83-96.

Cooper, C.L. and Marshall, J. "Occupational Sources of Stress: A Review of the Literature Relating to Coronary Heart Disease and Mental Ill Health." *Journal of Occupational Psychology*. 1976. Volume 49: 11-28.

Core Knowledge in the Drug Field. Volumes 1-12. Ottawa: Health and Welfare Canada, 1978.

Danish, S.J. and Hauer, A.L. *Helping Skills: A Basic Training Program*. New York: Human Sciences Press, 1977.

Egan, G. *The Skilled Helper: A Model for Systematic and Interpersonal Relating*. Monterey, Calif.: Woodsworth Publishing Company, Inc., 1975.

Farr, H.L., Gualtieri, P., and Leslie, C. "Training for Occupational Alcoholism Programmers." Arlington, Va.: National Center for Alcohol Education, May 1978.

Foote, A. and Erfurt, J. "Occupational Employee Assistance Programs for Substance Abuse and Mental Health Problems." Institute of Labor and Industrial Relations. The University of Michigan; Wayne State University, 1977.

Googins, B. "Employee Assistance Programs." *Social Work*. November 1975. Volume 20: 464-67.

Litterer, J.A. (ed.) *Organizations: Structure and Behaviour*. Vol. 1. 2d ed. New York: John Wiley and Sons, 1969.

Pincus, A. and Minahan, A. *Social Work Practice: Model and Method*. Itasca, Ill.: F.E. Peacock Publishers, Inc., 1973.

Schramm, C.J. (ed.) *Alcoholism and Its Treatment in Industry*. Baltimore: John Hopkins University Press, 1977.

Shain, M. and Groeneveld, J. *Employee Assistance Programs: Philosophy, Theory and Practice*. Lexington, Mass.: D.C. Health and Co., 1980.

Sheehy, Gail. *Passages: Predictable Crises of Adult Life*. New York: E.P. Dutton, 1976.

Thompson, J.D. *Organizations in Action: Social Science Bases of Adminstrative Theory*. New York: McGraw-Hill, 1969.

Torjman, S.R. *A Manual for E.A.P. Referral Agents*. Ottawa: Health and Welfare Canada, 1981.

Wrich, J.T. *The Employee Assistance Program*. Centre City, Minn.: Hazelden Books, 1974.

SECTION V

Research and Evaluation Methods and Issues within an EAP

Introduction

In this chapter, Roman and Blum will carefully analyze justifications for EAPs, including data collection and evaluation from the researchers' point of view. They note that EAPs continue to thrive in spite of weakly defined data bases and a lack of rigorous evaluation of what works and what does not. The authors call for even the busiest, harried EAP staff person to keep reasonable records, if for no better reason that to maintain continuity of client care in cases of a change in EAP staff. Such data should include the total activities of EAP staff, since a good part of the EAP function is interaction with other persons and units of the company, unions, and outside resources. These functions are as critical as clinical case work, and should be accounted for.

The need for an easily usable data base is emphasized, one which may or may not be computerized, but which should readily and frequently answer day-to-day questions, e.g., is this or that treatment center effective? does one EAP staff member yield different patient statistics than another? are some departments sending more tough cases than another, etc?

Considerable space is devoted to defining evaluation concepts and procedures and discussing the real problems with the use of job performance measures. For example, the ability of an EAP to document early alcoholism cases can be one form of measure. The treatment here of the subject of cost benefit analysis is also thought provoking, as is their discussion of the role of expert outsiders and researchers in regard to EAPs.

Can change brought about by the EAP be documented? Googins will address this question, targeting in on the critically important research questions, e.g., are EAPs responsible for increased productivity? Or–why do some EAPs work better than others? Is there really any good data? Often used to answer the latter question are changes in drinking behavior or in work performance, in cost reductions, or changes in penetration rates. He notes the need to clearly define what we mean by the terms *document, measure, reliability,* and *validity.* Further discussion illustrates the differences between changes of a "micro" and "macro" nature, i.e. between those wrought by the EAP in its clients as individuals, and in the company itself.

Among the other tough issues for the reflective EAP professional is the efficacy of broad-based EAPS, now emphasized so strongly, when compared with narrower alcoholism or chemical dependency models. The rationale for the broader programs has been that their reduced stigma would somehow encourage easier, earlier voluntary and supervisory referrals of cases, since pre-diagnosis (and the traps involved in having non-professionals attempt this) would be largely eliminated. In a study of ten broad-based programs in several countries, some interesting conclusions are reached. For example, about one-third of referrals were of the formal or supervisory type, of which a bit less than half were alcohol-related. The overall rate of alcohol cases, considering all forms of referral, was about 35 percent.

Durkin, in his section, laments the lack of standardization of definitions and measures, chiding the average company's records as being often poorly kept sources for such data as absenteeism and realistic performance appraisals. This set of circumstances is all too often compounded by the EAP staff, whose training (perhaps interest) in data collection and analysis may be wanting. In an effort to codify and correct such problems, a program needs to begin with an adequately detailed intake interview (exemplified in the text). As the data accumulates for eventual interpretation there are then several choices as to types of program analysis. These methods might include retrospective analysis, the use of control groups, or the comparison of EAP clients to norms of the average or comparable company employee.

Larkin, French and Ankers, of the Addiction Research Foundation in Canada, will review features of EAP development and operation, beginning with a description of one approach to an analysis of the organization about to initiate an EAP. Among the many descriptors to consider are its degree of specialization and centralized decision making; a company profile and analysis form assist in this effort. The second stage, development, can be systematically progressed with the assistance of a policy and program development form. Finally, two options are described for the evaluation phase; the first is by the meeting of objectives (e.g., number of cases, performance, efficiency); the second method uses the systems approach. The latter considers the degree in which EAP functions achieve integration within and among various systems or parts of the organization, and as they relate to the EAP and individual client.

20

Modes and Levels of Data Management Affecting the EAP Practitioner
Paul M. Roman and Terry C. Blum

Introduction

EAPs, developed within cultures that attach high value to science, are expected to conform to norms of rationality and reason, as contrasted to reliance on hope and faith. Both the design of EAPs and the strategies of intervention constitute arts that reflect the skills and ingenuity of particular individuals, rather than being grounded in scientific data and fact. The outcomes of EAPs are, however, believed to be subject to procedures of science in the form of evaluation and research. At issue are the questions of "Do EAPs do any good?" and "Why (or why not) do they do any good?"

As the EAP movement has rapidly emerged to constitute a recognizable new collectivity in the worlds of health care delivery and personnel management, there has been substantial confusion over research, evaluation, and the various role of data collection activities. On the one hand, there have been high expectations for applied research studies (Trice, 1980). The EAP specialty has mushroomed despite the slow and fitful development of this base of research evidence about the structure and dynamics of EAPs. On the other hand, claims about the extraordinary effectiveness of EAPs abound among EAP practitioners, yet most orientations toward EAP evaluation shortchange EAP impact, since they reflect a narrow perception of the functions of EAPs within work organizations. Most EAP evaluation remains focused on generic approaches to individual-based treatment assessment. A more challenging alternative is to tap the organizational phenomena resulting from the blend of substance abuse and parapsychiatric service delivery into the multiple species of work environment and their pre-existing mechanisms for dealing with troubled employees.

As research specialists, our own interests center on concentrating more resources and more attention to research and evaluation. Yet we must concede that deficiencies in the quantity and quality of such efforts apparently have not impeded the diffusion and adoption of EAPs or the attraction of new workers to the EAP practice specialties. Of course, we have no way of knowing what the consequences of more or better theory and data for EAP development during the past decade would have been. The specialty has grown and flourished, however, on a relatively slender research data base, coupled with evaluation studies that have concentrated on the clinical rather than the organizational impacts of EAPs.

In this section we explore issues in research, evaluation, and data collection that are germane to the work of EAP practitioners in terms of the development of their own programs as well as their own careers. Our experience has revealed substantial frustration with researchers among practitioners of all applied endeavors in human services, which seems to stem from confused expectations. We have also observed the paradox of practitioners who are mystified by the nature of research and evaluation strategies, yet are ready "on demand" to conduct their own studies with minimal consultation from experienced research and evaluation specialists. In this section we endeavor to bring some order to practitioner's perceptions and expectations of research and evaluation. We particularly desire to encourage the teamwork and cooperation that is vital to data collection and essential to the processes wherein data can be utilized to alter and improve EAP functioning.

We first examine some important conceptual distinctions that need to be made among different kinds of data collection and analysis activities. We then provide an overview of the EAP research community and its various relationships with the collectivity of practitioners. The next section focuses on evaluation studies, which are the kind of data collection endeavors most likely to involve and concern practitioners. Throughout this section we offer observations and recommendations for broadening the scope of evaluative concerns in EAPs, which in turn have implications for the scope and goals of EAP.

Clarifying Concepts of Measurement and Data Collection

Much of the confusion about research and evaluation among EAP specialists centers on interchanging various concepts of measurement and data collection, which indeed are very different types of activities.

The most fundamental measurement and data collection activity is recordkeeping. While nearly everyone recognizes the importance of records, "paper work" tends to be stereotyped as the mischief of minds which are incapable of designing real "action" and producing real "results." In other words, the pragmatist in North American culture is encouraged to "get on with the business" and leave "paper pushing" to lesser souls. This orientation may take on a somewhat different twist among clinicians who pride themselves in carrying all vital information about clients in their heads. These clinicians may indeed regard any kind of recordkeeping as a threat to the assured confidentiality of client information that is the foundation of their professional practices. Good clinicians indeed seem to be poor recordkeepers and this may present a major challenge to an EAP's needs for maintaining data.

It is unfortunate that many of us have developed our orientations toward forms and records on the basis of experience with public sector programs or with privately-based programs funded by public monies. For many clinicians, these experiences with paperwork, which indeed were useless in terms of impact on improving their organizations' efforts, left a permanent mark. Unfortunately, and inappropriately, these attitudes generalize to EAP experience, and support a reluctance to keep good records.

Recordkeeping is vital to an EAP in that all other levels of data collection we discuss here are dependent on the quality of these records. Despite worries about confidentiality, records are vital if for no other reason than protecting a client in the case of the unexpected demise of the therapist. Despite fears about breaching confidentiality, there is little difficulty in developing or maintaining records which assure anonymity and all appropriate safeguards of clients' identity.

EAPs are people processing systems, but too often they are viewed as only processing employees or employee dependents in need of counseling or treatment. While records of these client contacts are vital, there are a great many other people contacts about which data should be routinely collected and preserved. For example, EAPs commonly provide training and orientation for supervisors, shop stewards, upper management, and union officials. Education programs directed at different segments of the work force are common features of EAPs. Most EAP coordinators are also engaged in program diffusion activities involving "marketing" to upper levels of management as the EAP is implemented in different divisions or locations of their organization. Finally, a vital function of most EAPs is the provision of consultative assistance to supervisors who are dealing with a problem employee and need advice on what to do next.

It should be obvious that keeping records on all of these activities is important to EAP personnel. One of many possible reasons for maintaining such information is that busy people need mechanisms to preserve order across a wide range of human contacts, each for a different purpose, and each requiring a different follow-up at a later date. Other than maintaining order and compiling data which may ultimately be used in research or evaluation, there are at least three other very important organizational reasons for good recordkeeping on the part of EAP personnel.

EAPs which survive and flourish are those which become integral parts of work organizations. While much remains to be learned about how these processes of integration occur, it is clear that EAP personnel must adapt to the norms and the culture of their employing organization (Roman, 1982). This transition may be difficult for those whose prior employment has been exclusively in counseling or treatment organizations, where the technology utilized is common across the staff employees, and whose integration resulted from this commonality.

By contrast, the EAP administrator, coordinator, or counselor is "one of a kind" or at best a member of a small group whose technology and activities are unique in the organization served by the EAP. It is therefore crucial that the EAP staff carry out their activities in the same pattern as other organizational units and members. If other units maintain a careful budget, if they have stringent records about staff attendance and punctuality, if they freely interact with staff across units and departments at lunch and during breaks, and/or if they keep careful records of daily staff activities and time usage, then these are the norms for the EAP staff to follow. Thus, the scope and depth of recordkeeping will be in one way a response to organizational norms and culture, and conformity to these norms will enhance integration of the EAP into organizational functioning. By contrast, refusal to keep records or attempts to center EAP identity on personal charisma will likely be viewed negatively, and such efforts to be "special" may impede integration. Thus, a major reason for recordkeeping within the EAP is to conform to the particular norms of rationality and information management within the host organization.

A second and closely linked reason has already been mentioned, namely the importance of records to facilitate the possibility of staff succession. While unexpected events such as sudden death or accidents do indeed create a strong need for good records, they are rare events. On the other hand, turnover of EAP personnel is very common; tenure in a given EAP job may be relatively brief, especially when compared to the tenure of other organizational members. This is due in part to the age of the EAP specialty, and the fact that the only career ladders available to many EAP specialists require movement to a different organization for an enhanced level of responsibility and prestige.

These moves generally take place over a very short period, and often the individual who is moving on has no role in choosing or training his/her successor. We have seen the panic that occurs when a mobile EAP specialist realized that his/her successor will have great difficulty in picking up the progress of particular cases, understanding the pattern of prior supervisory training, or knowing who in the upper levels of management can be counted on to support the EAP at budget time. While records cannot communicate the full richness and the nuances of particular experiences in the organization and with particular clients, sketchy or non-existent records can be disastrous. While some clinicians may believe they are being especially conscientious by keeping recollections of clients and events only in their memories, these practices may indeed redound adversely on both the clients and the EAP.

We provide no specific recommendations for the content of particular records, for we believe that in order to be adequate, these forms have to be developed to accommodate the particular features of a given organization. A reasonable guideline for all such recordkeeping is its communicability to a total stranger, i.e., asking oneself how someone else could understand a document if I suddenly vanished and could provide no additional orientation or interpretation.

Management Information Systems

The third organizational reason for recordkeeping brings us to our first level of measurement, namely the development and use of a management information system (MIS). Commonly, EAP specialists keep records and perceive that this process constitutes an MIS or even program evaluation. It should be obvious that the data in the records must be tabulated in some fashion before it can provide the kind of information useful to a program. Concern about processing is, however, a major barrier to the use of an MIS.

We urge that this processing be kept as simple as possible, and particularly caution against a "rush to the computer" in dealing with the MIS. The purpose of the MIS is to develop information from records which indicates the efficiency of the EAP at all operating levels. An example of a use for an MIS is to assess the relative effectiveness of different treatment centers to which referrals are made. We often cannot rely on our own subjective judgments in recalling the cumulative effects of a series of events, such as referrals of individuals to the same treatment center. A simple tally and review of the outcomes across several treatment centers is an example of how an MIS may be used to enhance the efficiency of an EAP. It should be emphasized that while this kind of activity is indeed a type of evaluation, it is not program evaluation but is simply program management. The same kind of cumulation of data may be used to assess the performance of EAP staff in carrying out particular functions, i.e., records which indicate that a certain staff member seems to get much better results with clients when he/she spends an hour with them instead of 30 minutes. Another example is the assessment of supervisory training and orientation, where records of training attendance may be compared to subsequent referrals or requests by supervisors for consultative assistance. This type of information also provides insight into the utility of different approaches or modules used in supervisory training. At bottom, the MIS may be regarded as a major tool in day-to-day EAP management.

In most settings, the MIS can be developed and utilized through hand tabulations. It is not usually necessary to conduct statistical analyses at this level of information processing, and in fact the over-sophistication of an MIS can defeat its purpose in providing rapid feedback to enhance program efficiency. We generally believe that an EAP should "grow into" computer usage, first understanding its MIS needs through simple hand tabulations. The entry of records into a computer system is however contingent upon several considerations. If the EAP program is large, then computerization of records and their analyses may be important. Computer literacy among EAP staff is another important consideration, for such preexisting knowledge of computer technology can directly lead to an MIS which is considerably more efficient than hand tabulation. Availability of computer resources within the organization is a further factor to be considered, and it may be foolhardy to invest in these facilities for an EAP if resources are slim and the amount of MIS information is small.

Finally, since many if not most organizations have computer systems today for one or another purpose, the possibility of EAP data on a system used by others for other purposes may undermine the image of confidentiality. Even though it is clearly possible to code any kind of data entered into a computer in ways that make the data meaningless to others, the EAP's use of its own microcomputer might be important to assure confidentiality that is so important to the EAP's credibility.

The criteria for a good MIS is its accessibility and its utility. There are indeed programs which cumulate a great many records but never move to MIS usage because of a generalized fear of data analysis in general and computers in particular. Therefore the MIS should be informal and simple, and the kind of information it generates should be comprehensible to the entire EAP staff, since they will be the sole users of this information. Elegant systems of information storage and processing can too easily become ends in themselves, and too often these are foreboding to the potential users, with the consequence that recall and guesswork is the basis for managerial decisions about the efficiency of different program activities.

One key mechanism in maximizing the utility of an MIS is setting forth specific times at which the data in the MIS will be reviewed by the EAP staff. At this time it should be clear that changes in the program can occur and the staff affected can be given the opportunity to review the MIS data which is the basis for the change. It is a common problem to have established an MIS and yet have no specific times for using it. By formally setting such review times and possibly involving all staff, the utility of the MIS is more likely assured, together with supporting the staff's commitment to conscientious recordkeeping.

Evaluation

Program evaluation is frequently confused with an MIS, but is distinctly different in several very important dimensions. Most basic to program evaluation is the existence of a clearcut outcome goal for the EAP's expected activity, and a clearcut procedure for measuring the degree of achievement of this goal. There are indeed goals within the MIS, but these are defined broadly in terms of the efficient use of staff time, program resources, and maximal efficiency in the impact of services provided to program clients, organizational management, and union officers and members. Furthermore, efficiency goals are short-term and relatively immediate. The goal statement and its measurement in program evaluation must be considerably more precise than program efficiency, and less "lofty" than "helping of troubled employees." Examples are the number of employees who have received EAP program services, the rate at which the employees who have received EAP program services have resumed acceptable job performance, or the rate of the EAP's identification and service delivery to employees with alcohol problems.

It is most important to note that these are only three examples of an almost infinite number of possible goals to be included in an evaluation research design. One of the major problems in the perceptions of evaluation research among EAP specialists is the assumption that a single or several goals could be regarded as common to all EAPs. As we discuss in greater detail later in this section, the very nature of EAPs dictates variability in the goals that will be attached to any given EAP, and this matter must be developed and negotiated within the home organization, involving especially those who may use evaluation results in decision-making.

While goals must be stated in clear and concrete terms in order to be utilized in a program evaluation, this does not necessarily mean that the degree of achievement of these goals is easily measured. In the three goals that we used above as examples, it is clear that measurement could be problematic. In the case of the first goal statement, what do we mean by "receiving program services?" It is obvious that this could range from attendance at an employee education meeting to a lengthy number of intense counseling sessions. In the second goal, we have introduced the issues of acceptable job performance. How is this to be measured? What does "acceptable" mean? In the case of a given individual, are we going to use a company-wide standard of performance, or is it more appropriate to compare the post-EAP performance with the prior performance? In the third goal, we not only have the problem of measuring identification and service delivery, but also the question of what is an alcohol problem. Should we include in the data all cases which involved alcohol problems as a primary, secondary, or tertiary diagnosis, or only those cases involving primary alcohol problems?

How do we distinguish transitory alcohol problems that were indeed responses to other life stresses, or is this even important? How do we distinguish between alcohol problems and alcoholism, and again, is such a distinction necessary or important?

We have not provided this exercise to indicate how difficult it is to conduct an evaluation, but rather to indicate that a vast number of decisions are involved in translating the EAP's records into data for such an evaluation. Thus a key part of measurement is definition and the range of definition that is possible depends upon the range of information that is available in the records. This points us back toward the design of the recordkeeping system, but it is clear that any recordkeeping will set limits on later use of the information, so it is usually impossible to anticipate in the recordkeeping design the subsequent limits that will be encountered. The exception is in the highly unusual situation of beginning the program with the design of the evaluation already in order. There are some good approximations of this possibility, as we discuss in the next section.

A third feature of an evaluation, in addition to precision in goal statements and measurements, is the attribution of cause. If we find in the evaluation that change has indeed occurred, then we usually desire to attribute that change to the EAP and to the efforts of the EAP staff. This may be the case, although from a scientific point of view these attributions of cause are rarely legitimate. If, for example, the program goals are stated in terms of the reduction of absenteeism or reduction in health care costs, then it is obvious that changes in these indices could reflect a whole series of forces other than the EAP. In rigorous evaluation studies, the problem of causal attribution is often dealt with through control groups, which are essentially groups of people who have not had the opportunity to receive the EAP service, but which are identical in every possible respect to the group that does have the opportunity to receive the EAP services. It is also assumed in the ideal evaluation design that the control group and the program group have had the same set of environmental experiences during the time under investigation in the study. The use of control groups can assume considerable complexity when the investigators introduce groups which receive only the measurement instruments in order to ascertain the effects of having one's behavior measured on subsequent behavior. While this may seem like an idle waste of time and resources, an influential study of supervisory training about problem employees conducted in the late 1960s by Harrison Trice and James Belasco (1968) did indeed reveal the greatest change in attitudes toward problem employees in the control group that only completed the evaluation forms and attended none of the supervisory training, casting some doubt on the utility of training as compared to other kinds of sensitization devices which may be less costly.

EAP evaluations which include control or comparison groups which did not have access to EAP services are rare, and those that develop and utilize such control or comparison groups in a scientifically legitimate fashion are practically non-existent. The opportunities to conduct evaluations in this fashion within the context of work organizations are genuinely rare, because of the uniqueness of individual locations, and thus the problem of legitimate comparisons, as well as because of the problem of withholding EAP services from certain populations in the service of scientific evaluation. So, while we believe that the use of control groups is to be highly recommended, we are not optimistic about the frequency of genuine opportunities to employ these types of classical research designs.

Usually of greater potential in an EAP evaluation is the comparison of subgroups, such as those who enter the program through supervisory referral versus self-referral. Our experience indicates that most executives who are responsible for allocating resources to EAPs are not interested in highly sophisticated evaluation studies, and research on the utilization of research indicates that evaluation studies are less utilized the more complex their design and analysis (VandeVall, 1975).

Research has also shown, however, that two aspects of EAP's are central in most settings, and we would strongly recommend that consideration be given to the issues associated with their inclusion in evaluation design, namely job performance measurement and a focus on employee alcohol problems.

Job Performance Measurement

Job performance criteria are central to the evaluation of EAPs, since this is the base of problem identification and intervention. Experience with the implementation of EAPs indicates, however, that most work organizations do not have well developed job performance measurements other than those concerned with attendance, i.e.,absenteeism and tardiness.

In some instances, performance measurements are available where employees are directly involved in measurable production, but in today's society this tends to be the exception rather than the rule. Thus there are several problems involved in using job performance criteria in program evaluation that should be considered. First, the emphasis on performance-related criteria may result in the use of such criteria only for persons who are referred to the program. This is obviously unfair, but is a likely outcome if performance measurements are strongly emphasized as a basic part of the EAP, but are not otherwise developed as systems for all employees.

A more essential difficulty is related to the level of employee to whom measurable performance criteria are applicable. Research on programs has shown that they tend to generate referrals heavily from the lower echelons of the work organization (Trice and Beyer, 1977). There are a variety of explanations for this apparent disproportionate representation, but in considering evaluation of effectiveness, it is obvious that it may be easier to quantify measures of job performance criteria among lower level employees. This is a most important consideration in pooling information on rates of success which are reflected by performance criteria, when different levels of the organization are represented in the caseload. It may result in different measures for different levels of the organization, as well as different measures for different occupational categories in the organization.

A second general problem related to job performance criteria centers on the expectations that are associated with post-intervention job performance. Program literature frequently describes expectations for improvements in level of job performance or the return of job performance to an "acceptable" level. At issue are whether these standards are a fair reflection of the actual change in performance of employees who have received services. Particularly where ongoing measurement in the entire work force is lax, there may be tendencies toward expecting employees who have received program services actually to achieve superior levels of performance after receiving program services. In any event, a tendency to guard against in evaluative measurement is the expectation of greater-than-average job performance among program referrals because of the degree of scrutiny in measurement that is administered to persons who have been through the program.

In actuality, most organizations tolerate considerable slack in individual job performances. Therefore, it is imperative that carefully developed comparison measures with individuals who have not received program services be developed as part of an evaluation strategy. This does not necessarily require a full-fledge control group. The matching of employees who have and have not used the EAP on key characteristics such as sex, age, job level, and length of tenure may suffice for some reasonable comparisons. If such comparisons are not made, there is a tendency to escalate the expectations placed on individuals who have received program services, which in turn may reflect inappropriately heightened expectations for overall program performance.

Alcoholism Emphasis in EAPs

Most of the programs in the United States at the present time emphasize identification of problem employees on the basis of deteriorating performance and offer assistance to employees with a range of problems other than alcoholism. It is important, however, to maintain specific attention to the alcohol problem component of an EAP if the program design's proven effectiveness in dealing with alcohol problems is to be maximized (Roman, 1981).

In other words, basic program design which has evolved into a broad EAP has proven effective in dealing with employee alcohol problems; with the use of the constructive confrontation strategy, it is specifically capable of motivating action toward employee alcohol problems far earlier than would be possible in the normal course of events. Thus, it is strongly recommended that all program evaluations include specific attention to the extent to which the program is reaching employees with alcohol problems. While we recognize that many in the EAP field are concerned about alcohol-related identities for their own career futures, our experience indicates two salient points. First, there is no doubt that job-based confrontation is not only effective with alcohol problems, but is also a legitimate confrontation as compared to the use of family-based confrontation strategies. Second, there is no doubt that employees are attracted to EAPs because of their dramatic and clearcut utility in dealing with alcohol problems.

The alcohol problem emphasis in an EAP is a supposedly simple criterion, however it has multiple dimensions. Two distinctive outcome criteria are:

1) The extent to which the individual who has received assistance is performing adequately on the job
2) The extent to which the individual has successfully responded to the assistance directed at his/her alcohol problem

While it is likely that the individual who is achieving sobriety will also be showing improvement in job performance (since this is one dimension of sobriety), the employer in most cases will choose to focus attention on performance outcomes only. Consequently, an individual who was maintaining a pattern of abstinence and otherwise attending to the requirements of a treatment program, but who was persistently absent without adequate reason and who persisted with low quality performance, would not be regarded as successful at that point by a performance-oriented criterion.

It is essential for the maintenance of the distinctivenesss of a work-based program that issues of treatment outcome and job performance outcome remain separate in terms of measurement and evaluation consideration. It is emphasized, however, that such outcomes are likely to be highly correlated, and that the time dimension is an important consideration in terms of expecting adequacy of performance in all spheres of life after an extended period of personal disorganization due to alcoholism. In any event, performance-oriented criteria must be developed at the level of the individual work organization, and must be individualized in evaluation to reflect the expectations and agreements which characterize the local setting.

Another criterion consideration which is often regarded by employers and EAP specialists as relevant to alcohol problems is the extent to which the program is genuinely producing early identification. There is usually great value in the identification of any employee with an alcohol problem, in that expected rates of recovery in work-based programs are much higher than in other types of identification efforts. It is, however, desirable for programs to produce identification before extensive intervention is required, thus minimizing the discontinuity of job performance and individual life organization. The extensiveness and costs of formal treatment intervention required by employees whose performance problems have been identified to be associated with alcohol may be fairly good measures of the earliness of identification.

Among persons with interests in and commitments to dealing with alcohol problems, careful attention to the various dimensions of alcohol-related criteria are important. Such attention will fully establish and specify the effectiveness of these programs in identifying and providing assistance to the employed alcoholic, and will reduce the risks of losing attention to alcohol problems in the midst of other personal problems brought to the surface by the broad thrust of EAPs.

Experts and Outsiders

A final feature of program evaluation is the involvement of experts and the consideration of the involvement of outsiders. A major theme of this section is that data collection in an EAP requires the commitment and cooperation of EAP staff, but the design of data analysis and interpretation should involve persons expert in these techniques. Much of the perceived "shortfall" in evaluation studies about EAPs centers on the fact that they were designed and conducted by EAP specialists themselves (Trice, 1980). Consequently many of the studies do not meet the typical criteria for adequate measurement and analysis, and it is clear in almost every instance that the study would have been improved by consultation with persons expert in data analysis and interpretation. It is ironic that most EAP specialists readily utilize expert consultation in dealing with cases, but they are reluctant to do so in dealing with program evaluation. It is further irony that EAP specialists would not readily allow researchers to take over their clinical duties, but many clinicians readily "jump in" the enterprises of data analysis and interpretation. In large work organizations, finding appropriate experts may not be problematic because of the accessibility of expertise within the organization from units such as personnel research, but in most mid-sized and smaller organizations this expertise is not available and must be sought from outside.

Other than knowledge and experience with data collection and analysis, there are at least two additional major reasons for utilizing experts from outside the organization in the design and implementation of program evaluation. First is the enhancement of credibility. It is very difficult to accept conclusions about the efficacy of a particular EAP from the individuals who are operating the EAP. Thus the credibility of any evaluation will be enhanced by utilizing outside expertise, even if it is from within one's own organization. The second reason centers on the kinds of objectivity and indeed, naivete, that an outsider can bring to the evaluation of an EAP. Not only is the outsider lacking in personal commitments to the programs and their value, but he/she also is in a position to see things in ways that are not possible among insiders who are operating the program. This point is especially important when it comes to the interpretation of the evaluation results; the outsider will be in a superior position to perceive the dynamics of forces to which insiders have been inured or to which they are insensitive, due to their own commitments.

We return to the design of evaluation in the later part of this section, but at this juncture it is important to distinguish evaluation from research. The goal of evaluation is to ascertain how well an EAP has achieved certain goals, and it is usually concluded that the EAP has been the source of the desirable outcomes. Evaluation goals should be realistic in the expectations implied for the EAP that is under consideration. A most important consequence of an evaluation study should be alteration of the program in the direction that will increase the achievement of the valued goals, and thus the criteria used in evaluation should be within the scope of change and program improvement. Research, by contrast, is centered on why outcomes occur and usually should not reflect a commitment to maximize a given outcome which is believed to be desirable.

EAP Research

Evaluation studies should eventually provide the EAP specialty with a series of models of what types of programs seem to work best in given situations, given certain goals to be achieved by EAPs. Research, by contrast, provides the base on which EAP specialties may eventually establish the legitimacy of their claims to be "professions," and thus have unique claim over the activity which may come to be defined as the "core technology" of EAPs (as distinct from health promotion programs, safety programs, selection and placement, personnel counseling, etc.). Research on EAPs is thus not concerned with whether "they do any good" but is instead concerned with the organizational and individual dynamics that comprise the action in and surrounding EAPs. A very important distinction between evaluation studies and research studies is that the former may be mainly or exclusively intended for internal use within the organization where they were conducted and thus may never see "the light of day" outside that organization; research is useless unless published or otherwise available and "shareable" among those who benefit from the study's results. Finally, it is important to note that EAP practitioners would not only be well advised to utilize outside assistance in conducting evaluation, but that they also should not attempt to conduct their own research studies.

It is not surprising, however, that some practitioners have attempted to do research, in part as a response to the frustration of finding so little available research on EAPs. The researchers who might be qualified to carry out studies on the structure and dynamics of EAPs have not developed interests in EAPs, with the exception of a very small coterie of ten to twelve researchers who have produced a sizeable body of studies.

The "gap" between research data and the development of a new specialty interest is not unique to the EAP specialty though, and it is indeed rare that a body of practice develops only after the research base has been fully established and elaborated. The attraction of additional researchers represents somewhat of a vicious circle, in that published studies should be the main vehicle for attracting new personnel to research questions that they find both challenging and critical to their own area of theory and methodology. The absence of a "critical mass" of such published work is indeed an impediment to further research development.

A further problem centers on research translation. For the most part, research is not directly accessible to practitioners through the journals where most scientific research is published. Publication in journals which appear cryptic and esoteric to practitioners is vital for researchers for maintaining communication among their peers. This reduces the likelihood of research, meeting scientific standards, and being placed in publications which practitioners are likely to read and comprehend. There is thus a need for a middle-person or clearinghouse-type strategy, where scientific research is translated to reach the practitioner community. Unfortunately, this kind of translation has been very slow in developing in the EAP specialty. So, the practitioner who is genuinely concerned with research findings must either develop the expertise to comprehend research, or researchers' committees must adjust their reward structures to better accommodate the needs of practitioners.

A considerable potential for research translation exists through processes of consultation with experienced researchers, a potential which is rarely utilized. It is nearly absurd to assume that published research studies will be applicable to all EAPs; by definition, each EAP is in some (or many) ways unique in its accommodation to the particular work organization in which it is based. Thus, regardless of the researchers' commitment to the application of his/her findings in the "real world," written publications are limited to generalities or to very narrow case-study conclusions, often leaving the practitioner frustrated.

A middle ground for the practitioner between commissioning experienced researchers to conduct studies in one's own organization and total dependence on reading academic journals is the use of research consultation. A great deal can be accomplished at a very modest cost by inviting researchers on–site for several days to bring both their expertise and their "outsideness" to bear on the problems of a particular EAP. While this is by no means the same as intense empirical study, it does provide the opportunity for the practitioner to learn how the researchers' findings apply to the practitioner's EAP. Again, we are surprised at the rarity of such consultation in light of EAP practitioners' readiness to utilize direct consultation with various experts regarding clinical issues. Few clinicians will rely solely on studying their academic journals when faced with tough cases, yet there seems to be an expectation that research studies should be directly applicable to the EAP of every reader of the study's results.

A related and equally neglected use of consultation is the on-site visit to another EAP. We can regard this as a form of research by the EAP practitioner to the extent that visits to other EAPs are used to observe the mechanisms of solutions to problems that plague his/her EAP. It is expected that remuneration would often be involved in such visits to the extent that they involve extensive time of the host/hostess away from other duties and to the extent of exceeding norms of typical professional courtesies. In our own research we found that these two types of consultation comprised the primary research techniques which are deliberately used as the basis for planning and structuring the Australian occupational drug and alcohol abuse programming effort (Roman, 1983).

Designing Evaluation

One of the most common questions which we as researchers hear from practitioners in the EAP specialty concerns what they should measure in an evaluation. Much of what we regard as the inappropriate orientation toward standardized evaluation among EAP specialists stems from earlier career experiences in treatment agencies, in which client improvement was the universal criterion of program effectiveness. In this section we describe two very important considerations in the evaluations of EAPs that make them very different from typical treatment program evaluations.

Our earlier distinction about the significance of recordkeeping and the MIS is salient at this juncture because they are functions which every EAP specialist should undertake; by contrast, evaluation is not necessarily an EAP function toward which resources and efforts should be routinely directed. We regard program evaluation as the primary prerogative of the individual or the group which provides the funding resources for an EAP, and we believe that these decision makers should be intimately involved in the design of any evaluation that is focused on "their" EAP. There is obviously no reason to assume commonality in these criteria across different EAPs. These decision makers should also be the ones who decide when there is to be an evaluation.

While the logic behind this may seem obvious, experience within the EAP field shows that, from the early 1970s, EAP personnel were specifically told that program evaluation was one of their principal and most important roles. In this context, the concept of evaluation was inadvertently confused with the concept of a management information system, since there is no doubt that every EAP specialist should keep and utilize records of his/her work activities. Program evaluation, by contrast, is the province of the program sponsors, and it is indeed inappropriate, if not dangerous to the program's welfare, for program operatives to design and carry out program evaluation. On the one hand, since these operatives are not making the decisions about program funding, they cannot decide on the appropriate evaluative criteria. On the other hand, the production of a "voluntary" evaluation can indeed jeopardize a program if its results (which are usually unexpected when received by the decision maker) indicate that the program is doing something other than what the sponsor intended.

It is thus important to recognize from the outset that the design and timing of a program evaluation is the prerogative of the decisionmakers who control resources, rather than the program staff. An unsolicited evaluation can indeed produce trouble, especially if the decisionmakers find that the evaluation results underline their own exclusion from the program's development.

The prescription is therefore obvious. The program operatives should at the earliest possible date meet with the individuals responsible for making decisions about the program's resource allocation and establish with them their expectations for the program's achievements as well as their recommendations for the timing and design of program evaluation. In this manner the decisionmakers acquire genuine "ownership" of the evaluation and become more closely identified with the EAP's goals. This places the actual results of the evaluation in a much different context than if the program operatives design and conduct the evaluation while "second-guessing" the intent of the decisionmakers.

Evaluation Criteria

We have already indicated at several points our concern with the transfer of the treatment-model evaluation to the evaluation of EAPs. We believe that this model greatly underestimates the impact of EAPs on organizations. Our work indicates, for example, that EAPs may trigger substantial help-seeking outside the EAP umbrella. We are also aware of instances where the presence of the EAP stimulated and supported the presence of "natural" networks of help and support which existed within the organization and predated the EAP. As a final example, it is likely that the employer cares about the welfare of the workforce, and these positive sentiments in the workforce may be even more synergistic when the EAP is a joint effort of labor and management.

Many EAP specialists, however, tend to view managerial decision-makers in work organizations as solely concerned with costs and benefits of EAPs and have tended to place heavy emphasis on cost effectiveness. While this is an exciting and challenging enterprise, it carries with it several pitfalls and dubious assumptions which deserve comment. Programming specialists can easily exaggerate the importance of cost savings considerations. Belief in the importance of program cost-considerations is based on at least two assumptions:

1) Work organizations only sustain activities that are cost benficial
2) Programs have been adopted primarily for the cost savings that they are going to generate for the work organization

Both of these assumptions are erroneous. There are multiple reasons for maintaining organizational activities, especially those involving non-routine functions and services. This multitude of reasons applies equally to EAPs.

These comments are not an effort to avoid attention to costs and benefits, but rather to question the appropriateness of such an emphasis. If a work organization adopts an EAP on the basis of the perception that substance abuse and other personal difficulties are like other health problems, then it should support this program in the same way it would support other health-related interventions.

Positive health programs, such as exercise and smoking cessation as well as programs for the early detection of cancer and heart disease, are generally instituted by work organizations on the basis of a broad sense of corporate social responsibility and humanitarianism, rather that a cold belief in the cost effectiveness of such programs. Thus if alcohol problems, for example, are to be regarded as disease conditions, deserving the same attention as other disease conditions, similar evaluative criteria should apply, and cost efficiency is not a primary factor in the support of these other efforts.

The measurement of cost effectiveness of EAPs has other built-in difficulties. First are the factors which may be affected by an EAP which defy statistical measurement. These include the overall benefit of the employee's recovery to the community at large, the effects on his/her family, the effects on the morale of co-workers, and the unknown extension of the employee's productive career for the organization as a consequence of the intervention. Thus, a cost-benefit analysis is likely to underestimate program effectiveness.

A second problem is that of timing. We do not have adequate research evidence to understand the point at which visible "payoffs" from EAPs will occur. Consequently, the premature implementation of a cost effectiveness approach may produce inappropriate and unjustified conclusions.

Given the ambiguity of goals held across the various constituencies of EAPs, the results of a cost effectiveness analysis may be particularly meaningless unless undertaken after a number of years of program experience when earlier evaluations have sharpened the types of questions that need to be addressed about dimensions of program effectiveness.

Use of Results

A final pitfall in conducting program evaluation concerns utilizing evaluation results. Evaluations are usually launched with the unstated assumption that the results will be fed into the program to change it in the direction of improved effectiveness.

If an evaluation is to have an impact on a program, it is important to specify at the outset the means for reviewing evaluation data and the mechanisms for bringing about program change. The specification of a review group and a specific timing for their meeting to review evaluation results should be indicated as the evaluation is launched.

It should be pointed out that the results of evaluations are usually ambiguous. Rarely does one find an evaluation which clearly describes the ingredients of effectiveness or ineffectiveness or which clearly indicates highly superior or notably inferior components of programming activities.

Further, in considering evaluation feedback, it must be recognized that organizations resist change. Thus, even with the specification of feedback mechanisms and routes for "absorbing" the results of program evaluation, the implementation of change is far from a simple process. This is an important consideration in the context of involving behavioral researchers who can aid substantially this change process.

References

Roman, P., 1981, "From Employee Alcoholism to Employee Assistance: An Analysis of the Deemphasis on Prevention and Alcohol Problems in Work-Based Programs," *Journal of studies on alcohol*, Vol. 43, pp. 224-72.

_____, 1982, "The Pitfalls of Program Concepts in the Development and Maintenance of Employee Assistance Programs," *Urban and social change review*, Vol. 16, pp. 9-16.

_____, 1983, "Employee Assistance Programs in Australia and the United States: Comparisons of Origin, Structure, and the Role of Behavioral Science Research," *Journal of applied behavioral sciences*, Vol. 19, pp. 367-79.

Trice, H., 1980, "Applied Research Studies," *Alcohol, health and research world*, Vol. 6, pp. 8-19.

_____, and Belasco, J., 1968, "Supervisory Training About Alcoholics and Other Problem Employees," *Quarterly journal of studies on alcohol*, Vol. 29, pp. 382-98.

_____, and Beyer, J., 1977, "Differential Use of an Alcoholism Policy in Federal Organizations By Skill Level," pp. 44–68 in C. Schramm, ed., *Alcoholism and its treatment in industry*. Baltimore: Johns Hopkins University Press.

Van de Vall, M., 1975, "Utilization and Methodology of Applied Social Science," *Journal of applied behavioral sciences*, Vol. 11, pp. 14-38.

21

Can Change Be Documented?: Measuring the Impact of EAPs

Bradley Googins

Introduction

Despite the heralded acclaim which EAPs have received over the past several years, little substantive research has yet to be conducted to verify the effectiveness of these programs. In fact, the most basic question an evaluation would seek has rarely been asked: Do EAPs effect change? The simplicity of the question can be deceptive in light of the technical complexity of scientifically arriving at an answer. However, the programmatic and policy implications of not having an established body of research on the success and effectiveness of EAPs becomes an increasing problem as the field seeks professional respectability. Thus a number of critically important research questions await study.

- What type of changes do EAPs bring about?
- Are EAPs responsible for increased productivity?
- Why do some EAPs work better then others?
- What are the most important elements of an EAP?

The list could continue but the point is made. So little is known about what works, under what conditions for which people, that the existing body of research in the EAP field is embarrassingly thin. An example might best capture this point. The vice president of a 3,500 employee publishing concern has heard and read about the rapid development of EAPs. As one who prides himself on being in the forefront of personnel practices, he assigns a staff person to prepare a feasibility study within the company of establishing an EAP. As a businessman, he expects some answers to several questions which occur to him:

- What evidence exists on the effectiveness of EAPs?
- What percentage of the workforce would be expected to use such an EAP?
- What cost effectiveness figures are available?
- Does it make any difference whether he contracts out for the program or sets it up in-house?
- What effects will the EAP have on the company's health insurance—positive or negative?

These are fundamental questions that any responsible manager might and should ask prior to opting for setting up an EAP. They also happen to be areas with little data outside of anecdotal reporting and brief reports of programs, where the reliability and validity of the data render it little better than impressionistic.

All of this is stated to bring out a fundamental reality of EAPs in 1984. The EAP field is not in a position, based on existing studies, to back up most of the claims of success, cost savings, and effectiveness which are widely reported and accepted.

What has occurred over the past decade can be documented in terms of the numbers of programs established, the types of programs, different treatment interventions, employees who have stopped drinking and returned to "normal" work levels, etc. All of this is descriptive, captured simply by examining the form and shape of EAPs, and counting and documenting what exists. To move from this observational stage to one of inference and causality will require a more systematic and scientifically rigorous approach. Thus, in order to address the questions of the vice president of the publishing concern, or to present a body of widely accepted research on the success of EAPs, this section begins with a fundamental question for EAPs: Can change (defined as success, effectiveness or whatever) be documented? It is accompanied by a parallel question: How can EAP staff assist in documenting such change?

Measuring Change With EAPs

In order to examine the concept of change within the context of EAPs, it is necessary to first understand how change itself is at the heart of the EAP. One might say the business of EAPs is to bring about change. To the extent change occurs, the EAP and the EAP practitioner have achieved their goals. This is based on the assumption that, to justify EAPs, problems exist and a changed state is desirable. For example, an employee comes into the EAP office with a problem–alcoholic behavior has threatened both job loss and family disintegration. The desired change might be a lifestyle in which alcohol use is curtailed or cut off, such that job functioning is occurring at an acceptable level and/or family function has achieved a positive or steady state. Each of the words used to describe this desired state of change can be discussed from many angles: Who decides what changes are desired; are they measurable? How difficult will it be to measure these changes? But in all instances change is presumed. If no change is called for, then there would be no need for any program intervention.

For EAPs, most change goals are discussed in terms of success. Success could mean sobriety, improved job peformance, a cost saving, or some other measure. In a recent review of the literature, Kurtz, Googins, and Howard (1983) found measures grouped into four major classes:

1) change in drinking behavior–a measure of the degree to which a person has achieved an abstinent or sober state.
2) change in work performance–a measure of the degree to which the employee has improved job performance.
3) change in cost reduction–a measure of savings realized through improved work performance.
4) change in penetration–a measure of the extent to which a program reaches the target population of a given organization.

While there is much that could be discussed about these four types of measures, what is important here is the inclusiveness of the measures. That is, if change or success can be documented within EAPs, these are the traditional categories by which changes have been discussed. Each of these categories addresses different types or objects of change, emphasizing the lack of consensus on how program change or success has been conceptualized, targeted, and measured. While the obvious program goal is to help employees change those lifestyle patterns that have led to problems on the job, at home, or within themselves, the specific measures that have been used to determine the extent of change vary widely.

Documentation vs. Measuremnt

This is perhaps a good time to differentiate between documentation and measurement. While all measurement requires documentation, not all documentation requires measurement. Documentation is more of an enumeration or observation. For example, I can document or observe how many people of what type come into an EAP, what kind of treatment they receive, and even what their absenteeism rate is before and after treatment. All I am doing is documenting characteristics, frequencies, etc. I am not able to assign any association or implication for change beyond the observable data. Most EAP reports are indeed documentation of program characteristics.

Measurement, on the other hand, has a much more precise connotation, and represents an overriding concern in science. In essence, measurement consists of rules for assigning numbers to objects to represent quantities of attributes (Nunnaly and Wilson, 1975). Simply put, a thermometer or a yardstick offers an obvious form of measurement. Unfortunately, in most of science and in EAPs, the measurements of change are considerably more difficult and the absence of available tools such as a yardstick make it even more difficult. The value of measurement over documentation is that it allows us to be more precise and systematic in evaluating what we are doing. By scientifically measuring change in EAPs, we are better able to approach a certitude that the change occurring is due to the EAP and not to some external event.

What this distinction is suggesting is the desirability of measurement over documentation. It is a more powerful approach (although more complex) in being able to speak more authoritatively and with more confidence about outcomes or findings. Why this is so is best explained by briefly examining several key characteristics of all measures.

Reliability

This refers to the consistency of the measure, the extent at which measures are repeatable. If a measure is highly reliable, it will give similar results under similar conditions. The importance of reliable measures to the EAP practitioner is multifaceted. First, it is a good way to assess the value of a measure. Thus, if we were to have some measure of sobriety lifestyle patterns, one would like to have confidence that this measure is consistent, whether it is used at the General Motors EAP or the Atlantic Richfield EAP. Secondly, if we have such a reliable measure, we will know whether any changes that show up during the treatment program are due to actual changes in the problem, whether they are due to changes in the instrument, or in the observer's way of viewing or reporting the problem (Bloom and Fisher, 1982). Reliability can be determined through specific types of statistics which demonstrate the stability of a measure.

Validity

High reliability does not necessarily mean high validity. Validity refers to the extent to which an instrument measures what it sets out to measure. Thus, several have raised the question as to whether job performance measures really measure job performance, or instead constitute surrogate measures (measuring something else). Even though there may exist a job performance measure that consistently and with high repeatability measures absenteeism, tardiness, etc, unless it indeed is also a true indicator of job performance, it is not very useful.

These two classical components provide us with some indication of the rigor needed to assure an acceptable level of measurement. Without these there is little certitude or credibility in generalizing about findings. If I am to state that 70% of the employees who are treated by the EAP are "successes," then I have to be able to demonstrate that the measures I have used to test and arrive at this conclusion are both valid and reliable. If we were to review the state of the art in EAP evaluation research, we would find little evidence that those who set out to evaluate paid much attention to these issues. Because this is so, there is little ability to generalize the findings.

How Can Change Be Documented?

Let us return now to our original question: Can change be documented? Clearly, either the documentation or measurement of change is possible. Given the scientific paradigm and the existence of instruments, much change can and has been documented. What is more to the point are the dilemmas and difficulties in measuring change: There are many scientific obstacles to measurement; no research method is without bias; there will be sampling error, threats to validity, and interviewer bias. But all of these are not necessarily overwhelming obstacles, only limitations to approaching a scientifically sound measurement.

Several problems exist for EAP administrators as they face the measurement of the impact of their interventions. Schramm (1977) describes several difficulties in evaluating programs such as EAPs and reports that the most frequently encountered difficulty is the isolation of quantifiable programmatic goals which can be linked to and measured against program efforts. However, Schramm states that isolating program goals and assessing them is considerably easier for EAPs for two reasons: 1) The broad aim of the EAP is to rehabilitate employees who are abusing alcohol and to have them work at an acceptable level of job performance and 2) All behavior changes can be measured in value of lost productivity. Thus the very advantage and uniqueness of EAPs, i.e., their link to job performance, can also be used to introduce a primary evaluation measure. While EAPs may differ on a number of dimensions, all of them are set up to correct deviant behavior with the objective of returning the problem drinking employee to acceptable job performance (Trice and Beyer, 1981).

It should be noted that the use of job performance measures are not without critics. Trice and Beyer, for example, contend that measures such as absenteeism may not be anything more than proxies for job performance and productivity, unrelated to the quality of work (assumed to be the genuine object of study), but may instead be sensitive to the intervention strategy, thus biasing results that presume to generalize job performance (Howard, 1982). Foote et al (1978) assumes that these surrogate measures are related to more direct measures of work performance, and although they do not directly measure the quantity or quality of work performed, are available from company records; hence they are both accessible and tied to the real world, with all its drawbacks. They also cite the work of Mann et al (1963), consisting of a comprehensive study of work groups, that revealed low absenteeism to be significantly related to high productivity (actual rates) and overall high effectiveness (as rated by middle management).

Although these measures are often ambiguous, they are more concrete and precise than most measures of drinking behavior, and more useful and appropriate both for motivating individuals to seek treatment and for measuring program success (Howard, 1982). Shain and Groeneveld (1980) find considerable agreement on the dimensions of job performance which should be used in program assessment, but a consistent set of indices and criteria is lacking.

Having an effective program mechanism for measuring change con-stitutes a distinct advantage. Imagine the greater degree of difficulty for counselors in a community-based treatment center. In pursuing the same goal of documenting and measuring change, they are forced to rely almost exclusively on self reports and perceptions. For the EAP, the more objective measures of job performance allow for a considerably stronger and more valid assessment of change. Using these already existing organizational measures provides a unique opportunity for EAPs in more closely assessing the effectiveness of program intervention.

Relating The Documentation of Change to EAP Staff

All of this may sound fine, but still unrelated to practitioners within EAPs. After all, the uniqueness of the job performance measures and their role in documentation and confrontation is a treatment advantage, before it is an evaluation advantage. Nevertheless, the opportunity to document and evaluate change can be missed if EAP staff do not play some role in linking research to their practice.

Given the negatives and positives of available measures, what specific steps can EAP counselors and administrators take in documenting change? What, in brief, can active practitioners bring to an essentially research question? Several suggestions follow:

1. **Data Collection.** Before any change can be measured data must be collected. Such a simple statement has been the bane of many researchers.

EAPs, particularly in the early stages of development, rarely pay much attention to the function of data collection. With the rush of setting up the program, getting sanctions secured, identifying outside resources, getting the door open, assessing, treating, and referring, data collection is often relegated to little more than face sheet information. Understandable as this is, it does not allow for evaluating change or measuring effectiveness in EAP treatment.

All evaluation research begins with data. The one basic reason for recording–the systematic measurement of client and client system problems, and the keeping of records on those observations–is to enhance effectiveness through measures of change (Bloom and Fisher, 1982). The role of EAP staff in collecting baseline data in a systematic fashion is indispensible. This function, which is often perceived as secondary to the treatment function and a nuisance to be sure, is critical for evaluation, comparing information collected prior to intervention, to the intervention period itself, and again to a period following treatment.

Mainlining data collection procedures into EAPs does not come easily. Nevertheless, if the field is to be able to maintain a creditable position, front line staff will have to do their part. This will include developing and pretesting intake forms, examining program objectives, specifying appropriate measures, and insuring current recordkeeping systems which can be used for generating data. There are software packages developed which can assist in the computerization of data as well as facilitating data retrieval and conducting basic research.

2. Developing a Research Component and Resources. While collecting client and program data is a sine qua non of evaluation research, it is not sufficient by itself. Unless something is done with the data, it has only limited use. Consequently, a second step consists of developing a research capacity by which the program evaluates and routinely analyzes data to determine appropriate answers to research questions. These questions will differ from program to program depending on the political necessities of the corporation, the stage of development of the particular EAP, and the research agenda of the EAP staff or relevant corporate or union officials. Because of the lack of a universal EAP model, variables of organization staffing and treatment also introduce untested factors which need to be controlled and analyzed to determine effectiveness. Only by such repeated and widespread testing will a base of research be built which will allow the effectiveness of EAPs to be examined in a systematic fashion.

At present, few EAPs have the time or expertise to develop a research capacity. But given the desire, linkages with research in universities or consulting firms can achieve this goal. The research community is increasingly interested in creating these links. Indeed, if research is to take place, a truly collaborative model is necessary. The role of the EAP staff in this collaboration is critical. Their knowledge of the organization and skills in obtaining the necessary sanction for research is an absolute necessity. Because these partnerships have been few, less than a handful of research projects have taken place, a startling and detrimental development. When the expertise of the researcher is linked to the political skills and organizational savvy of the EAP staff, the chances of conducting significant research is greatly enhanced.

3. Dissemination of Results. A final factor relates to the dissemination of research findings. It may very well be that change can indeed be documented, despite all the technical difficulties, but unless the findings of such research can reach the EAP public, no one will know what, if any, change took place. Documentation of change implies an ability to communicate results. Much of the documented change has been conducted and transmitted by an insular group of educated individuals called researchers, whose arcane knowledge and narrowly written texts perpetuate the mysteries of research, while squandering their findings in little known journals read by each other.

Indeed, the absence of journalistic avenues has had a negative impact on the EAP field, One journal, *The Labor Management Journal of Alcoholism*, was recently discontinued. The *EAP Digest* represents the only existing journal in which occupational alcoholism research findings appear. However, most of what appears is focused more on programmatic innovation and practice pieces. While the *Journal of Alcohol Studies* has published some outstanding articles, its lengthy review process results in two-year delays between submission and publication. In summary, there exists a serious lack of "vehicles" by which research results are disseminated and to which practitioners and others can turn for data on EAP effectiveness.

Macro versus Micro Change

A final note on documenting change within EAPs raises the question of levels or goals of change. Because the EAP has closely aligned itself with the medical and clinical model, it primarily focuses on micro change or change within the individual. While this is a desirable and necessary focus, it is not necessarily the sole focus. EAPs are also related to organizations, and thus should be concerned with structural and institutional change. Although there is not much attention paid to macro practice or macro change, it is as much of a goal for EAPs as micro change. To downplay this factor is denying the very preventative thrust which characterizes EAPs.

Organizational measures of change are more cumbersome and more difficult to document and is one of the primary reasons why few attempts have been made within EAPs. For example, is the organization more likely to identify and refer employees to the EAP today than it was five years ago as the result of supervisory training, employee education, etc? Have environmental effects to stress been lowered over the past several years as the result of EAP intervention? Even raising these questions might seem inappropriate for some EAPs, but it serves the purpose of reformulating the goals of EAPs. A useful consequence of examining measures is the exercise in stating program goals and objectives. Such a process will inevitably raise the macro level changes desired by an EAP.

Documenting both macro and micro change within the same EAP can be difficult, due in part to the inadequacies of measures at the macro level. However, the management and organizational fields have developed a number of measures which might prove quite useful to EAPs. By adopting this dual focus, the EAP will enhance its mission by reflecting on the many dimensions of change it seeks to bring about within corporations.

Conclusions

As the EAP field matures and becomes more professional, it seeks a widespread respect for its activities and accomplishments. A primary vehicle for achieving respect and entering a professional mode rests with the state of research. As any field develops, it must put forth a body of research to substantiate its claim of effectiveness. The EAP field is no exception. Thus, the question of "can change be documented?" would better be stated "How *best* can change be documented?" For the field not to be able to document change within the accepted research protocols is to relegate the EAP to a practice based on intuition and good intentions. The documentation of change is both a challenge and an opportunity for the EAP field. It is a challenge to place increased emphasis on research and evaluation as an integral part of EAPs and not to be satisfied with anecdotal accounts, grandiose claims of success, and paper thin documentation to corroborate program success. It is an opportunity in which the perceived effectiveness which is felt by the EAP field can be translated into reliable and valid findings, which in turn will argue for the establishment of EAPs in the thousands of corporations who have not yet been convinced of EAP efficacy.

References

Bloom, M. and Fisher, J. 1982, *Evaluating Practice: Guidelines For The Accountable Professional,* Prentice Hall, Englewood Cliffs, New Jersey, p. 36 and 268.

Foote, A., Erfurt J., Stranch P., and Guzzards T. 1978, *Cost Effectiveness of Occupational Employee Assistance Programs: Test of an Evaluation Method,* Institute of Labor and Industrial Relations, University of Michigan, Wayne State University, Ann Arbor, Michigan.

Howard, W., "Evaluating Job Based Alcoholism Programs–A Substantive Paper," Heller School, Brandeis University, July 1982.

Kurtz, R., Googins, B., and Howard, W., 1983, "Measuring The Success of Occupational Alcoholism Programs," forthcoming, *Journal of Alcohol Studies.*

Mann, F., Indik, B., and Vroom, U., 1963 *The Productivity of Work Groups,* Ann Arbor: University of Michigan.

Nunnaly, J. and Wilson, W.H., 1975, "Method and Theory for Developing Measures in Evaluation Research" in *Handbook of Evaluation Research,* ed by E. Struening and M. Guttentag, Sage Publication, Beverly Hills.

Schramm, C.J., 1977, "Measuring The Return on Program Costs: Evaluation of a Multi-employer Alcoholism Treatment Program," American Journal of Public Health, 6, pp. 50–51.

Shain, M. and Groeneveld, J., 1980, *Employee Assistance Programs,* D.C. Heath, Lexington, Mass.

Trice, H. and Beyer, J., 1981, "A Performance-Based Evaluation of the Constructive Confrontation Strategy; How Effective is Discipline?" General Meeting of American Sociological Association, Toronto.

22

An Exploration of the Ability of Broad-Based EAPS to Generate Alcohol-Related Referrals

Martin Shain

The Concern of this Study

The merits of broad-scope EAPs as opposed to alcohol-specific programs in relation to their ability to generate alcohol-related referrals, are still very much a matter of debate. Dunkin's concern that broad-scope EAPs may dilute the effectiveness of more specific programs in relation to alcohol problems (Dunkin, 1982) appears to be reflected in fluctuations in the rate at which they were adopted during the 1970s (Roman, 1979). Roman reported in 1979 that there were only slightly more broad than narrow programs among the Fortune 500 companies and 250 leading banks, insurance, utilities, transportation, and financial organizations which he studied. This contrasts with Roman's earlier report of broad-scope EAP's greater popularity in the mid–1970s.

Few empirical data exist to test what seems to be a mixture of ideological assumptions and products of practical experience in relation to this issue. Foote and Erfurt (1981), in recognizing the vigor of the rivalry between the two camps, obtained data from 118 General Motors plants with various kinds of assistance programs, from broad to narrow. They found that, if the caseload within a given broad-based program contained in excess of 35% alcohol-related referrals, the absolute proportion of such cases relative to the workforce from which they came would be the same or higher than the proportion obtained in alcohol-specific programs.

The paucity of data on this subject prompted the study outlined in this section.

This chapter is a summary of a longer research report (Shain, 1983). The views expressed in this chapter are those of the author and do not necessarily reflect those of the Addiction Research Foundation.

Method of Study

A series of hypotheses was formed on the basis of arguments found in the literature about the supposed benefits of broad-based EAPs in relation to alcohol abuse. A principal source of such material in summary form was the Report of the Task Force on Employee Assistance Programmes (Smith et al., 1978) commissioned by the Addiction Research Foundation of Ontario. Further refinement of the principles discussed in that report resulted in an official goal statement by the Addiction Research Foundation (1982) in relation to occupational programs. The key points of the statement can be converted into the following hypotheses.

Hypotheses

1) The identification rate for programs that emphasize alcohol problems has been given as a range of 0.1% to 1.6% of the workforce with a mean of 0.64% and a median of 0.45% (Hitchcock and Sanders, 1976). The expectation of broad-based programs is that they will exceed the mean identification rate of narrower programs with regard to alcohol-related cases.

The usual explanation of this hypothesis is the belief that broad programs, in addition to identifying advanced alcoholics, will allow people with emerging problems of alcohol dependence to present themselves for help with other sorts of difficulties. In the course of exploring these difficulties it will often be discovered that alcohol is a problem and help may then be obtained in this regard. Then the supposed stigma of being referred for, or referring oneself for a primary alcohol problem is avoided. It is clear, nonetheless, that this rationale assumes the use of "voluntary" referrals or at least "suggested" referrals where the employee has an opportunity to take some initiative on his/her own behalf. Similarly, it implies that such cases of alcohol problem identification will be of the earlier rather than later variety. It is sometimes argued that more women will present themselves for help under the aegis of a broad-based program because they are more likely to define their problems as domestic, emotional, or financial, even though they may have fairly well developed alcohol and drug dependency problems.

2) Where broad-based programs offer employees a variety of pathways to care and assistance they are likely to attract more alcohol-related cases. Thus, if the program has a clearly enunciated voluntary component as well as a well worked-out formal component, and if there are ways of gaining direct access to the source of help without going through mediators (committee members, medical departments, supervisors, personnel managers, coordinators, etc.), but where such mediators are in place to facilitate care-

seeking when this is needed or wanted, the odds are much higher that potential clients will make contact with the service provider.

The corollary of this hypothesis is that managers and supervisors will be more effective in dealing with problem employees if they are free to consult the service provider about specific situations in which they are not sure what to do. This consultative level of intervention is often carried out without the service provider's knowing who the employee is. It also allows the service provider to identify cases in which the manager or supervisor may need help for a personal problem as well as the employee about whom the call was originally made.

3) Where assessment, referral, and subsequent service in a broad-based EAP is external to the workplace–and in that sense is conducted by a third party–the odds are raised that employees of the client organization will use the service. This hypothesis extends to employees with all sorts of problems, including alcohol dependence. The reasons advanced in support of this hypothesis are usually that this location of the service provides an independence from employers and their agents, which in turn suggests to employees that greater confidentiality exists. This perception of independence may also extend to seeing the service provider as more competent, although this may be thought to depend on a variety of other factors also. Accessibility is probably a factor too, particularly where self-initiated referrals are involved, in that it is easier to call a well-publicized number in town than to navigate through a perceived maze of mediators, such as committee members, supervisors, coordinators, personnel and medical officers, union counselors, and others.

It is important to note, however, that the principle underlying the hypothesis is concerned with employee perception of independence, credibility, competence, accessibility, and confidentiality. Consequently, a variety of apparently different arrangements may serve this principle equally well.

4) Where the development and implementation of a broad-based EAP is carried out jointly by management and union or other employee representative groups, the odds are raised that employees with problems will utilize the service. The logic of this argument is that employees will trust a program more if it is clearly endorsed by their elected representatives and that the joint auspice provides a strong support to the basis of the program, which is that people can and should be assisted in efforts to help themselves. Often the joint committees which emerge from this collaboration include one which designates each of its members as a contact person when help is needed. Since half, or a good proportion of this committee will be union representatives, this structure provides another pathway to care.

In the case of formal referrals, the union's role is extremely important in monitoring due process. The more effective this surveillance, the more likely it is that the policy will be used as intended, as long as there is joint commitment to making it work and a recognition of the need for a formal as well as a voluntary component to the program.

5) To be effective, broad-based EAPs have to be known about and understood by all those who will play a role in their activation. Consequently, supervisors and stewards must be trained in its use, and employees must be educated about the intent and procedures of the program. This is not a once in a lifetime undertaking: training and education are ongoing functions for which the employer and service provider (particularly if external) must budget and plan time. These are not simply program implementation functions, but also maintenance functions.

6) The greater the number of principles, 1-5, that are served, the greater will be the rate at which alcohol-related cases are identified. These principles are hypothesized to be synergistic.

Procedure

The data discussed here were gathered over a period of two years as they became available from ten broad-based programs. In all cases, I had personal contact with people intimately involved in these programs, either in their capacity as program directors or consultants. However, the primary sources of the data reported here are the written statistical reports emerging from the various sites. These documents are usually unpublished. Their publication status is given in references for each program discussed.

The information was not collected according to a pre-established protocol since it appeared impractical to impose a standard monitoring device across the ten programs, most of whose directors relied upon their own records for their statistical reports. In compiling the data, however, I used a standard format in so far as it was possible. The purpose of this standardization was not to encourage comparisons between programs in terms of any preconceived notion of effectiveness, but rather to ensure that the same sorts of observations were made about all of them.

We cannot generalize from the present data to broad-based programs as a whole, their variety is simply too great. The present set of examples, (see Table 22-1) is used in the present discussion either because I had the good fortune to be invited to help analyze records from a given program (Cases 3, 5, 8, 9) or because program directors or service providers were kind enough to share their data with me (Cases 1, 2, 4, 6, 7, 10). Where I was not involved in analysis I was sometimes invited to help interpret the data (Cases 4 and 10).

All cases, records permitting, were reviewed in terms of the following dimensions or variables.

Annual Identification Rate (Alcohol): This refers to the percentage of the workforce under consideration that was identified and actually seen by the EAP primary service provider for alcohol–related reasons in a given

TABLE 22-1. Comparison of Consortium Client Population

Case list	Date of program establishment	Period considered in this report	Type of work done by client organization(s)
1. London Employee Assistance Consortium (Ontario)	1976	1980–1981	Ten organizations are represented. They do widely differing kinds of work.
2. Family Service Association/Public Utility Company	1977	1981	Transportation.
3. Family Service Association/Computer System Company	1980	1981	Design and manufacture of computer hardware and systems.
4. An Ontario Government Ministry/ North Zone	1977	1978–1979	Transportation and communications.
5. A Federal Government Department, Canada	1978	1979 and 1980	Wide variety of tasks related to air, land, marine transportation.
6. Employee Counseling Consortium Programme [U.S. Federal E.A.P. Chicago Region]	1981	1981	16 sites—federal agencies of all types and sizes.
7. Occupational Assistance Service, Melbourne, Australia	1981	1981	Extremely wide variety of small (<200) organizations.
8. Lifeline Foundation Programme (Toronto)	1972	1978	75 member organizations, all affiliated with steel-workers. Typical size is less than 100 employees, but four have more than 500.
9. Coast Guard, Central Region, Canada ("Joint Venture")	1977	1981	Marine patrol, surveillance, rescue, ice-breaking, navigational aids.
10. "Interlock," Vancouver	1977	1980	15 employers ranging in size from 80 to 800 employees, and in activity from steel production to local government.

calendar year. It combines primary and secondary reasons for referral. Primary service provider, in this context, describes whomever is designated as the agency or individuals who make initial assessments and then refer clients elsewhere when appropriate.

Annual Identification Rate (All causes): This refers to the percentage of the workforce under consideration that was identified and actually seen by the EAP primary service provider for any reason in the given calendar year. This figure includes alcohol problems, while also referring to emotional, domestic, financial, and legal difficulties.

Percentage of Formal, and Informal Referrals (Alcohol): Information in this area was difficult to collect in any systematic way, with the result that standardization of terms between programs on this dimension became more than unusually hazardous. The language used to describe whether referrals were self-initiated, heavily coerced, or somewhere in between varied a great deal from one program to another. I suspect, as many others no doubt will, that the terms "voluntary" and "suggested" referral conceals a wide variety of degrees and types of coercion from many sources. We need to be particularly concerned with the relative proportions of formal versus informal referrals among alcohol cases, as opposed to the general caseload in a given program. These are within program comparisons, where we might hope for at least some consistency in the use of the terms formal, informal, voluntary, mandatory, and so on.

Location of Service refers to the location and affiliation of the primary service provider (assessment and referral being the minimal or "core" function). The main distinction is between services which are located in or affiliated with the managerial structure of the client organization(s) and services which are not.

Auspices (Management/Union): An attempt was made to determine whether or not joint union-management committees were functioning at the time the data were reported, and if so, at what level.

Services Beyond Assessment, Referral, and Direct Counseling: These services are described according to "levels." Level 1 refers to assessment, referral, and face-to-face counseling. Level 2 describes any advice or consultation that is given by the primary service provider to managers, supervisors, union officials, or medical or personnel staff about the best way to cope with problems presented by specific employees.

Level 3 activity refers to training of supervisors, union personnel, joint committee members, and medical and personnel staff with regard to the purpose and utilization of the EAP. It refers also to education aimed at the workforces in specific organizations, with a view to informing them about the policy and procedures. Sometimes these educational efforts extend to providing information about the nature and course of certain conditions for which employees might want to consult the primary service provider via whatever means are set up to facilitate this access.

Provision for Direct Access by Employee: Programs were identified in which employees could gain access to the primary service provider without having to go through one or more in-house mediators (e.g., coordinators, personnel, medical officers).

Type of Work Done by Client Organization (s): Clearly, the type of work carried out by organizations affects the sort of EAPs they are likely to have, by virtue of factors such as differing styles of management, the employment of people with widely differing socio-economic backgrounds, size, presence of external regulatory bodies, location, etc. In the case of the ten examples here, there are a number of multi-employer EAPs, with the result that many different types of organization may be represented within one program. In such cases, it will be evident that annual identification rates and all other statistics are averaged across the member organizations. This naturally conceals a considerable variation in practice, but the general trends are nonetheless reflected in the summary statistics.

Observations

The information resulting from the application of the framework just outlined was recorded on a master chart, which is not reproduced here because of space limitations. The hypotheses outlined earlier were then reviewed in the light of the compiled data, resulting in the following observations:

1) *"Broad-based programmes... will exceed the mean identification rate of narrower programmes with regard to alcohol-related cases."*

The mean identification rate with regard to alcohol-related cases in the ten programs reviewed here was 0.63% per annum based on one typical year. The range was 0.18% to 1.40% and the median was 0.58. These figures are very close to those reported by Hitchcock and Sanders (1976) in relation to a sample of occupational alcoholism (narrow) programs, where the mean was 0.64%, the median 0.45%, and the range 0.11% to 1.60%. However, in the cases which they reviewed, the identification rates were averaged over the life of the programs, although the results were still in annual terms.

It appears, then, that there is little difference between the "narrow" programs reviewed by Hitchcock and Sanders and the "broad" programs reviewed here. The significance of no real difference, however, is not easy to determine. Broad-based EAPs identify or help people to identify themselves a variety of problems other than alcohol abuse. In the present sample the mean identification rate for all problems combined (including those that were alcohol-related) was 2.15% per annum, the median was 1.90%, and the range 0.56% to 4.6%. One might argue, therefore, that since broad programs do as well as (or no worse than) narrow programs in the identification of alcohol problems, they are indeed superior because they also deal with a wide range of other problems. However, this would imply that the success rate achieved through broad-and narrow-based programs with regard to alcohol cases is the same, a subject which cannot be adequately explored within the confines of the present section. A key difference between the two types of programs, however, is thought to be the extent to which motivation to change is induced in the employee with alcohol problems as a result of applying the more formal coercive mechanisms often associated with narrow approaches.

In fact, the use of formal approaches to referral was not uncommon among the 10 cases examined here. Taken over the whole sample, 32% of all referrals were classed as formal, though the range was 5% to 90%. Among formal cases, 46% were alcohol-related, compared with 29% among informal referrals. The overall proportion of alcohol cases (primary and secondary reasons for referral combined) was just over 35%.

These results would seem to suggest that the formal components of broad-based programs are often maintained in order to deal with recalcitrant alcohol-related cases. However, Foote and Erfurt (1981) found in their study of a large manufacturing plant that more severe cases of alcoholism tended to be referred under union and medical departments rather than supervisory auspices. This implies that the value of the formal component in such programs may have been overestimated with regard to identifying severe cases of alcoholism, at least where other pathways to help existed.

Even so, the question still remains whether the auspices of identification affect the rate of treatment success that may be expected. Supervisory referrals have the element of implied or explicit coercion associated with them that is simply missing in most other referral sources—particularly union source. Other pressures, perhaps just as potent, are brought to bear from these sources, but they do not include the ultimate threat of job loss. Foote and Erfurt (op. cit.) showed that supervisory referrals, though less serious cases to begin with according to their sickness and accident records, responded best to treatment according to the same indicators. Self-referrals had sickness and accident records that were similar to those of supervisory referrals but their costs on these measures actually increased in the year after treatment. Union and medical department referrals were, as already noted, more severe cases at admission. Their costs increased also in the year after treatment.

Smart (1974), in an earlier study, had shown no difference of any significance between the treatment outcomes of alcoholics treated voluntarily and under coercion, in relation to drinking behavior, although a composite index including social behavior, work behavior, and family and financial adjustment favored the voluntary referrals. Unfortunately, there was no control for the severity of impairment at admission to treatment, so it is difficult to conclude from Smart's study whether voluntary referrals were originally less advanced in their alcohol problems than the mandatories. The likelihood is that even if the severity of problems in the two groups was identical before treatment, the people who were heavily coerced were different from the ones who were not, simply by virtue of the pressure it took to get them into treatment. Discussion of studies such as these, however, is plagued by difficulties in definition of terms such as voluntary, informal, formal, and mandatory. An approach to coercion which sees it as emanating in many different degrees from many different sources is preferable to the use of these terms.

2) *"Where broad-based programmes offer employees a variety of pathways to care they are likely to attract more alcohol-related cases..."*

The multiple pathways hypothesis can be approached from several points of view using the data at hand. The provision and use of voluntary (self-initiated) routes, the ability to have direct personal access to the primary service provider, and where appropriate, the presence of joint committee members acting as facilitators are all relevant factors in considering the multiplicity of pathways to care in a given case.

With regard to alcohol referrals, these factors did not differentiate sites with more than average numbers from those with less. However, if referrals for all causes are combined, we find the mean rate to be 3.0%, which is substantially greater than for the ten cases as a whole Possibly, then, the principles may be of greater importance for non-alcohol-related problems. Sometimes, too, variations in the alcohol-dependent populations at risk in different workforces can transform the significance of apparently similar referral rates.

3) *"Where assessment, referral and subsequent service... is external... the odds are raised that employees will use the service."*

Two of the three programs with primarily on-site service locations had above average alcohol referral rates (Cases 4 and 9 with a mean of 0.71%) while one was below average (Case 5, mean 0.35%). From this, it would appear that the hypothesis cannot be accepted as proposed. With regard to rates for all problems combined, the mean for the three programs was 1.8%, which is not significantly below the 2.15% avertage for the ten cases. It is arguable, then, that in-house programs can be managed in such a way as to generate levels of credibility comparable to those in external, third-party services.

4) *"Where... the EAP is carried out jointly by management and union... the odds are raised that employees... will utilize the service."*

Active union involvement was associated with referral rates that were both much higher or much lower than the mean rate for the whole sample. In itself, then, this factor appears not to be a determinant of referral rates.

5) *"Broad-based EAPs have to be known about and understood by all those who will play a role in their activation."*

Superficially, there was little variation in the extent to which training and education were carried on for supervisors, union officials, and employees across the ten sites. Where there was evidence of greater effort–e.g., scheduled retraining and educational campaigns–referral rates tended to be somewhat higher but not to a significant degree.

6) *"... these principles are hypothesized to be synergistic."*

The programs reviewed in this paper do not show any wholly consistent trend which would allow for a simple synergistic interpretation of the various "principles" of EAP operation outlined in the hypotheses, at least with regard to alcohol-specific identification, i.e., the rate of alcohol referrals does not increase in proportion to the number of principles served.

Conclusion

The broad-based programs reviewed in this study performed as well as narrower programs described in the literature in terms of their average rates of identifying alcohol-related problems. Variations in the rate of identification within this sample were not found to be related in any clear way to the variable application of a set of principles hypothesized to be important in maximizing this rate. The evidence was in some cases suggestive, and in others equivocal. All that can be concluded is that broad-based programs are often capable of maintaining a healthy alcoholism casefinding component while serving the needs of a large number of other people with a variety of other problems. There is no clear evidence from this sample that the impact of broad programs on alcohol abusers is diluted in comparison with the more specific programs. Nonetheless, it seems arguable that broad programs should maintain a vigorous formal mechanism for making referrals, since this appears to be the only way of guiding some alcohol abusers into treatment.

Research methods for studying the most effective ways of providing assistance to employees with problems unquestionably needs to be improved. One of the basic problems is the difficulty of making comparisons between workplaces that are not alike both in terms of organizational structure and in terms of variations in the prevalence of employee problems. These are factors which complicate the findings in the present study. A more useful model for the study of employee assistance may be one in which the criterion for an effective program or approach is the degree to which it has been fitted to the norms, expectations, and culture of a given organization or set of organizations. In some cases this may mean the development of an alcohol-specific program emphasizing formal referrals. In another, it may mean the development of a broad-based EAP with multiple pathways to care, a vigorous health promotion component, and an offsite third party service provider.

Case List References

1. Kaplun, J. *London Employee Assistance Consortium Annual Report*, 1980–1981 (and other such reports). 472 Ridout St. N., London, Ontario, N6A 2P7.
2/3. Wright, D. *Statistical Reports of the Employee Assistance Division of the Family Service Assn.*, Toronto, 1978–1982. 14 College St., Toronto.

4. Gray, R.H., and Poudrier, L.M. *A preliminary report on voluntary referrals in the work-place: A two year follow-up on a preventive approach to an EAP in a group of public employees.* Addiction Research Foundation, Substudy #1183, 1981.
5. Shain, M. and Lefebvre, P. *Factors influencing use of Employee Assistance Programmes: An example from Transport Canada's Counselling Services.* Addiction Research Foundation, Substudy #1191, 1981.
6. Koca, G. *The Federal Effort: Where we are, how we got there and where we're going.* Paper presented at Conserving Human Resources: Perspectives for the 80's. A.L.M.A.C.A. Detroit 1981. [Also, memoranda from Office of Personnel Management, Chicago Region, U.S. Govt.]
7. Ritman, T. *Occupational Assistance Service Annual Reports* (Melbourne), 1981. Hawthorn Square, Suite 17, 1st Floor, 104 Burwood Rd., Hawthorn 3122, Australia.
8. Groeneveld, J., Simon, J., and Shain, M. *The Problem Employee's Programme of Lifeline Foundation.* Substudy #971, Addiction Research Foundation, 1978.
9. French, P., Ankers, K., Larkin, E., and Shain, M. *EAP Monitoring System Reports,* Metro EAP Resource Centre, 175 College St., Toronto, 1982.
10. Lynch, J.A. *Variations in programme usage in different occupational settings.* Paper presented at the National Council on Alcoholism's "National Alcoholism Forum," May 6th, Seattle, Washington, 1980.

References

Addiction Research Foundation of Ontario. The Mandate, Functions and Goals of the Addiction Research Foundation. Addiction Research Foundation, 33 Russell Street, Toronto. April 14th, 1982.

Dunkin, W.S. *How and why to "sell alcoholism" in EAPs?* Labor-Management Alcoholism Journal, 12, 1, 26–30, 1982.

Foote, A., and Erfurt, J.C. *Effectiveness of comprehensive EAPS at reaching alcoholics.* J. Drug Issues II, (2), 217–232, 1981.

Hitchcock, L.C., and Sanders, M. *A survey of alcohol and drug abuse programs in the railroad industry.* National Technical Information Service, U.S. Dept. of Commerce, Springfield, Va. 22161, 1976.

Roman, P.M. *Employee Alcoholism and Employee Assistance Programs: Similarities and differences in major corporations in 1979.* Labor-Management Alcoholism, Journal IX, 6, 211–222, 1980.

Shain, M. *An exploration of the ability of broad-based EAPs to generate alcohol-related referrals.* Addiction Research Foundation, Internal Document #8, 1983.

Smith, D. et al. *Report of the Task Force on Employee Assistance Programmes.* Addiction Research Foundation of Ontario, 33 Russell St., Toronto, 1978.

Smart, R.G. *Employed alcoholics treated voluntarily and under constructive coercion—a follow-up study.* Quarterly Journal of Studies on Alcohol, 35: 196–209, 1974.

23

Evaluation of EAP Programming
William G. Durkin

Introduction

In 1980 a committee was established to develop standards for EAPs. The panel consisted of members of industry, labor, and the federal government, and was sanctioned by the major professional organizations involved in the EAP field (Almacan, 1981) Their work over the next year produced a set of standards that identified five major components of an EAP: 1) policy and procedures, 2) administrative functions, 3) education and training, 4) resources, and 5) evaluation. Of the five components, evaluation has been consistently recognized as being in highest demand but shortest supply.

Section Overview

This section will attempt to identify and discuss methods of EAP evaluaton and the practical issues that have to be considered when conducting evaluation in the industrial setting. It will not deal with the use of statistical techniques, such as measures of significance or appropriate sampling design. General textbooks on statistics should be referred to for this information. Definitions of what are "good" or "normal" results from operating an EAP will not be offered. To do so would assume that all EAPs are very similar in design and operation. This is not the case.

To Evaluate or not to evaluate

One would be hard pressed at this stage in the development of EAPs to offer any argument against the need for evaluation. Yet, there continues to be an element in the field which suggests that evaluation of a program may be counter productive. It argues that an inability to adequately measure all the benefits of a program may cause an evaluator to conservatively state program results. They caution that outcome may be measured against unrealistic program goals that may tend to obscure the broader social role and impact of programs (Shain and Groeneveld, 1980). Possible compromise of confidential information is also raised as a concern.

Some EAP managers feel they are being unfairly singled out when other organization functions such as supervisory training, medical, and public relations are rarely required to demonstrate their cost-effectiveness. Akabas and Donovan (1982) point out that cost-effective data is available in less than five percent of psychotherapy research studies, yet is expected in almost all EAPs.

Reasons for Evaluation

Evaluators need to know, or at least examine, their reasons for evaluation before embarking upon the task. Schulberg et al. (1969) identified two groups of reasons why evaluation is undertaken. Organization-oriented reasons center around the need to demonstrate positive impact, cost-effectiveness, and progress toward objectives. The second reason to evaluate is based on the administrator's personal needs. He/she may see evaluation as a means of receiving increased attention in order to get needed budget or staff changes or as an aid in furthering his/her career. From a broader perspective, evaluation of individual programs contributes to the knowledge of what is effective and what is ineffective in the field of employee assistance programming.

Problems in Evaluation

The difficulties faced in evaluation frequently have their basis in problems of methodology and definition. However, even underlying those two issues is the more basic consideration of what is realistically possible versus what is idealistically desirable.

Staffing

Most program administrators are ill-equipped by virtue of training to conduct sophisticated research. Additionally, most programs do not have sufficient staff to devote enough time to evaluation studies of a caliber that would hold up under rigorous examination (Presnall, 1981; Schlenger and Haywood, 1976). Scientifically valid studies would require laborious and sometimes impossible efforts at data collection.

Preparation

Often, programs have not given sufficient thought to an evaluation system in their initial planning process. Attention must be paid to an evaluation component of the program in its developmental stage. This issue will be dealt with in the development section.

Standardization

Because of the lack of standardized measures and definitions for such vital variables as "utilization rates" and "success," program administrators have difficulty in comparing their programs with others. The numerous qualifying remarks, exceptions, and other lengthy explanations of results found in EAP research studies reflect this. One of the most widely quoted indicators of success–the penetration rate–is frequently misused, mis-understood, and ill-defined (Schlenger and Hayward, 1976). Over time, organized efforts in the profession should resolve this problem.

Data Collection

Even in the largest and most sophisticated organizations the type and amount of data available is less than adequate for meaningful evaluation. Frequently, poor performance review programs will hamper an assessment of performance change over time. In addition, existing record keeping systems in the company may be incomplete, inaccessible, or will require so much work to get information that a meaningful evaluation becomes almost a hopeless goal. In the end, the researcher frequently settles for less than optimal research designs, data collection techniques, and analytical schemes. Indeed, the art of evaluation research may be appropriately described as an effort to make do with considerably less than what is ideally desirable (Rossi and Wright, 1977).

While the program administrator is faced with state-of-the-art EAP evaluation that is less than desirable, he/she should not use that as a license to retreat from evaluation efforts, or produce evaluation findings that can not be defended. Program improvement cannot take place without program evaluation.

Developing an Evaluation System

The maxim "we never have time to do it right the first time, but always find time to do it over again," should be borne in mind in the developmental stages of an EAP. This is particularly true in setting up the evaluation system, since you will want to compare the same or similar information from year to year over a long period. Therefore, it is not advisable to develop a system that may require frequent changes in design. If adequate thought is given to developmental stages, a large amount of work and frustration can be avoided in the future.

Stating Goals and Objectives

The first step in developing an evaluation system is the identification of specific goals. Without goals, progress or success cannot be evaluated. Goals can be stated in broad or general terms, usually preceded by such phrases as: reduction of; improvement of; enhancement of; or maintenance of. Wherever possible, goals should be stated in a way that they can be quantitatively measured and include specific time frames in which changes are to occur.

In setting goals, one must seek a consensus of the various parties involved, such as labor, health professionals, benefit plan administrators, and various levels of management. Caution must be taken to set goals that are reasonably attainable, and to recognize the expectations–which frequently may be quite limited–of management. It is advisable to break down long–range goals into sub-goals so that progress or lack of progress toward ultimate goal obtainment can be measured. This allows for periodic corrective action to keep the program on track.

In formulating goals, a realistic appraisal of the program's capability to measure them must be made. This appraisal must not be only in terms of data available, but must also take into account staff time and expertise available. A pragmatic view must be taken of what can and should be measured to adequately judge the effectiveness of the program.

Types of Evaluation

The main purposes of evaluation are:

1) To provide objective estimates of achievement
2) To guide staff in conducting program activities

To achieve these purposes, a program requires three types of evaluation:

1. **Process Evaluation.** If we do not evaluate a program periodically during its operation, we may not recognize errors in program conceptualization that are causing problems. Process evaluation, sometimes called progress evaluation, formative evaluation, or developmental evaluation, is useful in alerting staff to operational weaknesses of the program. Monitoring variables, such as supervisory and self-referrals, sex, age, how individuals heard about the program, union or non-union employee, and type of problem

presented, can give administrators early warning signals that their expectations of program activity, impact, or operation are not being met.

2. **Impact Evaluation.** Impact is measured by changes brought about in those employees and organization units participating in the program. A program that has a positive impact is not necessarily producing a positive cost-benefit result. The cost of producing change may exceed the productivity benefits gained by the corporation. For this reason, it is wise to identify impact measurement separately from cost-benefit measurement. It is, however, the rare instance when impact and outcome (cost-benefit) evaluations will not mirror each other's results if a program has been in operation for a reasonable period and has an acceptable utilization rate.

3. **Outcome Evaluation.** An outcome evaluation is normally presented in the form of a cost-benefit analysis. It is used to identify the benefits—both tangible and intangible—and the cost—both direct and indirect—of conducting a program. A ratio of benefits to cost is usually calculated to indicate the "return" that a company receives from its investment in a program, i.e., 2:1, which would indicate a two dollar return for every one dollar invested.

The major difficulties in conducting outcome evaluation involve measurement and quantification of all variables involved, and stating them in terms of dollars and cents. Most program administrators feel it is impossible to identify, much less quantify, all pertinent variables. Quantification of qualitative changes in performance is particularly difficult to accomplish.

Evaluation Design

With each type of evaluation conducted (process, impact, and outcome), various research designs can be used.

An EAP evaluation system should include one or a combination of the following elements:

1) Retrospective analysis
2) Control group
3) Comparison against organization "norms"

Retrospective Analysis. Retrospective analysis simply means the study of past events. In EAPs, it refers to the comparison of variables for two or more distinct periods of time, usually before intervention and after intervention. A retrospective evaluation design can be used in process, impact, and outcome evaluation. In impact and outcome evaluation, variables such as absenteeism, sickness benefits, measurable performance, or grievances, should be compared for at least two periods of time. Participants' absenteeism, etc., for the year prior to entering the program should be compared to absenteeism, etc., during a year after entering the program. Caution must be observed when measuring results shortly after a person seeks assistance, since it is in this period that higher medical costs and absenteeism can occur because of involvement in treatment. Presnall (1981) and Foote et al. (1978) advise a minimum two-year follow-up period. Hoffman (1983) suggests a five-year period should pass before reliable evaluation can take place. A problem in conducting retrospective studies is that there commonly is a lack of adequate data on individuals before they enter the EAP, most notably among white collar workers (Foote et al., 1978).

Control Group. The use of a control group is necessary to state with confidence that changes that have taken place result from the EAP, rather than from some other unknown factor. For instance, is a reduction in absenteeism by program participants a result of the EAP or a result of a strict new policy on absenteeism, which the company has just implemented? Only the method of comparing program participants (experimental group) with a similar group of employees who have not participated in the program (control group) can establish a cause and effect relationship between the program and changes observed. Considerations should be taken in establishing control group centers around their similarity to the experimental group (program participants). Efforts should be made to match them based on factors such as age, sex, job, and work location (see Jones and Vischi, 1979).

Comparison Against Organization "Norms". The use of this method presumes the ability to obtain information regarding company averages or norms for such variables as absenteeism, accidents, etc. The evaluator can compare organization norms for absenteeism, etc., before and after implementation of the program. However, an EAP may not be large or active enough to impact the absenteeism rates of the total organizaton. Therefore, use of norms in this fashion is often misleading. A better method is to compare a variable such as the "absenteeism rate" for program participants to absenteeism norms for the organization. However, absenteeism rates for program participants may be higher than the norm simply because the program deals with employees who commonly have serious problems in this area. Generally speaking, the use of normative data is the weakest and least desirable method of evaluating program results.

Variables

Listed in this section is a review of the variables discussed in EAP evaluation literature, followed–in some cases–by comments and reference citations regarding their use. A variable, as defined in this section, is an item or category of data recorded, evaluated, calculated, measured, or compared in the evaluation process. The review is not comprehensive, but it includes most variables that the literature deems as relevant. It is not recommended that evaluators attempt to measure and analyze all variables mentioned. Each program has different needs, different abilities to evaluate, and different qualities of data available, therefore each program will evaluate a different array of variables.

In choosing which variables should be evaluated, program administrators must compromise between their evaluation needs and their capabilities. In their excellent study, Foote, Erfurt, Strauch, and Guzzardo (1978) examine the use of many pertinent variables, but suggest that the practitioner must be reasonable in what can actually be transformed into dollar figures. They suggest that, at a minimum, absenteeism, medical costs, workers compensation, and sickness and accident benefits should be included.

The Necessity of Clear Definition

Sufficient thought should go into the description or definition of variables. For example, the variable "cases," which ultimately translates into the very useful and commonly used evaluation statistic "utilization rate," needs to be clearly defined. Does it include family members who may have access to the program? Does it include returning cases as opposed to a new case? Does it include telephone inquiries? If variables are clearly defined, then administrators will be better able to compare their program results with other programs, and to present their evaluation findings to others for study.

Client Variables

Any evaluation system must have, as its base, adequate information on individuals who use the EAP. Foote et al. (1978) utilized a data collection form that itemized the following client variables. For space purposes, they are presented below in a consolidated fashion.

- Name of the department or organizational unit
- Case number
- Problem identification:
- On-the-job problem (quality of work, quantity of work, absenteeism, etc.)
- Employee presenting problem (alcohol, drugs, family, marital, etc.)

- Counselor's evaluation (type of problem)
- Treatment agency diagnosis
- Acceptance of program intervention (yes/no)
- Employee occupational category (professional, managerial, clerical, laborer, etc.)
- Employee wage
- Age
- Sex
- Ethnic group
- Marital status
- Seniority (number of years employed by the company)
- Type of referral (self, management, union, medical)
- Type of treatment or service (in-patient, out-patient, other)
- Date of program entry

Other Client Information

- Absenteeism (hours)
- Number of visits to medical
- Number of disciplines
- Number of grievances
- Number of on-the-job accidents
- Workers compensation ($)
- Sickness and accident benefits ($)

Further examination of the literature reveals other client variables that can be included on a data collection or intake form:

- Work location
- Union represented (yes/no)
- Job title
- How employee learned of EAP (training program, bulletin board, etc.)
- Educational level
- Client category (employee, spouse, dependent, retiree)

Process Variables

To evaluate whether the program is being utilized in the manner and degree originally intended, the following process variables can be examined:

Casefinding

This is an assessment of the amount, types, and sources of cases a program is receiving. If the case load is not within expected parameters, it may be caused by a procedural or "process deficiency."

Treatment Agencies

Is feedback from clients concerning treatment agencies favorable? Does feedback from the agency indicate the client is making progress? Systematic procedures should be maintained to gather this type of data.

Acceptance of EAP Referral

High rates of rejection of EAP assessment and referral may indicate assessment deficiencies, misuse of EAP as a resource, or other program weaknesses.

Informal Evaluations and Reports about EAP

The program administrator should be aware of and solicit informal comments from employees, unions, and management.

Follow-up

Is the program following up on the client at appropriate intervals?

Awareness of Program

While utilization rates indicate that employees are aware of the program, other surveys–both formal and informal– can be used.

Sources of Referrals

Are various departments and functions, such as medical and personnel, referring employees in appropriate numbers? No referrals from the medical department may indicate a program weakness.

Supervisory versus self-referral

No guidelines can be given here, but the trend has been toward increased self-referrals. Past program experience can provide a yardstick to measure whether the program has taken an unexpected or unwanted direction.

Training

Upon intake, clients should be asked if it was a training program that motivated them to use the EAP. Additionally, questionnaires should be used as part of training programs to assess their effectiveness.

Other Types of Publicity

The effectiveness of other types of program publicity including mailouts, bulletin board posters, or articles in the company newspaper should be gauged. Charting changes in referral activity concurrent with various publicity efforts provides an indication of effectiveness, but no direct cause/effect relationship. Client interviews are better, more direct measurements.

Evaluation of evaluation

A personal, honest assessment of your evaluation effort should be made. For example, is your evaluation an acceptable research product? If not, the amount and type of data used, effort expended, or evaluaton design may not be satisfactory.

Impact Variables

Evaluation of impact is a method of measuring the direction and, if possible, the degree of change in program participants and the organization. Additionally, it is being alert to any unexpected effect of the program, either positive or negative. There is a wide variety of impact variables that can be evaluated. Most variables commonly used are listed in the Outcome segment of this section.

The most commonly studied impact variables are:

- Absenteeism
- Alcoholism referrals
- Productivity
- Success
- Medical Claims
- Turnover
- Minority groups
- Accidents

Success, probably more than most variables, needs to be clearly defined. It has commonly been applied to the outcome of alcoholism cases. Some programs define it as improvement in job behavior, others as a period of abstinence (Trice and Roman, 1972, Schlenger and Hayward, 1976). Between the two definitions there lies a range of other possibilities.

Outcome Variables (Cost/Benefit Variables)

While evaluation of outcome variables usually yields data that parallels evaluation of impact variables, such is not always the case. A program's impact may be quite positive in terms of direction of change, but its outcome in terms of yielding a return on investment may not.

Data on outcome variables is usually stated in both absolute terms and in dollars and cents terms, i.e., number of disability claims and their related cost. Outcome variables can be analyzed separately to determine whether special attention should be devoted to a segment of the program that does not show desired results. For example, treatment costs may be the "swing factor" that could produce a cost-effective program. It would then be appropriate to investigate use of less expensive treatment programs.

Commonly evaluated outcome variables are:

- Productivity (requires effective performance review program)
- Sickness
- Absenteeism (Some studies exclude a treatment period when using this data.)
- Turnover
- Medical benefit claims (The program should expect increased cost during client initial participation (Presnall, 1981).)
- Disability claims
- Tardiness
- Visits to medical department
- Grievances
- Discharges
- Workers compensation
- Disciplinary actions
- Overtime costs
- Insurance premiums

Normative Data

To assist in the evaluation of program impact and outcome, whenever possible, normative data should be gathered. Normative data plays a supportive role in evaluation when used in conjunction with data on program participants. As previously mentioned, caution should be taken in using only normative data.

Normative data frequently used in evaluation:

- Average replacement cost for a new employee
- Average training cost for a new employee
- Average cost of a grievance procedure

- Average cost of a medical department visit
- Average salary
- Average absences per employee
- Average sick benefits ($) per employee
- Average tardiness
- Average medical claims ($) per employee

Using medical department visits as an example, cost savings can be calculated as follows: Reduction in visits to medical department × Average cost of a medical department visit = Cost savings.

Intangible Variables

These variables are worth mentioning, but they vary in value, depending on how convincingly they are used and on the attitudes and values of company management. Their main deficiency is that they are subjective. However, an effort at quantification could lend them some limited statistical credibility.

Commonly used intangible variables:

- Family problems that did not happen
- Reduction of coworker and supervisory anxiety
- Improved morale
- Improved decision making
- Public relations value–internal and external
- Improved relations with labor unions
- Meeting the "corporate social responsibility of the organization"
- Ability to direct employees to less costly forms of treatment (Cummings, 1977)
- A particularly valuable or hard-to replace employee assisted by the program

Contractor Variables

Many programs utilize contractors or EAP consultants to deliver services to employees. It is important to motivate contractors to achieve optimal performance, by conducting separate evaluation studies of their activities and results, or closely scrutinizing those offered by the contractors. Most of the client, process, impact, and outcome variables mentioned in the previous sections should be utilized to evaluate the services of an EAP contractor/consultant.

Particular attention should be devoted to gathering client (employee) evaluations of services they received from contractors. A questionnaire designed to protect confidentiality should request the following information:

- General demographic data on the employee (age, sex)
- Type of problem for which assistance was sought
- Ease of access to the consultant
- Level of professional services received (poor, average, good, excellent)
- Degree of helpfulness in dealing with
  - personal life
  - occupational life
- A list of any difficulties with the consultant
- Would the client recommend the program to other employees? (yes/no)

Measurement

A program cannot hope to measure its total impact on the organization. Some organization effects are unmeasurable (see intangible variables) in quantifiable terms. The first step in developing an evaluation system is to set up goals that can be measured. Goals should relate to variables that can be accessed and measured with reasonable simplicity.

Two characteristics that goal statements should possess are that:

1) Variables identified in the statement must be well explained. The variables' parameters and characteristics must be explicitly defined. For instance, tardiness might be defined as reporting for work ten or more minutes after assigned starting time.
2) Variables identified should be capable of being quantitatively stated. This may not be possible in every case, but variables that can not be quantified should receive less attention and less emphasis.

Data Collection

With the advent of the desk-top computer and other advancements in computer technology, storing, processing and manipulation of data is increasingly less difficult. However, the quality, quantity, and accessibility to pertinent data still remains one of the larger problems in the EAP field.

It cannot be emphasized too strongly that a data collection system should be an integral part of initial program development. Intake procedures, follow-up methods, and determination of final case disposition must be constructed to allow for the collection of relevant data on each client. Program records should be designed to facilitate retrieval. Categories of information (variables) to be gathered and evaluated should be selected with care, taking into consideration usefulness, ease of access, and reliability. At a minimum, the system must provide data that will measure progress toward program goals. To ensure timely availability of data, input to a system should occur on a current basis or at regular intervals—probably monthly.

Computerize Your System

Computer systems are so widely available, there is practically no excuse for a program not to be storing information in this fashion. Before embarking on development of a computerized system, an administrator should thoroughly investigate existing data systems in the company, such as medical, employee benefits, and personnel and payroll systems to integrate with them or capitalize on their availability. Larger, mid-sized, and even smaller organizations have internal resources that could assist in setting up a system. Presnall (1981) suggests the use of outside consultants, because internal EAP staff lack the time and often do not have skills to conduct acceptable evaluation.

A system should allow for the maximum manipulation of variables on which data is collected. Each variable should be capable of being compared to each other variable or group of variables in the system. Such a system would be capable of answering questions such as: How many female alcoholism problems were identified in the 20-25 year-old age group? How many of these were management referrals? What was the total reduction in medical cost of this group? What was it for program participants as a whole?

Presenting Results

The final product of an evaluation is a written report detailing changes that have taken place as a result of the program, coupled with an interpretation of those results. The report should have a public relations function as well as an informative function. The less the report relies on estimates, "guestimates," and nonquantifiable data the better credibility it will have in the eyes of its reader. The use of graphs and tables is desirable.

Results are generally presented in the form of decreases or increases in the variables discussed in previous sections. A report should mention whether goals were accomplished and, if not, an explanation of why not, accompanied by recommendations.

Most EAPs have an implicit goal of providing a return on investment to the company. Therefore, most programs will attempt to quantify change in terms of dollars and cents. However, the program administrator should be aware that an economic return is not the only indicator of success. Management may not seek results in strict economic terms. They may realize that the company is receiving an economic return but one which is not wholly measurable. It is advisable for the program administrator to mention this reality when presenting results.

It is commonly acknowledged that, in the absence of an EAP, problems such as alcoholism fester for many years before action (usually firing) is taken. An evaluation report should emphasize that cost savings accumulate for a period of years. Savings are realized and should be calculated for each and every year a problem would have gone unnoticed or undealt with had there not been an EAP to deal with it.

When presenting results, two audiences should be borne in mind:

1) Management of the organization served by the EAP.
   Usually, this is the most important audience. Data should be presented in a manner that will be useful, interesting, and make sense to recipients. Where possible, breakdowns should be given to reflect separate data for larger sub-units in the company. Selectivity should be exercised in determining managers who should receive the report. Broad distribution can invite the scrutiny of individuals who may lack understanding of the function and purpose of the program. Yet, distribution should be broad enough to reach those people who need to know and who can make a positive contribution to the program in terms of support or constructive critique.

2) EAP professionals outside of the organization.
   To further professionalism of the field, reports should be presented in terms that can be standardly applied and compared across organizations. Increased publication of research in the EAP profession is resulting in the evolvement of commonly used terms, definitions, and methods of evaluation. Further coordinative efforts of the professional organizations in the field are necessary.

Confidentiality

Guarantees of confidentiality communicated by the program must be observed. Not to do so would have legal ramifications and potential negative impact on the trust employees place in the program.

The need for client confidentiality can inhibit the evaluation effort. Therefore, it must be considered at the earliest stages of developing a program. Program intake procedures, follow-up procedures, and associated data collection functions should be designed to allow easy access to needed information, while preserving the anonymity of the client.

A common situation is that the EAP intake procedure collects a certain amount of data on the client but must rely on other information systems in the organization to conduct a reasonably thorough evaluation. Strategies must be designed to provide linkage between these two sources that protects client confidentiality. This might involve seeking the help of computer systems specialists.

SUMMARY

Evaluation studies of EAPs have been infrequent. Some reasons are: 1) lack of standard definitions for variables measured, 2) inadequate staffing of programs, and 3) a less than desirable data base.

In the earliest stages of EAP development, administrators should incorporate procedures and record-keeping systems that will facilitate evaluation. Goals that can be quantitatively measured should be set.

The major areas of EAP evaluation are: 1) process, 2) impact, and 3) outcome. Each area has particular, and frequently the same, variables that should be measured.

When presenting results to management, attention should be paid to the intagible benefits of a program as well as to the tangible (cost-savings) benefits. Wherever possible, quantitatively stated results should be offered.

REFERENCES

Akabas, S. H., and Donovan, R. *Cost Containment and Cost Benefit Analysis in Employee Counselling Programs: An Annotated Bibliography.* New York: Industrial Social Welfare Center, Columbia University School of Social Work, 1982.

The ALMACAN. *ALMACA Approves Testing of Proposed New Program Standards.* Published by The Association of Labor-Management Administrators and Consultants on Alcoholism. Arlington, Virginia: Issue 11; Pg. 1, November, 1981.

Cummings, N. *Prolonged (Ideal) vs. Short Term (Realistic) Psychotherapy,* Professional Psychology. #8: 491–501, 1977.

Foote, A., Erfurt, J. C., Strauch, P. A., and Guzzardo, T. L. *Cost Effectiveness of Occupational Employee Assistance Programs–Test of an Evaluation Method.* Ann Arbor, Michigan: Institute of Labor and Industrial Relations, The University of Michigan–Wayne State Univ., 1978.

Hoffmann, J. J. *Guide to Evaluating Employee Assistance Programs and Staff.* The EAP Digest. Vol. 3, No. 1: 36–38, Jan./Feb. 1983.

Jones, K. and Vischi, T. R. *Impact of Alcohol, Drug Abuse and Mental Health Treatment in Medical Care Utilization: A Review of the Research Literature.* Supplement to *Medical Care.* 17:12, 1979.

Presnall, L. F. *Occupational Counselling and Referral Systems.* Salt Lake City: Utah Alcoholism Foundation, 1981.

Rossi, P. H. and Wright, S. R. *Evaluation Research–An Assessment of Theory, Practice, and Politics.* Evaluation Quarterly. Vol. 1, No. 1: 5–53, February, 1977.

Schlenger, W. E. and Hayward, J. *Occupational Programming: Problems in Research and Evaluation.* Alcohol Health and Research World. Spring Issue: 18–22, 1976.

Schulberg, H. C., Sheldon, A. and Baker, F. *Program Evaluation in the Health Fields.* Chapter 3: Knutson, A. *Evaluation for What.* New York: Human Sciences Press, 1969

Shain, M. and Groeneveld, J. *Employee Assistance Programs.* Lexington, Mass.: D. C. Health & Co., 1980.

Trice, H. M. and Roman, P. M. *Spirits and Demons at Work.* Ithaca, N. Y.: Cornell Univ. 1972.

24

Monitoring the Development and Operation of an EAP

Edward J. Larkin
Patricia A. French
Kim Ankers

Introduction

The development and operation of an EAP can be divided into at least two different tasks. The first task is the analysis of the organization within which the EAP is to function and the design of a program which fits the unique characteristics and needs of the organization and its employees. The second task is the setting in place of operational units for the continued maintenance and operation of the EAP.

The completion of the first task requires a detailed description and analysis of the organization in question, while the second task requires the development of a monitoring and feedback system for the long-term maintenance and operation of the EAP.

Organizational Analysis

Pugh, Hickson, Hinings, McDonald, Turner,and Luptom (1963) have developed a system for the analysis of organizations that relates to contextual and structural variables. Contextual variables include the origin and history of an organization (i.e., private versus public funding), the size of the organization (number of employees), the technology available to the organization (i.e., the degree of integration of the work process), and, the interdependence of the organization (i.e., the extent of dependence on customers, suppliers and other organizations). Structural variables include specialization, i.e., the division of the organization into specialized roles; standardization–the degree of standard rules and procedures; formalization–the degree of written instructions and procedures; and centralization–the degree of decision–making authority at the top of the administrative hierarchy.

In addition to these concepts, there are inventories for the description of the characteristics of individual organizations. For example, Likert (1967) has devised a complex method of measuring organizational performance. Litwin and Stringer (1968) have developed questionnaires concerning the relationship between organizational environment and different types of motivation. As the EAP task is relatively specialized, a form was designed specifically for EAP consultant use, and is described below.

Company Profile and Analysis Form

The Company Profile and Analysis Form (CPA) was designed (see Table 24-1) to be completed by an EAP consultant during initial inverviews with the representatives of client organizations. It collects information about the bureaucratic structure of the organization, performance standards, existing health care services, the companies' current policies regarding alcohol use, information concerning union-management relationships, and various aspects of the work environment.

The use of the CPA or some similar instrument can provide an EAP consultant with a quick, but focused, method of describing a given organization's current circumstances, structures, and procedures as they relate to the development of an EAP.

The Policy and Program Development Form

The development and design of an EAP for a particular organization may require many meetings to describe to the company and labor officials the problems, context, focus, and procedures of an EAP.

Following the initial decision to proceed with the development of an EAP, there is a need to design, and ultimately seek approval for, an

TABLE 24-1. Company Profile and Analysis Form

Organization Structures	Composition and characteristics of the work force
	Work environment
Organization Systems	Occupational health facilities
	Job standards/Goals/Specifications
	Conflict resolution/Appeal procedures
	Policy on alcohol in the workplace
	Performance management
	Attendance
Organizational Relationship	Management-union relationships
	Communication channels–formal and informal

employee assistance policy by the organization. Subsequent to this decision, union, management, and health care personnel must be acquainted with the intended purpose of such a program and the various systems, mechanics, policies, and procedures that it entails.

This can be a very long and involved process, extending for months and years in the case of some large and diffuse organizations. The Policy and Program Development Form (PPDF) was designed (see Table 24-2) for the purpose of describing and documenting these events. The PPDF is to be completed by the EAP consultant and logs the initial steps in program devlopment from the initail contact to the post policy implementation contacts. For example, the areas of interest include: the area of the organization that initially demonstrated interest in formulating an EAP policy; initial information sessions held to acquaint management and labor representatives of the organizaition about the EAP's policy development phase; a logging of the various implementation events; the creation of a community social/health care resource file for the EAP coordinator; the details associated with training sessions conducted to introduce the policy

TABLE 24-2. Policy and Program Development Form

Section I		
Pre-policy	I) Sources of interest	initial information session and number
	II) Consultation meetings	representative groups and their expectations number of sessions leading to commitment
	III) Policy and procedures formation	representative groups resources allocated chronology of formation
Section 2		
Implementation	I) Training sessions	attendees (participants) methods and materials duration
Section 3		
Follow-up	I) Follow-up periods	who, when, and what
	II) Annual survey	expectations met/not met effects of EAP on • procedures • job standards • performance review

and procedures of the program to management and labor representatives; and, employee information sessions introducing the program.

It can be seen that there are ways of analyzing organizations along variables which will assist the EAP consultant in the development of an EAP designed for a specific organization. As well, it is possible to document in a systematic fashion, the various steps involved in policy development and staff training. Completion of these tasks constitutes, for the EAP consultant, the initial phase, i.e., the design and establishment of an operating EAP. The next step is to put into place methods of assisting the maintenance and operation of the program.

Monitoring the Operation of an EAP

As has been noted elsewhere (Larkin, 1974; James, 1962), there are at least three major approaches to the monitoring or evaluation of programs put into place to achieve certain valued results. Two of them are of relevance here.

Evaluation By Objectives

The evaluation by objectives model is used to determine the degree to which previously selected objectives are achieved. As applied to an EAP, this model is used when attempts are made to designate existing levels of alcoholism or other employee problems and to set up methods to reduce or eliminate the existence of given problems. Usual measures for determining the degree to which such programs are successful have focused on four outcomes:

1) Effort
2) Performance
3) Adequacy of performance
4) Efficiency of methods

Evaluations of effort involve counting of activities or functions that are believed to be attempts at achieving program goals. For example, one might choose to evaluate an EAP by counting the number of seminars, leaflets, pamphlets, posters, or staff hours related to the program. Evaluation of performance includes counting the number of individuals who are assisted through the EAP. Adequacy of performance relates to the issue of the effectiveness of a program, i.e., the number of individuals who should have been referred for alcohol abuse as opposed to the number who, in fact, were referred for assistance. Evaluation of efficiency of a program involves the comparison of different methods to achieve the same objective. This level of evaluation would involve, for example, the number of clients referred through voluntary versus formal methods of referral or the number of employees seeking assistance from the company health unit as opposed to external treatment resources.

Systems Approach

A second model of evaluation involves the use of a systematic or systems approach to evaluation. A systems model rests on the belief that an organization is functioning at more than one level and towards more than one objective at any given time. In the current context, it is clear that the major objective of providing a service or producing a profit for shareholders competes for resources with the organization's EAP. As described below, the EAP monitoring system developed by the authors includes methods of feeding back to decision-making groups the information about the effectiveness of educational and staff awareness programs, as well as the outcome of requests for assistance by employees. The impact of greater or lesser resources allocated to the EAP can then be related to the outcome of the program.

The monitoring system described utilizes the systems approach to evaluation, as it includes feedback mechanisms that integrate the EAP and the organization environment, allowing for the continued modification of procedures and objectives. The selection of a systematic feedback approach to monitoring was done deliberately to avoid the pitfalls noted by Schulberg, Sheldon, and Baker, (1969), who note that the use of the evaluation by objectives framework seldom provides information that is useful in the modification of programs. In an EAP context, for example, this would include designating appropriate "penetration rates" and the setting up of organization systems to determine the extent to which the rate is achieved. The evaluation by objectives focus need not involve the simultaneous collection or information which might account for the extent to which the program fails to meet its objectives. Specifically, the use of predetermined rates of referral as a method for determining the success of an EAP is considered to be less satisfactory than the development of a monitoring system that includes systematic feedback to program officials. A systems evaluation approach can result in a balanced and measured allocation of resources that varies as programmatic success, organizational circumstances, and working climate vary.

The Information Requirements

The evaluation of an EAP involves the collection of information of interest by the EAP consultant, by management, and by labor. As a general rule, EAP consultants will want to know the information needs of management and labor. These needs will be in addition to the specific concerns reflected in the CPA and PPDF noted above.

Management Information

Based on the experience to date, the following categories of information needs are presented as representing concerns to be expressed by virtually all organizations contemplating the installation of an EAP.

1. Resources utilized to implement the EAP (e.g., the number of managers, supervisory, union representatives and employees attending training or information centers).
2. Changes in the rates of absenteeism, lateness, or accidents.
3. The number of voluntary and formal referrals to the program.
4. Characteristics of referred employees, such as the source of the referring agent, location for origin of the referral, the type of employee problem.

Union Concerns

Some of the major union concerns about the operation of an EAP include the following:

1. Are anonymity and confidentiality of employees utilizing the EAP maintained throughout the process?
2. Are individual employees treated fairly by the EAP?
3. What percentage of management and union members utilize the EAP?
4. The benefits derived from the program, i.e., number of employees who represent safety hazards for fellow employees; the number of additional hours involved for union stewards in the operation of the EAP?
5. What is the effectiveness of the program in assisting employees?

EAP Consultant

As noted above, the EAP consultant will be interested in the informaton needs outlined of management and union representatives. In addition, specific aspects of the design, implementation, and operation of the program are of importance to the consultant. Chief among these aspects are the following:

1. Is there visible support for an EAP by management and union?
2. How much time will be involved in the design and implementation of a program for a particular organization?
3. Is there an appropriate degree of trust by all members concerned?
4. Are initial referrals to the community treatment resources successful from all points of view?
5. Are all of the mechanics of this service and delivery system in place, i.e., is the design of the program appropriate for the company and its environment?

Information Needs and Concerns

Some concerns of the EAP consultant, management, and union have been outlined above. In addition to these concerns, there are more routine and important issues regarding the information collected to answer such concerns. Some issues to be considered and resolved before introduction of a monitoring system are:

1. Who has control of the information collected?
2. Is an appropriate level of confidentiality being maintained?
3. What basic organization information systems need to be in place, and how will confidentiality be maintained if existing systems are used?
4. What is expected of the EAP coordinator once the program is operational?

Systematic Feedback For Program Control

In order to develop a useful monitoring system that includes feedback of the results of the program, the EAP consultant is faced with the responsibility of designing data collection and feedback systems. The EAP consultant must design for the company, a system to document and feed back information about the effectiveness of services delivered to employees and their awareness of the program. This information gathered by the EAP coordinator should be provided to the EAP committee charged with the overall responsibility for the operation of the program.

Employee Referral and Follow-up Form

The Employee Referral and Follow-up Forms (Table 24-3) are completed by the EAP coordinator at the time of each employee referral under the program. These forms provide information regarding job classification, source of referral, disposition of referral, and, at selected intervals, job performance. Since the purpose of collecting the information is to determine program effectiveness, as measured by the use of the program, considerable attention must be paid to maintaining the confidentiality of the employees during this process. The EAP coordinator can describe the effects of the program by collecting and collating this information. It is then provided in group form to the company's EAP committee. Effectiveness of the program (as evaluated by the committee) can then be "fed back" to the operating structure of the program.

Employee and Supervisor Awareness Questionnaires

The Employee and Supervisor Awareness Questionnaires (Table 24-4) are designed to be used one to two years after the implementation of an EAP. These forms are an attempt to obtain, over time, an informed estimate of the awareness of company employees and supervisors of the program's existence and the procedures to utilize it.

TABLE 24-3. Employee Referral and Follow-up Form

1. Initial referral	Demographic data
	Employment data
	Type of referral
	Job performance
	Type of presenting problem
	Disposition of referral
2. Follow-up of referral	Time interval
	Duration of treatment/assistance
	Job performance data
	Termination data

TABLE 24-4. EAP Employee and Supervisor Awareness Questionnaire

1. Employee questionnaire	Demographic data
	Employment data
	Knowledge of EAP
	Utilization of EAP (voluntary)
	Non-EAP assistance
	Comment section
2. Supervisor questionnaire	Demographic data
	Employment data
	Knowledge of EAP
	Utilization of EAP
	formal referral
	results of referral
	Utilization of EAP (voluntary self-referral)
	Non-EAP assistance
	Comment section

Summary

In summary, the Employee Referral and Follow-Up Forms will provide the EAP committee with an informed perspective on the success of the EAP, and the Employee and Supervisor Awareness Questionnaires will provide similar information as to the extent to which company employees and management are aware of the existence of and steps necessary to utilize the program.

The EAP monitoring system described within (See Figure 24-1) has been implemented in six organizations in metropolitan Toronto. As well,

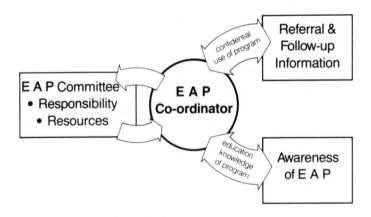

FIGURE 24-1

other organizations in Newfoundland, New Brunswick, Ontario, Alberta, and Australia (who has expressed an interest) have received authorization to use the system. Modifications to this EAP monitoring system have been and will continue to be made based on experience with its use.

References

Ankers, K., French, P.A., Larkin, E.J., Shain, M. *The MTR/EAP Monitoring System: IV. Staff Awareness of an Employee Assistance Program at a Toronto Area Hospital.* Substudy No. 1197, Addiction Research Foundation, 1981.

_____French, P.A., Larkin, E.J., Shain, M. *The MTR/EAP Monitoring Sysyem: VI. Development and Evaluation of an Alcoholism Recovery Program.* Substudy No. 1204, Addiction Research Foundation, 1981.

_____French, P.A., Larkin, E.J., Shain, M. *The MTR/EAP Monitoring System: VII. An Information Retrieval System for Employee Assistance Programs.* Substudy No. 1212, Addiction Research Foundation, 1981.

French, P.A., Ankers, K., Larkin, E.J., Shain, M. *The MTR/EAP Monitoring System: I. Employee Awareness of an Employee Assistance Program at a Toronto Hospital.* Substudy No. 1164, Addiction Research Foundation, 1981.

_____Ankers, K.,Larkin, E.J., Shain, M. *The MTR/EAP Monitoring System: V. Procedures and Forms.* Substudy No. 1198, Addiction Research Foundation, 1981.

James, G. *Evaluation in Public Health Practice.* American Journal of Public Health, 1962, 52, 1145–1154.

Larkin, E.J. *The Treatment of Alcoholism: Theory, Practice and Evaluation.* Addiction Research Foundation, Toronto, 1974.

Likert, R. *The Human Organization.* McGraw-Hill, New York, 1967.

Litwin, G.H., and Stringer, R.A. *Motivation and Organizational Climate.* Harvard University, Cambridge, 1968.

Pariser, P.C. and French, P.A. *Monitoring an Employee Assistance Program.* Substudy No. 912, Addiction Research Foundation, Toronto, 1977.

Pugh, D.S., Hickson, P.J., Hinings, C.R., McDonald, K., Turner, C., and Luptom, T. *A Conceptual Scheme for Organizational Analysis.* Administrative Science Quarterly, 1963, 8, 289–315.

Schulberg, A., Sheldon, A., and Baker, F. *Program Evaluation in the Health Field.* New York: Behavioral Publications, 1969.

SECTION VI
Preventive Approaches in an EAP

Introduction

The concept of EAPs having a strictly clinical function, dealing with the interesting diseases revealed in the workplace, and directing them to treatment, was, is, and always will be valid. However, it seems that the next evolutionary step for employee assistance programming may take it still further away from the "alcohol only" focus of the past, to a new role in the prevention of disease. As the medical model of intervention broadens to encompass the relationship of one's habits, emotions, and family relationships to health, EAP staff who are open to change will find exciting new opportunities to apply their skills.

Intergrating the EAP with health education (HE) and health promotion activities is the subject of Case's section, in which she examines the possible interactions and mergings which can take place between such programs, including a direct relationship to company medical departments, where they exist, EAP and HE programs are being found more and more in companies, but often they are under different direction or within different departments. Now, with *wellness*, *cost reduction*, and *early detection* as ideas whose time has come, there is reason to analyze the wisdom of combining and sharing such resources in order to improve the synergy of the "total" program.

Shain, in a later section also looks at the EAP/HE connection. A health education program, if totally successful, would remove entirely the need for an EAP, or even a medical program. However, that seems not about to happen very quickly. He notes the troublesome problem of documenting prevention programs, but suggests that better efforts at analysis of subsets of HE, such as stress reduction and smoking cessation programs, may indeed be worthwhile. Food for thought too is the proposition that the small positive changes wrought by an HE program can geometrically bring about a multitude of small changes in behaviors and actions, leading to improved states of individual health. In other words, progress may not by easily measured by "leaps," but by a steady small progression in the right direction.

Albert Ellis, pioneer of the Rational Emotive Therapy movement, has contributed a discussion of the approach to "acceptance." Referring to mankind's eternal global, yet individual, reluctance to accept what fate has in store, he discusses our tendency to become bound up in unfortunate belief systems. Can we step back and benefit from relatively simple approaches to our perceptions, from our attitudes toward the uncontrollable events of our lives? He speculates on the relationship of our belief and action systems to emotional disturbances, addictions, and even alcoholism. As to how this relates to EAPs, such behavioral approaches may have utility in the short-term counseling that many EAP practitioners do on an almost daily basis.

The defining, managing, and evaluation of "stress" is the subject of Klarreich's section. He reviews stress first as it evolves from the organization to the individual, caused by such things as mobility, work overload, and role ambiguity. These plus other personal life crises may then compound to give one the feeling of being stressed, perhaps leading then to illness. But what is the interface between the environment (workplace or otherwise) and the individual's reaction and perception of stress? Expanding upon some of the behavioral principles practiced by many therapists today, he notes the probable sequence of beliefs, perceptions, and inappropriate behavior responses that lead to stress and illness. Modifications of such maladaptive thinking may not always be easy, but the principles can be adopted and practiced within EAPs by staff members willing to invest some small amount of time in their learning.

Levine describes for us in her section, the principles of the chemical dependency program model, as put in place in Canada by Control Data. This program, entitled Employee Advisory Resource Program, concentrates on the need to accept alcohol and drug problems as being behavioral and medical disorders. Since 1982, the program has sponsored four-hour chemical dependency awareness seminars, which are offered to all employees. A discussion follows on other features of their program, and on the role of supervisor training as it rtelates to chemical dependencies.

Executives and their families are often relocated at company discretion to serve the company's needs. In the section by McGehee, the problems of relocation stress are examined in detail; it is nearly always a crisis, both before and after it happens, the question is just how severe. Spouses, usually female, suffer the consequences most frequently; the children nearly as often. Relocation, especially overseas to new cultures, is a summation of stresses which ranks high on the familiar Holmes and Rahe scale. Even "successful relocations," according to the section, would not often be voluntarily repeated, even though 95% of the queried executives thought them to be a valuable experience.

Returning home after such assignments is not always the end of problems either, since repatriation to a homeland after many years away may reveal such surprises as a changed community, higher costs, and the absence of inexpensive domestic help. What are the solutions proposed? Among them are an appropriate selection process, pre- and post-departure orientations, and an awareness of what may need to be done upon the return "home."

25

Integrating EAPs with Health Education Efforts
Jean B. Case

Introduction

" . . . people who live in unhealthy ways are more at risk for becoming excessive drinkers and inappropriate drug users than people whose lifestyles are healthier . . . " (Shain, 1983).

The potential relationship between an EAP and a health education/ health promotion program (HE/HP), may or may not be obvious, depending upon one's vantage point. If one is operating from within a company where an EAP is alive and well, and an intergral part of a company's well-established medical department, then EAP and HE/HP programs most likely will find the relationship comfortable, supportive, complementary, and logical. This situation does not always exist, since not all companies have EAPs, medical departments, or HEPs/HPPs. In addition, EAPs may or may not be integrated with a company's medical department, since, historically, human resources/personnel management department may have initiated a given company's EAP. Furthermore, some view HE/HP efforts as a logical part of an EAP, rather than an EAP as part of a larger health promotion program.

Whatever the historical and traditional cases may be, much can be gained through the cooperative interaction of EAP and HE/HP efforts.

There is a a scanty supply of literature which specifically addresses the integration of EAPs and HE/HP programs. The literature on stress management comes closest to addressing this issue. Indeed, the very exploration of the relationships between stress, health, and disease brings traditional medicine to interface with the behavioral sciences.

What Has Been the Traditional Pattern of EAPs and HE Efforts?

Traditionally, the early EAPs grew from organizations' perception that alcohol and drug abuse were lowering the productivity of the workforce, contributing to increased absenteeism, accidents, and the ultimate destruction of valuable employees. Programs were designed to deal with alcohol and substance abuse, and administered by human resources/employee relations departments or a company's medical department. While the early programs were directed at end stage problems, the more mature programs began to address the early stages of substance abuse and address the prevention of such problems. An ideal, mature EAP not only deals with end stage problems of the "troubled" employee, but also offers education and guidance in early detection and prevention of problems.

HE efforts, also called *Wellness Programs* or *Heath Promotion Programs*, are so relatively new that there is little that can be called traditional. Nevertheless, the general focus of these programs has been upon areas such as cardiovascular disease, musculoskeletal and back problems, cancer and accident prevention. Concomitant preventive courses might address smoking cessation, fitness, nutrition (lipids), hypertension detection and control, healthy back, cancer prevention and detection. Stress management courses might be included in the HP package, in due respect to the mind-body connection and the probable relationship of coping skills and level of self-awareness to health and disease.

In the above traditional models the HE/EAP connection was not necessarily apparent or strong and, if present, existed as the direct result of enlightened and committed staff.

What Recent Trends Are Bringing EAPs and HE Efforts Together?

First, the rising cost of health care in the United States has forced industry to face this problem and to become involved in its solution. When a large portion of the leading causes of death in this country can be prevented (e.g., heart disease, accidents, stroke, cirrhosis and lung cancer), it makes economic sense to use "disease prevention as a way to reduce health care spending;" indeed, "an ounce of prevention is worth a pound of cure . . . when one compares the cost of a smoking cessation [cost range of $50–$400], with the price tag of a coronary bypass operation [approximately $50,000–$75,000]" (Bernstein, 1983). Thus, wellness programs are sprouting in the fertile soil of industry's efforts to contain expenditures in the area of health care.

In addition, there is a change in the definition of "health" accompanying a growing national awareness that there is more to health than normal laboratory tests. Individuals are anxious to be more involved in managing their own health. Fitness, ideal body weight, and a sence of inner peace, to name a few, are beginning to be perceived as a part of "wellness." Furthermore, there is a general trend towards individual responsibility for his/her health, creating a broader ownership of health issues.

Third, there is the gradual acceptance by traditional medicine, as well as the general public, that the mind and body are indeed connected. In fact, there is a new and evolving field entitled psychoneuroimmunology, the very title of which connotes the intricate connections between the brain and the body's response to it; it assigns an important role to the mind in maintaining health and overcoming illness (Brody, 1983; Ader, 1981).

As recently as ten years ago, "psychosomatic" illness was neither the most acceptable nor the most traditional specialty for a physician to choose. Those physicians who were strong advocates of this concept were viewed with skepticism by their peers. With recent discoveries of such substances as endorphins, the body's own self-made "opiates" (which are thought to contribute in part to a runner's "high"), the mind-body connection is not so untenable and continues to be a challenge to those seeking to objectively confirm it. This confirmation is aided by discoveries of body substances which can mediate pain, anxiety, and even mood.

"Substantial progress in documenting the role of psychosocial stress in the etiology and development of physical and mental disease has been made in the past ten years." Any growth and understanding in this area "will hinge on the creative integration of behavioral and biomedical approaches." (Parkinson and Associates, 1982).

Acceptance of a broader definition of health and the recognition of the mind-body connection set the stage for the development of more comprehensive health education and wellness programs, which go beyond the traditional and include such topics as effective coping skills, healthy attitudes, and stress management. Indeed, "the newly emerging concern for health promotion also called the 'prevention' or the 'wellness movement'– offers a promising new opportunity for drug abuse and alcohol programs in the workplace." (Parkinson and Associates, 1982).

Another way of stating this is: " . . . certain types of health promotion programs . . . [are] highly *consistent with*, and logical *components of* comprehensive EAPs." (Shain, 1983). It is simply a matter of semantics of definition as to which (EAP or HE/HP) is the umbrella under which all the preventive and therapeutic programs fall.

Health education/promotion programs basically attempt to catalyze the adoption of healthy lifestyles. Educating individuals about what comprises a healthy lifestyle is a first and basic step in this process. Beyond this, the successful program is one which motivates behavioral change. Inasmuch as alcohol and drug abuse represent, in part, patterns of behavior, EAPs therapeutic approach is to a certain extent based upon motivating behavioral change towards a healthy lifestyle.

In the context of the above, a most critical connection between HPPs and EAPs becomes clear. Those who "experience high levels of stress, anxiety and depression are more at risk for the development of excessive drinking and inappropriate drug use than those who do not experience such conditions." (p. 40) In addition, those who abuse alcohol and drugs are higher risks for developing other unhealthy habits (e.g., lack of exercise, smoking). On the other hand, people who practice healthy habits are at lower risks for developing alcohol and drug problems; for example, an avid jogger is less likely to smoke or drink to excess, since these habits would not support high performance in jogging. So the "complex of behaviors expressed and implied in the state of 'wellness and fitness' perform a protective role against the development of other habits which, over the long run, lead to health problems . . . " (p. 40).

Optimally then, an EAP is an integral part of a wellness program (or vice versa) which is designed not only to detect and treat medical-emotional-substance abuse problems, but also to teach and facilitate employees' understanding and achievement of a healthy lifestyle. "The purpose of health education—is, of course, to help employees, make informed decisions and take actions in their own interest." (Pearson, 1980).

Specific Examples of Cooperative/Integrative Efforts

Increased and appropriate utilization of EAP and medical services

At the Exxon Corporation headquarters office, the health education effort is based in the medical department, and is managed by the EAP manager, the medical department physician in charge of clinical services, and its head nurse, with significant input from the employee relations/human resources department. These people are actively involved in hosting programs as well as giving them. This gives high visibility to the staff, enhances staff credibility, and identifies the medical department's concern with the "total person." Employees consequently think of utilizing the medical department for more than care of the common cold or the obtaining of a periodic health examination. For example, a significant number of self-referrals to our EAP occurred after the EAP manager gave a talk on "Coping with Loss." Thus, medical and EAP staff work together to educate employees while also responding to referrals that often arise from joint presentation and cooperative efforts. In this way the EAP and medical department services have increased utilization.

Program planning

The EAP staff is often tuned into the state of wellness of the overall organization (particularly when the EAP staff is working *within* the organization), and can be valuable in designing programs that suit the needs of the employees. For example, at a time when an organization is going through size reductions and/or significant relocations, programs or workshops on stress, change, and relocation are invaluable and well received by employees.

Other examples of programs which reflect the interaction of our EAP with the HE effort are seminars on balancing parenting with work, dual career families, depression, loss, and workaholism.

Synergism through integration

Many examples can be cited to show how "health education" efforts can blossom and multiply as the result of EAP/HE integration. One such example, is the story of the talk on "Coping with Loss" referred to above. This particular talk was developed by our EAP manager to address the general topic of loss (loss of a loved one, a job, divorce, etc.), and was well attended at a time when the corporation was going through significant change. As an outgrowth of this one presentation, the EAP manager was asked to work with several departments facing relocation (as one form of loss). Dealing with relocaton then became an EAP/medical/employee relations effort, and workshops included the participation of staff from these three areas. The physician role was to clarify the mind-body connection, to point out that relocation can be stressful, and that stress may or may not trigger disease, depending upon attitudes, coping skills, etc. The relocation seminar evolved further into a talk on "Stress, Change, and Health" given by the EAP manager and two physicians of the medical department for the entire employee population. Handout developed from the above have been sent to many upon request, and are being considered as part of a pre-retirement package of materials. This is just one example of the synergistic potential derived from the integration of an EAP with a HE effort.

Concluding Comments

- A wellness program that does not include coping skills, attitudes, mental health issues is not addressing the *total* person.
- An EAP that limits its horizons to "detection and treatment" without using its resources toward preventive measures is not recognizing its fullest potential.

- An optimal EAP includes a strong *preventive* element that is coordinated with the overall HE effort.
- An optimal HE effort accepts mental/emotional wellness as essential to health.
- EAP and HE programs *complement each other.*
- A high performance creative, effective wellness "team" should include committed occupational physicians and nurses, as well as EAP professionals.
- The integration of EAP and HE efforts enhances the overall wellness program and emphasizes the importance of prevention, and the potential of an individual, once educated, to make responsible decisions towards the optimal state of health.

References

Ader, R. *Psycho-neuroimmunology*, Academic Press, 1981.

Bernstein, J.E. *Handling Health Care Costs by Reducing Health Risks.* Personnel Journal, 1983, *62*, 882–887.

Berry, C.A. *An Approach to Good Health For Employees and Reduced Health Care Costs for Industry.* Washington, DC., Health Insurance Association of America, 1981.

Brody, J. *Emotions Found to Influence Nearly Every Human Ailment*, New York Times, 5/24/83.

Holmes, T.H., and Rahe, R.H. *The Social Readjustment Scale.* Journal of Psychosomatic Research, 1967, *11*, 213–218.

Kobase, S.C., Hilker, R.R.J., and Maddi, S.R. *Who Stays Healthy Under Stress?* Journal of Occupational Medicine, 1979, *21*, 595–598.

Kotz, H.J., and Fielding, J.E., eds., *Health, Education and Promotion, Agenda For the Eighties - A Summary of an Insurance Industry Conference on Health Education and Promotion.* Atlanta, Georgia, March 16–18, 1980 (sponsored by the Health Insurance Association of America).

Parkinson, R.S. and Associates. *Managing Health Promotion in the Workplace*, Palo Alto, Mayfield Publishing Company, 1982.

Pearson, C.E. *The Emerging Role of the Occupational Physician in Preventive Medicine, Health Promotion and Health Education.* Journal of Occupational Medicine, 1980, *22*, 104–106.

Shain, M. *Prevention of Substance Abuse Through Health Promotion in the Workplace.* EAP Digest, 1983, *3*, 39–41, 47–51.

26

Executives, Families, and the
Trauma of Relocation
Lockie J. McGehee

Introduction

The dramatic increase in international business by United States companies over the past several decades has brought about a rapidly increasing number of American expatriates. These American expatriates are expected to manage their companies' business abroad. Implicit in this expectation is the further expectation that these Americans will also successfully relocate their families and manage their families' "business" abroad. This section deals with the "trauma" of relocation, particularly international relocation, and points out a number of problem areas that arise and potential solutions to these problems. Among these solutions may be the assistance of the EAP.

The "Price" of Relocation

International relocation is an expensive proposal. It is costly both in terms of dollars spent and in terms of human factors. A current estimate by one of the largest multinational U.S. corporations of the "cost" of interntional relocation of an executive and the family is close to a quarter of a million dollars. If executives return prematurely due to an inability to adjust to their new assignment, such costs will include not only relocation expenses, but the efforts required to replace them, the "clean-up" time and lost time at the foreign office, and the efforts required to relocate such executives at home, or their loss to the company. There will also be costs in terms of the human factor. Premature return has often been euphemisitically labeled "people crashes." When people crash," they have typically reached intolerable levels of stress at work or at home or, in all probability, both. This cost in human terms becomes even greater when one considers that the executive was likely sent abroad in the first place because he/she was expected to succeed as the "best person for the job."

From a 1974 study by the Center for Research and Education, it has been estimated that upward to 37% of Americans working in foreign countries return prematurely from their assigment. This is a hefty figure, even without considering those Americans who remain abroad but perform marginally in their assignments. This figure also indicates that there are numerous problems involved in transferring Americans abroad. There are three major areas in which these problems can arise and can be dealt with. These include: 1) assessment and selection of the candidate for transfer; 2) management of crises abroad as they arise; and 3) fostering acculturation for the executive and the executive's family.

The Best Person for the Job

The following description of an executive from a multinational company, who returned prematurely from his assignment abroad, is a dramatic illustration of the poor selection of a candidate. Jim H. was transferred to his company's office in the Far East. He was selected for this transfer because he was the "best person for the job." His managerial record indicated that he would be able to get the job done, and his expertise in the required area was substantial. He was also being moved upward rapidly by his company. Jim admits to accepting the transfer not only for career reasons, but for family reasons. He had decided that this transfer was exactly what was needed to "shake things up" at home. His wife had begun to complain of boredom and was becoming distant, his 12-year-old daughter had become quiet and sullen, and his 8-year-old son had been living with the stigma of being a "learning disabled" child in his school. Jim was right, this move did "shake things up" for his family. But not in the direction that he had expected. When Jim's family returned home, from abroad, his wife had developed a drinking problem, his daughter had had a very phobic response to the new culture and had withdrawn further, and his son had lost valuable time in school, because he could not get the help he needed with his studies. Clearly, the case of Jim H. is dramatic. His unique combination of family characteristics, any of which might have precipitated a premature return, was a virtually certain indicator of failure overseas. One might wonder how the company ever selected Jim for this assignment overseas with this family history. He was selected because his company did not ask about his family history, and, from the perspective of the employer, he was the best employee for the job. This case also demonstrates that the candidate often erroneously evaluates his own family's chances for success in a move abroad. The human resource professional or the employee assistance professional can aid in both the company's assessment of the candidate and the candidate's own assessment of the family's response. Methods for dealing with these issues will be covered later in this section.

Relocation has never been a solution to family problems, as Jim's case demonstrated. In fact, relocation puts unusual stress on families. Using the "Schedule of Recent Life Events" developed by Drs. Holmes and Rahe, all of the life changes that would, by necessity, occur in an international relocation would receive a weighted value of 387 points of "Life Change Units." This score is dramatically above the level which would predict a 70 percent chance of a stress-related illness occuring within a year of the relocation (Holmes and Rahe, 1967). The items on the "schedule" which are reflected in this calculation include: business readjustment; change in financial state; change to a different kind of work; change in responsibilities; outstanding personal achievement; wife/husband begin or stop work; change in living conditions; change in residence; change in recreation; change in social activities; change in sleeping habits; change in number of family get-togethers; change in eating habits. This list of changes points out the variety of potential problem areas that the family may face, but does not include the more heavily-weighted items, such as marital discord and health problems. If these are co-occuring, simultaneously, the impact of the life change will be even more likely to result in a stress-related illness. These changes are among the many reasons that the family's response to relocation is so crucial to the success of the relocation. Paul Illman in his book, *Developing Overseas Managers and Managers Overseas*, makes this point emphatically when he reserves a paragraph for these two sentences, "Don't overlook wives. They can make or break their husbands, particularly in a developing country" (Illman, 1980). But it is not simply a matter of "making or breaking" the husband. There are very real reasons that the impact of the family is great, whether it is that of the wife, husband, or child. These reasons must be considered when the company goes about selecting the "right family for the job," and are reflected in the family's abllity to respond to the changes they are about to face.

Culture Shock is Real

Cultural shock, more popularly referred to as "culture shock," is a real phenomenon. Dr. Kalervo Oberg coined the term culture shock in his work. In a talk to the Foreign Service Insitute in 1958 he stated:

> Culture shock, an occupational disease of many people who have been suddenly transplanted abroad, is precipitated by the anxiety that results from losing all our familiar signs and symbols of social intercourse. These

signs or cues include the thousand and one ways in which we orient ourselves to the situations of daily life. . . . . When an individual enters a strange culture, all or most of these familiar cues are removed. No matter how broad-minded or full of goodwill he may be, a series of props have been knocked from under him. This is followed by a feeling of frustration and anxiety (Oberg, 1958).

All people will experience a certain degree of culture shock upon moving into a new culture. People differ though in the degree, the impact and the manifestation of culture shock in their lives. Drs. Harris and Moran, in their book *Managing Cultural Differences*, describe some symptoms that people suffering from culture shock would manifest. These symptoms include:

" . . . excessive concern over cleanliness, feeling that what is new and strange is dirty, this may be seen with reference to water, food, dishes, and bedding, or it might be evident in excessive fear of servants and shopkeepers relative to the disease they might bear. Other indications . . . are feelings of helplessness and confusion, growing dependence on long-term residents of one's own nationality, constant irritations over delays and minor frustrations, as well as undue concern for being cheated, robbed or injured. Some become mildly hypochondriac, expressing overconcern for minor pains and skin eruptions–it may even get to the point of real psychosmatic illnesses (Harris and Moran, 1981).

This list can be expanded upon to include more serious developments in culture shock, which include: alcohol and drug abuse; depression; isolation; unusual phobias, and more serious symptoms of anxiety disorders, such as disorientation and attacks of unreasonable fear and the inability to carry out normal life activities. It is reasonable to expect a variety of these manifestations of culture shock in the members of the family, but prolonged or exaggerated symptoms are a sign of the inability to adjust to the new culture.

Culture shock appears to emerge in stages. Dr. Peter Adler of the East-West Center of the University of Hawaii describes five stages that he believes mark the emergence and resolution of culture shock. These stages include: 1) **contact**, a stage of excitement and euphoria as the individual is immersed in an exotic and unusual environment; 2) **disintegration**, the stage when the impact of truly being in a different setting hits and the individual feels isolated and indulges in fears and anxieties; 3) **reintegration**, the stage of rejection of the new environment, and the individual's preoccupation with his/her likes and dislikes in the new culture emerge; 4) **autonomy**, the stage in which the differences are finally accepted and the individual develops new strategies for coping with these differences; and 5) **independence**, the stage in which the new-found coping strategies allow the individual to engage in a positive interaction with the new culture and gain enjoyment from this interaction (Adler, 1975). Psychologically speaking, the critical phase in determining whether the individual will be successful in coping with the new environment arises between the reintegration and the autonomy stage. At this point, the individual's appraisal of his/her life events and his/her own beliefs and personal philosophies will determine whether or not he/she can become autonomous and independent or reject his/her new environment altogether. Education for such employees on these issues and support systems will aid in the effective resolution of culture shock.

Problems of the Successful Expatriate

What about those executives who do not return early? These executives and their families appear to be successful at resolving the culture shock they may have experienced. These families also report a variety of problems and stresses. Korn/Ferry International recently polled 100 executives who had returned from their overseas assignments in Europe, the Middle East, Africa, South America, Central America, the Far East and the Pacific, and also polled their U.S.-based employers. The study had these essential questions: "Is the international experience satisfying–or frustrating? Does it prepare the executives for more important roles–or interrupt career growth? Can companies look forward to welcoming back happy, motivated people–or malcontents?" (Korn/Ferry International, 1981). They found that 93 percent of these executives believed that their overseas assignment was a valuable experience, but only 41 percent would accept the same assignment again. Their responses to the poll indicated that though they felt their experiences to be valuable, they experienced numerous difficulties. Table 26-1 describes the reactions of the executives themselves and their U.S.-based employers as to how they rated several categories of the difficulties in doing business abroad.

In this list of difficulties, problems in family adjustment was rated at "very" or "somewhat difficult" by 45 of the 100 executives surveyed. It is interesting to note that the executives' employers felt that the executives' family adjustment problems were similarly difficult in 74 percent of the cases. This discrepancy may be due to the reluctance of the executive to cite family difficulties or due to the employers' attribution of a relationship of family problems to the executive's work performance. Whichever is the case, these figures demonstrate that even in successfully completed assignments abroad, many families were in difficulty. It is also clear from this table that the American executive overseas is faced with a variety of difficulties doing business, and family adjustment problems can only compound the stressful situation. Table 26-1 also demonstrates that some of the more heavily-rated

TABLE 26-1. Difficulties Doing Business Abroad.

	Percentages	
	Very Difficult Employees Responses	Somewhat Difficult Employers Responses
Adjustment to production levels	43	53
Foreign work attitudes	50	70
Raising money	30	39
Currency fluctuations	51	66
Obtaining raw materials	32	42
Quality control	51	44
Accounting and financial controls	49	50
Marketing conditions	47	69
Personnel and labor philosophies	73	86
Meeting delivery dates	46	51
Language	51	80
Political Climate	38	60
Mentality of people	49	71
Family adjustment	45	74

Reprinted with permission from Korn/Ferry International, "A study of the repatriation of the American international executive," December, 1981.

problem areas included dealing with foreign attitudes, philosophies, and ideas. These are areas where some prior education concerning the culture in which the executive is about to work would be helpful, in an effort to diminish the stressful reaction to attitudes, philosophies, and ideas.

Table 26-2 illustrates the rating of the spouses' adjustment to the overseas assignment by the executive.

It is clear from this table that difficulties were experienced by the spouse in a majority of the cases (60%). Many of the difficulties appear to have been related to cultural differences (60%). This is an expected area of difficulty, as the spouse, who typically can not work while living abroad, must deal on a day-to-day basis with the new culture. The "work" of the spouse often becomes figuring out how to shop, manage servants, supply the children with needed support and supplies, deal with services and basically learn a new way of life. The working executive, of course, has the regularity of the job, with many familiar aspects to it, to keep occupied and reduce the novelty. Education about living in the new culture and how to proceed with daily activities would appear to be very useful to the spouse and family, and could possibly remedy some of the difficulty in adjusting to the new culture. Also,

TABLE 26-2. Spouse Adjustment to Overseas Assignments.

	Percentages of Employee Response
Difficulties	
Yes	60
No	40
Nature of Difficulties	
Language	44
Cultural differences	60
Family disruption	6
Climate	6
Socialization	4
Medical facilities	6

Reprinted with permission from Korn/Ferry International, "A Study of the repatriation of the American international executive," December, 1981.

some language training would appear to be a valid investment. This study by Korn/Ferry also indicated that for the executive, preparations for the overseas assignments included such things as introductory trips and a job definition, but there was no mention of preparation for the spouse or family. It is important to note that these were the successful families. Those who return prematurely would most likely have rated these difficulties not as "very" or "somewhat" difficult, but as intolerable.

The Adjustment of Repatriation

One final problem involved in adjusting to an overseas transfer is that of repatriation, returning home from that transfer. Curiously, the families who appear to have adjusted well to the new culture, often report the most problems upon repatriation. The Korn/Ferry poll of executives who had successfully completed their overseas assignment indicates that 53 percent of the executives felt that their U. S. jobs were not as satisfying as their overseas jobs in the areas of status, responsibility, authority, and decision-making autonomy, (Korn/Ferry International, 1981). This would seem to indicate that, once executives make a healthy adjustment to the rigors of their overseas assignments, they truly become "independent," as Adler's stage theory would predict (Adler, 1975), and develop strategies for enjoying the new environment with its difficult demands. When asked to return to a less demanding work environment, they appear to have difficulties readjusting. Fifty-three percent reported that they felt that the significance of their re-entry problems was great enough to discourage others from accepting an assignment overseas (Korn/Ferry International, 1981).

Social re-entry problems were reported as well by the returning executives. Forty-three percent encountered social re-entry problems, including change in living style (52%); adjustment problems to the new community (48%); and changes in the U.S. environment (48%) (Korn/Ferry International, 1981). A common experience for families returning from overseas assignments is that of a drop in the style of living that they had experienced abroad. This typically involves the loss of family servants and an increase in the cost of living. Another loss commonly reported is that of the very close friendships formed while abroad. These friendships were often the positive resolution of the early feelings of isolation and heightened differences, and by necessity became very strong. Children of families returning from abroad often report regret that they were removed from the culture just as they had become comfortable and accepted by their peers. What is apparant is that a positive resolution of the experience of culture shock while abroad often leads to a new form of culture shock upon their return home.

Potential Solutions through Human Resource Management

Sending executives and their families abroad is clearly a more complicated issue than assigning someone to a new job. It is critical that this assignment be viewed with family variables in mind. It is also critical that the human resource manager be aware of the potential problems that can arise, and respond with programs and support that can offset these problems. Suggestions are offered for programs in the following areas: selection and assignment, pre-departure educational programs, post-departure programs, and repatriation services.

1. **Selection and Assignment**.
   - Interview the candidate and secure a family history.
   - Provide the candidate with information concerning potential risk factors for family relocation. These factors include: drug or alcohol use problems by any member of the family; special educational needs of the children; special health problems of any family member; career aspirations of the spouse; particular political, religious or moral ideals that conflict with the potential culture; any history of psychological problems, especially depression and nervous disorders; peer group adjustment problems for parents or children.
2. **Pre-departure Education**.
   - Provide a workshop for the family on developing coping skills and strategies for dealing with change.

- Provide resources for language training and education surrounding the culture to which the family is being assigned. This should be provided for all family members.
- Establish an open line of communication between the human resource professional and the family, with the clear understanding that problems are expected to emerge and that there is support for dealing with these problems.

3. **Post-departure Programs.**
   - Introduce family members to expatriates in the new culture who have made a successful adjustment and set up social support groups for families abroad.
   - Provide a list of resources, such as medical services, counseling services, and cultural affairs available in the country to which the family has been assigned.
   - Periodically contact the family and follow their progress in adjusting to the new culture.

4. **Repatriation services.**
   - Provide information to the family about the changes they will experience upon their return.
   - Provide a workshop for the family on responding to their return home and developing coping strategies.
   - Consult with the executive concerning his/her response to the changes he/she will experience in his/her job.

Most of the services described can easily be carried out in the executive's company. Services of psychologists or counselors may be desired in the design and implementation of the workshops. A directory of organizations providing language training and cultural education is provided through the Society of Intercultural Education, Training and Research and Intercultural Press in Washington, D.C. There are also a number of programs specifically designed to orient the executive to managing business overseas that are typically offered through graduate schools of business, but these do not usually provide resources for the family.

Considering the cost in both dollars and human factors of an unsuccessful relocation, the cost of these programs designed to minimize risk is minimal. Drs. Harris and Moran quote a report from *Time Magazine* (January 8, 1979) as an example of the trade off of a small cost for a greater ultimate cost:

"Not long ago, . . . one U.S. firm proposed a 30-to 50-hour orientation course for new employees of 100 American, European and Japanese companies. It would have included elementary Farsi, a brief history of

Iran, and a cultural and sociological introduction to the country. Not a single company would agree to underwrite the cost, citing uncertainties of Iran's economic and political situation. The results are painfully obvious. (Harris and Moran, 1981)

When one considers the impact of a new culture on the family and the impact of the family on the executive, it becomes clear that these factors will affect the executive's job performance. Programs to help the family and the executive successfully relocate need to address the issues of culture shock and the successive stages of becoming independent, and provide needed support systems at appropriate times. They also need to address the specific risk factors of each family and attempt to provide appropriate resources for the family. One of the most important components of any program designed to aid international relocation though, is the awareness of management that difficulties are to be expected and considered "normal," and that a message of understanding and support is transmitted to the executive and the family.

References

Adler, P. The translational experience: An alternative view of culture shock. *Journal of Humanistic Psychology*, 1975, 15, vol. 3.

Harris, P.R. and Moran, R.T. *Managing Cultural Differences*. Volume 1, Houston, Texas: Gulf Publishing Company, 1981.

Holmes, T.H. and Rahe, R.H. The social readjustment scale. *Journal of Psychosomatic Research*, 1967, 11, 213–218.

Illman, P.E. *Developing Overseas Managers and Managers Overseas*. New York: AMACOM, 1980.

Oberg, K. Cultural shock: Adjustment to new cultural environments. *Practical Anthropology*, 1960. vol. 7.

Oberg, K. Talk presented to the Foreign Service Institute, December, 1958.

Korn/Ferry International, "A Study of the Repatriation of the American International Executive", Dec, 1981.

Tucher M.H., *Screening and Selection for Overseas Assignment Assessments and Recommendations to the US Navy*, Moran, Stahl and Boyer, International Division, Boulder, Colorado, July 1974.

27

Toward Coordination of Employee Health Promotion and Assistance Programs

Martin Shain
Bernard Boyle

Introduction

Employee Assistance Programs represent an attempt to achieve, in the workplace, a mutual accommodation of economic and public health goals. More specifically they are an illustration of an area in which there has been a mutual permeation of economic and public health values. This has expressed itself in the humanization of the process whereby employee problems are dealt with in a manner that considers the needs of the employee, the employer, and the union. The ethical system that has evolved to allow both the interpenetration of values and insulation against abuses is one of EAP's greatest achievements.

A further expression of the accommodation of these values can be witnessed in the relatively novel trend towards the proliferation of Health Promotion Programs (HPP) in the workplace. These programs, taken as a whole, attempt to mobilize the individuals' strengths and self-governing behavior by providing education and training in a variety of areas including cardiovascular health, smoking cessation, weight control, cancer prevention, alcohol consumption, and stress management (Parkinson and Associates, 1982).

In spite of their overlapping goals, EAPs and HPPs are rarely coordinated or integrated. Thus it is the intention of this paper to provide a rationale and framework for the consideration of a comprehensive approach to occupational programming.

In order to achieve a reasonable view of the usefulness of integrating EAP and HPP approaches in theory and practice, it is necessary to make some general evaluative comments about both of them.

Employee Assistance Programs

Although broad-based EAPs have been dealing with a wide variety of problems for some years, there seems to have been a disproportionate amount of interest in their ability to manage alcoholics. Indeed, it is hard to find published material dealing in any depth with the outcome of cases involving domestic, interpersonal, emotional, legal, financial, and related problems. Similarly, while we have some estimates of the prevalence of alcohol problems in the workplace, we have hardly any such estimates for the range of other problems dealt with by EAPs. This means that we have no valid means of relating the referral rates for a given problem to the population at risk for a given problem, a state of affairs which makes it very difficult to render anything but relative determinations of EAP effectiveness at the identification level.

Nevertheless, it is possible to extrapolate certain principles from studies of how EAPs have fared in relation to alcoholism for purposes of speculating upon the manner in which such programs cope with other problems.

The rate at which alcohol problems are identified under the auspices of EAPs has been estimated in the range of 0.6% to 1.6% per annum for established programs (Hitchcock and Sanders, 1976). This estimate appears to have been based on programs which emphasized alcoholism. A more recent estimate (see Shain, this volume), nonetheless, places alcohol-related referral rates in the same approximate range while using broad-scope programs as the referent. Thus, it appears that regardless of the size of the alcohol-dependent population at risk, the best referral rates in EAP are somewhat in excess of 1.5% per annum.

It is true that these figures do not account for the effect of variables such as turnover and re-entry of recovered people into the workplace. However, in any given year it is predictable that the alcohol-dependent population at risk will be much larger than the referral rate. How much larger depends on the criteria used to establish alcohol dependence. Conservative estimates would place it at twice the size, while more liberal estimates would see it as being five or six times the size of the referred population, even in the best programs (Shain and Groeneveld, 1980; Mannello and Seaman, 1979; Parker and Brody, 1982).

The disparity between average referral rates and the average size of populations at risk has caused considerable concern among some students and practitioners in the field. Nevertheless, it seems likely that this disparity may reflect an inescapable reality of EAPs as currently known, namely, that such programs have outer limits of effectiveness (Walker and Shain, 1983). Indeed, the key issue may lie in the definition of effectiveness: whose definition and using what criteria? There is some evidence to suggest that, from management's point of view, these referral rates are quite acceptable in that they reflect the identification of the worst loss-causing cases or the "critical few," as they are sometimes called in Loss Control Management. To the employer, it may not be worth the effort to push for the identification or even the self-referral of less severely impaired employees, since it is a small subgroup of the alcoholic population which accounts for a disproportionate amount of the loss (Borthwick, 1977; Orvis et al., 1981). Of course, from the perspective of employees and their representative groups (unions and associations) this method of accounting leaves much to be desired: if employees are out there who need help, they should be helped, even though they may be costing their employers a great deal extra in lost productivity, absenteeism and accidents, or in relation to numerous other cost lines. However, this is where public health and economic goals tend to conflict, since the cost-benefit ratio is perceived to decline in proportion to the push toward "earlier identification" of problem employees or simply employees with problems (Swint, 1982; Schramm, 1982). Part of this conflict, though, is attributable to the nature of the interventions typically available under the auspices of most EAPs. Such interventions tend to be oriented toward clinical treatment, that is, toward the kind of help that is provided by physicians, psychiatrists, nurses, social workers, and psychologists, These interventions involve the deployment of very expensive services, often on a one-to-one basis. In spite of evidence which points to the effectiveness of less intensive forms of intervention (Edwards, et al., 1977; Orford, et al., 1976; Orvis, et al., 1981), these models continue to occupy center stage.

In so far as employers are concerned about restoring order and predictability to the work situation, they may not become excited about extending the benefit of very expensive treatment to those employees who do not represent immediate threats to stability and order. Nonetheless, a considerable proportion of employees may at one time or another have problems which, taken in the aggregate, affect the general productivity, morale, and functioning of an organization, even though in any given case no job performance problem warranting supervisory intervention may exist (Weiner, Akabas and Sommer, 1973). At the same time, the individual employee may not see him/herself as being sufficiently troubled to justify self-referral to what is likely perceived as problem-oriented treatment or "therapy" via the EAP. Such an employee, rattled by troubles at home, poor sleep, eating and drinking too much, overwork, and not enough genuine recreation may be more likely to see him/herself as in need of a rest, or as losing their edge or their grip. If these problems create or are aggravated by superfluous stress over a long period of time, it is probable not only that such people will do poorly at work, but also that they will be victims of premature morbidity and mortality (Selye, 1976; House, 1974; McQueen and Siegrist, 1982). In other words, they represent present and future loss to their employer as well as to themselves and their families. However, this is clearly not the sort of loss that can be addressed by remedial, therapeutic interventions designed to deal with manifest problems.

It is at this stage that we require a fresh vision of what is meant by "assistance." This vision is required, we contend, not only or even principally in relation to alcohol use but also in relation to a variety of problems, the later manifestations of which are dealt with in broad-based EAPs. We have used alcohol as an example of the disparity between referral rates and populations at risk. There is every reason to believe, however, that for every domestic, marital, or emotional problem bad enough to warrant assistance through an EAP, there are three others that depress productivity and affect overall functioning, but which do not lend themselves to therapeutic intervention in the usual sense. These are problems with which people are, in a way, "coping," but which sorely tax their resources in doing so. It is, nevertheless, from this larger population that future candidates for EAPs will come. Consequently, intervention at this earlier level has preventive functions.

Health Promotion Programs (HPPs)

If HPPs do not embody the fresh vision of assistance referred to above, they may at least hold the promise of it. In the broadest sense, HPPs refer to a wide gamut of interventions having as their common denominator the intention to mobilize the self-regulatory drive of individuals and groups to govern their own health and well-being. Their variety is enormous in kind, degree, and quality. They range from highly specific education campaigns with low budgets, to heroically funded multirisk factor interventions aimed at changing the world. They deal with cardiovascular health, nutrition and weight loss, smoking cessation, hypertension control, stress management, fitness, lifestyle appraisal and reformulation, as well as a variety of other health-related matters. They vary, too, in their availability to the workforce as a whole and in the degree to which they receive organizational support (Parkinson and Associates, 1982).

In spite of this variety, there begins to emerge a set of principles for the government of effective health promotion activities in the workplace (for a review, see Boutilier and Shain, 1983). Some of these principles flow from the observation that health-related behaviors, attitudes, values, and beliefs are highly interdependent (ibid.). Thus, in order to modify any one behavior in any one health area on a lasting basis requires that we can at least demonstrate how it fits with and is influenced by a whole constellation of related behaviors. This does not mean that everything has to be radically changed at once. Indeed, almost the opposite is probably true; namely, that small, well-planned steps taken one at a time are more likely to result in lasting change than great leaps forward that fall short (Green, 1970; Leventhal, 1973; Janis and Mann, 1977).

Consistent changes in one area, however small, are likely to create pressure for change in other areas and in so doing provide a foothold for making such changes. For example, drinking less alcohol in the evening may result in better REM sleep. In the morning, less coffee may be required to allow the individual to get going. He or she, feeling more rested, may be in a better position to make decisions during the day which in turn, may be satisfying to the extent that the evening is less replete with residual stresses from the day. This provides more room and energy for recreation, which in turn reinforces the decision to drink less. Such a chain reaction, though exaggerated for the sake of example, demonstrates the importance of preparing people for such consequences, so that they can exploit the opportunities which they represent for further change.

Behind these principles of interdependence and graduated change lies a related concept, that of self-efficacy or mastery. Programs designed in such a way that people glean immediate satisfaction from small gains, which they are then able to sustain, should have a positive effect upon their self-image and feelings of competence and self-worth. The need to activate this sense of competence (self-efficacy) appears to be another emerging principle in the theory of health promotion (Wallston, Maides, and Wallston, 1976; Wallston, Wallston, and DeVellis, 1978).

Given this framework of interdependence, it matters little where intervention begins, so that the choice of starting point should be dictated primarily by employee needs and interests. Sooner or later all the other areas will become relevant too.

To be of interest to employers, of course, HPPs have to be able to demonstrate that they are cost-beneficial. The data in this area are confused and confusing, largely because a variety of approaches are being compared that should not be compared owing to their disparate natures.

Once the problem of apples and oranges is sorted out, there remains the question of what criteria will be used to determine "benefit." Clearly, absenteeism, sickness benefits, productivity, turnover rates, long-term disability and compensation claims are all relevant factors, but so too are morale, corporate image, and recruitment appeal. The best-run hypertension control and smoking-cessation programs are claimed to be cost-beneficial on some of the "harder" cost lines just listed (Fielding, 1982; Kristein, 1982), while certain fitness programs have been shown to be of equivocal value in these terms, but of great value in the "softer" domains of job satisfaction and morale (Fielding, 1982).

Stress management programs, themselves representing a huge class of interventions, have succeeded in showing some promise in spite of their variety. Currently, it cannot be demonstrated that they prevent premature morbidity or mortality, but it can be demonstrated that some of them reduce the physiological and psychological manifestations of stress (see Schwartz, 1980, for a review). In terms of benefit to the employer, this effect is of value in itself, given that superfluous stress is associated with poor performance (ibid.).

Hopefully, enough has been said to illustrate the powerful connection between the needs of those employees for whom current EAPs would be too much of the wrong thing and HPPs of certain types. While benefits to the individual have been clearly demonstrated, unequivocal demonstrations of such benefits to employers have been made so far in rather global terms. It is obvious that sound evaluative studies are urgently required.

An Integrative Model

In our rapid overview of EAP/HPP approaches we have illustrated some of the strengths and weaknesses of each. It is the contention of the writers that their integration will result in a potentiation of their strengths, and will go some way toward a correction of their weaknesses. The basic premise upon which the following integrative model rests is that the general characteristics of the workforce do not differ greatly from the total community population. Consequently, any plan for impacting the health of workers requires the same multi-faceted approach as would be utilized in the larger community group.

While this assumption may appear to be somewhat simplistic, it is the contention of the writers that worksite programs have tended to be focused on either the conspicuously well or the conspicuously ill, to the exclusion of the majority.

Absent from the philosophy and practice of most occupational workers, rather than those at extreme ends of the continuum. We believe that such a concept should be elaborated and translated into organizational policies which espouse the value of optimum health for all workers. Such policies can be developed by management, labor and employee health and assistance practitioners outside the sphere of adversarial models of negotiation, if there is an acceptance of the common goal of achieving the optimum health and well-being of workers at all levels and on all points on the health-illness continuum. Such a goal can serve the economic and humanitarian values often shared to some extent by employers and unions.

The continuum just referred to provides a framework against which the various components of a comprehensive health policy can be identified. The needs of the workforce will vary in specific cases. An average health risk profile for an organization might appear as in Table 27-1:

TABLE 27-1. Average health risk profile for an organization.

0%	10	20	30	40	50	60	70	80	90	100%
Low risk (Healthy)				Moderate risk					High risk (Ill)	

In practice, and it spite of program directors' best intentions, EAPs typically address the needs of the high risk population, while HPPs address the needs of the low risk population. On occasion, both types of program reach out to the moderate risk group. However, it is often found that no clear objectives exist for interventions at any risk level. Consequently, the balance of this section is given over to an expression of how such objectives might be conceived as part of a comprehensive approach.

Programs aimed at the low risk area, target that portion of the workforce whose members have no personal or social problems impinging upon their workplace relationships or responsibilities. Their behavior can be described as "acceptable." However, this does not preclude the possibility that some people within this group may be experiencing difficulties that are not related to their state of health or well-being. For example, having duties or responsibilities that are beyond one's capability or having unclear or ambiguous job expectations may cause serious problems, but these are normally beyond the purview of such programs and must be dealt with through other organizational mechanisms or processes.

Within the group referred to as "healthy," an important distinction should be made between those whose behavior and attitudes serve to maintain their condition and those whose youth or genetic endowment enable them to remain healthy in spite of various abuses to which they expose themselves. The former group may be at low risk but the latter may be edging toward moderate risk by virtue of practices which in the long run have a high probability of undermining their health.

The objective of programs at this level therefore is to reach both these subgroups through education and promotion of the acceptance of healthy lifestyles as well as through reinforcement of the resolve of those already committed to such ideas.

The program component aimed at the moderate risk group provides perhaps the greatest challenge as well as the greatest benefits within the comprehensive model. Although the people within this group can by definition be said to be in a problematic situation, their behavior at work may have undergone only minimal or subtle changes, and they are not yet in a position where formal or disciplinary responses are appropriate or permissible.

However, if one were to apply the normal bell curve to the health-illness continuum, it would follow that this moderate risk group constitutes the largest proportion of the workplace population and, consequently, the group in whom gains could have the most impact on the present and future well-being of the total population.

As with the low risk group, those who are at moderate risk should not be viewed as a homogeneous entity. There is again a major distinction to be made in examining this group. Within it we should expect to find both those whose present health-related behavior is causing them current chronic loss in terms of wellness, productivity or both, and those who are suffering acute, severe difficulties or crises which might prognosticate serious future harm or loss if not adequately resolved.

The focus of programs at this secondary prevention or problem resolving level is avoidance of the personal and functional deterioration that can be expected to follow such unchecked situations. The objective here is to provide an awareness of the nature and consequences of these types of problematic situations in order to promote self-appraisal and self-directed problem resolution. Self-direction, however, does not preclude the selective use of community or workplace resources in the resolution of problems.

For example, a strategy that is currently being adopted in many work sites is the use of trained co-workers as primary care or referral agents in order to facilitate this process of self-appraisal and problem resolution. Referral agents can, on a proactive or reactive basis assist their fellow workers to become aware of a problematic situation, identify the nature of the problem, and refer them to an appropriate community agency or self-help group for the required assistance. Early observations of this strategy in the context of innovative EAPs indicate that, when utilized in conjuction with off-site community assessment and counseling services, program user rates increase significantly.

The final program component to be dealt within this model is for that part of the workforce who are at a high risk level. This is the designation used to describe those workers whose personal problems are such that their ability to function at work has deteriorated, such that they are not able to meet the expectations of their job, and are therefore in an unacceptable position.

This is the situation that calls upon the employer or manager to formally intervene in the problem, in a fashion that is usually referred to as constructive confrontation. The objective of this component is to assist these workers to recognize the situation and accept a referral for assistance as an alternative to the normal disciplinary action.

This is the aspect of EAPS that is most widely described in the literature and for that reason further elaboration is not required here.

This multi-risk level approach to health programming is summarized in Table 27-2.

TABLE 27-2. A Comprehensive Model for Employee Health and Assistance Programs.

GOAL: To establish in the workplace policies and procedures that will help workers maintain or regain satisfactory health and well-being.

	HEALTH		ILLNESS
	Primary Prevention Component	*Secondary Prevention Component*	*Tertiary Prevention Component*
Target group	Workers who are at low risk and whose behavior is acceptable.	Workers who are at an early stage of problem development and whose behavior is undesirable.	Workers who are at a late stage of problem development and whose behavior is unacceptable.
Component objective	To reinforce the resolve to maintain good health.	To encourage self appraisal and self correction of problems.	To establish identification and referral procedures.
Suggested interventions	Implementation of ongoing awareness campaigns aimed at disseminating health information and promoting healthy lifestyles through modification of beliefs, attitudes and behavior. Implementation of skill-building/training interventions, such as stress-management, smoking	Implementation of health awareness campaigns promoting self appraisal and correction. Utilization of trained resources (union counselors and referral agents) to assist fellow workers recognize problems and to motivate actions toward resolution on an informal basis.	Utilization of policies and procedures to have employers and managers provide referral to assistance as an alternative to discipline. (Formal) Provision of pathways to interventions at secondary level where indicated.

(continued next page)

TABLE 27-2 (continued)

GOAL: To establish in the workplace policies and procedures that will help workers maintain or regain satisfactory health and well-being.

HEALTH		ILLNESS
Primary Prevention Component	Secondary Prevention Component	Tertiary Prevention Component
cessation, weight reduction, nutrition, exercise courses.	Utilization of trained supervisors, managers and stewards to assist workers recognize problems and motivate actions toward resolution on an informal basis.	
	Training, self-management, skill-building courses in relation to stress, smoking, drinking, exercise, nutrition, hypertension, diabetes, etc.	

Conclusion

Achievement of a comprehensive model for employee health and assistance programs requries a philosophical, theoretical, and practical leap forward on the part of both EAP and HPP practitioners. The challenge to both lies in the recognition that a large body of workers with quantifiable health needs has been largely unreached by either health promotion or employee assistance interventions. Practitioners in both areas have much to learn from one another, provided that a mutual respect can by formed. Health promotion practitioners are in possession of valuable technology for changing and consolidating health-related attitudes, beliefs, and behavior. Employee assistance practitioners have developed excellent models for collaborative arrangements between management and labor, building upon the organizational power base which is a prerequisite to the successful implementation of any employee-related policy. This power base has been sadly neglected by health promotion programmers, who would do well to observe the principles to which their more treatment-oriented colleagues adhere when seeking to reach the greatest possible proportion of employees in need.

Representatives of management and labor, as well as employee health and assistance practitioners, need to further examine the opportunities that exist in every organization for the extension and integration of programs from both ends of the health continuum, so that the health needs of the whole workforce may be addressed. In this way we can expect to see each type of program lending power to the other so as to become synergistic. The alternative is for practitioners of EAP and HPP to compete for resources, to the frustration of both, and the detriment of employees in general.

References

Borthwick, R.G. *Summary of cost benefit study results for Navy alcoholism rehabilitation programs.* Technical Report #346, Presearch Inc., July, 1977.

Boutilier, M. and Shain, M. *Health practices, "lifestyle" and future disease: Implications for the prvention of excessive drinking.* Internal Document #13, Addiction Research Foundation, 33 Russell St., Toronto, M5S 2S1. 1983.

Edwards, G., et al. *Alcoholism: A controlled trial of "treatment" and "advice."* Journal of Studies on Alcohol, 38(5): 1004–1031, 1977.

Fielding, J.E. *Effectiveness of employee health improvement programs.* J. Occupational Medicine, 24, 11, 907–916, Nov, 1982.

Green, L.W. *Should health education abandon attitude change strategies?: Perspectives from recent research.* Health Education Mono. #30, 1970.

Hitchcock, L.C. and Sanders, M. *A survey of alcohol and drug abuse programs in the railroad industry.* National Technical Information Service, U.S. Dept. of Commerce, Springfield, VA. 22161, 1976.

House, J.S. *Occupational stress and coronary heart disease: A review and theoretical integration.* J. Health and Soc. Behaviour, 15, 12–27, March, 1974.

Janis, I.L. and Mann, L. *Decision making: A psychological analysis of conflict, choice and commitment.* New York. Free Press, 1977.

Kristein, M.M. *The economics of health promotion at the worksite.* Health Education Quarterly, 9, Special Supplement. 27–36, 1982.

Levens, E. *The cost benefit and cost effectiveness of occupational alcoholism programs.* Professional Safety, 36–41, Nov. 1976.

Leventhal, H. *Changing attitudes and habits to reduce risk factors in chronic disease.* American Journal of Cardiol., 31: 571–ff., 1973.

Mannello, T.A. and Seaman, F.J. *Prevalence, costs and handling of drinking problems on seven railroads.* University Research Corporation, Washington, D.C., 1979.

McQueen, D.V. and Siegrist, J. *Social factors in the etiology of chronic disease: An overview.* Social Science and Medicine, 16, 353–367, 1982.

Miller, R.E. *Incorporating health promotion into Employee Assistance Programmes.* Health Education, 14(4), 983 (in press).

Orford, J., Oppenheimer, E. and Edwards, G. *Abstinence or control: The outcome for excessive drinkers two years after consultation.* Behav. Res. Ther., 14: 409–418, 1976.

Orvis, B.R., Armor, D.J., Williams, C.E., Barras, A.J., Schwarzbach, D.S. *Effectiveness and cost of alcohol rehabilitation in the U.S. Air Force.* Rand, Santa Monica, 1981.

Parker, D.A. and Brody, J.A. *Risk factors for occupational alcoholism and alcohol problems.* In Occupational Alcoholism: A review of research issues. Research Monograph #8, National Institute on Alcohol Abuse and Alcoholism, Rockville, Maryland, 1982.

Parkinson, R.S. and Associates. *Managing health promotion in the workplace: Guidelines for implementation and evaluation.* Mayfield Publishing Co., Palo Alto, 1982.

Schramm, C.J. *Evaluating occupational programs: Efficiency and effectiveness.* In Research Monograph #8, National Institute on Alcohol Abuse and Alcoholism, Rockville, Maryland, 1982.

Schwartz, G.E. *Stress management in occupational settings.* Public Health Reports, 95, 2, 99–108, 1980.

Selye, H. *Stress in health and disease.* London: Butterworths, 1976.

Shain, M. and Groeneveld, J. *Employee Assistance Programmes: Philosophy, theory and practice.* Lexington Books, D.C. Heath Co., 1980.

Swint, J.M. *Critique of "Evaluating occupational programs: Efficiency and effectiveness,"* by C.J. Schramm. In Research Monograph #8, National Institute on Alcohol Abuse and Alcoholism, Rockville, Maryland, 1982.

Walker, K. and Shain, M. *Employee Assistance Programming: In search of effective interventions for the problem-drinking employee.* British Journal of Addiction, 78, 291–303, 1983.

Wallston, K.A., Maides, S. and Wallston, B.S. *Health-related information seeking as a function of health-related locus of control and health value.* Journal of Research in Personality, 10, 215–222, 1976.

Wallston, K.A., Wallston, B.S. and DeVellis. *Development of the multidimensional health locus of control scales.* Health Education Monographs, 6, 160–170, 1978.

Weiner, H.J., Akabas, S.H. and Sommer, J.J. *Mental health care in the world of work.* Associated Press, New York, 1973.

28

Stress: An Intrapersonal Approach
Samuel H. Klarreich

Stressors, or, What Starts the "Stress" Ball Rolling?

For years, occupational stress has been considered to be any work-related factor or set of factors which creates a maladaptive response (McLean, 1974). These work-related factors are typically labeled "stressors," and there has been a considerable amount of research regarding the impact of stressors (Selzer and Vinokur, 1975; Sheridan, 1981; Morse and Furst, 1979).

Mobility, as an organizational stressor, has received attention. Syne, Hyman and Enterline (1965) reported greater instances of stress-related disorders among those who were geographically mobile as opposed to those employees who remained stable and somewhat immobile. Underpromotion and overpromotion were other stressors which were examined by Brook (1973). This researcher noted that there were a variety of behavioral disorders and stress-related symptoms in four case studies of overpromotion, where the individual had been given responsibility exceeding his abilities, and underpromotion, where the person was not given responsibility equivalent to his ability.

Work overload has been researched extensively (French and Caplan, 1973). Margolis and Kroes (1974) found that work overload significantly contributed to a variety of stress symptoms, including absenteeism, alcohol misuse, poor work motivaton, poor self-esteem, and a general malaise.

Role ambiguity, another stressor, has also been researched. It involves a lack of precise information and clarity about the objectives and requirements of a role or position. Kahn et al. (1964) discovered that employees who experienced role ambiguity displayed a variety of distressing signs. These included lower job satisfaction, greater frustration and futility, poor self-confidence, and increased job tension. Role conflict, another stressor, occurs when an employee is being "pulled" by conflicting job demands, or is performing a task which he/she simply does not want to do, or feels is not part of his/her job. Kahn et al. (1964) discovered that individuals who experienced greater role conflict had, in fact, greater job-related stress and lowered job satisfaction.

Relationship with the superior has also received attention. Buck (1972) indicated that various pressures and strains can be felt by those employees who experience a "lack of consideration" from their superior. When a superior is highly critical and authoritarian, and in general "pulls rank," this tends to frustrate and pressure the employees. Relationship with subordinates is another critical stressor. Donaldson and Gowler (1975) discussed the fact that many managers may experience extreme stress and anxiety simply because they may not be used to the "participation model" of management. The managers may feel that their powers and their rule have been stripped.

Marshall and Cooper (1979) devised a very elaborate model which pointed out the many organizational factors that can cause stress. The various categories of stressors included those "intrinsic to the job," those related to "the role in the organization," those related to "career development," those related to "relationships," and those related to "organizational structure and climate."

Another category of stressors is referred to as extra-organizational stressors (Marshall and Cooper, 1979), situations and events which occur outside the organization. The study by Holmes and Rahe (1967) highlights the many potential life occurrences which cause stress. In fact, they developed a social readjustment rating scale, containing 43 life events. All of these events had a stress value attached to them; the greater the stress value, the more stressful the event. The items included: death of a spouse–stress value 100; divorce–stress value 73; marital separation–stress value 65; jail term–stress value 63; death of a close family member–stress value 63; and so on. The emphasis throughout their research was on obtaining events which represented changes "from the existing steady-state."

This research seems to indicate that stressors cause stress and illness. Stressors are, as Holmes and Rahe (1967) indicate, changes from a balanced state. Therefore, changes cause stress and illness in individuals. It would logically follow that in order to manage stress, simply eliminate change or the stressors. If the working environment is free of change, a "stress-free" existence will be ensured.

Is it, in fact, realistic to view stress in this way? Is it simply a matter of eliminating change? Can there be an existence free of change? Could the world of business and industry exist without change? Are we not constantly experiencing stressors or change, especially technological change? Alvin Toffler (1971), in his book *Future Shock*, talks about the fact that changes are here to stay.

The Meaning Of Stress

What does stress really mean? Is it a matter of encountering stressors and then experiencing stress? I don't think so. There has been considerable research discussing the importance of "mediating variables." Mediating variables are those processes which are located "in our heads," namely thinking, perceiving, judging, and appraising.

Bowers and Kelly (1979) made the point that stressors are not stressful until they are perceived to be as such. In fact, any particular changes are stressful only if they are viewed that way. McGrath (1976) said, "There is a potential for stress when an environmental situation is perceived as presenting a demand which threatens to exceed a person's capabilities and resources for meeting it" (pg. 352). Goldberg and Comstock (1976) indicated that life events may in fact be important as stressors only if they are viewed that way by the individual. French (1973) suggests that stress is a function of "the person-environment fit." The implication here is that a person's perception of a situation, as well as the perception of personal capabilities to deal with the situation, are the critical determinants of whether stress will be experienced.

Arguing, therefore, that stress is basically caused by factors or stressors extrinsic to the person is rather too simplistic. Furthermore, such an explanation would lead us to manage stress by unrealistically trying to eliminate the so-called stressful features of the environment, namely changes, while paying little attention to the perception of those changes.

Some of the most profound research has been conducted by Lazarus (1966). He states that the experience of stress is based on the concept of "cognitive appraisal." Events in the work environment or outside the work environment are not significant unless the person attributes significance to them and perceives them to be stressful. Once these events are appraised and judged to be a threat to one's own well-being, the term stress may be applied. This notion was further reinforced by later research conducted by Lazarus, Averill, and Opton (1970) and Lazarus and Launier (1978).

For the remainder of this discussion, stress will be considered a response (symptoms such as racing heart, dizziness, sweaty palms) to events which are believed and perceived to be a threat to one's own well-being and, in turn, are managed ineffectively. The three key elements in the definition are belief, perception, and ineffective management or behavior.

The Relentless Burden of Unrealistic Beliefs

The belief system is a prominent feature in the development of stress. The basic assumption is that people create their own stress because of their unrealistic beliefs. In fact, there is considerable research to substantiate this premise (Ellis, 1973; Ellis, 1971).

Dr. Albert Ellis (1962), from his practice and research, developed the theory that irrational beliefs create emotional disturbance. People adopt irrational or unrealistic beliefs, which in turn create considerable distress, and tension, and ultimately lead to what we know as stress-related disorders.

What is a belief? The Funk and Wagnalls dictionary (1976) defines a belief as "something held to be true or actual" (pg. 58). It is synonymous with faith, conviction, and a strong, deep feeling of certainty. A realistic belief is consistent with the real world, and there is sufficient evidence to point to this consistency. Additionally, the belief is not overly demanding, is not necessarily absolutistic, and usually results in moderate and not severe or extreme emotions (Walen, DiGuseppe, Wessler, 1980). A realistic belief assists one to fulfill his or her goals.

On the other hand, an unrealistic belief is typically unverifiable and inaccurate, and is usually not true (Walen, DiGuseppe, Wessler, 1980). Often the best indicator that a belief is unrealistic is that it usually leads to uncomfortable and disturbing emotions and symptoms, which may in fact be labeled as stress or stressful. As well, these unrealistic beliefs usually hamper one's goal-fulfillment and attainment (Wessler and Wessler, 1980; Walen, DiGuseppe, Wessler, 1980).

At this point, to illustrate the concept of unrealistic beliefs, I will describe a number of these. Before proceeding with the examples, it is worth noting that these beliefs are very global and general, and determine our philosophy of life. When they are unrealistic, they tend to distort information about self, about others, and about situations. In fact, these unrealistic beliefs tend to create and reinforce faulty perceptions and ineffective behaviors, both of which will be discussed in the next section.

Some examples of unrealistic beliefs are:

1. *"Something terrible will occur if I make a mistake."* This means that I may be fired by my manager; or I may be criticized by my supervisor or my spouse. In a sense, mistakes, errors of judgement, etc., are viewed as terrible and horrible occurrences.
2. *"There is a 'right and wrong' way to do things."* Obviously, it is right to succeed and it is wrong to fail. Furthermore, it is right to make my spouse happy, and it is wrong to make my manager angry.

There is an absolute way to do things. There are clear rules "carved in stone" which obviously indicate to all of mankind that certain things are "right" and certain things are "wrong."

3. *"It is awful to be criticized."* If I am criticized, it must mean that I am a failure in the eyes of management; and it further must mean that I am incompetent in the eyes of my spouse.

4. *"I must be approved of all of the time."* This means that management must tell me that I am doing a fantastic job, not some of the time, not most of the time, but all of the time. Furthermore, my spouse must tell me that I am successful. In fact, individuals who subscribe to this belief, vigorously seek out approval. However, if they do not acquire it, terrible things will happen. Their egos may be shattered.

5. *"People in authority should not be challenged."* If I disagree with my supervisor, I'll be fired. If I quarrel with my parents or in-laws, they'll disown me. With this unrealistic belief, then, you have really no choice but to run in fear of these "god-like individuals." If you run in fear, then how is communication maintained or how can problems be resolved?

6. *"Life must be fair and just."* For example, my supervisor should be fair in the distribution of work. My child should not have a learning disability. My stock broker should be able to project the financial dips of the future.

7. *"I must be in control all of the time."* I must be bright and alert. And I must respond brilliantly, especially in the presence of my manager. People who irrationally believe this invest a tremendous amount of energy in creating this unrealistic image.

8. *"I must anticipate everything."* I must know what is going on in my manager's head. Also, I must be prepared to handle "anything which my spouse dishes out." In other words, you are setting yourself up as "a mind-reader." But if you act upon every piece of guesswork which you contrive, you may experience considerable difficulty.

9. *"I must have things the way that I want them."* For example, I must have a prestigious position; I must have a beautiful office, and I must make a good salary.

10. *"I must have someone's shoulder to cry on."* That is, I must have support, especially from my spouse; also, I must have people feel sorry for me, such as my colleagues, peers, etc. When I have a problem, the world around me must share in my misery.

11. *"I must feel perfect all the time."* For example, I must not feel nervous or anxious; as well, I must not get discouraged or down. There are many people who, in fact, believe that the "ideal"

company man or woman feels "positive and up" to the exclusion of other feelings.

12. *"I am judged according to my performance."* That is, if I receive a poor performance rating, then I must be "a poor human being." Additionally, if I fail at a task, therefore I must be "a failure." With this unrealistic belief, people tend to generalize from a specific aspect of their performance to all of their performance and worth as a human being.

13. *"I was promised a rose garden."* For example, my work must always be rewarding and satisfying. As well, my colleagues, my peers, and my manager must be considerate, kind, and show respect for me. Certain individuals believe that "the world owes them something," and when this "something" is not forthcoming, discomfort typically sets in.

Rigidly adhering to one or more of these unrealistic beliefs tends to create a distorted sense of self and others, and an irrational view of situations. Leading your life on the basis of these unrealistic beliefs will create considerable stress. However, there are some other significant processes which also play an important role–perception and behavior.

Faulty Perception and Ineffective Behavior–"Two Peas in a Stress-Pod"

Perception, according to Funk and Wagnalls dictionary (1976), is "any insight or knowledge arrived at by the process of understanding or apprehending with the mind" (pg. 486). Accurate perception is based on the interpretation of experience without distorting it. However, certain distortions can take place. Distorted perceptions, in fact, cause and exacerbate psychological stress (Raimey, 1975; Cameron and Meichenbaum, 1982). Distorted or faulty perception involves a misinterpretation of experience, that is, misinterpreting various benign situations as being very problematic and threatening.

Perception, although influenced by beliefs, is a process which significantly differs from beliefs, because it is very situational and immediate. It is more specific, more tailored to the situation, whereas, beliefs are more general and global, taking a longer period of time to develop.

Perception is synonymous with appraisal, judgement, and inference (Christensen, 1977; Klarreich et al., 1980). Because perception is influenced by beliefs, if the beliefs are unrealistic, they will probably lead to faulty perception. Once the faulty perception exists, based on unrealistic beliefs, the behavior that results will probably be inappropriate, maladaptive, and ineffective in that situation. This entire process is, basically, the stress cycle.

Faulty perception is illustrated by the following examples: When there is an expression of anger, a faulty perception might be that "my angry spouse is attacking me." Or, "that angry manager is out to get me." When someone expresses criticism, a faulty perception might be that "my colleague is critical because I was at fault." Or, my spouse is upset because I performed poorly." When an individual expresses rejection, a faulty perception might be that "the manager is always trying to hurt me." Or "my spouse is terrible and destructive towards me." When someone is unresponsive or does not offer feedback, a faulty perception might be that "my manager doesn't care about me." Or, "my spouse thinks that I am useless and not worth anything."

In essence, faulty perception is the process whereby a conclusion is drawn prematurely, without a full understanding of the situation. This inaccurate conclusion, which is profoundly influenced by unrealistic beliefs, often produces very uncomfortable feelings.

Behavior is the final element which completes the cycle. As was previously indicated, behavior is influenced by perceptions and beliefs (Cameron and Meichenbaum, 1982). Funk and Wagnalls' dictionary (1976) defines behavior as "the way a person . . . acts under different circumstances" (pg. 57). Ineffective behavior includes acts which are maladaptive or do not properly "fit" or adjust to a given situation (Goldfried and Davidson, 1976). I will illustrate three prominent ineffective behaviors.

The first ineffective behavior is "aggression" (Christensen, 1977). Examples of aggression include screaming, shouting, "desk pounding" at a peer or a subordinate. The individual, to deliver the aggressive message, may use the word "you" before a number of sentences that are used. What transpires is a method of attack in which one individual attempts to overpower the other. Usually when an individual is attacked, one of two reactions may occur. The individual, in fear of the aggressor, may flee. If the individual is suitably upset by the aggressor he/she may, in fact, fight and become aggressive in return. The exchange then usually becomes a very heated one, and constructive dialogue literally "goes out the window." Little is accomplished, and, therefore, this aggressive behavior is regarded as ineffective.

The second type of ineffective behavior is termed "avoidance" (Christensen, 1977). This may typically involve leaving a meeting because of anxiety, or running away from a debate with a colleague or supervisor. What the individual temporarily avoids are the uncomfortable feelings engendered by the problematic situation. However, these uncomfortable feelings usually recur once the situation is again encountered.

A third type of ineffective behavior is "passivity" (Christensen, 1977). This may include remaining silent when one is feeling angry inside. Or, it may be expressed as doing absolutely nothing when someone has "dumped upon you." This is a very awkward form of behavior, because the individual remains in the situation, yet is immobilized. He or she strongly wishes to do something differently and more effectively, but does not. The frustration that builds may be discharged in some other fashion. The individual may argue with his/her spouse, discipline the children more harshly, or sulk for days.

In summary, then, if the behavior is ineffective, and is in combination with faulty perception and unrealistic beliefs, the outcome is predictable–stress. And what of stress management techniques? It is important to realize that this refers to the management of stress, rather than the elimination of stress. Management implies utilizing strategies that permit control of the stress symptoms, so that satisfactory functioning is restored in and/or outside the work environment.

Relaxation and Stress

Today, relaxation techniques appear to be among the most prominent stress management strategies. Many researchers seem to believe that stress and its related problems can be controlled through the systematic application of relaxation procedures (Bowers, 1976; Luthe, 1969). Examples of these relaxation procedures are biofeedback, yoga, transcendental meditation, progressive relaxation, autogenic training, and hypnosis.

Benson (1974) developed the term "the relaxation response." He pointed out the significance of this response in decreasing a variety of stress-related disorders. These include elevated blood pressure, increased heart rate and respiration, and other nervous system activities. He stated that, once this response is elicited, (which resembles transcendental meditation), a variety of positive changes can occur. Blood pressure can be reduced, heart rate can be lowered, and oxygen consumption can be reduced. Frew (1974) examined the application of transcendental meditation to the work environment and the extent to which it could influence productivity. The employees instructed in meditation indicated that they experienced better job performance, greater job satisfaction, decreased desire to leave their work environments, improved relationships with peers and management, and a reduced desire to "push for the top."

Elder et al. (1973) and Patel (1973) employed biofeedback training, a relatively new therapeutic procedure, and produced a significant decrease in blood pressure for the treatment of essential hypertension.

The above research illustrates the variety of such techniques, all of which produce similar relaxed states. It would be safe to say that "relaxation" is a very useful tool which is spreading, as corporations "learn its mantras and chronic worriers unwind their minds" (Wallis, 1983).

But what does relaxation accomplish? What it seems to bring about is a variety of biological changes. Secondly, it seems to reduce levels of tension. Basically and simplistically, it is a profound method of distraction. In a sense, it distracts one away from those troubling situations which ultimately need to be resolved. It allows one a short time-out or respite away from the troubling events at work or at home. But is this a desirable state? Is it being suggested that one should strive for a constant state of relaxation? Is it, in fact, possible to be constantly relaxed? And, if it is not, then, is it being suggested that temporary states of relaxation ultimately allow one to control stress?

It was explained earlier that unrealistic beliefs, faulty perception, and ineffective behavior ultimately lead to stress. Does the relaxation training and the relaxation response address these three ingredients? No, of course not. Relaxation training is virtually useless in changing what I believe to be the three essential ingredients to stress and stress management. That is not to say that relaxation training brought about by a variety of techniques is not valuable. Relaxation training does have value. But it must be pointed out that its value is short-term in nature. It is a powerful way to temporarily relieve tension, yet it clearly has its limitations, and these should be carefully noted. What I am also suggesting is that attention and energy should be directed towards a re-examination of beliefs, perception, and behavior (Shea, 1980).

Shea (1980) points out that "Much stress is a result of negative thinking in that the development of new habits and the controlling of negative moods can substantially reduce stress" (pg. 30). Relaxation does not significantly affect these areas, but in the remaining sections, I will attempt to describe techniques which do.

Restructing Beliefs, or, "Debunking"

What is important throughout the restructuring process is the individual's willingness to accept the principle that unrealistic beliefs are the chief sources of stress. Then it is important that the individual be willing to challenge and to dispute those unrealistic beliefs with the understanding that a more realistic framework will evolve (Ellis and Abrahms, 1978; Ellis and Grieger, 1977).

Disputation is, then, a logical and empirical process in which the individual is helped to stop and think. Its basic goal is to help the person internalize a new philosophy, epitomized in statements such as: "It would be too bad if I don't succeed but I can bear it." "I'm merely fallible and that's not awful." (Walen, DiGiuseppe, Wessler, 1980).

In the restucturing process, doubts and questions and reservations are raised about the precise nature of the unrealistic beliefs. They are challenged with the ultimate purpose of developing alternative, more realistic philosophies. There are ways to challenge these, mainly through the use of questions. Some questions might include the following: "What is the proof for your belief?" "What evidence exists for that belief?" "How do you know that to be true?" "What is the worst thing that could happen to you?"

What is also critical throughout this process is humor (Walen, DiGiuseppe, Wessler, 1980). In a sense, by recognizing the humor and the silliness which is sometimes involved in these unrealistic beliefs, you are already restructuring your thinking. You are beginning to take less seriously what was previously viewed as very serious and critical. Stress does not necessarily have to be a devastating, debilitating, and destructive force.

What is also being disputed are a number of philosophical "givens" which people seem to possess. The first of these is that there are many "universal truths" to living, and these are often reflected in the words "should" and "must." Furthermore, if these universal truths are not upheld, horrible, catastrophic and awful things will occur (Walen, DiGiuseppe, Wessler, 1980; Ellis, 1978). Another of these is that human worth is established by the ability to perform according to these universal standards, so that if these universal standards are not met, a state of worthlessness and uselessness is the outcome. Another of these "givens" is that these universal standards are needed in order to remain happy (Walen, DiGiuseppe, Wessler, 1980).

Allow me to illustrate the restructuring process by returning to a few unrealistic beliefs which were stated in the section entitled "The Relentless Burden of Unrealistic Beliefs." In disputing these, it is hoped that the reader will begin to see that there is a more realistic, flexible and rational approach to adopt. This approach embodies the fundamental principles of stress management.

If you make a mistake, will something terrible really occur? Are you certain of that? How do you know what will occur? Do you not, in fact, learn from mistakes? Is not trial and error a valuable process?

Is there really a "right and wrong" way to do things? Is the world really black and white? When you look around, you can obviously see that things are not that simple. Is it always right to make people happy, and is it wrong to make people angry? By the way, can you really make a person happy and make a person angry? If you can do that, you must have tremendous control over people.

How awful is it to be criticized? If your actions are criticized, does that mean that you are a complete failure in every phase of your existence? When others have been criticized, how do they survive? Is there no such thing as constructive criticism? If you are criticized, how long will you feel uncomfortable? Is that so bad?

Why do you have to receive approval all of the time? What will happen to you if you don't? What is other people feel uncomfortable always offering approval? Wouldn't the positive effects of approval wear off if you were to receive it all the time? Might you not question the truth of the approval if it was forthcoming a hundred percent of the time? And is happiness totally based on approval? Is approval truly necessary for you to function?

Once beliefs are restructured, for certain people this may be sufficient in managing their stress. They may be comfortable to the point where they are, once again, happy and living their lives and managing their work environment satisfactorily. On the other hand, this restructuring process may make it possible for other individuals to continue to make additional changes in their perceptions and their behavior.

Correcting Perceptions, or, "Cleaning The Windows Of Your Mind"

The difference between changing perceptions and changing beliefs is the distinction, as Walen, DiGiuseppe, Wessler (1980) point out, between elegant and inelegant solutions. In modifying perceptions, the difference between observation and inference is taught (Christensen, 1977). You are taught to pay closer attention to your environment, and then to draw conclusions that are consistent with your observations. However, people make many errors and seem to repeat this process, especially if there are prominent unrealistic beliefs prevalent, which heightens the probability that faulty perceptions will be made.

Therapists such as Beck (1976), Raimey (1975), and Maultsby (1975) highlight the importance of correcting people's errors in gathering information and also correcting people's errors in drawing conclusions from that information. People also tend to generalize too quickly, and draw conclusions from one single event and apply them to all events (Beck, 1976).

Changes will occur in perceptions once they are challenged. I will illustrate how perceptions may be corrected by returning to a few faulty perceptions described earlier in the section on faulty perceptions.

When your spouse is angry with you, is he/she really attacking you? When your manager is angry is he/she truly out to get you? What other reasons might there be for this angry behavior? What additional information could you gather about this behavior that might lead you to another conclusion?

When your spouse is critical, does that conclusively mean that you performed poorly? When your colleague is critical are you always at fault? What other conclusions could you draw about these critical comments?

When you cross-examine your perceptions, your faulty perceptions will change, and more accurate conclusions wil be formulated. Once the faulty perceptions have been corrected, it is another facet to the management of stress. For some, it may be sufficient to simply restructure their beliefs and correct their perceptions. For others, however, it may also be important to modify their behavior as the final step needed to manage their stress.

Modifying Behavior And "Going For It"

Behavior change is the last dimension which is relevant to the management of stress. Poser (1970) discussed the importance of a variety of behavioral approaches. Such behaviors as information-seeking, anticipatory problem-solving, and general coping skills are significant in the management of stress. Lang and Jakubowski (1976) discussed the importance of a direct, honest, and appropriate discussion of one's opinions, beliefs, feelings, and wants as a way of managing one's interpersonal environment and thus controlling stress.

Changed behavior is simply those actions and expressions which increase the probability of a favorable outcome. If your beliefs are more realistic and your perceptions are accurate, this prepares you for a more reasonable approach and more effective behavior (Rimm, 1973; Ellis and Harper, 1975; Wolfe, 1975).

Effective behavior initially involves approaching the situation and/or the person, in other words, physically moving forward. This includes maintaining eye contact, especially in communication with others, and maintaining an erect posture while in the presence of others. As well, this involves asking questions, rather than drawing inappropriate and inaccurate perceptions. Questions which begin with the words "how" "what" "why" allow you to seek out information. Information-seeking is, in fact, very important, as the derived data will assist you to more accurately form your perceptions. In asking these questions, it would be important to speak clearly and audibly and not to convey an apologetic or fearful stance [Lange and Jakubowski, 1976].

The next stage is self-expression or assertion. In this instance, you clearly express your feelings, thoughts, and ideas. It would be important to begin sentences with "I." "I feel . . . ;" "I believe . . . ;" or "I am thinking about . . . " are examples. There is no attempt to attack or berate the other individual; simply, there is an attempt made to express yourself. Ellis (1978) indicates that "self-assertion is one of the healthiest goals imaginable and one that is likely to help you become and remain efficient" (pg. 121). He further points out that "assertion is healthy, because it states that you want something, and that you are determined to do something about getting this want satisfied, even though some of people you are involved with have different preferences" (Ellis, 1978).

Summary

"Stress—is it me, or is it the organization?" Basically, it is "me" that is causing stress. Although the organizational environment may create a variety of stressors, and although the organizational environment may subtly reinforce certain behaviors that you feel are inappropriate, stress basically relates to what you believe, what you perceive, and what you do.

References

Beck, A.T. *Cognitive Therapy and the Emotional Disorders*, New York, International Universities Press, 1976.

Benson, H. *The Relaxation Response*, New York, Avon Books, 1974.

Bowers, K.S. *Hypnosis for the Seriously Curious*, Monterey, Brooks, Cole Publishers, 1976.

Bowers, K. S. and Kelly, P. "Stress, disease, psychotherapy and hypnosis," *Journal of Abnormal Psychology*; 1979, 88, pp. 490–505.

Brook, A. "Mental stress at work", *The Practitioner*. 1973, 210, pp. 500–506.

Buck, V. *Working Under Pressure*, London, Staples Press, 1972.

Cameron, R. and Meichenbaum, D. "The nature of affective coping and the treatment of stress-related problems: a cognitive-behavioral perspective" in C. Goldberger and A. Breznitz (eds.) *Handbook of Stress*, New York, Free Press, 1982.

Christensen, C. *The Interpersonal Coping Skills Program*, Toronto, University of Toronto, 1977.

Donaldson, J. and Gowler, D. "Perogatives, participation and managerial stress" in D. Gowler and K. Legge (eds.) *Managerial Stress*, Epping, Gower Press, 1975.

Edler, S. T., et al. "Instrumental conditioning of diastolic blood pressure in essential hypertensive patients", *Journal of Applied Behavioral Analysis*, 1973, 6, pp. 377–382.

Ellis, A. *Reason and Emotion in Psychotherapy*, New York, Lyle Stuart, 1962.

_____. *Growth Through Reason*, Hollywood, Calif., Wilshire Books, 1971.

_____. *Humanistic Psychotherapy, the Rational Emotive Approach*, New York, Julian Press, 1973.

_____. *Executive Leadership: A Rational Approach*, New York, The Institute for Rational Living, 1978.

_____., and Abrahms, E. *Brief Psychotherapy in Medical and Health Practice*, New York, Springer Publishing Company, 1978.

_____., and Grieger, R. *Handbook of Rational-Emotive Therapy*, New York, Springer Publishing Company, 1977.

_____., and Harper, R. *A New Guide To Rational Living*, New Jersey, Prentice-Hall, 1975.

French, J. R. P. "Person-role fit," *Occupational Mental Health*, 1973, 3, pp. 15–20.

_____., and Caplan, R. D. "Organizational stress and individual strain" in A. J. Marrow (ed.) *The Failure Of Success*, New York, AMACOM, 1973.

Frew, D. R. "Transcendental meditation and productivity," *Academy of Management Journal*, 1974, 17, pp. 362–368.

Funk and Wagnalls Dictionary, New York, Funk and Wagnalls Publishing Company, 1976.

Goldberg, L. and Comstock, G. W. "Life events and subsequent illness," *American Journal of Epidemiology*, 1976, 104, pp. 146–158.

Goldfried, M. R. and Davison, G. C., *Clinical Behavior Therapy*, New York, Holt, Rinehart and Winston, 1976.

Holmes, T. H. and Rahe, R. H. "The social readjustment rating scale," *Journal of Psychosomatic Research*, 1967, 11, pp. 213–218.

Kahn, R. L., et al. *Organizational Stress*, New York, Wiley, 1964.

Klarreich, S. H., Cole, J. R., Fryatt, M. "A coping skills approach to the treatment of adult psychiatric outpatients: a pilot study," *Canada's Mental Health*, 1980, 28, pp. 5–7.

Lange, A. J. and Jakubowski, P. *Responsible Assertive Behavior*, Illinois, Reasearch Press, 1976.

Lazarus, R. S. *Psychological Stress and the Coping Process*, New York, McGraw-Hill, 1966.

_____., Averill, J. R. and Opton, E. M. "Toward a cognitive theory of emotion" in M. Arnold (ed.) *Feelings and Emotions*, New York, Academic Press, 1970.

_____., and Launier, R. "Stress-related transactions between person and environment" in L. A. Pervin and M. Lewis (eds.) *Perspectives in Interactional Psychology*, New York, Plenum, 1978.

Luthe, W. *Autogenic Training*, New York, Grune and Stratton, 1969.

Margolis, B. L. and Kroes, W. H. "Work and the health of man" in J. O'Toole (ed.) *Work and the Quality of Life*, Cambridge, M.I.T. Press, 1974.

Marshall, J. and Cooper C. L. *Executives Under Pressure*, New York, Praeger Publishers, 1979.

Maultsby, M. *Help Yourself To Happiness*, New York, Institute for Rational Living, 1975.

McGrath, J. E. "Stress and behavior in organizations" in M. Dunnette (ed.) *Handbook of Industrial and Organizational Psychology*, Chicago, Rand McNally, 1976.

McLean, A. *Occupational Stress*, Springfield, Thomas, 1974.

Morse, D. R. and Furst, M.L. *Stress for Success*, New York, Van Nostrand Reinhold Company, 1979.

Patel, C. H. "Yoga and biofeedback in the management of hypertension," *Lancet*, 1973, 2, pp. 1053–1055.

Poser, F. "Toward a theory of 'behavioral prophylaxis," *Journal of Behavior*

Therapy and Experimental Psychiatry, 1970, 1, pp. 39–43.

Raimey, V. *Misunderstandings of the Self: Cognitive Psychotherapy and the Misconception Hypothesis*, San Francisco, Jossey-Bass, 1975.

Rimm, D. C. "Thoughtstopping and covert assertion," *Journal of Consulting and Clinical Psychology*, 1973, 41, pp. 466–467.

Selzer, M. L. and Vinokur, A. "The role of life events in accident causation," *Mental Health Society*, 1975, 2, pp. 36–54.

Shea, G. F. "Cost effective stress management training," *Training and Development Journal*, 1980, July, pp. 25–33.

Sheridan, P. J. "NIOSH puts job stress under the microscope," *Occupational Hazards*, 1981, April, pp. 70–73.

Syme, S. L., Hyman, M. M. and Enterline, P. E. "Cultural mobility and the occurrence of coronary heart disease," *Journal of Health and Human Behaviour*, 1965, 6, pp. 178–189.

Toffler, A. *Future Shock*, New York, Bantam, 1971.

Walen, S. R., DiGuiseppe, R., Wessler, R. L. *A Practitioner's Guide to Rational-Emotive Therapy*, New York, Oxford University Press, 1980.

Wallis, C. "Stress: can we cope?," *Time*, 1983, June 6, pp. 54–61.

Wessler, R. A. and Wessler, R. L. *The Principles and Practice of Rational-Emotive Therapy*, San Francisco, Jossey-Bass, 1980.

Wolfe, J. L. "Rational-emotive therapy as an effective feminist therapy," *Rational Living*, 1975, 11, pp. 1–6.

29

Educating Employees in the Area of Chemical Dependency
Janis L. Levine

Introduction

Today, alcohol and other drug problems are a major health issue in North America, resulting in severe consequences for business and society at large. Alcoholism, the most common dependency, ranks as one of the most serious health problems, along with heart disease, cancer, and mental illness. It is estimated that alcoholism affects approximately 10 to 12% of the working population, and costs industry millions of dollars each year in lost productivity, absenteeism, and injuries (U.S. Department of Health and Human Services, January, 1981; Galt, 1982; Neil, 1982).

Although chemical dependency is similar to other personal problems in its ability to interfere with an employee's work efficiency, of all such problems, it is one of the *most* destructive and widespread. If permitted to run its course unchecked, it has the ability to destroy both physical and mental health, and often ends in death.

Society has only recently begun to recognize chemical dependency as an emotional and physical crippler. In turn, the business community has also accepted that it has a noticeably destructive impact on employees and their work.

For many, chemical dependency is tragically and fundamentally misunderstood, distorted by myth and misconception. The Roman philosopher and lawyer Seneca (4 B.C.–65 A.D.) pronounced an opinion about drinkers and drunkenness that continues to mold public opinion: "Drunkenness is nothing but a condition of insanity purposely assumed," (Milam and Ketchan 1981).

Yet, recent research and statistical evidence have indicated that alcoholism and other drug dependencies are illnesses that can happen to anyone. This is the rationale behind educating employees–to root out and replace myths and misconceptions with facts. It is then, with awareness and education, that the disease can be fully understood.

Historical Overview

Control Data Corporation has always had, by written policy and corporate mission statement, a commitment to employee welfare and to meeting human needs. In 1973, Control Data instituted a corporate-wide counseling program. Although not identified as an alcoholism program, it developed out of a growing recognition in the late 60s and early 70s that employers could do something constructive about alcoholism, rather that just tolerate the problem until termination became inevitable.

The expansion of the program to cover a broad range of personal problems came as a result of experience in the beginning months of the program, when very few calls indicated chemical dependency problems. It was believed that people with these problems were not coming forward due to stigma and a lack of recognition. From this early experience, it was concluded that the program should focus on the "troubled employee," individuals with an issue of problem that is interfering with the attainment of their personal or work objectives.

In April, 1974, the Employee Advisory Resource (EAR) Program was formally announced and made available to 48,000 employees and their families through a special mailing sent to their homes. The new service was not identified as an alcoholism-oriented program, but simply as a counseling program designed to help employees and their families through personal and work-related problems. EAR was set up to provide a confidential, 24-hour counseling service for evaluation and referral.

Control Data's policy is to approach chemical dependency, which includes alcoholism and addiction to other drugs, as a behavioral-medical disorder that can be successfully treated, like other illnesses. The company does not wish to intrude into its employees' private lives and become involved only when the use of drugs or alcohol, or the effects of other personal problems, interfere with an employee's health and job performance, the performance of other employees, or the company's ability to carry on its business.

The company's managers are responsible for recognizing deteriorating job performance. Supervisory training sessions were introduced seven years ago as tools to aid in awareness and capability in the recogniton, proper administration and referral of performance problems which may or may not be related to alcohol and/or other drug abuse. Diagnosis of alcohol and other drug problems on the basis of physical symptoms is discouraged, as supervisors are not qualified to make such judgments. The course provides management with:

1. an awareness that alcohol and other drug problems often underlie performance difficulties.
2. guides them toward earlier recognition, intervention, and referral of *performance problems* to EAR for evaluation.

The Management Training and Awareness on Alcohol and Other Drugs Course is mandatory for everyone that works in a supervisory capacity at Control Data.

Control Data Canada

In July, 1982, the EAR Program was introduced to Canada by Control Data Canada, Ltd. to provide couseling services for personal and work-related problems to the company's 2000 employees and their families across the country. It was decided to begin a program of chemical dependency awareness seminars in the fall of 1982, as a means of increasing the visibility of the EAR program and educating employees. A four-hour seminar was offered to all employees, regardless of job title or responsibilities, based on the assumption that chemical dependency can rear its head at home as well as at the workplace, and that it affects approximately 25% of all North American families (Control Data, 1980).

"The National Council on Alcoholism estimates that there are 10 million alcoholics in the United States and that each one of these profoundly affects the lives of at least six other people" (Woititz, 1979). Chemical dependency is a disease that may start with one person, but eventually each family member becomes part of a dysfunctional family system. To live in a distressed family and not have the courage to talk about the situation is an emotionally painful and difficult experience for family members. They experience fear, anger, loneliness, hurt, guilt, and shame as the disease progresses, and they eventually become part of the problem. Thus it is that chemical dependency is often referred to as a *family illness*.

Goals

The goals of the chemical dependency awareness seminar are as follows:

1. To identify personal attitudes about drugs and alcohol.
2. To describe the difference between social use of alcohol/other drugs, and chemical dependency.
3. To describe the characteristics and progression of chemical dependency and various treatment alternatives.

4. To gain an understanding of company policy on alcohol, drugs, and other personal problems.
5. To be aware of the EAR program, how it operates, how it can be helpful, and how to use it effectively.

The following goals focus specifically on supervisory responsibilities:

6. To explain the importance of early identification and referral, and the characteristics of the pattern of performance decline.
7. To explain the difference between problem identification and referral, and diagnosis.
8. To examine feelings about dealing with a problem employee.
9. To describe procedures for conducting a job performance interview with a problem employee.
10. To identify elements of the supervisor's role during and after treatment.

Content

A key feature of the seminar is the utilization of "I'll Quit Tomorrow," a three-part film developed by The Johnson Institute, Minneapolis, Minnesota. Part I follows a businessman, his family, and his employer, as they struggle with his progressing alcoholism. By lacking knowledge about alcoholism, both the family and employer permit the illness to progress by covering up and making excuses for his behavior. In Part II, one form of intervention sometimes used in employment settings is shown. The family members, manager, and employer meet with the businessman, describe to him the personal and social effects of his drinking behavior, and encourage him to accept treatment. Part III portrays a comprehensive treatment program and the beginning of recovery.

At the beginning of the four-hour seminar, participants introduce themselves and indicate their supervisory responsibilities and personal expectations of the seminar. This helps the instructor to tailor content to either a heavier focus on supervisory responsibilities or personal experience.

Alcoholism has been desribed as a disease and has been recognized as such by the American Medical Association since 1956. Recognizing alcoholism and other drug abuse as an illness implies:

- The illness can be described.
- The course of the illness is predictable and progressive.
- The disease is primary–not a symptom of some underlying disorder.

- It is chronic–it can be arrested but not cured.
- It is terminal–it results in death unless the progression is stopped.

A functional definition is introduced: Alcoholism occurs when one's usage of alcohol causes problems in any one or more of the major life areas, and despite the development of these problems, the person continues to use alcohol and continues to experience problems in one or more of these areas: 1. **Family**, 2. **Friends**, 3. **Legal**, 4. **Financial**, 5. **Job**, 6. **Health**.

From a Control Data standpoint, a chemical dependency includes any continuing use of drugs (including alcohol) which impairs a person's ability to perform his or her duties.

As the seminar progresses, the film is used to prompt questions and discussion in an open, accepting atmosphere. The film explores the effects of one man's drinking on his family, resulting in their increasing social isolation, and it describes his deteriorating job performance as the illness progresses. An intervention by his employer and family members is demonstrated in the film, which eventually results in treatment being accepted.

During the seminar, defense mechanisms, the role of denial, the incidence of blackouts, and "loss of control" are discussed. The key question presented is, "What happens when someone drinks?" The emphasis is on indicating whether individuals can safely predict what will happen when they start drinking. The process of intervention is discussed along with various forms of treatment:

- Inpatient/Outpatient
- Alcoholics Anonymous
- Half-way houses
- Detoxification centers

Because alcoholics significantly affect several people in their life, a majority of the seminar attendees will have some personal experience with an alcoholic. The key is to create an open, accepting atmosphere where individuals feel free to ask questions and engage in discussion.

Supervisors are given guidelines on how to confront an employee on job performance (performance, attendance, behavior), rather than trying to diagnose and counsel. A supervisor's job is to monitor performance, and if performance declines, his/her task is to discuss the performance decline with employees and encourage them to seek assistance. EAR is a strictly confidential resource that Control Data has developed to provide assistance to employees as well as consultation to managers.

By focusing on the educational aspect of the seminar, attendees will hopefully gain knowledge that will help them in turn to help others, and in the future that will not allow the disease to progress. People close to a chemically-dependent individual usually permit the disease to progress further by not calling attention to the harmful consequences of the chemical usage on behavior and/or performance. They do this by letting individuals use excuses to rationalize their behavior. The "enabler" sympathizes, covers up, and protects the individual from harmful consequences and the progression of the illness goes on unchecked.

As a logical extension of Control Data's recognition of chemical dependency as a behavioral–medical disorder, a program was introduced in 1983 whereby the company will reimburse employees for taxi fares when alcohol use in social and work-related situations may prevent them from driving safely. The program has been developed to encourage responsible decision-making about drinking and to reinforce the message "If you drive–don't drink."

Conclusion

Chemical dependency is having a devastating effect on our society, and all of us have been, will be, or are currently affected by it, whether on the job or in our personal lives. It is a disease that ranks with cancer, heart disease, and mental illness, yet it has the relative advantage of being arrestable–the earlier the better. Factual knowledge about the disease and its early symptoms will help individuals make effective decisions when confronted with chemical dependency, whether at home, at work, or at social gatherings. Education is the key to prevention.

References

Control Data Corporation, Chemical dependency awareness and training for managers, Minneapolis, Minnesota, 1980.

Johnson, V., *I'll quit tomorrow*, New York, Harper and Row, 1980.

Johnson Institute, *"I'll Quit Tommorow,"* film, Johnson Institute, Minneapolis, Minnesota.

Milam, J. R. and Ketcham, K., *Under the influence–A guide to the myths and realities of alcoholism*, Seattle, Washington, Madonna Publishers, 1981.

Neil, B., *Accidents on tap: Drinking on the job*, WCB Report, Summer 1982.

Brecher, J. et al, *Taking drugs on the job*, Newsweek, August 22, 1983.

Galt, V., *Hard times force firms to face alcoholism;* The Globe and Mail, Toronto, Ontario, August 28, 1982.

Shain, M., *Prevention of substance abuse through health promotion in the workplace*, in EAP Digest, Sept/Oct 1983.

U.S. Department of Health and Human Services, Alcohol and Health; Fourth Special Report to the U.S. Congress. (DHHS Publication No. (ADM) 81-1080), Washington, D.C.; U.S. Government Printing Office; January, 1981.

Woititz, J.; *Marriage on the rocks*, New York, N.Y., Delacorte Press, 1979.

30

A Rational-Emotive Approach to Acceptance and its Relationship to EAPs.
Albert Ellis

Introduction

The philosophy of acceptance of the inevitable or unchangeable is one of the most time-honored parts of the self-help movement. Various forms of it are included in ancient scriptures–including those of the Jews, Buddhists, Christians, and Moslems; and many self-help groups and EAPs use it to good effect.

The term acceptance, as it is used in mental health fields, is often ill-defined and even contradictory. I shall attempt in this paper to clarify its usage in rational-emotive therapy (RET), and to show how it can be efficiently applied to psychotherapy, to self-help groups, and to EAPs.

What Acceptance is Not

Let me first try to outline what acceptance, according to RET, is *not*:

1. It does *not* consist of liking, loving, or approving of other people (nor oneself), but of unconditionally accepting them as fallible and forgiveable humans, even when you distinctly dislike some of their traits and characteristics. When you fully accept people you do not necessarily feel friendly toward them, and may even choose to always avoid them (as, for example, you might refuse to be friendly with Hitler and Stalin). But you do accept their humanity, even when it erupts in vicious forms, you do view them as fallible humans, and have no illusions as to their being superhuman or subhuman. Acceptance means trying to help people change for the better–but not damning or condemning them when they don't change (Ellis, 1962, 1972, 1973, 1976; Ellis and Harper, 1975).

2. Acceptance does not mean rating people's behaviors as "good" or "bad," "efficient" or "inefficient" in accordance with the goals these people (and others) try to achieve. But it means making a real effort only to measure their acts and performances and not their "self," "essence," "totality," or "personhood." If these higher order abstractions can be accurately defined at all (and to some degree they probably can not be), they are too complex and ongoing (processes rather than products), and therefore can hardly be given a single, global rating, Acceptance means acknowledging people as they are and not for who they are. You rate their deeds, but not their being, and you honor their aliveness, but not necessarily what they do with it. If sinners, you accept them, but not their *sins*. You give them grace, but not always plaudits.

3. Acceptance does not mean that you tell people that they act well when you think they don't, nor that you refrain from severely criticizing some of their deeds. It means that you do not criticize, blame, or damn them. But you do, often enough, frankly tell them that you abhor their behavior, and that you profoundly hope that they will change it for (what you think is) the better.

4. Acceptance does not mean that you never restrict people or penalize them for their obnoxious deeds. On the contrary, it means that you do your best to refrain from damning or condemning them, but that you sometimes do reward them for good behavior and unvindictively penalize them for their poor or unethical act, not to get back at them or "punish" them (for that implies damnation as well as penalization), but to try to discourage their continued deprecations.

5. Acceptance, as used in RET, does not mean that you merely are aware of others' limitations or have insight into how and why they are acting in an unpleasant manner. Awareness and insight are fine and may lead acceptance, But not necessarily. Acceptance means seeing people's fallibilities and giving them the right to be fallible. It means forgiving them in spite of their iniquities–discouraging their acts but not themselves as people.

What Acceptance is

If this is what unconditional acceptance of people is not, what then is it? It includes several things which have already been strongly implied, but now will be delineated more concretely. When you really accept people you tend to think and act as follows:

1. You respect people (including yourself) when they fail, and you refuse to denigrate them as complete failures, losers, or hopeless

foulups. You acknowledge their past and present ineptness but refrain from labeling them as thoroughly incompetent and worthless people, and you refrain from predicting that they have to keep failing in the future. Preferably, you encourage them to keep trying, and show them that they probably can succeed in some ways. You certainly do not discourage them and throw doubt on their ability to learn and develop today and tomorrow.

2. You respect people (and yourself) when they are rejected by others and are disapproved or unloved. You refrain from viewing them as totally unlovable or undeserving of any attention or approval. You attempt to see that they do have some lovable traits and possibly to help them develop and use these to future advantage. Although you may never particularly care for them as friends or partners yourself, you stop assuming that no one under any conditions could find them lovable.

3. You accept people (including yourself) even when they are lazy, procrastinating, or inert, and when they are doing little to help themselves. You sometimes try to show them that they can change and can work to improve their lot. But at least you do not condemn them to oblivion and insist that they have to get off their rumps or else they are worthless, hopeless basket cases.

4. You acknowledge the common occurrence of frustration, pain, crises, and injustice, and you stubbornly refuse to demand that they absolutely must not occur. You do your best to change and better the inconvenient aspects of your life; but you do not whine and scream when they are temporarily or permanently unchangeable. You work against, not whine about unpleasant reality.

5. You accept others not only with their incompetencies and inadequacies but also with their disturbances about having these failings. You realize that humans, as part of their normal nature, frequently become anxious and depressed—and then become anxious about being anxious and depressed about being depressed. So you accept them with (yes, in spite of) their disturbances—and you accept them with their disturbances about their disturbances. "It's too bad," you tell (and convince) yourself, "that people (like me) are frequently moody and nutty. Okay, so they're moody and nutty. It's not the end of the world. And although I'll never like it, I can certainly live with it and still lead a happy existence."

6. Most importantly, while accepting others in the ways just described, you also fully and unconditionally—yes, unconditionally—accept yourself. You accept (i.e., acknowledge, respect, and forgive) yourself with your failings, with your rejections by others, with your laziness and avoidance, with the unchangeable and unavoidable frustration, pain, injustice, and crisis that life commonly brings you.

And, as in the case of others, you accept yourself with your emotional disturbances and with your disturbances about your disturbances.

Unconditional Acceptance

RET-oriented acceptance, in sum, means that you respect (though not necessarily like) all humans–yourself and others. And, after you strongly try to change obnoxious conditions but are unable to do so, you accept all unmodifiable situations–not as "good" or as "fair" but as indubitably existent and as quite annoying and inconvenient, but not as "awful," "horrible," or "unbearable."

Can you really work on yourself and make yourself feel this almost ideal, unconditional kind of acceptance. Yes, you can–but not with ease, not without real hard work. For, by both heredity and training, you naturally and easily are prone to non-acceptance of grim reality. You have a strong human tendency to whine and wail when people perform badly and when they are treated poorly by other people or by unavoidable conditions. You often insist on nonacceptance of reality and you have a very hard time forgiving and forgetting.

Nonetheless, you had better. For nonacceptance of yourself leads to anxiety, depression, and self-hatred. Nonacceptance of others leads to rage, fury, violence, wars, and genocide. Nonacceptance of unchangeable conditions leads to self-pity, depression, avoidance, withdrawal, and addiction. Acceptance is hard, very hard. But nonacceptance is a whale of a lot harder. And it produces more, much more, failure, disapproval, crisis, and hassle than you dreamed of in your philosophy, Horatio! (Ellis, 1972; Ellis and Becker, 1982; Miller, 1983; Young, 1974). Try it and see.

A few final words about self-acceptance. Unless you fully, unconditionally accept yourself with your failings and unlovable traits, can you really succeed at rationally accepting others and the world in which you live? Most probably not–because if you disrespect yourself, your "you-ness," your totality, how can a "bad," "inadequate," or "hopeless" *you* have the confidence to achieve almost any important goal, including that of accepting others? Not very easily. Self-acceptance, therefore, is practically a prerequisite to any other kind of sensible world philosophy and activity (Ellis, 1962, 1972; Lazarus, 1978; Tillich, 1956).

Self-Acceptance

And self-acceptance, to be more precise and practical, means exactly what? In RET, we try to help you define it as follows:

"I am alive and strongly choose to remain alive and to make myself (and help some others to be) happily alive. To do this, I will frequently measure or rate my performances, deeds, and traits to see whether they really help my (or sabotage my) remaining alive and happy. When they aid me (and the community in which I choose to live) I will call my acts "good" or "efficient" and when they impede me (and my community) I shall term them "bad" or "inefficient" and shall do my best to modify them. But, whether or not I behave well and whether or not others approve of my behavior, I shall never give a global or total rating to me, myself, or my being. Instead, I shall always fully *accept* myself no matter *what* I do or do not do. Under normal conditions, I shall cherish my aliveness and try to make it a happy as feasible. And I shall never rate, damn, condemn, or devil-ify my self or my being at all.

Why? Why shall I unconditionally accept myself, and try to live and enjoy myself, in this unwavering manner? For several reasons: 1) Because I simply *choose* to do so and need no special reasons nor accomplishments to make this choice. 2) Because I think unconditional self-acceptance will bring me better results—a longer, healthier, and happier life. 3) Because I think it proper to respect and honor *all* humans, including myself, just because they are part of my species, just because they are human. 4) Because I believe that if I have unconditional acceptance (though not necessarily love) for all people, many of them are more likely to follow my example and also have it for me. My and their mutual acceptance will probably help create a longer and happier life for all of humanity."

This kind of RET-oriented self-acceptance, and its corollaries of other-acceptance and world-acceptance, will presumable encourage people to become more reliable, disciplined, competent, and caring, and less likely to be addicted to emotional disturbance and to alcohol and substance abuse. It consequently can be of immense help in EAPs and other efforts to facilitate mental health and personal happiness. That is why RET places the concept and the practice of acceptance at the very core of its EAP and other helping programs. If millions of employed (and self-employed) people will learn through RET and other effective forms of therapy to accept themselves and others, no panacea will result and no utopia will suddenly erupt. But many more satisfied and effective workers, I strongly hypothesize, will rise and shine.

References

Ellis, A. *Reason and emotion in psychotherapy.* Secaucus, NJ: Citadel Press, 1962.

_____. *Psychotherapy and the value of a human being.* New York: Institute for Rational-Emotive Therapy, 1972.

_____. *Humanistic psychotherapy: The rational-emotive approach.* New York: McGraw-Hill, 1973.

_____. *RET abolishes most of the human ego.* New York: Institute for Rational-Emotive Therapy, 1976.

_____., & Becker, I. *A guide to personal happiness.* No. Hollywood, CA: Wilshire Books, 1982.

_____., & Harper, R. A. *A new guide to rational living.* No. Hollywood: Wilshire Books, 1975.

Lazarus, A. A. Toward an egoless state of being, In A. Ellis & R. Grieger (Eds.), *Handbook of rational-emotive therapy.* New York: Springer, 1978.

Miller, T. *So, you secretly suspect you're worthless, Well you're not a shit and I can prove it.* Manlius, NY: Tom Miller, 1983.

Tillich, P. *The courage to be.* New York: Oxford, 1956.

Young, H. *Rational conseling primer.* New York: Institute for Rational-Emotive Therapy, 1974.

SECTION VII
Critical Issues Relevant to an EAP

Introduction

Like many programs with wide support, the EAP carries with it a credibility that may be more based upon the belief of its initiators and supporters than upon its real day to day effectiveness. Reidiger will examine the various barriers to effectiveness of the EAP, beginning with a review of the spread of the EAP concept from its "alcoholism" predecessors in the late 1950s to the present versions. The proposition that broader programs will increase the uncovering of cases of alcoholism is questioned. There is a disparity of percentage rates of such cases found among broad-based programs. While some regularly yield a rate of 1%, fairly respectable, there are programs that bring that number to 5%. What are the differences? Is the one broad-based EAP less accepted in the workplace; is the marketing deficient, or what?

This same chapter focuses heavily also on the reasons for insufficient supervisor referrals; perhaps the emphasis of EAPs should be on the relief of the supervisor's dilemma and the aggravations surrounding his/her troubled employee . . . rather than on emphasizing the help directed to the employee. In addition, the supervisor's reluctance to refer employees without something more substantive than simple job deterioration needs to be addressed by EAPs in some more dramatic, effective manner. In short, our programs need to better match what Riediger calls the "creative rationale" used to sell them to management.

Santa-Barbara explores the unique role that EAPs can have in the influencing of mental health resources and their utilization in the community. Since the EAP represents the corporate funnel of regular patients and fees to the community resources, the implicit power held can be very constructively used to improve their accountability, as well as the nature and degree of their services. Also examined are the methods whereby these same resources can be cooperatively drawn into in-house services provided by the EAP. Several potential conflicts of interest are examined. One of these is clearly not uncommon; i.e., the internal EAP in which much or most counseling is done by EAP staff, at the detriment of outside resources. This and other similar concerns are discussed in detail.

What position should the EAP take, if any, on the larger issue of influencing social policy making in the community? Corneil's section contains many interesting viewpoints on this new question for EAPs. The EAP can wield considerable influence by its selective use and financial support of various private and/ or public community agencies. It is, indeed, the intermediary between the workplace and such services, and may be the primary reason for a sudden boost in a company's use of them. Pre-EAP mental health referrals from a company (e.g., a nurse or medical department) were usually less frequent and less centralized. The responsibility inherent in the new EAP relationship to the community can be ignored of course, but perhaps we should explore the constructive uses of that potential influence existing in the new realignment.

Ethical concerns are probed in the section by Briar, in which she reviews the history of social services within industry, going back to the days when company personnel departments administered housing and welfare programs, coming into frequent battle with employees and unions. Such programs were often and correctly viewed as being administered by and for the company, with the always present threat they could be withdrawn or otherwise manipulated at the discretion of management. Care must be exercised that the EAP is properly positioned and not used as a manipulative tool. For example, it may be useful for the EAP to assist in stress reduction programs during layoff periods, but how does the program avoid being used by management simply to reduce union complaints about how the layoff is handled? It is important not to become the referee between management and labor, risking the enmity of both. Ways are discussed by which the EAP can serve its clients, assist in the democratization of the workplace and remain ethically proper in the middle of difficult circumstances.

Alcoholism at executive levels has particularly worried and challenged EAP professionals. Shirley's section describes the TOPEX (for "top executive") study, in which the New York City Affiliate of the National Council of Alcoholism examined a sampling of well-recovered senior level executives in several companies. The study sought to define the natural histories and progress of their alcoholism, from teenage days to the time of their "discovery" and entry into treatment. Curiously, they were often high achievers in the business world, with "deteriorating performance" not apparently an issue. Several lessons for EAPs are useful, for it is clear that there are significant variations in how the EAP can reach, educate, and bring this class of alcoholic to treatment. The summary may well be "must" reading for the EAP which hopes to reach the executive level employees. Another study, following up on this subject, is underway and will be released shortly by the author of this chapter.

Byers and Quinn will review the devastation wrought by alcohol misuse and alcoholism. They review in detail the many statistics that underlie our rationale for past and current programs, in industry and elsewhere, to deal with this serious condition. The authors remind today's broad-based EAPs of the continuing need to rigorously look for and include (or exclude) alcohol problems in performing their differential diagnoses. The principles of constructive confrontation are still important to learn, particularly since many current EAPs are under the direction of staff whose background fails to provide an understanding of why it is a critical skill.

Quality of work life programs (QWL) as they relate to EAPs is the core issue of Ferman's section on the reorganization of the workplace. The QWL represents one of the newest variants on organizational programs in recent years. The goals of QWLs have included the improvement of inter-level communications within companies, and the development of ways to solicit and use problem-solving skills engendered from all manner of employees, not just management. He describes the manner in which these QWL programs, commonly known also as quality circles, form, interact and pass information to the management. As to EAPs in relation to QWLs, there has been extremely little experience with joining the two. Although more and more companies may have elements of both, they are usually organizationally unconnected.

EAPs, of course, tend to be clinical, rehabilitative, and cure-focused, while the QWLs, as described above, deal with communications, collecting good ideas of merit regarding the company's performance and work force quality. However, there are several intriguing methods by which the two can interact and contribute to each other's goals. For example, the QWL can act as the ears of the company, detecting departments, groups or individuals in need of one or more EAP services/interventions. As voices of the common man and woman of the company, with direct access to management, the QWL can also become the impartial marketer of the EAP to higher levels. This may be quite useful if the EAP has otherwise had trouble being heard. These and other interesting interactions are probably the beginning of a productive new varient in ways to spread the good news of the EAP.

31

Social Policy Issues and EAPs
D. Wayne Corneil

Introduction

Just as they must become integral parts of the organization in which they operate, EAPs must function within the context of the community where they are located. As a result, EAPs cannot avoid becoming involved in social policy issues.

While many in the field vigorously claim that EAPs have no role in social policy questions, and a few may acknowledge potential involvement, there has nonetheless been a studious avoidance of any public discussion of such issues. However, failure to address such social policy concerns as the distribution and funding of social services will result in EAPs being unable to fulfill their present mandate and in losing their potential promise of expanded services.

What is social policy

EAP personnel need not be reminded of the importance of policy statements. Most would accept a definition of policy as being a statement of general principles, plans, courses of action, practices, or programs to be pursued by an organization. Those working in the field know that policies are practical tools which state a desired objective and simply outline the direction to be pursued in attaining that objective. Policies are not elaborate, nor are they detailed sets of procedures and directives. "Dynamic organizations don't have fat policy manuals" (Atkey, 1975).

Social policy is also a statement of objectives and the elaboration of directions to be pursued. Most often social policy is concerned with issues related to the priority in which social problems need to be addressed and how society should organize to ameliorate social conditions.

Social policy is concerned not only with government practices and the allocation of public monies but also with how private services are organized and supported. The way in which governments respond is normally called "public" policy, which should obviously be formulated in the context of the broader social policy. Therein lies the nexus of the difficulties that will beset EAPs over the next decade.

As Bryan and Crawshaw (1978) note:

> "Few social policies are absolutely clear-cut. Furthermore, for several problems no clear policy has been adopted. Because most programs developed to support a social policy are left intentionally or by default in a state of ambiguity that people implementing a program are obliged to assume a policy making function."

For EAPs, the very nature of the type of service they provide places them in the role of formulating social policy. Acting as the intermediary between the work organization and the community service provider, EAP staff are forced to make at least *ad hoc* social policy decisions. Even for those who restrict themselves to a straightforward acceptance of the status quo regarding treatment services, decisions are still made which influence the nature of the service available.

This aspect is usually limited to advising clients which of the many agencies in an urban setting are the most suitable. Yet this screening of agencies is in itself a social policy function. Making decisions based on other than hard scientific data is a social policy decision. For example, to choose between two equally competent treatment facilities based on the fees charged to clients is a resolution of a social issue.

Whenever EAP personnel meet as a group in a given community to discuss the care providers, they are engaged in a discussion of social policy. The exchange of information and the often informal endorsement of an agency, in fact, influences the social policy not only of that agency but also of others in the community as well. Certainly private agencies will respond very quickly to adapt their programs and methods to either real or peceived trends in EAP. One need only trace the evolution of treatment for alcoholism from primarily inpatient services to the present burgeoning outpatient modalities to see the influence of EAPs. Public insitutions are likely to be somewhat slower to change, however, they will alter their programs in response to the subtle pressures of EAPs, as witness the testimony of health maintenance organization program offerings to the employment settings since 1980.

Role of EAPs in social policy issues

If EAPs cannot avoid being involved in social policy matters, the question then becomes what is their proper role? This question goes to the heart of the philosophy and origins of the EAP movement. It provides a host of options for the conduct of EAP personnel engaging in social policy discusssions:

- should they simply seek to create a climate of awarenesss and concern in the hope that other institutions for the community at large will seize the initiative and respond to the issue?
- should they be entirely passive and responsive only to others, such as government initiatives, and then capitalize upon these?
- should they actively promote and attempt to facilitate social policy making to the adoption of objectives determined by EAP people rather than by the service providers?
- do they have a role in monitoring not only the formulation and development of social policy but also in evaluating its implementation?

One may assume the stance that, because EAPs are based within the work setting, the corporation has no responsibility for involvement in formulating social policy. However, how then does one reconcile this with the finding that, of senior corporate executives surveyed, the predominant single reason for initiating an EAP has been and remains "corporate social responsibility" (Roman, 1980). Moreover, how can one justify creating in an organization an internal system which identifies distressed persons, may increase their level of anxiety, and then refers them into a community lacking adequate resources? Where does corporate social responsibility lie in relationship to advocating what, in its best judgment, represents for example, an effective treatment delivery system and method, or preventive program and method?

Historically, EAP people have tended to be ambivalent about their role in advocacy. This ambivalence can be attributed on the one hand to a concern for adequate treatment facilities, and on the other hand to the leap from the corporate setting to offering advice on the manner in which social and health services should be structured. While is is true that corporations do not have a mandate telling society how to decide such issues, that is not sufficient reason for EAPs to shrink from offering their best advice and advocating what they believe to be wise from the point of view of public interest, especially in terms of efficiency. In fact, social policy would benefit enormously if the vast resources and experience of business were committed to the solution of social problems on a business-like basis. One needs to remember that business motivation is both economic and social. The economic motivation for involvement in social policy stems from a pragmatic interest in shaping a social environment in which business can continue to operate five to ten years from now.

Policy Issues

What are the social policy questions that EAPs need to address? The already mentioned expansion of services to meet broader-based EAPs is only the most obvious. Closely related is the requirement for expanded insurance coverage beyond addiction treatment to services for other types of problems. These two issues in turn lead to the next, standards in certification of service providers. The last major issue relates to the opposite end of the continuum from treatment–the relationship of prevention activities to EAPs.

The natural evolution of EAPs beyond an alcoholism-specific focus to respond to an expanded range of psychosocial problems has not been accompanied by a concurrent shift in community service infrastructures. Short-term attempts to resolve the situation on an individual-by-individual basis will not suffice. Even those which attempt to provide parallel services by hiring in-house counselors simply postpone the inevitable. Business and industry are not organized to provide social services. Nor, regrettably, does it appear, that communities are adequately structured to respond to all of the demands being generated by EAPs.

The advent of the assessment and referral center, or the consortium type EAP, has implications for community services apart from flooding them with clients. Who is in a better position than EAP staff to assist in the long-term planning and co-ordination of community services? EAP personnel should be actively seeking out seats on local social planning councils so that their expertise can guide the long-term planning process. They have a double interest at stake–the services their clients require, and the tax burden their sponsoring corporation must assume for uncoordinated and inefficient services.

The funding of services is important for both the public and private agency. Corporations not only pay significant taxes; they are also the primary contributors to insurance schemes. The costs of employee benefits, including health insurance, are rising at a rate four times greater than wage settlements.

EAPs were instrumental in influencing the coverage for inpatient treatment of alcoholism and are currently shaping coverage considerations for outpatient services. They will also have to address the nature of insurance coverage for other types of services, such as family and marital counseling or individual therapy for emotional and mental distress. Presumably, with an increase in legal actions stemming from such matters as divorce or custody, coverage for legal services might also become more feasible.

Studies (Egdahl et al, 1980) have already established that comprehensive coverage does not necessarily mean greater utilization or increased costs over the long-term. The opposite is clear. If employees increased their use of services early on, while the matter is still relatively simple, there would be a reduced cost, because fewer people would require the costly involved services for a problem that has become exceedingly complex over time (Muldoon et al, 1978).

Once again, EAP staff have a particular insight and a vested interest in becoming involved in the setting of social policies regarding insurance coverage.

No movement of the size and impact of EAP can expect to avoid the issue of social accountability, which leads to the creation of standards in some form of regulation. EAP personnel cannot expect to exert an influence over community service providers, and over business and labor organizations, and still avoid this issue. While it may not be necessary to adhere to rigid credentialing or licensing structures, some form of voluntary self-regulation is necessary.

For example, if insurance coverage does expand to include a wide range of services, those who are called upon to assess and refer clients to the appropriate facility will require some means of certifying that they are capable of making such decisions. Moreover, if the employee and the employer are dependent upon such decisions for both their well-being and economic livelihood, stricter limits of liability will be imposed on EAP practitioners.

As such, they will be faced with the decison either to participate constructively in the discussion of credentials or simply wait until pressure forces government to impose controls.

The last issue to be discussed is the relationship of EAPs, which are primarily oriented towards helping those who are having a problem, and the emergence of prevention/promotion initiatives. In the 1970's, public health studies (Lalonde, 1974) revealed that the majority of people suffered from disorders caused by their lifestyle. This has lead to the subsequent trend of lifestyle modification programs or wellness promotion programs.

Given that most lifestyle disorders occur with adults and that most adults work, the employment setting has become the natural target site for these activities. Indeed, many EAP practitioners have embraced the lifestyle approach as being the natural, logical extension of their original mandate. Others have been a little more wary of these approaches (Shain et al, 1980). The issue is not merely a matter of company paternalism. It is a more fundamental question about the environmental and organizational factors which may cause or exacerbate such disorders. The workplace is never neutral in respect to such problems. It has as much potential for adverse as beneficial effects.

While there has been a steady resistance to any acknowledgement of environmental or organizational factors playing a role in the genesis of alcohol-related disorders or other mental/emotional health disorders, one cannot avoid this issue. Workmen's Compensation has already ruled on a number of precedent-setting cases (Egdahl et al, 1980). These have accepted the premise that both the work environment and the structure of the employing organization can, under certain circumstances, be responsible for the generation of problems. There is a growing trend to force greater responsibility on the employer for the mental well-being of workers. At what point will such fiscal responsibility be translated into social responsibility and organizations be required to undertake preventive measures or further wellness promotion programs?

EAP's appear to be attempting to straddle the fence in their efforts to move from a clinical orientation (direct provision of services to those affected) to the adoption of preventive or promotional stances which try to ignore environmental factors. These latter tend to lapse into a "blame the victim" stance. Such an approach has eroded the credibility of not only the promotional elements of the program, but the EAP service in general. Employee confidence is reduced as they begin to question the impartiality of EAP staff in dealing with health issues.

Another serious threat to the credibility of EAP is for persons in this field to isolate themselves from both the health promotion movement and the "quality of working life" field. It is not necessary that EAPs should embrace in their entirety either of these social forces. They must, however, not hold themselves aloof from the discussion which these two areas concern at the workplace. Both are influencing social policies and the nature of work organizations, which will in turn have an impact on the future of EAPs.

The spotlight is on EAPs as never before to perform as a socially responsive movement, well beyond their original intent as a means to the treatment of alcoholism. Based as they are in the corporate structure, they will be perceived as having access to a citadel of concentrated economic power. EAPs will be called upon by government, media, community activists, stockholders, employers, and others to play a larger role in the formulation of social policy.

EAPs will become the target of the social change movement, because they are seen to have access to corporate economic resources. With governments cutting funds to community agencies, many more will be seeking out the private sector as a source of continuing support. EAPs are already promoted as a means to handle many of these social problems.

The pendulum can swing either way for EAPs. They can choose to take a leadership role in advocating social policy or they can become its mute recipients.

References

Atkey, R., *Practical policy development*, Optimum Volume 6, No. 3, 1975.

Bryan, C.M., and Crawshaw, P., *Law and Social Policy*, Volume 3 of Core knowledge in the drug field, edited by Philips, L.A., Ramsay, G.R., Blumenthal, L. and Crawshaw, P., Ottawa, Canada,: Government of Canada, 1978.

Egdahl, R.H. and Walsh, D.C., (eds) *Mental wellness programs for employees*, New York, N.Y.: Springer-Verlag, 1980.

Lalonde, M., *New perspectives on health*, Ottawa, Canada: Government of Canada, 1974.

Muldoon, J.A. and Berdie, M., *Effective employee assistance*, Minneapolis, Minn.: Compcares Publication, 1978.

Roman, P.M., *Employee alcoholism programs in major corporations in 1979*: Scope, change and receptivity, in fourth special report to the U.S. Congress on alcohol and health, Washington, D.C.,: U.S. Government, 1980.

Shain, M. and Groeneveld, J., *Employee assistance programs: Philosophy, theory, and practice*, Toronto: D.C. Health and Co., 1980.

32

Ethical Questions Concerning an EAP: Who Is the Client? (Company or Individual?)

Katharine Hooper Briar
Michele Vinet

Introduction

The emergence of EAPs prompts discussion about ethical issues and dilemmas in many camps, among advocates as well as critics. Not all advocates agree on the value of raising ethical issues while the field is just emerging. In fact, it is often argued that ethical discussions can deter the progress of human services in the workplace, especially if future service developers perceive value dilemmas as hazardous roadblocks. Counter arguments hold that gaining entry into the workplace can only be fueled by explicit attention to practice standards and the unique ethical dimensions of EAP practice. This counterpoint suggests that attention to ethics strengthens the field and reduces the gulf between critics and advocates. Discussion of ethics can help recent entrants stop looking over their shoulder at those who criticize them for abandoning the poor, promoting market values in professional practice, and aiding capitalism.

Exposing the ethical dilemmas inherent in the promotion of human welfare in the workplace cannot but only help to fortify practitioners, but also compel them to transform some workplace practices. Ethical standards may help to guide the EAP away from an ancillary toward a more central role in responding to human needs in the workplace. While alterations in workplace practices will not necessarily replace the overriding profit-making mission of private sector institutions, they may intensify corporate responsibility for promoting employee, family, consumer, and community well-being. Reconciling the push for profits (and profit maximization) with corporate responsibility for human welfare, creates challenges as well as pitfalls within evolving EAPs. Discussion of dilemmas also sets the stage for establishment of standards of practice, and possibly for the resolution of the ethical dilemmas themselves.

Values guiding employee assistance professionals derive from ethical beliefs in the integrity and human potential of each individual, his or her right to self-expression and self-actualization, and the centrality of human welfare above and beyond other potentially overriding organizational goals, such as profitmaking, efficiency, and productivity. In all settings for human service practice, collisions in values among human services professionals, clients, employing organizations, and society are commonplace (Briar et al, 1983; Vinet and Jones, 1981). The fact that a host system's values may be inherently antithetical to human service values may heighten ethical dilemmas confronted by the practitioner.

Drawing on some of the observations from two years of demonstration projects, promoted by the Washington State chapter of the National Association of Social Workers, this section will outline some of the ethical dimensions and issues in EAP practice. Guided by Levy's (1974) exhaustive review of ethical standards that crosscut many of the human service professions, this section will attempt to address issues applicable to the multiple professions represented by employee assistance practitioners.

Because EAPs are still in an early stage of development, it is premature to catalog the variety of emergent ethical and value issues with which EAPs must contend. Instead, the authors will attempt to apply some of the commonly shared ethical standards identified by Levy (1974) to discussions of auspice, sponsorship and funding dictates, employee assistance roles and mission, adversarial conditions for service delivery, client interests, implications for systems change, treatment issues, practitioner competence, workplace and societal effectiveness. Discussion of ethical components of practice is guided by several rationales for human services practitioners in the workplace. The authors assume that human service workers bring valuable skills, knowledge, and perspectives not only to alleviate personal problems and needs of all workers and their families, but also to address structures, policies, and practices that: 1) damage or impede effective functioning of workers and their families, 2) develop the human potential of workers by enhancing opportunities for individual self-actualization and collective well-being, and 3) produce harmful effects on consumers and the broader community. To begin the discussion, historical antecedents of current practice help to illuminate some potential impacts and cautions associated with utilizations of human service professionals in the workplace.

Historical Antecedents of Employee Benefits and Services

The legacy of earlier human service involvement in the workplace sharpens concerns about ethics. A brief review of the contributions and pitfalls of our forerunners may illuminate some of the ethical issues that pertain today. The provision of employer benefits and services and cushioning of the human costs of the workplace have long been hallmarks of industrial development. Such protections, emerging first with worker guilds, were replaced later by benefit programs of labor and management (Akabas, 1977).

Employer-sponsored benefits and services for workers can be traced back to the late nineteenth century in the United States. Human service personnel, called "welfare workers" or "welfare secretaries," administered such programs as company housing, sanitation, safety and family care programs (Brandes, 1976). Described as "welfare capitalism," such services were instrumental to management's attempts to foster loyalty, prevent strikes and unionization, and to obligate and control laborers. These services generated such distaste among labor that it led Samuel Gompers, a vocal labor leader, to rename the activities of the cadre of human service personnel as "hell-fare" work (Akabas, 1977). Indeed, the animosity felt by some employees over such programs appeared to heighten the tendency for violence among insurgent striking workers (Brandes, 1976). Human services professionals became labeled as instruments of management rather than as agents of workers. The provision of benefits and services for workers were not ends in themselves, but instead were mechanisms for policing and reporting on discontented workers, their personal morality, and union organizing efforts.

In contrast to these historical trends are the collective efforts of other human service workers, such as Jane Addams and Florence Kelley, who developed service and policy initiatives to accommodate the needs of working women and children. With footholds in private and public sector auspices, they were able to organize consumers as allies in developing improved services and policies. Employed by settlement houses and public agencies, these reformers and others like them were able to press for initiatives that management-based human service providers were unlikely to develop.

Union-based social services, well documented through the work of Bertha Reynolds and the National Maritime Union, provide another historical precedent for re-emerging human service programs (Reynolds, 1951). Her efforts to aid and advocate for the needs of workers and their families in the 1940s are reminders of the way in which auspice and funding shapes service options as well as evolving service initiatives.

EAPs: "Welfare Capitalism" Revisited?

The recent evolution of management and jointly sponsored labor-management EAPs provides enormous opportunities for developing comprehensive services for workers and their families. The re-entry of human service practitioners in the workplace is fortified by policy and service shifts in modern-day worksites, thereby altering some of the conditions that led to earlier welfare capitalism. An array of social legislation, coupled by employer and labor initiatives, mark the workplace as a dynamic environment–not just for the increased production of goods and services, but for systematically addressing unmet human needs and rights (Akabas and Kurzman, 1982). EAPs draw strength from laws and practices created by mandates such as affirmative action, vocational rehabilitation programs, safety protections, and shifts in retirement age limits. Well developed departments of personnel, medical services, and employee or labor relations may provide a value-consistent backdrop against which one's professional allegiance to ethical practice can be protected and supported.

Nevertheless, the historical rift between management and labor persists today and has implications for some of the demands that might be placed on human service workers. Such a rift is derived in part from the exclusion of workers from decisions governing the distribution of the fruits of their labor, terms of employment, and work conditions. Moreover, company values promoting profits rather than human well-being, are reinforced by primary corporate accountability to stockholders, rather than to employees and their families, consumers, and the community. However, many companies, for their internal policies, draw heavily on professionals whose mission and identity transcends that of the employing organization. Consequently, some of the pitfalls of prior employee welfare programs may be avoided.

The department housing the EAP may share ideological views of the EAP. Such a reference group with similar ideologies should not only sanction but foster value advocacy by the EAP practitioner.

Dictates of Auspice and Sponsorship

Ideological support by the department housing the EAP does not ensure that values promoting employee well-being will prevail in workplace decision-making. Practitioners in all settings recognize the power of the organizational auspice and funding source to dictate the appropriateness of certain problem definitions and interventions.

Bakalinsky (1980) argues that the value conflicts posed by the entry of social work into industry can be best resolved if the human service delivery system remains outside the purview of industry altogether. She argues that sponsorship will affect accountability, confidentiality, referral processes, and service delivery and utilization. Such claims constitute empirical questions that can be the subject of future studies which compare the functioning of programs with independent auspices to those sponsored by industry.

The dictates of auspice and funding may circumscribe the innovations that the EAP can offer. For example, counseling services for strikers and their families regarding income, interpersonal and mental health stress, sometimes crucial to employee and family well-being, do not fit well within the purview of a management sponsored program. Funding dictates in some sites may preclude the corporate-based employee assistance staff member from working on plant closure regulations or activism. In different ways, human service professionals contracting for externally provided services realize rather quickly the limits that are placed on programs not located at the worksite. One human service worker turned down a contract when she realized that her efforts might be viewed as union busting. Another EAP consultant, concerned with conditions that might result in violations of client confidentiality, terminated the negotiations with a prospective employer (Briar et al., 1983).

Some limits inherent in EAPs are in actuality no different than those imposed on other agency-based practitioners. The parole officer cannot organize parolees to question sentencing practices nor can the United Way planner readily organize efforts to fight mortgage foreclosures. Clearly, the purpose of the EAP depends on the auspice of the program, but also on the kinds of problems the practitioner is prepared to confront. Auspice and sponsorship may shape the perspective on problems the EAP practitioner is expected to hold. As with public sector social services, an individual, rather than systemic change model predominates. Even so, the EAP can offer multiple perspectives on employee issues and needs, so that they are not defined too narrowly.

For example, the EAP director in a boat building organization is encouraged by the personnel department to explore the viability of introducing a health promotion program. He is aware of the increased accidents associated with some seemingly unsafe work conditions and equipment. While health promotion will add a new dimension to employee well-being, he is concerned about health and safety problems which may continue to go unaddressed. He decides to explore ways to link the health promotion effort to the need for improved safety and reduced accidents.

Auspice and sponsorship decisions can positively shape the scope of practice by prompting more deliberate public-private sector problem solving. Integrated public and private sector approaches to certain human needs can help ensure that worker needs do not fall through the cracks. Other examples of ways in which auspice and funding arrangements have prompted such problem solving are reflected in services to layoff victims. While few EAPs are in positions to prevent massive layoffs, corporate relocation, and capital flight, or even offer counseling help to laid-off employees, some employee assistance directors do attempt to mobilize community services on behalf of the worker. Such initiatives include promoting self-help groups under other auspices, referrals to other employers who are hiring, as well as support groups for the newly laid-off employee (Briar, 1983). These services reflect ethical missions to extend service boundaries to either directly or indirectly aid stressed employees and to set in motion new service arrangements beyond those currently provided within the EAP.

Such beginning efforts attest to the human service professional's commitment to worker well-being, which transcends the dictates of service entitlement, so often limited to already employed workers.

EAP Roles and Missions

Some professional roles in EAP programs may intensify the value divergence between human service and corporate goals. If the EAP is solely focused on clinical service, its staff performs primarily treatment-oriented services. Yet, those EAP professionals who also sense their mission to span preventive as well as remedial interventions, will address those workplace policies and practices that are harmful to workers and their families. In a cogent analysis of the philosophical underpinnings for industrial social work practice, Kurzman (1983) argues that social workers must be motivated by values that prompt advocacy and promote equity. The workplace is replete with structures and processes that are oppressive and discriminatory and that inequitably mete out goods, services, and opportunities. Human service workers must be as much concerned with removing injustices as they are with addressing personal problems and promoting more therapeutic, self-actualizing experiences.

Despite this, it is not uncommon to hear newly established EAP practitioners wonder whether to stand on the sidelines during company reorganization, lay-offs, or employee reassignment to potentially dangerous equipment. As the example from the boat building company EAP illustrates, effective client-focused service compels the practitioner to make incremental inroads into decision-making structures to advance, when appropriate, alternative practices, especially when in the long run they can be shown to benefit not just the employee but the employer as well.

As EAPs reach new thresholds in their organizational contributions, the guiding answer to such queries and uncertainties is derived from their mission. The mission found in most codes of ethics provides for, if not requires, the advancement of collective social welfare above and beyond individual clients (Levy, 1974). The mission-oriented EAP will reflect such values. However, to expect an EAP to transform decision-making structures before becoming fully established, prematurely assigns it intervention responsibilities for which it may not be prepared. The EAP must establish a track record for competent service. Once it is well accepted within the infrastructure of the corporate and/or labor setting, enhanced levels of trust and commitment will permit change strategies to be fostered.

Ozawa (1980) delineates four stages of development for the maturing EAP. Moving from occupational alcoholism to "broad brush" services, to the redesigning of jobs and interpersonal relationships, the EAP eventually will aid the workplace with more democratic practices (e.g., placing workers and consumers on boards) and with the pursuit of social welfare rather than profit-oriented corporate objectives.

Even now, the EAP requires more than the mere application of human service skills. Elements of various stages are currently being addressed in EAP practice although not as explicitly as Ozawa's stages might suggest. EAP practitioners must assess organizational readiness for their programs to use a broader skill repertoire and weigh carefully the risks in pressing reformist agendas. Incremental changes may be possible before organizations are convinced about the utility of such interventions. There are some who argue that one cannot function as a human service worker, specifically as a social worker, without a reform edged agenda (Walden, 1978).

Service Integrity in an Adversarial Environment

It is assumed that practitioners will place themselves in roles that ensure the maximum service for the client (Levy, 1974). However, observers of EAPs presume that because of the managerial auspice and funding and because employers have seemed to be ideologically at odds with employee needs, the EAP practitioner will be compromised (Bakalinsky, 1980). To counter, EAP practioners remind us of the wrenching compromises they once were forced to make when employed in traditional public and voluntary social service programs. They recall how assaults on services by conservative agency board members or legislators curtailed client access to services in their publicly funded human service programs. Even within public sector social services, efforts to ensure the fullest delivery of service are approximations of an ideal.

Such reminders suggest that meeting client needs and promoting access to services have been challenging in many settings. Some EAP professionals experience a major challenge to employee access to services because of the presumed difficulty they will have in maintaining confidentiality about client disclosures. Unions are especially suspicious of the EAP practitioner's ability to maintain confidentiality. It is hard for union leaders, particularly, to believe that employers will honor the practitioner's standards regarding confidentiality, given the distrust that has enshrouded labor-management relations. Workers may fear that disclosure and the consequent violation of confidentiality will lead to dismissal.

Practitioners sensitive to employees' mistrust and fear of job jeopardy take measures to prevent it from becoming an issue. If they receive client referrals through supervisors, they build their service intervention into an early stage of the employee grievance process. Their accountability to the supervisor is then limited to formal procedures that preclude disclosure of confidential, treatment-related information. If clients prefer that the EAP staff talk with their supervisor, they are asked to sign a release of information.

Maintaining the employee's right to confidentiality is another way of developing trust. The practitioner may facilitate better communication between the employee and supervisor, and arrange more appropriate ways to give supervisors feedback, by not breaching confidentiality. They build trust in both employees and supervisors by structuring open communication as their goal, rather than solely protecting privileged communication.

Adversarial relationships between management and labor organizations lead unions from time to time to interpret employer sensitivity to worker needs as an attempt to weaken the power of unions, or as a deliberate tactic to prevent worker insurgence and union organizing. Ethical responsibilities of human service workers preclude engaging in actions that diminish the legal or civil rights of clients (Levy, 1974). Thus, the explicit use of an EAP and its staff to preempt labor organizing, when such activities indeed are legal, places the practitioner in an ethically untenable position reminiscent of earlier welfare capitalism.

Programs associated with improving the "quality of worklife" have been met with such distrust that unions have successfully stopped them. The EAP, occasionally thought of as a variant of such efforts, can be cast as a threat to employee empowerment, labor union organizing, and benefit development. The fact that some unions have seen the development of EAPs as unfair labor practices attests to the depth of animosity engendered in some labor-management relations. Obviously, the employee assistance professional faces ethical dilemmas derived from labor-management conflict. As an aid in confronting these conflicts, Levy reminds us that "practitioners should be scrupulous about not representing opposing parties" (Levy, 1974). For example, when the EAP is established only by management without the participation of labor unions (in the organized workplace), workers may perceive this arrangement as management-oriented. Ultimately this may obstruct client access because of fears stimulated among union members. The most well-meaning EAP service provider, because of labor-management tensions, may be caught in a situation in which union members believe that only a union-sponsored program can assure worker protection and individual confidentiality.

Unions may perceive EAPs as threats to the health of labor organizations. The dilemmas inherent in such distrust compels vigorous trial and error problem solving to better link the EAP to the employee or union culture. The labor organization that is prompted to develop its own EAP in reaction to the management-initiated version is sometimes responding to forces beyond the control of the EAP. Thus, the EAP practitioner must respect the legacy of labor management conflict and find ways to either remain neutral or offer mutually agreeable solutions.

Adversarial relations may exist in the non-unionized workplace as well, and may create dilemmas for employee assistance practitioners. Consumers and community representatives may be set against the employer, employees (even in the non-unionized workplace) against supervisors or managers, rank and file union members against union leaders, ethnic minority against caucasian workers, women against men workers, disabled against non-disabled workers, part-time against full-time workers, smoking against non-smoking workers, feminist against non-feminist workers, laid-off employees against workers on overtime, and so forth.

On one hand, the service mission of the EAP must be shielded from counterproductive involvements which might limit service access and viability. On the other hand, certain injustices may necessitate that employee assistance practitioners take a stand and intervene, Such situations may cause employee assistance paractitioners to face difficult ethical decisions about the best way to maintain professional standards and service integrity. Discriminatory and harassing practices, consumer boycotts, picket lines, and community protest activities may compel allegiances to client needs and codes of conduct that in some settings might ultimately place one's job and the future of the EAP on the line.

Ethical dilemmas in certain situations may preempt the introduction of services altogether. In one situation, massive reorganization and layoffs occurring in a large public institution prompted the employer to introduce employee assistance services especially for those being terminated. The employer hoped that a counseling program would reduce the likelihood of lawsuits and a poor image in the community. As an EAP service developer, one would have to weigh carefully the service benefits to those terminated against the costs engendered by hostile attitudes toward management and toward the service itself.

In the Best Interest of the Client

EAPs rest, ultimately, on the premise that what is good for the employee is good for employer (Akabas, 1980). Much progress in the marketing of the EAPs has occurred because they could be shown to produce positive benefits to employers (e.g., cost savings, increased productivity) and to employees (e.g., more comprehensive assessment and intervention, job retention, improved well-being). In the spirit of linking such programming to the mutual interests of employer and employee (and often union as well), service development has proceeded, in many instances, remarkably well.

How does the EAP handle service needs that, from time to time, may not be good for the employer, but nevertheless are good for the employee? Since we are still in the early stages of development, it is premature to predict what successes may accrue to the EAP when client-centered advocacy falls short of proving explicitly beneficial to employers. Efforts to promote employer-sponsored child care reflect the emergence of this dilemma. Many employers currently see child care benefits and centers to be beyond their purview. Because they may perceive child care as women's or family needs, which traditionally have been discounted as workplace concerns, they may not pursue such service benefits. In fact, despite valiant efforts to foster employer-sponsored child care, the track record so far is rather limited.

The promotion of human welfare occurs within a political as well as an ethical context. Thus, service providers may advocate what will be well received and may find themselves resisting efforts to promote initiatives less popular with management. The EAP, serving a workforce of single parent, low wage women, may be hard pressed to meet the needs of its stressed workers without innovative work policies or benefits from employers. While long-term plans need to evolve, insufficient responsiveness or unreadiness on the part of the employer, while discouraging, still can lead to alternative forms of problem-solving in the short run. For example, if child care is a need, the practitioner can mobilize improved information and referral services, and provide workers with links to existing community-based child care programs.

Guided by a client-centered mission, the employee assistance practitioner does not stop expanding service options simply because of acquiescence by the employing organization. A common theme among human service professions is the practitioner's responsibility to advance a client's cause as far as knowledge, ethics, and competence permit (Levy, 1974). Thus the pre-eminence of the client's needs over employer or others' needs infinitely expands opportunities for the professional to address unmet needs of employees. Meeting these needs will often extend beyond what is possible within the resource system of the employing organization, often requiring a commitment to linking the public and private service sectors.

Advancing the Client's Cause

Advancing the needs of the client may require a range of workplace interventions. Some ethical codes for human service professionals prescribe preventive interventions as a natural complement to remedial problem solving (Levy, 1974). Growing emphasis on systemic intervention requires an assessment of the environmental shapers and reinforcers for stresses and problem behaviors of employees. Worker harassment, dangerous work conditions, job dissatisfaction, and under-employment may be precipitants or shapers of employee stress. Thus, it is incumbent upon the EAP practitioner to offer multiple assessment and intervention perspectives to ensure appropriate and complete services.

Multi-level, multi-targeted interventions may become ethically perplexing at times and thus difficult to fashion, especially when confidentiality issues prevail. For example, despite the prevalence of environmental stimuli or reinforcers to employee's problems, specifying the nature of such stress may increase the employees' vulnerability. Thus, seeking a release of information, even in the interest of changing workplace practices, must be weighed against circumstances that may not be in the employee's best interest. A delicate ethical balance must, then, be struck between addressing clients' needs as ends in themselves and as symptoms of workplace dysfunction.

Ethical mandates in professions like social work require a social change focus as an integral part of practice. Social work practitioners are encouraged to adopt a "case to cause" orientation which addresses the systemic roots of the client's problem. While attention to the social cause of problems increases one's practice repertoire on one hand, it also requires greater ethical sensitivity in weighing clients' best interests against multi-level interventions. This balance is particularly important to maintain in EAP programs. In other settings, policy advocacy on behalf of a class of clients involves clients who usually are anonymous to the policy maker in the public policy making arena. Promoting shifts in policy and practice in the workplace may increase the likelihood of detection of those involved and thereby jeopardize trust and threaten the right to confidentiality.

There are many ethical dilemmas created by the tension between organizational and individual needs. These are most apparent when the employee's needs and problems figure centrally in one's practice, yet organizational expectations thwart the EAP from fully addressing them. For example, pressures for increased productivity may intensify demands on workers, resulting in declining work performance as well as health and family problems. EAPs may not be able to prevent stepped-up productivity nor its human costs, should they occur. However, documentation of the human impact may be useful for employer review of the human and corporate costs and benefits. The following case illuminates some of these issues:

> Sales are down in an advertising sales company. Its new management has decided to double the minimum monthly amount of sales required from its sales personnel. Tony, age 30, and Jane, age 25, have both had a steady and successful track record in sales. Tony's recent divorce has made him preoccupied and has intensified his difficulties in making the additional required sales. Jane finds the pressure to be counter-productive, as she

worries so excessively that she is unable to make efficient use of her time or present herself effectively in sales promotion. Both are concerned that they will lose their jobs if productivity doesn't increase. They individually seek help from an EAP practitioner, who provides Tony with a counselor and Jane with stress management, self-help techniques. Uncertain about the new management, neither Tony nor Jane want to discuss their difficulties with their supervisors.

The EAP practitioner is faced with several questions reflecting the tension between individual and organizational needs. For example, in this case, should the practitioner seek release of information from her clients so that she can document the impact of such problems as increased productivity standards? Or, should she work to empower Tony and Jane to detect among co-workers stress levels which may be helpful in directly confronting their supervisors with their difficulty with productivity requirements? How far the EAP practitioner can press with his/her human service values, perspectives, and skills without losing a job or threatening the viability of the EAP may depend on many factors—including his/her credibility and that of the EAP; interpersonal trust between EAP practitioners, supervisors and managers; prior successes in promoting human welfare in similar times of employee versus organizational conflict and so forth.

In many cases, the EAP professional will be able to expand options so that ethical compromises are reduced—not just for the EAP but for the employing organization. In fact, the EAP becomes a vehicle for expanding supervisors' options, so that the human side of decisions is not sacrificed for expediency and efficiency. By showing managers, supervisors, shop stewards, and co-workers new ways of dealing with work performance and interpersonal issues, the EAP is building a base for the promotion of a broadened array of choices available to decision makers. The prevention-oriented EAP practitioner fosters changes in the definition of the problem by tying client needs to alterations in environmental precipitants. Decisions that are not now within the purview of the EAP may eventually become more directly affected by the value base, increased problem restatement, and decision option repertoire promoted by the EAP.

Treatment Issues

The belief in the right to client self-determination and to autonomy in decision making cuts across many helping service professions (Levy, 1974). The EAP practioner is an enabler as well as an empowerer. Thus, respect for the integrity of individuals, and their right to chart their own life course, and to do so without undue intervention, may be difficult to uphold when the stakes (such as salary reduction and job loss) are so high. The employee reluctant or unable to seek alcoholism treatment and on the verge of job loss may pose dilemmas and self-doubts for the EAP counselor. While respecting the client's autonomy in decision making, the employee assistance practitioner, pursuing all possible avenues, may nevertheless work with the client to overcome all possible obstacles to help-seeking, such as a co-worker subculture fostering problematic drinking (Fine, Akabas, Bellinger, 1982).

Professional judgment regarding employees' treatment needs can be a major source of ethical concern. Limited by company benefit coverage, some benefit programs fall short of covering the actual treatment requirements of clients. Insufficient coverage may increase the emotional and financial hardships of employees, who may feel coerced into covering the remainder of the services, particularly when concerned about treatment as a condition of job retention. Because of the heavy utilization of private practitioners and treatment facilities, the scrupulous EAP practitioner will want to ensure that clients are not unnecessarily required to continue treatment at their own expense. Given the variety of treatment philosophies and approaches, some of which by their very nature require long-term care (as opposed to others offered on a short-term basis), the client's best interests must be upheld. On the other hand, by documenting insufficient benefit coverage and the burdens on workers to cover remaining costs, practitioners may successfully alter benefits to more realistically reflect the actual costs of care.

Employee assistance staff may spend many hours monitoring, assessing, and adjusting referral patterns and practices. Client choice among treatment philosophies and providers is a desirable outcome, especially important if the referral to the EAP is involuntary. Infusing the assessment and referral process with choices—not only to accept or reject treatment, but to do so on an informed basis, having inventoried various provider treatment options—aids the client in his or her ethical right to self-determination. Such practice also protects the EAP from appearing to be excessively aligned with some and not other treatment approaches and providers.

Ethical codes prompt practitioners to monitor the course of treatment, to the extent that failure may be attributable to the treatment approach or other variables, such as client motivation. Given the fact that for some clients, treatment effectiveness may mean the retention or loss of one's job or other disciplinary action, employee assistance referrals must be guided by an ethical concern for ensuring successful treatment approaches, whenever possible. Divergent views of employee assistance practitioners and those providing treatment should not put the client in uncomfortable or vulnerable positions in which they fear that the choices they make may influence the extent and quality of care they will consequently receive or will interfere with their work conditions.

Practitioner Competence

Issues pertaining to competence in EAP practice have ethical consequences. Being equipped to provide appropriate services to workers involves special dimensions of preparation, ones less often required in practice in a community-based agency. In some respects, the EAP represents to the workplace what the myriad of social service agencies may be to the community. Employees bringing personal problems to the EAP require that the practitioner be knowledgeable about an array of presenting problems. In this age of specialization, the EAP practioner is asked to function as a generalist and expert diagnostician, competent to assess not just alcoholism and drug abuse, but other facets of employee functioning, such as mental health, marital, family, legal, and financial concerns. Preparation for differential assessment among this wide range of problems may exceed the educational experience of some human service training programs. While much emphasis has been appropriately placed on requisite knowledge and experience in alcoholism and substance abuse treatment through standards promulgated by ALMACA, the same requirements should be made for appropriate preparation to assess psychosocial and psychological problems, and family stresses and stressors.

Ethical standards governing human service practice mandate ongoing training and skill upgrading (Levy, 1974). Inherent in these ethical standards is the requirement that the practitioner be qualified before taking on EAP roles and only respond to those client needs which he or she is competent to address. Thus, while the EAP practitioner must often have a multi-problem assessment capability, resources must be available to ensure that consultation or additional staff with complementary skills be available.

The EAP practitioner is placed in a position of being a human needs problem solver in a new frontier. Such pioneering may place practitioners in ethically compromising situations in which client needs for service exceed their practice capability. Resources not only need to be available for contingencies and emergencies–to aid the practitioner–but practitioners need to be frank and open with clients about the limits of their skills and capabilities, and their contingency plans for backup service.

It is over such issues as practitioner competence that major debates erupted in the early years of EAP development. Controversy over alcoholism versus broad-brush programs derives as much from the ethical responsibility of practitioners to make sound assessments as from the significance of alcoholism as a presenting problem in the workplace. However, the strong emphasis on practitioner competence in alcoholism does not preclude effectiveness in addressing other client problems.

It is almost axiomatic that problem definition is a function of the resources and response repertoire one has available. It would follow that effective practice rests not just on assessment, counseling, brokering, and case management skills but on a repertoire that spans systems as well as psychological interventions. Workplace interventions add new dimensions to assessment and to intervention possibilities. Promoting organizational development, corporate social responsibility, or workplace democracy without additional training may come less easily to the clinically prepared practitioner. Thus, the expanded intervention repertoire inherent in work-place practice requires the practitioner to perform multilevel intervention, which necessitates additional skill acquisition, or a division of labor within the EAP.

Training of supervisory staff is an integral part of program effectiveness. Skill preparation for such tasks is essential for imparting program knowledge to supervisors, shop stewards, volunteer referral agents, and employees and their families. Skill in helping supervisory staff to respond non-punitively to a troubled employee involves more than the application of clinical wisdom. In a sense, the EAP professional may be helping the supervisor respond therapeutically as well as ethically. Setting up expectations for changes in supervisory responses to troubled employees, followed by reinforcement for altered approaches, may increase the incidence of more desirable behavior (Hegarty, Sims, 1978).

Ethical Practices in the Workplace

While an examination of ethical and unethical practices in profit making settings is beyond the scope of this section, it is appropriate to examine the impact of the EAP practitioner on the values and ethics of supervisors, managers, and employees. Clearly, the EAP practitioner is not a moral entrepreneur for the workplace. On the other hand, the infusion of new approaches to troubled workers and to troubling work conditions by management, unions, legal, and legislative bodies, consumer groups, as well as EAPs, may help to build an alternative value basis for selective corporate decisions. Such infusion of alternative practices–whether the expanding opportunities for workers to control allocative decision-making bodies, or changing policies regarding hiring and firing practices–may help to diversify the values that guide corporate practices, especially as they affect workers and their families.

EAP staff can look to the experiences of human service practitioners in other host settings (such as jails, schools, and hospitals) for evidence that such value impacts are feasible. At a time when the world of work is undergoing major transformations, and decisions are increasingly based on presumptions about the need for American industry to stay competitive in world markets, a myriad of experiments in the ever-changing work environment are possible. The EAP practitioner, joined by others in the workplace with similar humanistic functions, can help to promote new perspectives on corporate investment in employees and their families, consumers, and the wider community.

Society, Ethical Practice, and the EAP

The employee assistance practitioner, operating under a professional code of ethics, is expected to promote social justice and to address social problems (Levy, 1974). Such broad sensitizing terms as social justice lack easy prescriptions for practice, but their intent must be, for example, to mobilize employee assistance practitioners to transcend their workplace focus to support broader community and societal problem solving.

Such mandates may involve the mainstreaming of new workers into the workplace, such as recent immigrants, displaced home-makers, and the handicapped. EAP practitioners can help to inform discussions about whether service responses to needs of such groups should have public or private sector auspices. For example, discussions may transpire over whether housing, transportation, training, or skills in English as a second language should be provided by the public sector, private sector employer, or both.

Given the increasing private sector provision of services traditionally offered in the public or voluntary sector, and the infusion of market values into services traditionally within public sector domains, intensified planning is required to determine the appropriate mix of funding and collaboration between private and public sector service arrangements. Employee assistance practitioners are in preeminent positions to combine efforts with private sector and public sector providers in offering planning and resource development ideas. Organizing efforts of this sort are evolving around such issues as child care, "latch-key" children, and youth employment. Employee assistance practitioners, discharging their obligation to be concerned about social problems, can thus extend their service mission so that it has a broader-based community and societal impact.

Public sector social services have long been considered cushions for the negative human consequences of industrial decisions. Even though viewed as remedial, selective, piecemeal, and victim-blaming in orientation, such programs have been a primary employment base for most human service professionals. Now EAP professionals have opportunities to provide services for their employing organization on a more universal, rather than selective, basis to prevent progressive deterioration of individuals and to infuse humanistic and social welfare values into the industrial sector. Because of such new responsibilities, this cadre of pioneers occupies key positions to implement more preventive services in the arena that exerts the most profound impact on the well-being of individuals and society (Kurzman, 1983). While remaining aware of the historical pitfalls of being agents of employers rather than employees, the employee assistance practitioner is in a strategic position to advance the highest ideals and visions of the human service professions.

References

ALMACA, *Standards for Employee Alcoholism and/or Assistance Programs*, Arlington, Virginia.

Akabas, S.H., "Keynote Address," Human Services and the Workplace Conference, Washington State Chapter, National Association of Social Workers, Seattle, 1980.

_____, "Labor: Social Policy and Human Services," *Encyclopedia of Social Work*, Washington D.C. National Association of Social Workers; Seventeenth issue, 1977, pp. 737–744.

_____, Kurzman, P.A., "The Industrial Social Welfare Specialist: What's So Special?" *Work, Workers and Work Organizations*, ed. Akabas, Kurzman, Englewood Cliffs, Prentice Hall, 1982, pp. 197–235.

Bakalinsky, R., "People vs. Profits: Social Work in Industry," *Social Work*, 19 May 1980, pp. 471–475.

Brandes, S.D., *American Welfare Capitalism, 1880–1940*; Chicago; The University of Chicago Press, 1976.

Briar, K.H., "Layoffs and Social Work Intervention," *Urban and Social Change Review*; Summer, 1983.

_____, Bennet, A.L., Crump, L., Darling, E., Taylor-Degnan, L., Dethlefs, W., Stier, F., Vinet, M., *Initiating Industrial Social Work Services*, (Silver Springs, Maryland; National Association of Social Workers), in press.

Fine, M., Akabas, S.H., Bellinger, S., "Cultural Drinking: A Workplace Perspective," *Social Work*, 27; September, 1982. pp. 436–440.

Hegarty, W.H., Sims, H.P., Jr, "Some Determinants of Unethical Decision Behavior: An Experiment," *Journal of Applied Psychology 63*, 1978, pp. 451–457.

Kurzman, P.A., "Toward a Framework for Considering Ethical Issues in Industrial Social Work Practice," *Social Casework*. Feb. 1983.

Levy, C.S., "On the Development of a Code of Ethics," *Social Work*, March 1974, pp. 207–216.

Ozawa, M., "Development of Social Services in Industry: Why and How?" *Social Work*, Vol. 25, No. 6, Nov. 1980, pp. 464–470.

Reynolds, B., *Social Work and Social Living*, New York; Citadel Press, 1951.

Vinet, M., Jones, C., *Social Services and Work: Initiation of Social Workers into Labor and Industry Settings, Procedures and Professional Identification*

Issues, (Silver Springs, Maryland; National Association of Social Workers) 1981.

Walden, T., "Industrial Social Work: A Conflicting Definition," *NASW News*, 23 (Sept, 1978), p. 9.

Yelaja, S. ed., *Ethical Issues in Social Work*, Springfield, Illinois, Charles C. Thomas, 1982.

33

TOPEX Study
"Hitting Bottom in High Places"
Charles E. Shirley

Introduction

Although EAP's have proven to be highly effective in helping employed alcoholic people to accept and deal successfully with their alcoholism, the strategies and techniques utilized in such programs are considered by many people in the field to be generally ineffective for identifying and recovering the top executive alcoholic individual.

The New York City Affiliate of the National Council on Alcoholism. Inc., through its industrial department, became interested in exploring this problem in an effort to discover possible methods to reach this difficult group.

During our initial discussions it was brought out that we knew of several high-ranking corporate people who were not only recovered alcoholics but who had gained and maintained their recovery while holding top executive status.

What was needed, then, was for us to identify and talk with a number of such recovered people in order to find out what it was like for them as working, active alcoholics, what happened, how they found help, and then to determine whether or not we could use that information to develop more effective programs.

Exploratory Study

We decided to conduct an exploratory study using a one-to-one interviewing method of inquiry. With the aid of a research consultant we

Reprinted with permission from *Labor Management Alcoholism Journal*, Vol. 11: No. 4. Jan-Feb 1982, pp. 130–135.

designed a questionnaire that would provide the information we needed.

Once the questionnaire was constructed and adjusted, we immediately began to identify and query top executive people who had held the positions of vice president or above during their drinking years and who were in recovery at least one year at the time of the study.

We had very little difficulty in finding our subjects or getting their consent to be questioned. The subjects were interviewed by one of our professional staff and the questionnaire was filled out at that time. Confidentiality and anonymity were assured and proper controls and precautions were implemented and have been carefully followed.

Once the interviews were completed, the data that had been collected were extracted, evaluated and studied.

Limited Group

At the time of our study all of our subjects but one were maintaining their recoveries as active members of Alcoholics Anonymous. All were employed by corporations located in New York City. That means, of course, that we are dealing with a small sampling of a very select group of people. Those limitations must be kept in mind as we explore our findings.

Most of the questions we asked required hindsight on the part of our subjects. Recall on the part of anyone can be challenged. How accurate sober alcoholic people can be in looking back on their active drinking days could be very seriously challenged.

However, since we were questioning AA members, there is another element that enters that situation. Successfully sober AA members have, almost without exception, spent a good bit of time honestly exploring their past life histories as part of their recovery process. Hence, I feel quite comfortable with their ability to report accurately on the conditions and events about which we questioned them.

25 Subjects

The study was conducted over a period of six months during 1980/81. We identified and queried 20 males and 5 females. At the time of the study our 25 subjects consisted of 3 corporation presidents, 2 chief executive officers, 6 general managers, 12 vice presidents and 2 full partners. At some point during their active alcoholism, all of them had held positions equal to or above that of vice president. There were many types of corporations represented by our subjects, reflecting the diversity of the New York City industrial mix.

For the most part we went out to the subjects' offices during work hours. We found them all to be open about their recoveries within their organizations.

Usually they requested a secretary to hold the calls and devoted the following hour and a half to the project. The reasons for the study had been explained to them prior to our meeting.

Each question was carefully considered before being answered and clarifications were often requested and given. It was hard work, that hour and a half, and we were grateful for the quality of cooperation we received from each and every subject.

The average age of the people we questioned was 50, with a spread of 32 to 65. The average length of sobriety was 7 years, with a range of 1 to 18.

Other Demographics

These were basically middle-class people with college degrees or the equivalent. In the opinion of the interviewer, they could be characterized as energetic, ambitious, and bright. Thirteen were married at the time of the interview, 5 divorced, 4 single and 3 widowed. Eighteen came from homes where at least one parent was alcoholic.

The average age for having their first drink was 14 years. Sixteen had been drunk at least once during that first year and the rest before the next year was finished. This sounds early, and may be significant since there was only one exception to this early drink/drunk experience.

The majority of our respondents were daily drinkers; there were only 2 who could be considered periodic in their drinking pattern. Thirteen did not use drugs other than alcohol; 9 used prescription drugs as directed by a physician, and 3 were steady, addicted users of both prescription and illicit drugs.

Late-Stage Cases

It is important to realize that all of these people were seriously alcoholic when they entered recovery. Twenty-three had experienced shakes, all had had blackouts, 21 had had sleep problems, 23 had experienced serious interpersonal problems within their families and 19 with work associates.

Twenty-one reported that they frequently drank openly and at times heavily in work-related situations away from the office such as business lunches, conventions, seminars, business conferences, and on semi-social occasions with office peers.

If any drinking in the office took place, it was usually hidden from view.

The idea seemed to be that drinking off-campus in a work-related situation was condoned and even expected, but drinking in the office, except on special occasions, was considered to be taboo.

Only 15 of our subjects reported drinking in the morning and then only during the later stages of their alcoholism.

Performance

This study supports the opinion expressed by many experienced people in the field that it is unrealistic to hope that job performance deterioration in the usual sense will help to identify the top executive alcoholic in the earlier stages of his or her alcoholism. Quite the opposite, actually.

The theory is that, if we wait for the executive's work performance to deteriorate to the point where he or she can be confronted with it, we will be dealing with a group of very well-dressed, late stage chronic alcoholic people.

One possible explanation for this is fairly simple: Performance for the executive is often measured by the long-term financial results rather than day-to-day productivity. This person's current record of achievement is often the result of past actions. He or she may have brought important accounts to the firm or developed a new product, a unique service, or a production system that continues to show results through a considerable length of time. It may require only a minimum of current effort on the part of that executive to keep that account, product, service, or system producing.

High Achievers

Another possible explanation is that these people appear to be high achievers. What may happen is that the high achievement work pattern compensates for the downward progressive nature of the alcoholism, keeping the person within the boundaries of acceptable performance or better.

What these individuals could have accomplished without the handicap of alcoholism would, I believe, stun most people, if we could only measure it. But this is pure conjecture.

As it is, once in recovery, 15 advanced their careers almost immediately. Others, surprisingly, had reached the top in their careers in spite of active alcoholism and, for some, drastic physical debilitation.

All of our respondents reported that they believed that others around them saw their performance as acceptable or better. They themselves, however, knew they were slipping but didn't really understand why.

Career Histories

Sixteen of our participants reported that they achieved steady advancement in their positions throughout their active alcoholism.

One young man confided in us that he made a sincere suicide attempt only two days after having been made first vice-president of his firm. His reason was simple: "In spite of seemingly fantastic success in my career, I could find no satisfaction at all in my life."

Five others reported that they advanced in their companies to a certain point and then their careers stalled until they entered recovery. The remaining 4 either resigned their position, their companies failed, or they were actually fired.

Not one of our participants reported an attempt to cover up the fact of alcoholism for a very good and simple reason–they didn't know that they were alcoholic.

What they were attempting to hide was what they felt to be their inadequacy, possible insanity, a loss of drive, and the fact that they were often so physically sick or emotionally upset that they couldn't concentrate on their work.

Memory Lapses

They often resorted to elaborate measures to cover up the lapses in memory that were being experienced.

One highly placed executive was puzzled and baffled by his failing memory for day-to-day details. He missed appointments, forgot decisions, telephone calls, etc.

He responded to this supposed early onset of senility by hiring a stenographer who noted down everything that happened during his business day. The next morning he would have the previous day's notes read to him before he embarked on the new day's business. He didn't learn about alcoholic amnesia (blackouts) until he entered a rehabilitation center for treatment.

In order to keep abreast of their jobs, 11 of our respondents reported that they often came to work early, left late, and sometimes came in on weekends. In spite of their over-achieving efforts, many reported that they managed only two or three real working hours in any given day when they were able to get anything accomplished. The rest of the day was lost.

Nevertheless, they managed to look good for long periods of time. Sixteen reported that eventually they would miss days, arrive late, and find excuses to leave early, but they noted that that pattern emerged only towards the end of their active alcoholism.

Drinking Encouraged

Most of our participants were known by their peers and superiors to be heavy drinkers and were often sought after as being "fun" people. The women in our study reported that they were actively supported in their drinking by male peers and superiors who either thought it was "cute" or enjoyed having female associates who could and would drink with them.

As might be expected, there were others who were covering up for our interviewees. We were very interested in those activities and spent considerable time in exploring this area. I believe we were rewarded with some significant data that should be more directly studied.

For instance, 21 of our subjects reported that their personal secretaries conducted extensive and skillful cover-up operations. We assume that, in the spirit of loyalty to the boss and also to protect their own positions, these secretaries consistently acted in ways that would prolong and intensify the alcoholic problem but were completely unaware of the destructive nature of their activities.

Covered By Superiors

According to our subjects, the No. 2 cover-up artist turned out to be the subjects superior.

Why would a boss cover up for one of his executives? Possibly to avoid an embarrassing confrontation; because he was afraid of losing a good executive, and, possibly, not wanting to admit that he, the boss, could have chosen as a top-ranking executive someone who was flawed in this way.

We also found a number of situations where the subject's secretary and his or her superior were both covering up, neither one being aware of the other's activities. There were also peers, subordinates, and family covering for our subjects from time to time, they reported.

If the executive was involved with clients outside the corporation, then those clients often became involved in the cover-up system as well. Usually, it turned out that the clients who willingly covered up for our respondents were perceived by our subjects to be alcohol-troubled themselves and as expecting the cover-up to work both ways.

Time Factors

We often hear the opinion that the top executive is at high risk to develop alcoholism because of stress and the permissiveness concerning drinking at that level of management. That viewpoint is not generally supported by this study.

As we pointed out earlier, these people were drinking to drunkenness in their mid-teens. They reported that by their early 20s they were experiencing problems with drinking but didn't realize it at that time. Generally, they became aware in their 30s that alcohol and trouble were somehow connected for them.

These and other answers we got to our questions in this area led us to suspect that, for the majority of our subjects, the alcoholism had progressed to the middle or late stages by the time they were into the top executive slots. This appears to be just as true for the younger executives in the study as for those more advanced in years.

Hence, we would be tempted to conclude that the stress and permissiveness that exist in the executive suite could be considered to be factors contributing to the *progression* of the alcoholism but not necessarily the cause. It appears that our subjects, at least, brought their alcoholism with them to those corner offices. This is compatible with *some* of the subjects in a study made some years ago by Trice and Belasco which covered over 600 individuals. The Trice-Belasco study, however, also found a type in which the alcoholism developed simultaneously with the executive or professional career in individuals who showed no signs of alcoholism in earlier college days.

Long Delay

Six years after they had acquired some awareness that an alcohol problem existed for them, our participants report that thoughts of getting help began to form. Another 4 years passed, on the average, before help was actively sought out by them or made available to them–a total loss of 10 years.

We asked our executives to make a judgment of how long they were open to help before they actually found it. The average reply was 7 years. They usually related their readiness to some traumatic experience such as a suicide attempt, hospitalization, surgery, death of a family member, or an out-of-town blackout misadventure.

The basic block to getting help appeared to be the lack of information on alcoholism.

One man finally went to the public library and looked up alcoholism. He read about shakes, sweats, blackouts, and other details describing the disease, and immediately identified himself as fitting all the criteria for being alcoholic. Since AA was recommended as a source of help, he quickly became successfully involved with that fellowship.

What is important is his statement that he would have been entirely ready to act on that information, if he had had it, 8 years prior to that desperate trip to the library. To me this is tragic. The study indicates that the lack of factual knowledge cost these people from 7 to 10 years of active alcoholism.

Intervention

How did our subjects finally get help?

Seven found their own way into treatment, driven by the fear of death, insanity, loss of family, loss of work abilities, or because of sickness, desperation, despair, or the simple lack of any other route to follow.

Three knew of friends who were AA members and asked them for help. Two were influenced to accept treatment by a physician and 3 were urged to get help, finally, by their employers. But there was no one who was helped to treatment through an EAP, though 3 of our subjects worked for companies that had a program at the time.

Ten were influenced to accept counseling and treatment for their alcoholism by members of their families or by close associates. The majority of those family members had sought professional guidance for themselves in order to initiate the process of intervention.

We have known for many years that intervention through the non-alcoholic, reactive family member is a viable process if carefully implemented. It was, however, surprising and gratifying to find that that sort of help was being sought out and utilized by enough people so that it would show up strongly in a small study such as this one

Treatment

Ten of our people were detoxified in a medical setting and 8 followed detox with a longer stay in a rehabilitation center. The remainder stopped drinking "one day at a time" in AA without medical supervision or hospitalization. Seven reported having one relapse for which 3 were hospitalized.

In addition to their involvement with AA, 23 of our sampling had sought professional help of one kind or another at some point in their struggle to gain and maintain a comfortable sobriety.

All of their family members who had become involved with the recovery process had received professional guidance and many had become involved in the Al-Anon Family Groups as well.

When we asked our people if they would reach out to a peer executive who was showing signs of alcoholism, 19 reported that they had already done so. The others were willing to do so, with one person hesitant to answer in the affirmative.

Those who had helped another executive, instinctively used a peer pressure technique coupled with an AA "12th Step" approach. Our 25 had led 19 others, usually in the same company, into the helping network.

Summary

Our experiences in designing, conducting, and evaluating this exploratory study lead us to certain tentative conclusions that we would like to explore further.

For instance:

- The study suggests that the view that the standard EAP design, which leans heavily on declining job performance, absenteeism, and close supervision for its effectiveness, will not be effective with the top executive group. A separate program with separate policy, procedures, coordination, training, intervention, and educational components might be neccessary if we wish to reach the top executive alcoholic on the work site.
- The study suggests that a shift of work habits towards overworking manifested by arriving early, leaving late, and working weekends may signal that the top executive is in trouble. This should be explored by further study.
- Inappropriate drinking behaviors in offsite but work-related situations should be considered to be serious breaches of discipline which reflect negatively on the corporate image.
- Inappropriate behavior on the worksite, whether or not it is perceived as being alcohol-related, should be noted and documented, particularly when the behavior is troubling to other workers and interferes in their performance and morale.
- Since corporate advancement appears to happen in spite of developing alcohol problems, any threat to that continued evidence of success should have great impact on the troubled person.
- Confidentiality and job security should be extended to any subordinate who becomes in any way involved in the intervention process.
- The program coordinator should be outside the corporate power structure and reporting directly to the highest level of authority in the company.
- Carefully planned and conducted education seminars must be provided at the top executive level in order to spark self-referrals.

Other educational efforts should be made for the executive secretary group and for the other people in sensitive positions where "cover-up" operations would usually set in as alcoholism progressed for the executive.

- All intervention procedures at this level of management should be carefully orchestrated by the consultant/coordinator in each individual case.

Much of what has been said here should be further evaluated and researched. Our hope is that this can be done so that, eventually, we will be able to offer the same hope for recovery to the alcoholic top executive in the corporate structure as we do to his or her subordinate workers.

34

Alcoholism as a Major Focus of EAPs
William R. Byers
John C. Quinn

Introduction

The largest human resource problems facing American industry today are the costs of absenteeism, accidents, increased workers compensation, inappropriate utilization of health care benefits, and poor quality work related to employees with alcoholism.

EAPs have evolved from occupational alcoholism programs (OAPs), which initially focused primarily on identifying, motivating, and referring employees with alcoholism to treatment. OAPs were staffed largely by recovering alcoholics, volunteers, and medical personnel who had developed a specific base of expertise in alcoholism. The modern day EAP provides a wide range of services for employees and family members with alcoholism and problems such as substance abuse, emotional, marital, financial, and compulsive gambling. Issues such as job-related stress are also being addressed by EAPs, under the popular rubric of "wellness in the work place." Modern day EAPs are being staffed primarily by social workers, psychologists, and other helping professionals, many of whom have little education or experience in alcoholism. EAPs staffed by professionals unskilled in alcoholism will identify fewer alcoholics, and may engage in an "enabling" process. It is possible that alcoholics at the workplace will no longer receive adequate attention, due to the lack of alcoholism expertise of the helping professionals and the reduced focus on alcoholism in the promotion and educational materials provided employees by the EAP. It is important that helping professionals working in EAPs receive adequate training in alcoholism to insure that employees and their families with alcoholism receive quality services.

Prevalence, Scope and Costs of Alcoholism and Alcohol Misuse

Alcoholism is a multi-faceted illness that affects the individual, the family unit, the employer, and society. The U.S. Department of Health and Human Services estimates a prevalence of alcohol misuse and alcoholism ranging from 9,652,209 to 10,273,883 people in the U.S.[1] Of the nation's 90.5 million employed workers, it is estimated that seven million have alcohol problems.[2] According to the National Council on Alcoholism, between six and ten percent of employees have alcoholism; while 50% of fatal accidents involve alcohol; over 80% of fire deaths, 65% of drownings, 22% of home accidents, 77% of falls, 36% of pedestrian accidents, and 55% of arrests are linked to alcohol use. Violent behavior associated with alcohol use is of major concern, with 65% of murders, 40% of assaults, 35% of rapes, 30% of other sex crimes, 30% of suicides, 55% of fights or assaults in the home, and 60% of cases of child abuse are related to alcohol misuse.[3]

It is estimated that each alcoholic has a negative impact on an average of four other people, who may be family members, fellow employees, or significant others. While this statement is difficult to verify, experienced professionals treating alcoholics consider this 1–to–4 ratio conservative at best.

The costs of alcoholism and alcohol misuse are escalating at a significant rate. In 1975, the U.S. Department of Health and Human Services estimated the total economic cost of alcoholism and alcohol misuse at 42.7 billion dollars annually.[4] A report recently commissioned by the U.S. Health Subcommittee of the Senate Finance Committee estimated the current cost of alcohol abuse at $120 billion in the U.S. each year.[5] The National Highway Traffic Safety Administration of the U.S. Department of Transportation estimates the cost of alcohol-related auto accidents at over $24 billion per year, including losses in productivity, hospital, and health care costs, vehicular damage, auto insurance costs, etc. In New York State in 1979, the estimated societal costs for alcohol involving highway crashes were $727.5 million with the costs escalating to $900 million in 1982.[6]

Rationale for a Major Focus on Alcoholism

Alcoholism and alcohol misuse is the largest human problem at the workplace, due to the economic costs and pervasive impact on industry. Alcoholic employees have more absenteeism, more frequent accidents and illnesses, and a higher utilization of health care benefits and workers compensation than the average employee.

Various studies indicate that employees who misuse alcohol and/or are alcoholic are absent from 1.5 to 3 times more than the average employee. A study of absenteeism among alcoholic and non-alcoholic employees published in the *Quarterly Journal of Studies on Alcohol* in 1959 showed that problem drinkers average absenteeism rate was 2.9 times more frequent than the control group.[7] In 1979, a study by Mannello of drinking practices of workers on seven railroads employing 234,000 workers found that "problem drinkers missed an average of 15.3 days, while non-problem drinkers missed an average of 8.6 days," a rate of 1.7 times that of the non-problem drinkers.[8] The cost of absenteeism in the Mannello study is estimated to be 3.1 million dollars.[9] The costs and impact of absenteeism are difficult to identify, because there are many types of absences and the methods of documenting absenteeism vary from company to company and are different for management and union employees.

Several examples of absenteeism that are difficult to identify are on-the-job absences and casual absences. An alcoholic employee for example, may show up late, have extended coffee breaks, longer than average lunch periods, and leave early, but be able to provide acceptable excuses for a long period of time. The alcoholic employee who is drinking during the day will also be absent on the job, in the sense of an inability to concentrate, which also affects work quality, productivity, and decision making.

The alcoholic employee has more frequent accidents and sickness-related absences than the average employee, which is very costly, resulting in a higher utilization of health care benefits and workers compensation. D'Alonzo and Pell in 1970 studied a group of 764 alcoholics and found that their rate of accidents was 3.5 times higher than the control group. Sickness-related absenteeism for the alcoholic study group ranged from 1.3 to 3.3 times higher than the control group.[10]

Foote and Erfurt, in a study of EAP clients from 1976 to 1977, found that the average amount of benefits paid for alcoholic clients ranged from 1.3 to 2.2 times more than the company norm.[11] Joseph Follmann, Jr., in his book "Alcoholics and Business" states the following relative to absenteeism, disability, sickness, and accident costs of alcoholic employees.

- Absenteeism 2 1/2 times the norm.
- 3.6% of alcoholic employees are disabled daily, compared to a norm of 1.6.
- The average alcoholic employee is off work 22 days due to drinking or related physical complications.
- 12.8% of alcoholic workers are disabled for 30 days or more, and 3.8% are disabled 90 days or more per year, compared to 6.5% and 0.6% for the average employee.
- Alcoholic employees collect more than three times the amount of sickness payments than the average employee.

- Employed or retired alcoholics have a mortality rate from two to three times that of others.[12]

Follmann also lists the costs of alcoholism to various businesses:

- United California Bank–$1,000,000 annually.
- North American Rockwell–estimated cost of one alcoholic employee at $50,220.
- Gulf Oil Canada, Ltd.–estimated total cost of all alcoholic employees in excess of $400,000.
- The Scovill Manufacturing Company –estimated the average cost of an alcoholic employee at $4,550 annually for absenteeism alone.[13]

It is important for EAPs to have a major focus on alcoholism, due to the enormous economic impact on business and because the alcoholic rarely volunteers for treatment. The cost efficiency of identifying, referring, and following-up with alcoholic employees has been documented through various outcome studies of EAPs. The cost savings realized further support the rationale for EAPs providing a major focus on alcoholism, since a body of literature is not available to demonstrate similar savings for other employee problems.

Conservative estimates indicate that a four dollar return can be realized for every one dollar invested in EAPs and the rehabilitating of alcoholic employees. Follmann details various studies showing savings for rehabilitated alcoholics, summarized as follows:

- Recovery rates from 50-80%.
- Reduction in sickness and accident benefits as high as 60%.
- Accidents reduced by a much as 50%.[14]

The National Institute on Alcohol Abuse and Alcoholism distributed a "Summary of Alcoholism Offset Studies," which detailed the cost savings in ten organizations. The results are very similar to studies detailed by Follmann, with a few additions, summarized as follows:

- 40% decline in hospital, medical and surgical costs.
- $0.41 savings for every dollar spent on general health care.
- Hospital days down 60%, all illness diagnosis down 79%.[15]

Types of Employee Problems Identified by EAPs

There does not appear to be a single source to provide a definitive description of the percentages of employees seen by type of reporting problem or what the norm should be for those EAPs that desire to have a major focus on alcoholism. While it is difficult to project estimated levels of problems identified by an effective EAP, from our perspective the following ranges of identification would be reasonable (see Table 34-1).

The importance of these studies is that alcoholism is the single largest problem identified by EAPs that maintain a major focus on alcoholism and are staffed by people with expertise in alcoholism. Such high percentages of employee problems identified by EAPs will fluctuate over time, but it is our opinion that alcoholism, if properly addressed, will remain the largest identified problem. In the study of the Kennecott Corporation cited by Presnall, the percentage of alcoholism in a later study from 1970-1976 was only 18.1% of the total of reported problems, but was still 5% more than the next highest reported problem.[21] As a contrast, a mental health center staffed by industrial social workers servicing various industrial sites, who apparently were not skilled in alcoholism, listed the presenting problems of their clients as 88% psychotic, neurotic, and personality disorders. There is no indication that this project identified a single alcoholic employee.[22]

The EAP that is successful at identifying and referring alcoholic employees utilizes certain methods that are important to review briefly.

EAP Methodology

The method of intervening with the alcoholic employee utilizing work performance measures as a means of motivation has been well documented. Trice and Roman, in their classic book, *Spirits and Demons at Work,* named this method constructive confrontation; it has been and is being utilized very successfully in identifying and referring alcoholic employees to treatment. Constructive confrontation is a process often involving labor,

TABLE 34-1

	BYERS AND QUINN (EST)	ALMACA SURVEY (16)	FOOTE AND ERFURT (17)	KENNECOTT (18)	KELSEY HAYES (18)
ALCOHOLISM	35-60%	59%	58.3%	46.6%	38.4%
EMOTIONAL/ MENTAL	25-30%	22%	18.8%	8.7%	27.9%
FAMILY/ MARITAL			8.3%	11.2%	12.9%
OTHER:	5-40%	14%	4.2%	19.0%	12.5%
DRUGS	-	5%	10.4%	4.5%	8.3%

management, the employee, the family, the EAP staff, and treatment agency staff. An alcoholic employee with declining work performance is confronted at the work site, and is encouraged by labor and management to seek assistance from the EAP for any personal problems that are causing the work performance problem. The EAP staff also confronts the employee's declining work performance and, during an assessment interview, helps the employee to see the primary cause. Most often the cause is untreated alcoholism. The employee is given the direction toward treatment and, dependent on the policy, may or may not receive disciplinary measures for declining work performance. The treatment agency staff initially focuses on the declining work performance and attempts to have the employee see its relationship to the alcoholism and the need to accept treatment.

This systematic application of direct confrontation has been relatively successful in breaking through the denial system that most alcoholics maintain. Alcoholism, after all, is a disease of denial. The alcoholic is often stigmatized by society and is viewed as mentally ill, or physically and morally weak. In the mind of an alcoholic, initial acceptance of alcoholism carries a heavy psychological price. The stigma does not automatically end when the alcoholic becomes sober. Society does not easily remove negative labels once applied to diseases such as alcoholism.

Constructive confrontation, while highly successful when used with alcoholics, is often antithetical to the training received by social workers, psychologists, psychiatrists, and other helping professionals. They are more oriented to working with the client's definition of problems in a relatively non-confrontive fashion. Some helping professionals even have negative views of alcoholics, views whose presence holds little hope for promoting recovery from alcoholism, views which see business and industry as oppressive and responsible for employee problems.

Helping Professionals, Limited training in alcoholism

The crux of the problem for many helping professionals moving into EAP jobs is that their education and training has not prepared them to adequately recognize and assist persons with alcoholism. They have been trained to believe that the *effects* of drinking are a symptom of broader psychopathology. This view leads the helping professional on a never ending search for the underlying cause of alcoholic drinking that will somehow change the alcohlic's drinking. This approach to alcoholism is still being taught, despite many years of public education on alcoholism, and no data to support the idea that the incidence of mental illness among alcoholics is any higher than the general population's. What helping professionals are often missing in their formal education is awareness; that the pathological behavior in the alcoholic is chemically induced by the drug alcohol; that alcoholism therefore needs to be addressed as a *primary* illness; that professional assessment and/or psychological testing should be repeated following a period of abstinence; and that abstinence is a mandatory prelude to arriving at any secondary diagnoses. Helping professionals generally are not taught the skills needed to adequately confront the alcoholic to overcome the denial system. Helping professionals often re-focus the attention away from alcoholism, by labeling the alcoholic's problem as a family or emotional problem, which enables the alcoholic to rationalize the use of alcohol. According to Levinson and Straussner, for example, "the alcoholic is able to trigger a social worker's need to rescue, to comfort, to be liked, and to feel omnipotent.[23] A review of the literature points out that many helping professionals have strong negative views of alcoholism that block their ability to appropriately treat alcoholism.

In a 1969 study by Dorsh, less than 40% of helping professionals studied were willing to treat people known to have drinking problems. A 1973 study by Knox of helping professionals' attitudes toward alcoholics showed that social workers were more willing to treat alcoholics than psychologists or psychiatrists, but only 15% were willing to treat alcoholics full-time. A 1980 study by Peyton, Chaddick, and Gorsuch of graduate social work students found a significant bias against selecting alcoholics as clients, pessimistic predictions about their treatment outcomes, and a disregard of alcoholism indicators during assessments.[24] This negative bias around alcoholism logically carries over into treatment planning and outcomes, EAP program design, and implementation. It would seem that education in the schools that train helping professionals needs to eliminate the negative bias against alcoholism. Wechsler and Rohman, in a 1979 random sample survey of 2,000 students, found the opposite to be true. The students responding were enrolled in nursing programs, medical schools, social work programs, and in counseling programs. While these students had a high rate of exposure to alcohol education, only a small percentage had little hope for an alcoholic's chances of achieving recovery.[25]

A study by Smith in 1982 showed that education on alcoholism has not prepared physicians to adequately treat alcoholics. Significant findings in the Smith study show a distinct bias, in the 90% of the internists studied, prescribed drugs for alcoholism and nothing further.[26]

Some helping professionals have a bias toward industry, which could have a negative impact on the acceptance of EAP. A view expressed by Jacobsen in 1974 was that a strong contingent of the social work profession involved in social welfare believe that large industries tend to exploit people, injure their health, exploit natural resources and labor, and shirk accountability to the public they influence.[27] Some concerns about alcoholism programs in industry are evidenced by the statements of two academicians who promote a concept called industrial social work. Kurzman and Akabas state that "the considerable success achieved by these alcoholism programs has done a disservice in some ways to the aim of expanding counseling programs for workers. The development of alcoholism programs lulls the industrial parties into believing that they share a counseling service that meets employees' needs."[28]

The staffing of EAPs is changing, in that the majority of job openings, based on our observations, now require a master's level degree in one of the helping professions, and usually in social work. It is obvious that without adequate training in alcoholism and an understanding of the purpose and nature of complex business organizations, EAPs may become so broadly focused that alcoholism will no longer receive adequate attention. It is important, therefore, to establish what is considered to be adequate training in alcoholism.

Education and Training

We have established that most helping professionals need additional education and training in alcoholism and the complexities inherent in providing helping services in industry. Due to a dearth of alcoholism educational opportunities within professional schools, there has been an emergence of specialized institutes and summer schools of alcohol studies.

These educational forums continue to provide training and educational experiences for teachers, clergy, physicians, social workers, industrial and labor leaders, directors of EAP services, and other persons interested in alcoholism education, research, and rehabilitation.

In 1977, Kolben surveyed schools of social work and found only four with curricula oriented towards industry.[29] Certainly, many professionals working in the EAP field require an increased training concerning alcoholism. In a study published in 1981, of 325 people seen by Hazelden Employee Assistance Services, only 19.1% were identified as presenting an alcoholism or drug problem. Upon completion of a professional assessment, 41.2% of this group were found to have an alcoholism or drug-related problem.[30]

In order to insure that helping professionals have sufficient information regarding the illness of alcoholism, we suggest that the following material be included in the basic curriculum to train and educate helping professionals prior to their entry into the world of work: information defining alcohol as a drug, the medical aspects of alcohol addiction, and the disease concept of alcoholism. Since it is important for the helping professional to recognize the disease, training and education should also include an understanding of alcoholism's progression, with the identification of signs and symptoms at each stage of the disease.[31]

Additional information, training, and skill development in how to identify alcoholism and how to facilitate an appropriate referral for treatment should also be presented.

Alcoholism assessment, motivation, and referral resource development would focus on material concerning the use of psychosocial evaluation as a tool; key drinking history questions; confrontation techniques and information on how to organize, develop and determine which treatment resources are available in the community. Services, such as emergency care, detoxification, inpatient rehabilitation, outpatient clinics, and self-help groups such as Alcoholics Anonymous, would be developed for the resource list, to support the EAP alcoholism referral component.

Since most EAP services extend to family members, training and education should provide an understanding of the effects of alcoholism on children of alcoholics and the family. Educational objectives would include discussions of the alcoholic family, symptoms and characteristics of children of alcoholics, and descriptions of family treatment resources in the community.

Finally since the helping professional will be functioning in the workplace, education and training need to be provided which describe the complexities of industry and identify the inter-relationship and appropriate roles of the EAP service to labor and management.

The overall mission of the educational content presented here is to support and insure the development of a highly effective EAP assessment and referral component, one which recognizes the needs of the employed alcoholic.

Summary and Recommendations

Alcoholism is a multi-faceted illness that affects the individual, the family unit, the employer and society. It is estimated that over 9 million people in the United States are alcoholics. Alcoholism is estimated to cost society $120 billion dollars annually, a large percentage of which is attributable to lost production. Alcoholic employees have more absenteeism, more frequent accidents, more illnesses affecting a higher utilization of health care benefits and workers compensation than the average employee. EAPs need to maintain a major focus on alcoholism, due to its high prevalence, its enormous costs to industry, and its potential for cost savings realized through the rehabilitation of alcoholic employees.

EAPs are currently being staffed by helping professionals, many of whom have little training in alcoholism or understanding of the purpose and nature of complex business organizations. As a result, EAPs may become so broadly focused that alcoholic employees and their family members will no longer receive adequate attention and services. It is recommended that schools and universities provide training in employee assistance programming and the complexities of business and industry, including an understanding of labor unions and all aspects of the disease of alcoholism.

References

1. U. S. Department of Health and Human Services, Public Health Service-Alcohol, Drug Abuse and Mental Health Administration, National Institute on Alcohol Abuse and Alcoholism, *First Statistical Compendium on Alcohol and Health*, Feb. 1981, Pg. 72, U. S. Printing Office, Washington, D. C.
2. Association of Labor-Management Administrators and Consultants on Alcoholism, *Fact Sheet-Information about ALMACA and Occupational Alcoholism Programs*, ALMACA, Arlington, Va.
3. National Council on Alcoholism, *Facts on Alcoholism*, Feb. 1979, NCA, N.Y., N.Y.
4. U. S. Department of Health and Human Services, Pg. 67.
5. Saxe, et. al., *The Effectiveness and Costs of Alcoholism Treatment*, March 1983, Office of Technology Assessment, Congress of the U.S., Washington, D.C.
6. Williams, T.P., and Lillis, R.P., *Societal Costs Associated with Highway Crash: Development of County Level Estimates*, NYS Division of Alcoholism and Alcohol Abuse, Bureau of Alcohol and Highway Safety Research Brief 82-2, Winter 1982, Table I.
7. Quarterly Journal of Studies on Alcohol, Vol. 20, 1959, *Absenteeism Among Alcoholic vs. Nonalcoholic Employees.*
8. Mannello, T.A., *Problem Drinking Among Railroad Workers: Extent, Impact and Solutions*, University Research Corporation, Washington, D.C., 1979, Pg. 30.
9. Ibid., Pg. 6
10. De Alonzo & Pell, *Frequency of Sickness-Related Absenteeism Among Alcoholic vs. Nonalcoholic Employees*, Journal of Occupational Medicine, Vol. 12, No. 6, 1970.
11. Foote, A., & Erfurt, J.C., *Effectiveness of Comprehensive Employee Assistance Programs at Reaching Alcoholics*, Journal of Drug Issues, Spring 1981, Vol. 2, No. 2, Tallahassee, Florida, Pg. 223.
12. Follmann, Jr., J.F., *Alcoholics and Business-Problems, Costs, Solutions*, "Effects on the Business Community", New York, N.Y., AMACOM, American Management Association, 1976, Pgs. 82–83.
13. Ibid., Pgs. 84–85.
14. Ibid., Pgs. 166–172.
15. National Institute on Alcohol Abuse and Alcoholism, "Summary of Alcoholism Offset Studies, NIAAA, Rockville, Md. (Unpublished-Undated).
16. The Association of Labor-Management Administrators and Consultants on

Alcoholism, "Occupational Employee Assistance Programs, What do they look like?": Byers, William R., Bykowski, Robert J. and Hampton, Phyllis, (Unpublished) 1979 ALMACA, Arlington, Va.

17. Foote, A. & Erfurt, J.C., Pg. 222.

18. Presnall, L.F., *Occupational Counseling and Referral Systems,* Utah, Alcoholism Foundation, Salt Lake City, Utah, 1981, Pg. 54

19. Ibid., Pg. 136.

20. National Institute on Alcohol Abuse and Alcoholism, *Women's Occupational Alcoholism, Demonstration Project,* U.S. Department of Health and Human Services-NIAAA, Rockville, Md., 1980, Pg. 15.

21. Presnall, L.F., Pg. 51.

22. Weiner, A. and S., *Mental Health Care in the World of Work,* Pg. 134, Association Press, 1973.

23. Levinson, V. and Straussner, "Social Workers as Enablers in the Treatment of Alcoholics", *Social Case Work, Dimensions of Alcoholism Treatment,* Vol. 59, No. 1, Jan. 1978, Pg. 19.

24. Peyton, Chaddick and Gorsuch, "Willingness to treat Alcoholics: A study of Graduate Social Work Students", *Journal of Studies on Alcohol,* Vol. 41, No. 9, 1980, Pg. 935–939.

25. Wechsler, H., and Rohman, M., "Future Caregivers Views on Alcoholism Treatment, A Poor Prognosis", *Journal of Studies on Alcohol,* Vol. 43, No. 9, Sept. 1982, Pg. 939–955.

26. Smith, B.E., "Medical Education: The teaching of Alcoholism & Drug Abuse", *Submitted to the New York State Study on Heroin and Alcohol,* New York State Division of Alcoholism and Alcohol Abuse, 1982, Pg. 11.

27. Jacobsen, R., "Industrial Social Work in Context: Points and Viewpoints", *Social Work,* Nov. 1974, Pgs. 655–56.

28. Kurzman, P.A. and Akabas, S.H., "Industrial Social Work as an Arena for Practice", *Social Work,* Vol. 26, No. 1, Pg. 52, NASW, Washington, D.C., January 1981.

29. Kolben, N., "Graduate Education for Social Work Practice in Labor and Industrial Settings", *Social Work,* Vol. 26, No. 1, Pg. 52, NASW, Washington, D.C., 1981.

30. Plant, T., "Education & Prevention through EAPs", *Labor-Management Alcoholism Journal,* National Council on Alcoholism, N.Y., N.Y., March-April 1981.

31. Caldes, J., *Alcoholism Primer,* New York State Division of Alcoholism and Alcohol Abuse, Albany, N.Y., September 1983.

35

EAPs: An Opportunity for Improving Mental Health Services
Jack Santa-Barbara

Introduction

The main theme of this section is that the presence of EAPs in the workplace provides a unique opportunity for improving the existing mental health delivery system. An underlying assumption is that an improved mental health system will not only benefit employees, but business as well. To take full advantage of this opportunity requires critical discussion and clarification within the EAP movement, as well as within business and industry.

The most unique aspect of EAPs is that they provide mental health services through the workplace. This involves a more direct funding, and therefore control, of mental health services by those immediately affected. This increased involvement by employers and employee groups is likely to lead to an increased interest in the effectiveness and efficiency of the entire mental health care system. Given this increased interest, and fresh perspective, it may be a most appropriate opportunity for all parties to consider what improvements can and should be made in assisting employees and their families to maintain high levels of mental health.

Several recent trends have provided what may be a truly unique opportunity for improving mental health services through the presence of EAPs in the workplace. This happy synchronicity involves: 1) the fact that EAPs have established a respected, albeit small, presence in business and industry; 2) business and industry's growing awareness of the relationship between mentally healthy workers and a productive, committed workforce; 3) the realization that the rapid and dramatic changes in business and industry mean that there will be increasing sources of stress at the workplace over the coming years, requiring some type of planned response; 4) the recent cutback in services provided by many public agencies due to fiscal restraints and long waiting lists; 5) the increasing importance assigned to a "people" orientation in the workplace (e.g., Peters and Waterman, 1982); 6) a business commitment to increasing productivity through a variety of means; and 7) the restructuring and readjustment occurring in many corporations, which are encouraging an openness to new ideas.

EAPs provide a major link between business and industry and the mental health field, and are therefore in a unique position to take advantage of this singular opportunity. EAP providers and businesses must decide whether they are satisfied with providing the resources of the existing mental health services to the workplace, or whether significant improvements can be made with the increased involvement of the private sector.

But what are the issues? What are the major difficulties with the current system and how can EAPs make an improvement? Let us count the ways.

1. EAPs Provide an Opportunity to Actively Promote the Use of Mental Health Resources.

Public agencies and private practitioners rarely engage in the active promotion of mental health in general, or their services in particular. The mental health field operates on a demand model and is therefore basically reactive to individual clients and referral sources. Consequently, many individuals who might benefit from mental health resources are uninformed about their availability, and ignorant of what they offer.

EAP's provide an opportunity for mental health resources to be promoted to employees and their families on a proactive basis. Upon implementing an EAP, it is vital to promote its use among employees and their families. Potential users need to be made aware of the services available, educated about what these services can accomplish, and encouraged to overcome their resistance and actually use the services as required. The more "at risk" individuals who receive counseling, and the more effectively protective lifestyles encouraged, the greater will be the benefit to both employers and employees. In contrast to their colleagues outside of EAPs, professionals working within business and industry generally have a mandate to promote mental health services to the workforce.

Related to this issue of promoting mental health resources within an EAP, there is also a need to market EAPs to business and industry more broadly. Currently, only a relatively small percentage of employees are covered by some type of EAP. Setting aside for the moment that many of these EAPs may only be "paper programs" and not effectively reaching the workforce, it is clear that relatively few employees' lives are currently affected by the presence of EAPs. Apparently, the link between mental health and productivity has not been clearly made or marketed. New strategies and techniques are needed for EAP providers to more convincingly make this link, so that more employees and their families will have access to these services.

Part of the EAP marketing challenge is created by the fact that EAPs are generally a large corporation phenomenon. But the majority of the workforce is found in small and medium-sized businesses. One way of maintaining an economy of scale is for several smaller businesses to join together and form an EAP consortium. These programs have been successfully operating in several Canadian locations, some for as long as seven or eight years (Kaplun, 1983). EAP providers need to link up with business and trade associations to further promote these programs in small businesses—where the majority of workers are employed.

2. EAPs Provide an Opportunity for Preventive Programming.

To date, the demand model of mental health services has meant that services are "demanded" only when the personal pain and suffering is considerable. Mental illness is still regarded with fear and suspicion. Denial and avoidance of problems is the norm. Consequently, services are often not requested until the situation is serious, making treatment that much more difficult, costly, and uncertain. There is little "demand" for preventive services, services which contribute to positive mental health, which help people identify early warning signs, or even avoid unnecessary stressors to begin with.

However, within the EAP movement, interest in these preventive services is growing. Employers are realizing the enormous costs associated with waiting for employees to become so seriously dysfunctional that their work performance is adversely affected. Many EAPs include a preventive component, at least on paper. Few, however, have planned sufficiently for these types of activities to have a real impact. EAP providers, therefore, have an important responsibility to clarify what impact can reasonably be expected from a particular level of preventive effort. EAP providers will need to become very knowledgeable about the planning, implementation, and evaluation of primary prevention programs. The skills involved are often quite different from those involved in operating a treatment (or secondary prevention) program (Allen, 1978; Greenberg, 1982; Kotler and Zaltman, 1971; Lewitt, 1981; Novelli, 1980; Puska, 1979; Rothschild, 1979; Farquhar; et al, 1977; Public Health Reports, 1980).

Furthermore, planning for a preventive component in an EAP must give careful attention to the balance desired between the allocation of resources to primary and secondary prevention. How much of the resources should focus on those individuals who are already dysfunctional or at high risk for becoming dysfunctional (secondary prevention), and how much should focus on individuals who are not currently at risk, but whose protective characteristics could be enhanced? A careful needs assessment in a particular work setting might assist this process. However, in the absence of this type of data, the allocations will be made on the basis of the value orientations of the program planners. At the very least, these should be made explicit.

3. EAPs Provide an Opportunity for Improved Matching of Clients to Services.

Mental health resources in most metropolitan areas are diverse and highly specialized. From a prospective consumer's point of view, the available resources often present a bewildering array of unknown approaches and services (Bassuk and Gerson, 1978; General Accounting Office, 1976; Landau, 1969; Rae-Grant, 1976, Test, 1979). More often than not, the particular services an individual receives are based on happenstance rather than a careful matching of the individual's needs with the expertise of a particular agency or therapist (Glasser, 1979). Whatever effective treatment emerges from this chaos is probably due at least as much to the non-specific effects of therapy as to the appropriate matching of clients and services.

It is known from a large number of fairly well-controlled psychotherapy research studies (Bergin and Garfield, 1978; Edwards, et al., 1977; McLachlan, 1972, 1974; Skinner, 1981) that different types of therapies have greater impact with different types of clients. EAPs based on a referral or case management model have an opportunity of increasing the appropriateness of the match between client needs and service expertise. In this way, the specific benefits of particular therapies may be added to the non-specific benefits provided by most helpers, and the client outcomes will be more successful. Often, outcomes will be more cost-efficient with appropriate matching as well (Berkeley Planning Associates, 1977; Caragonne, 1979; Gans and Horton, 1975; Human Services Coordination Alliance, 1976).

More attention is required within the EAP field to this issue of matching clients and services. Familiarity with the intricacies of psychotherapy research is needed, as well as careful and detailed knowledge of the resources available in the community. These are the skills of a sophisticated generalist, rather than those associated with any particular type of therapy.

Procedures for educating clients to be good consumers of mental health services are also likely to be useful. We need to help clients make knowledgeable choices about the type of treatment they want, the goals which can be pursued, what to expect from a therapist, and about how they can best participate in the therapeutic relationship.

It should be noted that there is a potential conflict between an EAP model based on direct counseling by the EAP provider and the requirements of an improved matching process. Counseling-type EAPs are less likely to emphasize matching. The natural tendency will be for the EAP counselor to treat the individual directly, rather than match him or her with the best possible service. This EAP model comes closest to maintaining the status quo of the publicly funded services. In these situations, service providers are rewarded for delivering their own services rather than appropriately matching the client with the best possible service

One way of protecting against this is to assure the independence of whoever is conducting the initial interview with a client from the party or parties providing the treatment. In this way, breadth rather than depth may be explored in the initial interview and priorities negotiated based on client need, rather that on the specialized interests of the service provider. The referral and case-management model EAPs provide this opportunity. An EAP model which combines these advantages with a provision for short-term, general counseling by the EAP staff, overcomes the discontinuity of care which can result from a pure referral model. But the counseling and matching roles are distinct, and require different sets of skills.

4. EAPs Provide an Opportunity for Increased Accountability and Effectiveness.

Accountability in public agencies generally focuses on staying within a budget and considers such statistics as number of clients served. Some agencies also gather client satisfaction data as a means of justifying their services. Rarely are client outcomes considered in any systematic or rigorous way. And little attention is generally given to individuals who might benefit from the services, but who for a variety of reasons do not demand them.

The situation in the workplace may turn out to be quite different. EAPs are generally funded by employers and/or employee groups. Because their funding is more direct than that provided through the public agencies, it is not unreasonable to expect that increased accountability will be demanded of EAPs. Because the employee groups are the direct recipients of the program's benefits, the accountability procedures may focus more on results than on budgets and numbers of clients.

If the early reports regarding EAPs cost-effectiveness (Borthwick, 1977; Gaeta, et al, 1982; Shain and Groeneveld, 1978; Weaver, 1979) are borne out by more rigorous studies, accountability may be more concerned that sufficient effort has been made to encourage those who could benefit from assistance to seek it. If an EAP not only helps employees, but also cuts the company's operating expenses by four to twenty dollars for every dollar spent on the program, it is in everyone's interest to maximize the EAP effort.

Unlike public agencies, EAPs have a very well defined and accessible target group–employees and their families. And if the EAP is well promoted to these individuals, all individuals in need should at least be aware the program exists and view it as a positive resource. It will also be easier for the EAP to promote its services to the workforce, because its target group is so well defined and accessible. Consequently, it is reasonable to hold an EAP accountable for making staff well-known and respected to this target group.

As EAP providers we should welcome this closer scrutiny. It will help us clarify how effective our services are. It will also provide us with an opportunity to clarify to the funders just what the requirements are for an effective program. Public agency budgeting often has to compromise quality because the priorities are on numbers rather than effectiveness. EAPs are more likely to concentrate on effectiveness because positive outcomes will have a more immediate and direct impact on both the employees' well-being and the company's productivity.

But EAP providers will have to take a stronger stand than their colleagues in the public sector have done with respect to budgeting for services. Any compromises with quality services must be clearly identified for the funder and the implications made explicit. Because the funder is closer to the client (i.e., employer and employee, respectively), and both are beneficiaries of the service, maintaining quality services should be easier to justify. The EAP provider, however, must be able to adequately justify the requirements for quality services. Along these lines, procedures to obtain client outcome data should be a standard part of all EAPs.

5. EAPs Provide an Opportunity to Identify Work Environments which Contribute to Employee Distress.

There is increasing evidence that certain characteristics of the work environment contribute to employee distress and poor mental health (Suurvali and Shain, 1981a and b). An EAP is often in an excellent position to identify these problems, therby providing an opportunity for prevention of distress for large numbers of individuals.

It is fortunate in a way that the workplace characteristics which contribute to distress and poor mental health also contribute to reduced productivity. Consequently, it is in the interests of the employer, as well as the employee, to identify these problems and have corrective action taken. This point is not well understood or accepted in business and industry, and it is our responsibility as EAP providers to promote the concept more energetically.

Mental health workers in the public sector generally focus on helping their clients adjust to their environments. They have no mandate to act on the client's environment. As mental health professionals, if we simply transpose this perspective into our EAPs, we will be doing a disservice to both employees and employers. In negotiating a new program, it would be useful for EAP providers to explicitly deal with this issue in the preparation of policy and procedures. To be persuasive, EAP providers will have to assure themselves that they are sufficiently knowledgeable about those workplace characteristics which contribute to distress. As knowledge of the workplace is typically omitted from the training of most mental health professionals, special preparations will have to be made to fill this gap.

The more successfully the EAP interacts with the workplace environment, the more likely are benefits to be realized from preventive activities (Shain, 1981). Indeed, the EAP's successful interaction with the workplace environment may prove to be analogous to the enormous impact of such basic public health actions as sewers and clean drinking water on the community's physical health several decades ago (McKeown, 1971).

Lest employers cringe at the thought of EAPs dictating management style and otherwise "interfering" in the way a company is run, several reassuring points should be made. The EAP's role need only be to identify problem issues as they relate to employee mental health. In the final analysis it is the company's decision as to how to deal with the issues raised. Again, it will be the EAP provider's role to indicate the benefits to the company of dealing with these issues constructively.

Another issue which is important to clarify is that mental health professionals are not interested in removing all stressors from the workplace. Positive mental health involves an individual operating within their "optimal stress range." This is a construct used to describe the level of demands (stressors) placed upon individuals so that they are in neither an underload or overload situation. Both extremes of the demand continuum are dysfunctional. They create distress, which is objectionable because it cuts down on personal and corporate productivity. The "optimal stress range" describes the level of demand which is regarded by the individual as an exciting challenge, an attainable, and desired goal. Operating at this level of challenge contributes to an individual's sense of self esteem, competence, and pride. It brings out an individual's enthusiasm, energy, and creativity (Warr and Wall, 1975). Companies which try to create these types of working conditions for employees will have a mentally healthy, satisfied and productive workforce. And, of course, EAPs are only one of many resources to assist individuals to operate within their optimal stress range. Selection, placement, career counseling, training, supervision, and employee relations are all resources aimed at the same goal.

Obstacles

The opportunities identified above are by no means certainties. There are formidable obstacles which must be overcome if they are to be realized.

1. Territoriality of Various Departments and Professional Groups.

The growing interest in EAPs, corporate wellness programs, quality of working life, and new management techniques, is occurring at a time of major reorganizations in many sectors of the economy. Industrial and employee relations, and a host of other human resource functions are being rethought and restructured.

The jockeying for position is natural and necessary. Unfortunately, at times it is also distracting. Programs may be competing for the same dollars and may therefore be viewed as competitive. Emphasis is required on careful planning to determine how these various approaches to meeting employee needs can be integrated into a supportive and reinforcing network.

EAP providers need to become increasingly aware of these planning and organizational issues in order to understand the role of EAPs, and to contribute to the planning of such an integrated network. The principle of "client-centered" services may be applicable here, in that a focus on employee needs will serve to facilitate the integration of resources, rather than enflame unproductive competition. This principle of service planning starts with an examination of the individual's needs and then proceeds to develop programs and services to meet those needs. The opposite is often the case in public sector human services (and perhaps in corporations as well). Often, programs are created for political or other reasons, and their delivery and maintenance becomes the dominant focus, rather than the meeting of individuals' needs.

2. The Degree of Change Occurring in the Workplace.

The effects of the temporary recessions, as well as the simultaneous introduction of new technologies into the workplace have made "future shock" a way of life for many companies. The rate and extent of change are enormous and create stressors at many levels within the corporate hierarchy.

Given the profound impact of these events at the worksite, there is a danger that the mental health of the workforce will be overlooked. While the current changes are on the one hand providing opportunities for EAPs, the extent of these changes may make it difficult for EAPs to get a fair hearing. As EAP providers, we must be prepared to make forceful and well-reasoned arguments as to how EAPs can be part of the solution.

Also, change of any kind is often resisted. There is a perversity to perseverate, to maintain the status quo. This often creates considerable resistance to any innovations, which we must recognize and deal with if EAPs are to become more available and more effective than current mental health resources.

3. The Issues of Control and Values

There is a danger that some businesses and industries will view EAPs as a sophisticated mechanism for controlling employees, to make them more productive and loyal to the company. While these outcomes are often associated with EAPs, the major focus of an EAP needs to be determined by the joint participation of management and employee groups, whether the latter are organized or not.

I would argue that business and industry will obtain the most benefits from an EAP which values employee mental health as its dominant goal. Productivity enhancement will be a natural consequence of a focus on improved mental health in most cases. However, if productivity enhancement is the primary goal of an EAP, it does not follow that employees' mental health will be improved. In the long run, placing the individuals' needs first will have the greatest benefit for all parties.

Participation in a joint employee management EAP committee is one mechanism for clarifying these issues of control and the basic value orientation of the program. Both the policy statement and the procedures developed by a joint committee become important means of defining and maintaining the desired focus.

The development of professional guidelines or standards would also help EAP providers. Such guidelines would protect our integrity and help guide us through any ideological debates within such joint committees, which do not have the interests of the individual as the primary focus.

As mental health professionals, EAP providers have an enormous opportunity to bring a "new wave" (Toffler, 1981) of mental health resources to the community. By doing this through the workplace, significant contributions can also be made to the business of business. To set our own "optimal stress" level high, we must emphasize quality services, prepare ourselves with the new knowledge and skills required, and be sure of our own values and goals.

References

Allen, R.F., Changing Lifestyles Through Changing Organizational Cultures, Presented at the 14th Annual Meeting of the Society of Prospective Medicine, St. Petersburg, Florida, October, 1978.

Bassuk, E.L., and Gerson, S., Deinstitutionalization and Mental Health Services, *Scientific American,* 1978, *238,* 46–53.

Bergin, A.E., and Garfield, S.L., (Eds) The Handbook of Psychotherapy and Behaviour Change, 2nd Ed., New York, John Wiley & Sons, 1978.

Berkeley Planning Associates, The quality of the case management process: Final Report, Vol. III, in U.S. Department of Commerce, National Technical Information Service, *The Evaluation of Child Abuse and Neglect Projects 1974–1977,* Washington, D.C., 1977.

Borthwick, R.B., Summary of Cost-Benefit Study Results for Navy Alcoholism Rehabilitation Programs. Technical Report #346, Presearch Inc., 1977.

Caragonne, P., *Implications of case management: A report on research,* Presentation at conference on Case Management, Buffalo, N.Y., April 6, 1979.

Edwards, G., Orford, J., Egert, S., Guthrie, S., Hawker, A., Hensman, C., Mitcheson, M., Oppenheimer, E., and Taylor, C., Alcoholism: A controlled trial of "treatment" and "advice." *Journal of Studies on Alcohol,* 38(5)1004–1031, 1977.

Farquhar, J.W., Maccoby, N. and Wood, P.D., Community education for cardiovascular health. *The Lancet,* 1977, June, 1192–1195.

Gaeta, E., Lynn, R., and Grey, L., AT&T Looks at Program Evaluation, *EAP Digest,* 1982, May/June, 22–31.

Gans S.P. and Horton, G.T., *Integration of human services. The state and municipal levels,* New York: Praeger, 1975.

General Accounting Office, *Returning the mentally disabled to the community: Government needs to do more.* Comptroller General's Report to the Congress, Washington, D.C., 1976.

Glasser, F.B., Anybody Got a Match? Treatment Research and the Matching Hypothesis. Presented at the international conference Alcoholism Treatment: Finding New Directions (Institute of Psychiatry, London, 1979; Substudy No. 1045). Addiction Research Foundation, 33 Russell St., Toronto, Ontario.

Greenberg, R., Developing Mass Education for Community Health Programs, a Social Marketing Approach. *Health Education,* 1982; Summer, 6–9.

Human Services Coordination Alliance, *Case Accountability: Case Management Service Provision, Reporting, Service Outcome Assessment.* Louisville, Kentucky, Human Services Coordination Alliance, September 1976.

Kaplun, J., The Employee Assistance Consortium Approach: A Communal Employee Benefit. Presented at "Input '83, 5th Biennial Canadian Conference on employee assistance programmes and alcohol and addiction problems in the workplace," Toronto, Canada, 1983.

Kotler, P. and Zaltman, G., Social Marketing: An Approach to Planned Social Changes, *Journal of Marketing,* 1971, *35,* 3–12.

Landau, M., Redundancy, rationality, and the problem of duplication and overlap. *Public Administration Review,* 1969, *29,* 346–58.

Lewitt, T., Marketing Intangible Products and Product Intangibles, *Harvard Business Review,* 1981, *59,* 94–102.

McKeown, T., A Historical Appraisal of the Medical Task, from "Medical History and Medical Care," Oxford University Press, 1971.

McLachlan, J.F.C., Benefit from group therapy as a function of patient-therapist match on conceptual level. *Psychotherapy: Theory, Research and Practice,* 1972, *9:*317–323.

————., Therapy strategies, personality orientation and recovery from alcoholism. *Canadian Psychiatric Association Journal,* 1974, *19*(1):25–30.

Novelli, W.D., Tremendous Need Is Seen Ahead for More Effective Social Marketing, *Advertising Age,* 1980, 51:92.

Orford, J., Oppenheimer, E. and Edwards, G., Abstinence or control: The outcome for excessive drinkers two years after consultation. *Behavioral Research and Therapy,* 1976, 14(6):409–418.

Peters, T.J. and Waterman, Jr., R.H., In Search of Excellence, New York, Harper & Row 1982.

Public Health Reports, Health Promotion Programs in Occupational Settings–A Special Section, 1980; Vol. 95:2.

Puska, P., The North Karelin Project: An Example of Health Promotion in Action, In: The Promotion of Health: New Trends and Perspectives, 1979.

Rae-Grant N. Roadblocks and Stopgaps: A Review of Factors Obstructing the Development of Comprehensive Child Mental Health Services, *Canadian Psychiatric Association Journal,* 1976, *21(6).*

Rothschild, M., "Marketing Communications in New Business Situations or Why It's So Hard to Sell Brotherhood Like Soap," *Journal of Marketing,* 1979, *43,* 11–20.

Shain, M., The Value of Health Promotion in the Presentation of Alcohol Abuse, 1981, Addiction Research Foundation, 33 Russell St., Toronto, Ontario.

————, and Groeneveld, J., Employee Assistance Programs, Lexington, Ma.: D.C. Health & Company, 1978.

Skinner, H.A., Different Strokes for Different Folks: Differential Treatment for Alcohol Abuse, In Roger E. Meyer et al (Eds.), *Evaluation of the Alcoholic: Implications for Research, Theory and Treatment.* Research Monograph No. 5, National Institute on Alcohol Abuse and Alcoholism, Rockville, Maryland, 1981.

Suurvali, H., and Shain, M., The Relationship Between Environmental Aspects of Work, Mental and Drinking Practices: Evidence and Proposals. Addiction Research Foundation, Substudy, 1981a, #1172, 33 Russell St., Toronto, Ontario.

————, and Shain, M., Workplace Innovations: Implications for the Incidence and Management of Problems due to Alcohol and Drug Abuse, Addiction Research Foundation, Substudy #1176, 1981b, 33 Russell St., Toronto, Ontario.

Test, M., Continuity of Care in Community Treatment, in L. Stein (ed.) *Community*

Support Systems for the Long-Term Patient, San Francisco: Jossey-Bass, 1979.

Toffler, A. The Third Wave, London, Pan Books Ltd., 1981.

Warr, P., and Wall, T., Work and Well-Being, Baltimore: Penguin Books Inc., 1975.

Weaver, C.A., EAPs–How they Improve the Bottom Line, *Risk Management,* 1979, *27*:7, 22–26.

36

EAPs: Barriers to Effectiveness
A.J. Riediger

Introduction

Within the extensive promotional literature regarding EAPs, the matter of effectiveness is seldom questioned. Impressive "success" rates of obscure origin are cited, with little recourse to verification or empirical analysis. However, attempts to scientifically evaluate various aspects of the efficacy of such programs invariably become mired in definitional ambiguity, fragmentation of data, and philosophical double talk. This section therefore, will be devoted to a re-examination of basic employee assistance programming concepts and assumptions rather than a prescription of quick fixes for ailing programs.

What is an Employee Assistance Program?

The historical development of EAPs has consisted primarily of promotional efforts, changes in terminology, and the emergence of conflicting interest groups. Whether programs are labeled "occupational alcoholism," "troubled employee," "broad-brush," or "union-management," the major philosophical impetus still derives from the marriage of Alcoholics Anonymous and industrial alcoholism.

The EAP concept originated in the industrial alcoholism programs of the early 1940s. The idea was that alcoholics were a drain on productivity. Supervisors were expected to spot their symptoms and refer them to AA for "treatment," under threat of dismissal. After the war, the concept remained essentially dormant until the 1960s, when the concept was sponsored by the National Council on Alcoholism (NCA), and the basis for referral was shifted from symptoms of alcoholism to decreases in work performance, in order to remove diagnosis from the supervisor's responsibilities. It was assumed, however, that poor performance signalled alcoholism. The major impetus for widespread popularity of EAPs came from the Hughes Act in 1970. The establishment of the National Institute on Alcohol Abuse and Alcoholism (NIAAA) led to allocation of demonstration grants, which funded consultants to disseminate occupational alcoholism programs throughout the United States. During this decade, union involvement became a significant factor, and terms like "troubled employee" and "broad-brush" programs were popularized. The 1980s appear to be characterized by intensified promotion of programs, experimentation with a wide variety of program models, and keen competition for "turf" among various factions in this growth industry.

Each program constituent has a different rationale for participating in the program. The alcoholism industry sees the program as a case finding mechanism, employers are encouraged to implement programs in order to save money, unions are interested in enhancement of job security and health benefits, program staff usually want to help troubled employees, and public relations departments use the program to illustrate corporate responsibility.

As a result of the disparity in viewpoints, the concept of EAPs has not developed any consistent identity. Roman and Trice (1976) state that " . . . while most persons . . . refer to 'programs' in a rather glib fashion, we lack an operational definition of a program" (p. 513). They go on to suggest that we " . . . regard this set of ideologies and activities as a federally-funded social movement . . . ." (p. 509). Santa-Barbara (1983) states, " 'Employee assistance program' is a catch-all phrase which encompasses a broad range of activities" (p. 16). In short, we do not really know what an EAP is, if indeed such a thing exists at all.

What does exist is a set of beliefs and ideas about people who do not perform well at work. These ideas may be summarized as follows:

- A significant number of employees have problems which interfere with work performance.
- Many of these problems can be successfully treated.
- The workplace can identify and motivate such employees to accept treatment.
- Everyone concerned benefits from a corrective, rather that a punitive approach.

EAPs, then, include a variety of approaches which utilize the employer-employee relationship in order to identify problem employees and motivate them to accept treatment, with a view to restoring personal health and adequate work performance.

How Effective are Employee Assistance Programs?

Given the lack of program definition, the dearth of adequate research, and the conflicting program goals, it is extremely difficult to evaluate the effectiveness of any EAP. "The simple truth is . . . good data on any aspect of occupational programs is relatively nonexistent" (Trice, 1977). Several broad measures, however, may prove instructive.

Program Dissemination

By 1959, it was estimated that no more that 50 companies had implemented formal alcoholism programs (Archer, 1977). Current estimates range from 700-800, according to NCA records (Thede, 1983), to as many as several thousand programs, based on undocumented estimates. Desjardins (1977) located 175 programs in Canada. These figures suggest a dramatic rise in the rate at which programs are being implemented. This popularity is often cited as proof that many employers are recognizing the programs' worth.

Closer inspection of the NCA figures, however, reveals that the rate of dissemination has declined markedly. The number of programs doubled between 1971 and 1973 during the NIAAA funding programs. The next ten years have witnessed a further increase of only 50%. Further, it should be noted that current programs exist in a mere .0004% of the 1.8 million American employer organizations which Cloud and Gruhn (1977) estimate to exist. A current study by Health and Welfare Canada suggests that 5% of Canadian workers and 12% of American workers have access to an EAP.

An even greater concern is reflected in the percentage of "paper" programs, i.e. programs adopted on paper but not implemented in any meaningful fashion. Von Wiegand (1974) found that only 25 of 300 to 400 programs were achieving "anywhere near their possible potential" (p. 5). Habbe (1969) surveyed 160 companies which were thought to have a program. Of these, only 27 indicated that they had a "fairly good" program. Another survey of 300 company programs revealed only twelve successful and efficient programs. If these estimates are accepted as valid, 90% of existing programs must be considered ineffective.

Success Rates

Most outcome studies report impressive success rates and substantial cost savings. However, Edwards (1975) found only 16 programs out of 300 which had conducted evaluation studies. Thus, the estimates of program effectiveness can probably be generalized only to the elite 10% of relatively well-implemented, active programs, and do not represent the situation throughout the employee assistance movement.

In addition, Edwards identifies a number of biases which tend to inflate success rates. Most of the programs defined success as job retention. However, it is well-documented that very few problem employees are dismissed, even when performance does not improve (Schollaert, 1977; Riediger, 1979). Success rates also tend to ignore the employees who refuse referral or who are not offered referral because the supervisor anticipates resistance.

Program Utilization

The most serious indictment against many programs and their effectiveness is their inability to generate sufficient referrals. Conservative estimates suggest that 20% of employees suffer from problems which can affect work performance. In comparison, most of the best programs are highly ineffective in reaching the employees they are designed to help. Von Wiegand (1972) spoke with dozens of program representatives, who unanimously reported a lack of referrals. Edwards (1975) was able to derive penetration rates for only 2 of the 16 programs which had conducted an evaluation study. Estimates of program usage among a number of "model" programs ranged from .0002% to .5% of employees per year. In contrast, Miller (1981) and Pellegrino (1981) reported annual referral rates of 5% to 14% respectively, suggesting a much greater potential. One company referred over 1,000 employees in a 20-month period.

Van Wagner (1978) notes that the NCA has suggested that "a penetration rate of 1% per year can be considered adequate...many programs are not even approaching this rate" (p. 64). In addition, Sherman (1976) points out that such low referral rates reflect that only severe, late-stage problems are being identified. Cutler and Jones (1976) found, further, that the rate of referrals tends to decline over time.

Clearly, the present state of the art leaves little reason for complacency. EAPs constitute an indefinable collection of activities, subject to intense controversy, with little evidence of their much publicized merit. However, the fact that they do continue to exist and expand suggest that they represent a needed response to some serious problems. Therefore, the basic concept deserves serious reconsideration.

Why Employee Assistance Programs Fail

Like a typical gold rush, the employee assistance movement has been characterized by just enough glowing reports of success to keep masses of workers toiling on their barren claims. In reality, the tantalizing indicators of potential effectiveness obscure widespread, deep-rooted problems. Roman and Trice (1976) point out that "...program design and development have proceeded without a firm research base . . . [therefore] it is likely that any assumptions will become embedded and vested interests developed, making research-based change difficult" (p. 514). Trice (1977) goes on to warn that, in spite of demonstrated potential, " . . . unless future efforts reduce the glaring flaws of the past few years . . . the strategy could become a footnote in the history of efforts to deal with alcoholism and other drug abuses" (p. 5,6).

Lack of program utilization represents the Achilles heel of the employee assistance movement. It indicates that, in spite of a heavy promotional emphasis, the employee assistance movement has failed to become an integral part of the workplace. It has, typically, received token support, which may well disappear when its lack of effectiveness becomes apparent and discredits the promotional claims which has fueled the movement thus far.

In order to determine why referrals are not being made, we need to examine who benefits from referrals and who is responsible for generating referrals. It is clear, however, that the program does not work for those who are responsible for its utilization. Accordingly, each program constituent's perspective must be examined.

The Alcoholism Industry

The employee assistance movement owes its existence to the early dedication of Alcoholics Anonymous and to the recent impetus from what Trice refers to as the "Alcoholism Industry." Unfortunately, this industry, like many parents, has also smothered its offspring's attempt to attain maturity.

The alcoholism industry views occupational programs as a case finding mechanism on which it depends for profit, growth, status, and security. APs provide major sources of funding from insurance programs, government grants, and business contributions. Consequently, it is considered to be in the industry's best interest to limit programs to alcoholism. The effect on program development has been disastrous.

The obvious fact is that alcoholism represents only a fraction of the employee problems which affect performance. Documented estimates of the incidence of alcoholism in the workplace indicate an incidence of 3 to 5% (Roman and Trice, 1976; Schlenger and Hayward, 1975). Comparable statistics on the incidence of behavioral or mental health problems suggest an incidence of 20 to 25% (Yolles, 1970; Fletcher, 1979; McMurray, 1973). However, performance-based referrals in broad-scope programs inevitably generate a majority of non-alcoholism referrals (Riediger, 1979; Rostain et al., 1980; Wright, 1981). If these are excluded, the employer's potential cost benefit (and commitment to the program) are significantly decreased. There is evidence that the employee with personal problems is no less costly to the employer than is the alcoholic (Winslow et al., 1966; Trice, 1965; McMurray, 1973; Conley et al., 1973). Ironically, many of these "second class" employees are much more amenable to treatment than are the late-stage alcoholics who enjoy the program's best efforts.

As a result of the special status accorded alcoholic employees: a) Many programs are restricted to alcoholism, thereby excluding most problem employees; b) Most "broad-brush" programs are ineffective because they fail to provide the necessary program components for other problem types; and c) Supervisors are caught in the same old dilemma of being obliged to diagnose problem employees to determine which are eligible for the program. The greatest irony lies in the fact that well-utilized comprehensive programs refer more alcoholics than do typical, underutilized alcoholism programs. Indeed, performance-based referral systems preclude a program's ability to discriminate vis a vis alcoholics.

The Employer

Alcoholism programs are traditionally marketed to employers as a cost-cutting strategy. A secondary appeal is to the employer's social conscience. These arguments are invariably relegated to a low priority consideration, even when public relations factors dictate adoption of a program. APs are generally viewed as an artificial adjunct to the workplace, which may distract from organizational goals such as profit. The addition of new expertise and procedures is potentially threatening to established lines of authority and communication.

Successful businesses can point to a healthy profit picture and suggest that the program is simply "gilding the lily." Failing businesses are unlikely to regard alcoholism treatment as a savior. Governments and social service agencies can point to an absence of a profit motive and a lack of standards by which efficiency can be measured.

Obviously, the cost of alcoholism represents a small fraction of the organization's total inefficiency. Further, alcoholism counselors can lay little claim to recognition as efficiency experts.

Unless programs establish their relevance to existing goals and priorities in the employing organization, they have no chance of gaining the high level support needed to ensure successful implementation. Frequently, the program is relegated to front-line supervisors, with an implicit message to ignore it. Essential training is neglected, and consultation is unavailable. Use of the program becomes a risk to the supervisor's own job security.

The Employee

Programs which encourage self-referral have found that employees are, themselves, best qualified to identify early problems and that the vast majority of self-referrals are appropriate and legitimate. However, traditional EAPs are designed to confront and coerce recalcitrant employees to accept help. They are designed as disciplinary procedures rather than as a tangible offer of help. Usually the supervisor or shop steward is the only entry point to the program. Therefore, the employee must risk serious job consequences in drawing attention to his/her problem and is strongly motivated to avoid program involvement. Seldom does qualified, professional treatment exist as part of the program. In addition, most employees do not adequately understand or even know about the program. Meanwhile, employers tend to fear that ready access would result in costly abuse of the program by employees. Clearly, employers do not believe their own literature on cost effectiveness of programs.

The Union

In recent years, the unions have increasingly demanded full partnership in program implementation and administration. This much heralded development has imposed serious restrictions on the program. Labor and management do not, in fact, jointly administer the workplace, and their involvement in an EAP is not parallel. It is specifically the manager's prerogatives that provide for identification and motivation of problem employees. Perlis (1977) notes that management is concerned with the alcoholic as a productive worker, whereas labor is concerned with the alcoholic as a fellow worker with a problem.

The union's insistence on joint program administration is considered necessary in order to ensure workers' rights. However, as a joint administrator, the union protects workers through policy and procedural input, but abdicates its right to defend the individual employee. Joint programs tend to proliferate policy statements and watchdog committees. Thus, the programs become cumbersome, focusing on political processes rather than problem employees, and become suspicious of external influences, such as treatment professionals. In this environment, troubled managers are tacitly excluded from the program, thereby deleting some of the most valuable employees from coverage.

Labor has also lobbied strongly for limitation of programs to alcoholism. Perlis (1977) claims widespread union opposition to the basic tenet of performance-based referrals, "...to convert what should be a purely alcoholism referral and treatment program into a broad-brush troubled employee assistance program...is not only diversionary and unscientific but pie in the sky to boot" (p. 73). Unions feel more comfortable with alcoholism programs, because most cases are identified in the late statges, when the job is already threatened and coercive intervention is not only justifiable as a means of job retention, but is viewed as therapeutic in itself. The tradition of lay intervention appeals to the notion of union brotherhood.

Program Staff

"Employee assistance" is considered by many managers as a euphemism for a process in which the employer obliges problem employees to "shape up or ship out." The program forces employees to seek help but does not offer help. Typical staffing patterns in EAPs support this view.

Most programs are staffed by company managers, union representatives, or personnel administrators. Program coordinators, where these exist, usually provide a purely administrative and educational function. Programs staffed by counselors frequently are limited to expertise in alcoholism. Because of their lack of clinical expertise, such programs are seen by employees and supervisors as coercive mechanisms rather than as valid sources of help. The source of the much touted treatment is presumed to exist in the community, where it can be as reasonably and easily accessed by the employee himself/herself as by the program. However, the program, by definition, is targeted on employees who fail to take this initiative. The referral-to-treatment function is, therefore, a critical program task which requires specialized skills and knowledge within the program. The program must identify not only problem employees but employees' problems and appropriate sources of help as well. In addition to expertise, this function requires professional confidentiality to ensure that personal information is not used as a basis for discipline. In addition, the supervisor is left to make major decisions regarding management of troubled employees, with no source of clinical support and consultation. Without a professional diagnostic and referral service, treatment success becomes a function of sheer luck.

Treatment Resources

Traditional programs are based on a number of naive assumptions about the availability, accessibility, and efficacy of treatment. In fact, most treatment resources are highly specialized, over-utilized, difficult to locate, and unaware of the problems in the workplace. Mental health and social service agencies are particularly isolated from the concerns relevant to EAPs, because they have historically directed their services to the home or the individual rather than to the workplace.

Philosophically, treatment services are also frequently incompatible with sound EAP principles. The model of Alcoholics Anonymous implies that destructive behaviors such as alcoholism are signs of moral illness and degeneration, requiring confrontation, with natural negative consequences, and a need to return to realistic, proper life choices. The medical model treats personal problems as symptoms of disease; therefore, the individual is excused from responsibility and needs to receive treatment from an expert. The behavioral health model, however, focuses on the individual's responsibility to choose to receive treatment from an expert. The behavioral health model, however, focuses on the individual's responsibility to choose effective behaviors. Where problems interfere with tha ability to function effectively, the individual is responsible for accepting assistance as required. This approach is seldom understood by treatment agencies, which tend to adhere to the medical model and see only self-motivated clients. Accordingly, then, EAPs must provide a means for effective utilization of existing treatment resources.

In order to be effective with employee assistance referrals, treatment agencies need to be closely coordinated with the workplace. Deficits in work performance do not by themselves provide an adequate basis for accurate diagnosis and may well result in inappropriate referrals. In addition, treatment agencies require a high level of motivation in their clients. Simply showing up at the treatment agency is not sufficient to produce behavior change. Even well-motivated employees often need help in coordinating treatment when more than one agency in involved. Less motivated employees may subvert the entire program by playing one agency against the other.

The vital treatment function is largely ignored in the EAP literature. Because of their lack of professional expertise, programs are incapable of effectively utilizing available treatment resources or of providing their own. This problem is not reflected in research on program effectiveness, primarily because the studies are limited to those employees who were motivated enough to complete treatment and fortunate enough to receive appropriate referrals. The true victims of this shortcoming are those employees who were never included in the program, because it was not perceived as helpful.

The Supervisor's Perspective

Effective utilization of the program rests almost entirely on the supervisor's shoulders. Most programs state that as the employer's representative, the supervisor is responsible for identification, motivation, and referral of problem employees. The supervisor's compliance is blithely assumed or elicited through coercion (Brooks, 1976), with no consideration of the supervisor's needs and concerns.

Trice (1969) had cautioned that the supervisor's needs and concerns must be a primary factor in program design. " ... A policy can be more effective if its main target is frankly recognized to be the relief and aid of the immediate boss of an alcoholic employee, plus helping the employee himself. In a very real sense these two make up the 'hard core' of resistance to policy. All other parts of a program lead up to these two people ... " (pg. 23). Current referral rates clearly indicate that some EAPs do not work well enough for the supervisor to elicit his/her active utilizatoin of the program.

In order to determine why EAPS do not work for the supervisor, the present writer conducted a study including 145 supervisors from six employing organizations which had active programs (Riediger, 1979). Their response indicated that programs are based on a number of ill-founded assumptions.

Supervisors acknowledged that behavioral health problems are prevalent and costly and that employers are entitled to implement programs to reduce this cost. However, they made it clear they do not identify with the employer's goal or authority. Rather, they felt "caught in the middle" in conflicts between employer and employee. They considered the program as an added responsibility for the benefit of troubled employees rather than as an aid to themselves in their normal job function.

Identification.

Supervisors had no problem in determining which employees were not performing adequately. They identified over 12% in this category. However, they were most reluctant to formally identify these employees for program involvement. They considered poor performance to result from situational factors, lack of training, and inadequacies in the workplace. In spite of performance-based criteria, supervisors believed they must accurately diagnose the health problem, obtain voluntary compliance, or find a behavioral justification for referral in order to preserve their managerial credibility and personal sense of fair play. Absenteeism due to obvious excessive drinking in one employee, for example, was ascribed to his wife's nagging, and therefore beyond the scope of the program.

Lack of identification of problem employees, then, represents a deliberate choice not to use the program. If, in fact, poor performance does often result from personal problems, it is unecessary to impose responsibility for this judgment on the supervisor. One of the best identification rates was achieved at Kennecott Copper (Jones, 1975), when all disciplinary actions were automatically referred to the program for professional consideration.

Motivation.

Supervisors believed that motivation to accept treatment was the employee's responsibility. They objected to constructive coercion, especially for non-alcoholic employees. They saw this technique as a legitimate action in the employer's interest, but not beneficial to the employee. Also, it violated their deep commitment to avoiding confrontation generally, and helping (or covering for) employees who are in distress. Supervisors also noted that they lacked the authority to threaten dismissal. They had no concept of their potential role for assisting therapists to develop progressive motivational improvement in defensive clients, as Finlay (1975) suggests. The supervisor's essential question was, "Why should I risk my credibility in confronting a poor employee for his own good when there's probably nothing in it for either of us?"

It is not surprising that supervisors question the integrity of a program which purports to help distressed employees by subjecting them to added pressure. Rather than trying to re-educate such supervisors, it would be much simpler to define discipline as a management function and the assistance program as a positive alternative.

Referral

Because of their simplistic view of personal problems, supervisors considered the majority of problem employees as unsuitable treatment candidates. When treatment was considered appropriate, they expressed a rather naive optimism regarding the availability and efficacy of treatment.

Supervisors expressed deep personal concern for their employees. However, they had trouble relating coercion to treatment. Ravin (1975) has emphasized that it is the provision of treatment which makes coercion constructive and it is the blend of coercion with the offer of treatment which makes the program effective.

The supervisors did, however, strongly endorse establishment of a professionally staffed service to provide consultation to the supervisor, select appropriate treatment resources, and enhance cooperation between the workplace and the treatment agency. Supervisors wanted to be involved in this process, with adequate managerial and professional support. They did not consider the personnel officer or union steward as appropriately involved, and medical departments were not considered as relevant to this function. Supervisors lacked any appreciation for their own potential value in enhancing the treatment process through modification of the work environment, ongoing monitoring of performance improvement, and provision of rewards for improved performance.

Key Concepts in Effectiveness

A few unique programs have demonstrated that the employee assistance concept can work, not only as a rescue mission, but as an integral part of an employing organization's system of human resource management. In order to make EAPs work on a large scale, however, we need to clean up our act. Most of our current programs do not work, especially for the people who are responsible for making them work. In actual practice, the programs bear little resemblance to the creative rationale we use to "sell" programs. Finally, development of program improvements is mired in false, untested assumptions, ambiguous terms, woolly logic, and diplomatic double talk which obscures the real issues.

Comprehensive Scope

Programs whose referrals are based on performance deficits are fundamentally different from those directed at a specific disease entity. Employee assistance philosophy requires that referrals be based on performance criteria. Performance deficits do not discriminate between alcoholism and other behavioral health problems. Accordingly, EAPs must include, and be designed to deal with, a comprehensive range of personal problems. This broad scope is also vital to employer acceptance.

Integration with the Workplace

To be effective, programs must be an integral part of the workplace. Sonnenstuhl and O'Donnell (1980) suggest that the EAP should be considered to be a health plan aimed at the organization. Zeigenfuss (1981) points out the powerful correspondence between the employee's personal problems and group organizational problems. Thus, the EAP supports the organization's legitimate corporate goals without imposing an artificial philanthropic role. The program, in fact, resolves the perennial management problem of how to elicit responsible behavior from employees when their performance deficits may be due to ill health. Thus, the EPA is an essential component of good management.

Employer Support

Responsibility for program implementation rests with senior management. As true representatives of the employer, they benefit from the program and control the dynamics that make it work. Management's commitment must be operationalized through: a) adoption of a clear and comprehensive policy statement; b) specific assignment of responsibility and accountability for program implementation and utilization; c) development of formal links between the EAP and all other educational, disciplinary, health service, and human resource development systems in the organization; and d) assurance of adequate funding, program stability, and accountability. A simple policy encouraging self-referrals and requiring routine referral of all disciplinary cases would dramatically increase utilization rates.

Professional Clinical Resource

Referral of a broad range of problems based on performance deficits necessitates provision of a professional clinical resource as a central component of the program. This service may be in-house or under contract with a number of program. Its role is to: a) consult with supervisors, especially about problem employees who are not treatment candidates, b) ensure clinical confidentiality, c) diagnose the personal problem and refer appropriately, d) provide prompt crisis intervention, e) provide direct treatment for work-related problems, and f) coordinate the corrective efforts of the workplace and the external treatment resource.

Positive Program Definition

EAPs profess to be unique in their ability to capitalize on the standards and sanctions of the workplace as a means of motivating employees to seek help. Then they proceed to overhaul the company's entire disciplinary system in order to ensure good referrals. The program becomes associated with coercion rather than help.

A more fruitful approach would be to accept the workplace as it is, on the understanding that the program will free management to become more effective. However, the program encompasses only a viable offer of qualified treatment to employees who require this and consultation for supervisors who are seeking to resolve related management problems. Thus, the program cooperates, but does not identify with the disciplinary process and is appropriately regarded as a fair, positive option.

Use of Natural Roles

The employee assistance movement has inherited a distinctly anti-professional bias. In encouraging lay people in the workplace to cope with mental health problems, assistance programs tended to distort their normal roles and responsibilities. Supervisors were required to make clinical decisions under the guise of work performance issues, personnel officers became social case workers in their liaison with treatment agencies, union stewards monitored performance and initiated discipline, and unions adopted a managerial role in joint administration of programs.

By defining discipline as a management function and treatment as a professional function, an effective program facilitates the effectiveness of each program constituent. The employer is free to concentrate on his/her original profit or service goals; management is able to concentrate on effective management; the union is free to defend the rights of workers and to demand adequate provision of employee assistance services; supervisors are freed from their dilemma of covering for or punishing sick employees; the employee is actually given a change to overcome his/her problems; and the treatment agency gets a motivated, appropriate referral.

Behavior Health Model

EAPs have developed a useful concept of alcoholism as a self-defeating behavior which is amenable to treatment, if the individual actively chooses and participates in the process. Many personal problems are now being regarded similarly. Adoption of this model clarifies the troubled employee's responsibility and permits application of the basic employee assistance approach to a variety of personal difficulties and dysfunctions.

In order to become truly effective, the employee assistance movement will need to enlist the support and cooperation of the mental health service delivery system. Incredibly, the relationship between employee assistance and industrial psychiatry "had never been explored" (Roman and Trice, 1976). By relying on the behavioral health model, existing community treatment agencies may discover ways to adapt a home-oriented system to the special requirements of the workplace.

Program Education

Effective programs do not demand a superior level of supervisory skill or expertise. However, they do provide extensive, clearly focused educational programs.

1. Preventive mental health and informational programs are aimed at all employees to help them identify early problems and remedy them if possible. These programs also provide visibility and encourage self-referrals.
2. Staff development and management training programs are designed to incorporate program information in all relevant skill and knowledge areas.
3. Senior managers are given intensive training in the philosophy and process of the program, with emphasis on the integration of management and mental health concerns.
4. Supervisors are provided with specific training on the techniques of using the program.

Responsibility for Ongoing Development

EAPs need much broader sponsorship. The "alcoholism industry" has provided almost the only enduring support. Although this is highly commendable, it also represents a serious shortcoming in the program's capacity for futher development. Mental health service delivery systems in general, and occupational and mental health services in particular, need to get involved. Organizations of personnel and management administrators need to take ownership of their stake in the program. Professional and academic bodies need to contribute specialized professional training, research, and theoretical support for program advances.

EAPs are over-promoted and underdeveloped. If the concept is encouraged to fulfill its potential, these programs may become a highly significant factor in the operation of work organizations and in the delivery of mental health services. Those who have had a part in pioneering this collaboration will have every reason to be proud of the contribution.

References

Archer, J. Occupational alcoholism: A review of issues and a guide to the literature. In C.J. Schramm (Ed.), *Alcoholism and its treatment in industry*. Baltimore, MD: Johns Hopkins University Press, 1977.

Brooks, F.C. Who motivates the motivators? *Labor-Management Alcoholism Journal*, 1976, 5(4).

Cloud, L.A. & Gruhn, A. J. Labor-management luncheon. *Labor-Management Alcoholism Journal*, 1977, 7(2), 7–13.

Conley, R.W. An approach to measuring the cost of mental illness. In R.L. Noland (Ed.), *Industrial mental health and employee counselling*. New York: Behavioural Publications, 1973.

Cutler, R. & Jones, B. A study of occupational alcoholism programs in British Columbia. Vancouver, B.C.: Water Street Research Group, 1976. (Supported by a Non-medical Use of Drugs Directorate Grant.)

Desjardins, C. *A study of occupational alcoholism programs in Canada* (a report on research conducted for the Canadian Addiction Foundation). Ottawa, Ontario: Department of Health and Welfare Canada (Non-medical Use of Drugs Directorate), 1977.

Edwards, D.W. The evaluation of troubled employee and occupational alcoholism programs. In R.L. Williams & G.H. Moffat (Eds.), *Occupational alcoholism programs*. Springfield, IL: Charles C. Thomas, 1975.

Finlay, D.G. *Constructive coercion and the alcoholic employee: Problems and prospects*. Vancouver, B.C.: Education Department, Alcohol and Drug Commission of B.C., 1975.

Fletcher, B. Occupatonal psychology: An unexploited resource. *Occupational Health*, 1979, 8.

Habbe, S. *Company controls for drinking problems* (A research from the Conference Board). New York: National Industrial Conference Board, 1969.

Jones, O.F. Insight: A program for troubled people. In R.L. Williams & G.H. Moffat (Eds.), *Occupational alcoholism programs*. Springfield, IL: Charles C. Thomas, 1975.

McMurray, R.N. Mental illness: Society's and industry's $6,000,000,000 burden. In R.L. Noland (Ed.), *Industrial mental health and employee counselling*. New York: Behavioural Publications, 1973.

Miller, L. Giving a helping hand with personal problems. *Advanced Management Journal*, 1981,46(2).

Pelligrino, J.F. Teaching stress management: Meeting individual and organizational needs. *Advanced Management Journal*, 1981, 46(2).

Perlis, L. Unionism and alcoholism: The issues. In C.J. Schramm (Ed.), *Alcoholism and its treatment in industry*. Baltimore, MD: Johns Hopkins University Press, 1977.

Ravin, I.S. Formulation of an alcoholism rehabilitation program at Boston Edison Company. In R.L. Williams & G.H. Moffat (Eds.), *Occupational alcoholism programs*. Springfield, IL: Charles C. Thomas, 1975, Pp. 194–223.

Riediger, A.J. Employee Assistance Program: The supervisor's perspective. Unpublished doctoral dissertation, University of Alberta, 1979.

Roman, P.M. & Trice, H.M. Alcohol abuse and work organizations. In B. Kissin & H. Begleiter (Eds.), *The biology of alcoholism* (Vol. 4). New York: Plenum Press, 1976. Pp. 445–517.

Rostain, H., Allan, P. & Rosenberg, S. New York City's approach to problem-employee counselling. *Personnel Journal*, 1980, *59*(4).

Santa-Barbara, J. Will Employee Assistance Programs survive? *CTM: The Human Element*, August-September 1983, 16–17.

Schlenger, W.E. & Hayward, B.J. *Assessing the impact of occupational programs*. Raleigh, NC: The Human Ecology Institute, October, 1975. NIAAA No. OI00003.

Schollaert, P.T. Job-based risks and labor turnover among alcoholic workers. In C.J. Schramm (Ed.), *Alcoholism and its treatment in industry*. Baltimore, MD: Johns Hopkins University Press, 1977.

Sherman, P.A. Are we reaching the alcoholic? *Labor-Management Alcoholism Journal*, 1976, *6*(3).

Sonnenstuhl, W.J. & O'Donnell, J.E. Employee Assistance Programs: The whys and hows of planning them. *Personnel Administrator*, 1980, *25*(11).

Thede, G. Employee Assistance Programs: How they began and where they stand. *CTM: The Human Element*, August-September 1983, 14–15.

Trice, H.M. Alcoholic employees: A comparison of psychotic, neurotic and normal personnel. *Journal of Occupational Medicine*, 1965, *7*, 94–99.

Trice, H.M. *Alcoholism in industry—Modern procedures*. New York: Christopher D. Smithers Foundation, 1969.

Trice, H.M. Testimony before subcommittee on alcoholism and drug abuse, Senate Committee on Human Resources, May 18, 1977. Senate Hearing on S–1107.

Van Wagner, Hon. R.W. A simple measure of program effectiveness. *Labor-Management Alcoholism Journal*, 1978, *8*(2), 62.

Von Wiegand, R.A. Alcoholism in industry (U.S.A.). *British Journal of Addiction*, 1972, *67*, 181–187.

Von Wiegand, R.A. Advances in secondary preventon of alcoholism through the cooperative efforts of labor and management in employer organizations. *Preventive Medicine, 1974, 3*, 80–85.

Winslow, W.W. et al. Some economic estimates of job disruption from an industrial mental health project. *Archives of Environmental Health*, 1966, *13*, 213–219.

Wright, B. Helping employees help themselves. *Skyworld*, April 1981.

Yolles, S.F. Presentation at Institute of Management and Labor Relations, Rutgers University, June 10,1970.

Ziegenfuss, J.T. Responding to people problems. *Business Horizons*, April 1980, *23*(2).

37

Quality of Work Life Programs and EAPs: The Reorganization of the Workplace
Louis A. Ferman

Introduction

Coincidental with the growth of EAPs in industrial locations has been the development of industrially-based programs to reorganize the workplace. These latter programs have a number of objectives: 1) to improve communications across different levels of the organization (union-management, skilled-unskilled, blue collar-white collar, supervisors-subordinates, 2) to develop mechanisms to solicit inputs for problem-solving from all levels and groups in the organization, and 3) to distribute decision-making power across a wide spectrum of the organization. This movement goes under different names: "quality of work life," "humanizing the workplace," "employee involvement," "workplace democracy," and "participative management." A basic assumption of these programs is that involvement and participation of employees in the operation of the plant results both in a more humane and efficient organization of work.

It is anticipated that these programs yield benefits both for the individual employee and the company. The individual employee may realize increased control over the way work is organized; find a more challenging and interesting work environment; experience better social relationships with supervisors and co-workers; and receive more job security in the workplace. For the company, quality of work life programs (QWLs) may result in greater employee involvement with company goals, increased productivity, and more attention to qualtiy or product/operations.

A central feature of generic QWL programs is the establishment of employees into some form of work group organization (quality circles, problem-solving groups, participation groups). The goal, in many cases not to be realized immediately, is the development of these units into semi-autonomous or autonomous groups where the members engage in self-managment of their affairs, with little intervention form higher authority. Self-management means the establishment of group standards, the identification of work problems, and the selection of means to meet these standards or to resolve these problems. The underlying assumption is that these group members have the "grass roots expertise" to make a significant contribution to the organization of work and that, in doing so, they develop more positive attitudes toward work and become more productive workers. This assumption does not preclude the inputs of professionals. Actually, the group members are dependent on information about what is happening elsewhere, conceptual/theoretical formulations of an issue or problem, and the options for action that exist. Group deliberations in building consensus will inevitably use information both from within the group and from outside of the group. "Grass roots expertise" does not replace professional knowledge, but is mixed with it to produce a more adequate decision or judgment.

These QWLs exist independently, and in most cases, of the EAP, although EAPs and these programs both deal with different aspects of the human resource development of employees. The gulf between EAPs and these programs is not accidental, but reflects differences in objectives, technology, and staffing. There are also some structural factors that separate EAP from QWL programs. This raises a number of questions. Is the EAP compatible with these restructuring programs? Does the EAP have a role in workplace reorganization, and if so, what is that role? What factors act as barriers to EAP involvement and participation with work reorganization efforts? In this section, we will address these questions.

The Nature of EAP and Work Reorganization Programs

EAP Programming

The purpose of an EAP program is clear enough: 1) to detect employees who have impaired performance in the workplace or employees who are in a preimpairment stage and 2) to restore the workers to acceptable performance, or to prevent actual impairment. An ideal EAP strategy usually involves three sets of interrelated activities. The first is case finding or identifying of employees who may benefit from program services. Some of these employees may be walk-ins or self-referrals; others are detected through work performance reviews, formal disiplinary procedures, or the use of informal social networks. These employees are induced or encouraged through persuasion or "constructive confrontation" to seek treatment for their problems. The second activity involves problem assessment, short-term treatment if necessary, and follow-up or monitoring of work performance if the worker is returned to the job. Finally, there are treatment services, usually external to the work place, to which employees may be referred, and the monitoring of the employees' progress.

In the EAP, the unit of concern is the impaired, or potentially impaired, employee. The outcome to be expected is improved performance or the prevention of impaired performance by an individual employee. The EAP is not for everyone in the plant. It is concerned only with those workers impaired or at risk for impairment. The technology to achieve results in EAPs is a combination of interpersonal and social strategies to bring about a change in individual behavior. The staff in an EAP unit may range from lay personnel, who have some acquaintance with work impairments and their treatment, to professional psychologists or social workers, who are usually located in the medical unit or an offshoot of the personnel department. The range of variations in such units is extremely broad and diverse and permits no simple generalization. There are instances where the personnel are not part of the company but of contracting agencies that provide case finding, assessment, or treatment services for the EAP.

Finally, the EAP has a limited focus on the employee. It is not concerned with the totality of his/her interaction or behavior in the workplace, but emphasizes only those aspects of the employee that are related to the impairment or possible impairment. The EAP does not try to deal with all of the stresses and strains that impinge on the employee, but only with those that are problem-related. The emphasis is clinical and rehabilitative rather than developmental. The EAP is heavily cure-focused.

QWL Programming

QWL programs show a considerable contrast with EAPs. QWL programs are concerned with better communications and interactions among various groups in the organization; improvement of decision-making by soliciting inputs from all levels of the organization; developing higher morale and solidarity in work departments; and establishing higher productivity and quality levels in work performance. In QWL programs, the level of concern is the work department or some functional work group. The outcome to be expected is a group measure (productivity, quality improvement, or morale). The QWL program may be restricted initially to a pilot program or a limited number of departments, but in the long run the program is designed to encompass everyone in the organization. The concern in this program is with organizational change in the broadest scale possible. The technology to achieve results in QWL programs is a combination of group process, work redesign, organizational development, and training activities.

QWL programs are concerned with many different social and technical relationships in the workplace. It seeks to alter relationships between supervisors and employees and among co-workers in the same or related departments. The intention is to develop a more human work environment and also to provide a structure to involve the employees in decision-making matters and in problem-solving. The QWL program's focus on the employee is not clinical or problem-focused. Instead, the emphasis is on employee capabilities or skills to communicate, interact, and solve problems. Consequently, QWL programs concern themselves with a more diffuse view of employee behavior.

The staff of the QWL programs tends to be small, with a reliance in many instances on outside consultants for specialized expertise. Typically, staff members are administrators of facilitators, rather than practitioners, with little specialized expertise. It is not unusual for such staff members to come from the ranks of the local union, the labor relations office, the personnel department, or even from the floor of the shop. Their knowledge centers on an in-depth understanding of the organization, how it operates, and how to expedite group contributions to problem identification problem-solving and decision-making.

The essence of QWL programs is that they represent an attempt to change employee behavior from one of responding solely to management initiatives to some kind of participation in decisions and problem-solving which will affect what happens in the workplace. The concern in QWL programs is with long-term fundamental changes in employee behavior and the organization, not with a short-term, quick fix. The success of QWL programs is not measured by immediate changes in employee behavior but in long-term changes in group productivity, job satisfaction, morale, grievance rates, quality, and absenteeism. While short-term gains are possible, most of the returns from QWL programs will take time to develop.

Finally, in a generic QWL program there is a central group or plant steering committee coordinating the efforts of the program. In unionized facilities, this group is usually a blend of management and union leadership. It may include the chief executive officer, plant manager, personnel director, union president and/or bargaining chairman, or the international representative. It can add to this committee any management or union staff person to follow-up and implement policies determined by this assembly. This committee is a resource to the multitude of groups in the plant, not simply a controlling authority. The activities of the committee may include: developing and maintaining communication systems in the union and company to make members aware of QWL program activites and progress; assisting the groups when called upon; making available information and technical help when needed; evaluating the effectiveness of groups working on a problem; and providing training to improve group capabilities. The committee will often receive and evaluate suggestions from employees who wish to see particular problems worked on or who want departmental problem-solving teams set up in their areas. The major contribution of this central committee is to provide the resources and know-how to facilitate the work and to implement the decision of the groups.

Can EAPs and QWL Programs Be Reconciled? Some Observations

We have suggesed that EAP and QWL programs are basically different both in objectives and in structure. Both are, however, programs designed to deal with the human resource development of employees. We pose the question: Is there a role for EAPs in the reorganizaton of the workplace? Can QWL programs further the work of EAPs? Until now, EAP personnel have played minor roles in QWL program activities and are almost never represented on the plant steering committees that control QWL programs. The QWL programs have combined the talents of administrators. Organizational developers, and trainers, focusing on the improved performance of workers in the production system through improved communicaton and better decision-making processes. EAP personnel have not shared this emphasis, but have concentrated on the improved work perfomrance of a specific group of workers.

There are a number of ways in which the EAP and QWL programs can reciprocally influence each other in positive directions. Let us discuss each one of these in turn.

Information Diffusion

The establishment of a network of autonomous or semi-autonomous work groups can provide a new mechanism for the diffusion of information on the goals, resources, and activities of EAPs. One of the paramount concerns of the EAP is to make known to employees how the program operates and how to access it. The QWL programs offer both an organized learning and discusson structure for such information. The QWL program provides the further advantage of being a relatively stable group structure where information can be disseminated on a continuous basis for the prevention and treatment of behavior problems and diseases. The groups can become a powerful influence in the interpretation of this information for the employee, and can be the means to adapt the information to the cognitive, emotional, and behavioral structure of its members. Group consensus can become important both in legitimatizing the information and providing inducements for using it. The use of these groups for dissemination of information can result in reaching a greater number of employees within a framework that suggests a greater potential for utilization of the information.

Practitioners have long been aware that diffusing information by itself is not enough. The QWL program network of groups offers the opportunity to disseminate EAP information through structured training efforts with the groups. These efforts might well be integrated withing the framework of QWL program training given to improve the capabilities of the group members and thus tie EAPs closely to the core concerns of the groups. Such training might include: the etiology of different diseases; options for treatment; work performance reviews; symptoms of deteriorated work performance; and strategies for handling the impaired, or potentially impaired, employee. In the give and take of training sessions, the participants not only receive information but consider questions involved in the application and utilization of the information in their own situations. Such training sessions can result in concrete plans of action to utilize the EAP information.

These training efforts with QWL program groups may have yet another consequence. In training sessions, the EAP information would be presented both to impaired, or potentially impaired, employees and their peers in the groups. For the first group of employees, such information might provide a framework for self-assessment of the impairment and what should be done about it. The second group of employees might develop a better under-standing of the impairment, its etiology, and its treatment. In both instances, EAP information can be translated into practical guidelines for dealing with human problems in the workplace.

Identifying and Referring Potential EAP Clients

Given the mandate and responsibility for managing their own affairs, QWL program groups may begin to consider how human problems (absenteeism, tardiness, alcoholism) impede group performance, Group interest and action on these problems would be a reflection of the extent to which members perceive the problems to be impediments to group main-tenance of functioning. A major concern would be the costs incurred by group members because of a deteriorated work performance of impaired employees. Such costs may include a loss in the quality of product, the necessary assumption of more responsibility by group members and the greater dangers in working with impaired employees. Interest may become focused on such problems in the group by making information available on the extent of a problem in the plant or by providing information on individual employee work performance to the group as a whole (with appropriate consideration for confidentiality).

In some plants, supervisors and stewards have been trained, usually by EAP staff, to identify employees with deteriorated work performance for referral to EAPs. Such training usually involves detailing the symptoms of deteriorated work performance, conducting a work performance review and engaging in constuctive confrontation, to induce the impaired employee to seek assistance. In a like manner, the QWL program group can be trained to identify employees in need of assistance and provide the needed inducements for EAP self-referral. The QWL program group is a setting in which the behavioral problems of some group members may become apparent to other group members. By encouraging such activities in the QWL program group network, it is possible to extend the case finding system of the plant to identify impaired employees.

EAP and QWL programs can establish a close partnership in the identification and referral of impaired employees. EAP staff specialized expertise and can provide specific information for the QWL group–how to identify work impairments; how to engage in constuctive confrontation; and what strategies/options exist to deal with the problem. The QWL program members can select the strategy or option that is most appropriate to the social reality of the group and implement the proposed plan. The relationship between both programs is collaborative, with each contributing from its strengths.

Creating Employee Assistance Task Teams

In addition to a network of stable and permanent groups, QWL programs may include problem task teams. These teams consist of plant-wide volunteers who are interested in a particular problem. They collect and analyze information on the problem, make action recommendations for solution, monitor the implementation, and then disband. Such teams may be established to deal with any problem at the behest of the company, union, or employees.

Employee assistance teams can be established to deal with an impaired employee problem (alcoholism, absenteeism, tardiness). Such teams operate under QWL program principles of autonomy in decision-making, blend the experiences of the members with the information on the problem received from staff units, and have their work supported at the highest levels of the organizations. In such task teams, EAP staff can contribute in a number of ways. First, they can supply information on the problem. This may include data on incidence at the plant, an analysis of costs to the employee and the company, and clinical discriptions of work-impaired employees, Second, they can present strategies to handle the problem and options for action. These strategies and options may reflect the experiences of handling the problem at other companies,the results of recent research or theoretical/conceptual thinking on the problem. Finally, EAP staff members can critique the recommendations of the task team. This can be done in the terms of: 1) what has been tried and what has or has not worked at other companies, and 2) what are the organizational constraints on a particular option. The work of the task force combines with the expertise of the EAP staff and results in a collaborative approach to the problem.

Using an employee assistance team presents several advantages in approaching impaired employee problems.

1. The concern with the problem is not imposed on the employees; rather, the employees have an opportunity to make inputs into the definition of the problem and what is to be done about it. Such involvement and participation may guarantee that the solution to the problem will be accepted by the employees as their plan and reduce resistance that may have been forthcoming.

2. Such teams can be the basis for a dialogue between different groups of employees in the plant. Consequently, any plan would take into account different views and interests that exist among the employees. The agreed upon plan would be a negotiated agreement among employee groups rather than serving the interests of any one group.

3. The involvement and participation of employees can result in a significant learning experience about employee impairments. Insofar as the task team members have ties to other employees, a new information network on employee impairments and assistance can be developed.

4. Since the task team has a broad base of support from plant departments and upper echelons of the company, employment assistance activities become very visible and legitimatized. The employment assistance team is able to mobilize resources from a wide variety of staff departments to further its work. The situation is ripe to "open any door" for information and technical resources. The task team is freed of the restrictions frequently imposed on a EAP staff unit because it does not have the legitimacy or the support to perform its work.

5. Task team members know the social reality of the plant. Their knowledge of departmental circumstances and employees' attitudes can be used to enrich analyses or proposals on employee impairment. Such knowledge can be extremely useful in the adaptation of EAP proposals and practices to local department conditions. The knowledge of the team members is not antithetical to EAP staff expertise. Actually, both kinds of knowledge are required for implementation of action plans.

6. The task team is usually established with strong support from the "top dogs" of the organization. The team is given a strong sense of legitimacy and influence in defining problems and issues for

consideration. Employee assistance issues may assume a higher priority when they are identified or raised by the task teams themselves than by EAP staff members. The perspective may be that these problems are being raised at the grass roots level by the employees themselves and thus are in need of immediate attention. In this sense, the task team can be a mechanism of expanding political support in the organization for employee assistance activities.

7. Since membership on the task team is plant-wide, the monitoring of accepted recommendations or action plans can utilize the services of employees–task team members–who are geographically dispersed in the organization and have a detailed knowledge of what has been proposed. These employees can serve a double purpose: 1) interpret the recommendations to other employees in their departments, and 2) identify problems of implementation for EAP staff members.

The task team approach to EAPs has been tried in only a few locations. The effectiveness of this approach has not yet been established, but it would seem to hold considerable promise. It is a mechanism that combines the employee's knowledge of the workplace with the technical expertise of EAP staff members. Furthermore, it involves the employee in the program as an active participant in the retrieval of information on the problem and the development of the action plan.

Summing Up

We have suggested that EAP and QWL programs are different with respect to goals, technology, staffing patterns, and emphasis on expertise. QWL programs, however, do offer new opportunities to advance concerns with impaired employee problems. The QWL program groups can serve as channels to disseminate information about the EAP; to identify/refer poorly performing employees for treatment; and to provide political support within the organization for EAPs. The use of employee assistance task teams offers an opportunity to combine the grass roots expertise of the employee with the technical knowledge of staff experts in a new collaborative approach to employee problems. The end result will be a much different EAP than we have seen in the past, with employee assistance efforts closely tied to the quality of work life in the plant.

Postscript
The Future of EAPs and
New Directions

James L. Francek
Samuel H. Klarreich
C. Eugene Moore

We are living on the crest of waves in a sea of change. We are asked to chart the maps of our journey. Yet we know not the target nor the path. At best we are living each day to its fullest. At worst we are overcome and paralyzed by the fear of what could be.

At no other period in the history of man has change come in such successive and rapid waves. We travel across the continents of the earth in a matter of hours. We communicate by satellite and the world becomes a village. We can now, with the assistance of a home computer, our telephones, and our televisons, do our banking, our shopping, our travel arrangements, take college courses, send electronic mail, seek medical advice, gather research abstracts, and receive family therapy. Some of us do our office work at home via computers; futurists tell us that we will soon have wrist watch telephones that will link us to the world.

We have moved from a steel-energy-locomotive type of industry to a bio-technological informational workplace. We have gone from periods of financial abundance and security to a period where survival is paramount, where no one is secure. We have moved from a society that was more solid state in its structure, to one that is more an open flow state.

What does all of this have to do with EAPs? It has a great deal to do with them. Traditional EAP practitioners have seen themselves as specialists hired by the host organizations to do direct service interventions with individuals who have problems functionng. They have often been observers of the workplace and its processes, with little interest in changing it. They have often segregated themselves from the mainstream, thus limiting their effect on the organization as a whole. The future of EAPs will be dependent upon a number of variables. Those variables include:

- The EAP staff's openness to change
- The level of integration that the EAP has within the workplace
- The level of sophistication that the EAP staff has as facilitators of change
- The skill of EAP staff in applying a "system approach" to their program
- The level of credibility that EAP staff enjoy within the organization
- The level of ownership of EAP efforts that has been generated within the host organization

As we see it, a number of critical things are happening, all within short periods of time. Within the last few years, most work forces have undergone considerable shifts, downsizing, and reorganization. The introduction of "high tech" into the workplace has been both a boom and a bust. More work is being expected and done by less people in a shorter amount of time. Robots replace manpower in unsafe and unrewarding positions. The electronic office system replaces both middle management and secretarial staff as progress "moves forward." Employees are left to fend for themselves. For those working in the area of new technology, some may feel more isolated and unable to communicate. Prolonged periods of using this technology may leave some with rigid black and white thinking patterns; still others may use the new technology to avoid emotion and unevenness in affect. In the long run many of these positive innovations may create new patterns of organizational, social, and health dysfunctions. This is not to argue against the implementation of new technology, for companies need to stay competitive, but rather to argue for a more rational and human implementation of those new forms of work. Such an approach would allow for adequate time to process and integrate these multiple changes. To do otherwise would be to run headlong into massive change without consideration for the human element.

EAP staff need to integrate their efforts with the overall medical efforts in the area of wellness. A "total person" perspective allows for looking at all of the elements that preserve one's physical and mental health. By aligning some of our EAP goals with those of other health professionals, we can work towards a new joint definition of mental health. Perhaps M. Scott Peck's definition of mature mental health will even have a chance to be realized.

"Mature mental health demands . . . an extraordinary capacity to flexibly strike and continually restrike a delicate balance between conflicting needs, goals, duties, responsibilities, and direction."

Another area for staff members of EAPs to consider is their relationship to other allied professional activities within the workplace, such as those of the organizational development (OD) staff. OD staff are often involved in developing creative responses to organizational change, as they move toward organizational transformation (OT). In managing the energy of change, OD staff often focus their efforts on the values, vision, viscera, and ventures of the company. The perspective of an EAP staff member in such efforts, if properly focused, can assist in developing solid preventive measures that improve and preserve the health of the individual and thus the organization. EAP staff are in critical positions to see the unhealthy practices of both the individual and the organization. Their input can affect policy directions and procedures, as companies and individuals swim the river of change. EAP interventions with individuals stress the need for individuals to take responsibility for their health and use self-help methods to improve "survival." Keeping the balance becomes a major goal in surviving (see Figure 1). These are only a few of the new directions that EAPs may take in the future.

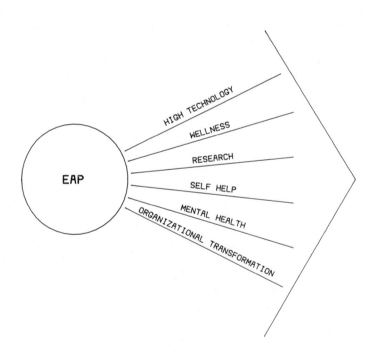

FIGURE 1

Closure

For those who would engage the future, there is much excitement, challenge, and opportunity to grow and become.

For those who would limit their focus and stay in a solid state, further isolation and possible future irrelevance may be in store.

The future is what we make it.

References

1. Hamilton, D., "A Clinician Comprehends the Computre Mentality," *Practice Digest*, Winter '83, Vol. 6, No. 3, pp. 27–30.
2. Peck, M.S., *The Road Less Traveled*, Simon & Schuster, N.Y., 1978, p. 66.

Index

Absenteeism, in alcoholism, 371–372

Acceptance, rational-emotive approach to, 325–330

Accessibility of services; in adversarial environment, 348; in assessment/ treatment model, 81; and utilization of EAPs, 234, 237

Accountability of programs; in assessment/treatment model, 81; in mental health services, 385–386

Achievement motivation, in alcoholism, 363

Adaptability of programs, in assessment/treatment model, 82

Administrative component of EAPs; management support of, 172–176; in service center model, 62–64

Adversarial environment, service integrity in, 348–350

Advocacy role of EAP staff, 337

Aggressive behavior, in stress, 310

Airline industry, employee assistance programs of, 172, 173; peer intervention model of, 103, 105, 106

Alcohol use and alcoholism, 3, 332–333, 360–380; absenteeism in, 371–372; achievement motivation in, 363; and age at first drink, 362, 366; attitudes and biases toward, 117–118, 376; awareness seminars on, 321–324; constructive confrontation in, 374–375; definition of, 323; delays in seeking help for, 366–367; disease concept of, 377; employee education in prevention of, 319–324; at executive levels, TOPEX study on, 332–333, 360–369; family approach to, 378; future areas for research on, 368–369; identification of, 373–374; in broad-based programs, 232–242; early, 214; rate of, 292–293; memory lapses in, 364; peer encouragement of drinking in, 365; prevalence, scope and costs of, 371–373, 378; recovery from, TOPEX study on, 360–369; referral rates for, 292–293; in broad-based programs, 202, 232–242; staff training on, 370, 375–378, 379; TOPEX study on, 360–369; treatment programs for, 8, 95–96, 367–368; in broad-based services, 232–242, 331, 398; in Control Data Corporation, 320–324; effectiveness of, 212–214, 397–398; historical development of, 393–394; work environment affecting development of, 340; work performance in, 320–321, 363–364, 374–375

Alcoholics Anonymous, TOPEX study on, 360–369

Announcement of program, in implementation stage, 85

Assessment; of candidate for international relocation, 282–283, 288; of employee(s), 37–38; in assessment/referral model, 43–44, 69–79; in assessment/treatment model, 80–94; evaluation of, 251; in implementation stage, 37–38; initial procedures in, 45, 48, 49, 50, 51; by psychologists, 157–158; in screening programs, 164; supervisory orientation on, 184–186; work performance reviews in, 184–186. *See also* Work performance reviews; of employee assistance programs, 76, 201–269; for alcohol-related problems, 202, 212–214, 232–242; in assessment/referral

Assessment (*cont'd*)
model, 72, 76; in assessment/
treatment model, 85, 87, 89;
attribution of cause of change in,
210; in broad-based services, 202,
232–242; client information in,
249–250; compared to research,
215–216; confidentiality of
information affecting, 257–258;
control groups in, 210–211, 248;
criteria for, 219–220; data
collection and management in, 23,
201, 203–221, 227–228,
235–237, 245, 255–256; design
of, 217–218; in development stage,
261–263; on dissemination, 395;
documentation in, 224–230; on
effectiveness, 395. *See also*
Effectiveness of EAPs; on
evaluation effort, 252; feedback
in, 266–267; goal statement and
measurement in, 209–210, 226,
246, 255, 263–264; informal, 251;
job performance measurements in,
211–212, 226–227; macro and
micro changes in, 229–230;
measurements in, 223–224, 245;
normative data in, 248, 253–254;
organizational analysis in,
260–261; on outcome, 247, 253;
outside experts involved in,
214–215; problems in, 244–245;
on process, 246–247, 250–252;
reasons for, 244; reporting results
of, 256–257; responsibility for,
218; retrospective design of,
247–248; on success rates,
395–396; system for, 245–248,
264–265; types of, 246–247; in
union-based services, 100–101;
use of results from, 220; on
utilization rates, 396; variables in,
248–255; of employing
organization, 260–261

Assessment/referral model, 43–44,
69–79; interviews in, 70–71;
matching concept in, 75–76;

professionalism in, 74–75;
resources in, 70; staff
qualifications in, 73–74; treatment
methods in, 72, 76; working
definitions in, 70

Assessment/treatment model, 44,
80–94; confidentiality policy in,
82, 88–89; historical aspects of,
80–81; implementation of, 82–85;
office location in, 81, 88; program
evaluation in, 85, 87, 89; rationale
for development of, 81–82; staff
qualifications in, 89–92

Attending behavior, training of referral
agents on, 193

Attitudes of EAP workers; toward
alcoholism, 117–118, 376; training
related to, 195

Auspice of programs, ethical decisions
in, 345–347

Availability of services, in assessment/
treatment model, 81

Avoidance behavior, in stress, 310

Awareness of services; evaluation of,
251; questionnaire for, 267–268;
in quality of work lie programs,
413

Behavior; ineffective, as sources of
stress, 310–311; modification of,
315–316; of referral agents,
training related to, 190–191

Behavior health model, 405

Behavioral therapy; in assessment/
treatment model, 86; definition of,
93

Belief system, as source of stress,
307–309; restructuring of,
312–314

Broad-based programs; alcohol-related
problems identified in, 202,
232–242; compared to
alcohol-specific programs,
232–242, 331, 398; effectiveness
of, 403; referrals to, voluntary and
suggested, 233, 236, 238–239;
social policy issues in, 338

Brochures describing EAPs, distribution of, 38

Capitalism, welfare, 344–345
Case finding, 45, 46–48; alcohol-related, 214, 232–242, 292–293, 373–374; supervisors in, 401–402
Case management; assessment of, 23; psychiatrists in, 135–136
Chemical dependency, 319–324. *See also* Dependency, chemical
Child care programs, 351
Clients. *See* Employees
Clinical component of EAPs, 9; management support of, 176–179
Clinical psychologists, occupational, 155–162
Cognitive-behavior therapy; in assessment/treatment model, 86, 90; definition of, 93
Communication; training of referral agents on, 193, 197–198; in workplace, in quality of work life programs, 411, 412
Community; social policy decisions related to, 335–341, 357–358; treatment resources in, 51
Company. *See* Employing organization
Company Profile and Analysis Form, 261
Competence of EAP practitioners, 355–356
Computer systems; in EAP data collection and management, 208, 228, 256; in workplace, as future concern of EAPs, 419

Confidentiality of information, 168; in adversarial environment, 348–349; affecting evaluation of program, 257–258; in assessment/treatment model, 82, 88–89; in computer systems, 208; of physicians, 121–122; of psychiatrists, 139; of referral agents, 194; of social workers, 153

Confrontation strategies; in alcoholism, 374–375; inducing employees to seek assistance, 47, 48; of nurses, 169; of physicians, 119; of referral agents, training on, 198
Consortium, EAP; compared to service center model, 60; definition of, 68
Consultation services; in assessment/ treatment model, 87–88, 91; evaluation of, 254–255; information requirements of, 266; in marketing of EAPs, 29; psychiatric, 134, 136; in service center model, 61; in supervisory orientation, 188
Contractors providing services, evaluation of, 254–255
Control Data Corporation programs, 172, 320–324; on chemical dependency, 320–324
Control groups, in evaluation of EAPs, 210–211, 248
Cost-effectiveness of EAPs, 173, 219–220, 244, 247, 253; alcoholism industry affecting, 397–398; in assessment/treatment model, 89; in health promotion, 295–296; for less severely impaired employees, 293; in mental health services, 385–386; per employee, 173; reporting results of study on, 257
Counseling, 16–17; appropriate clients for, 385; in assessment/treatment model, 86, 89–90; in Control Data Corporation, 320, 321; non-directive, 94; nurses' role in, 166; in service center model, 61; short-term, 45, 49

Credibility of services; in adversarial environment, 348–350; in assessment/referral model, 73–74; in assessment/treatment model, 81; staff qualifications affecting, 73–74
Credit union use monitoring, for early intervention, 99

Crisis intervention, training of referral
agents on, 193
Culture shock, in international
relocations, 283–285; and in
returning home, 288; stages of,
284–285

Data collection and management, 201,
203–221; accessibility and utility
of information in, 208; on alcohol-
related problems, 212–214; in
assessment/treatment model,
83–84; in broad-based programs,
235–237; on case activity, 23;
computerized, 208, 228, 256;
confidentiality of. See
Confidentiality of information
conforming to norms of employing
organization, 206; on
demographics of cases, 23;
documentation in; on changes in
employees, 226–230; compared to
measurements, 224–225; in
elevation of EAPs, 23, 201,
203–221, 235–237, 245,
255–256; facilitating staff
succession, 206; importance of,
204–207; job performance
measuremens in, 211–212,
226–227; in management
information systems (MIS),
207–208, 209; outside experts
involved in, 214–215; of
physicians, 121–122; policy
statement on, 22–23; prior to
implementation of EAPs, 31–33,
265–266; of psychiatrists, 139;
reliability of, 225; in research,
215–217, 228–229; in service
center model, 63–64; of social
workers, 153; time capture in, 23;
validity of, 225–226; variations in,
49, 51

Decision-making processes in
workplace, in quality of work life
programs, 411, 412

Democracy in workplace, 409
Demographics of cases, assessment of,
23
Dependency, chemical, 319–324; on
alcohol. See Alcohol use and
alcoholism awareness seminars on,
321–324; Control Data
Corporation program on, 320–324;
definition of, 323; employee
education on, 319–324; preventive
approach to, 272, 319–324
Designs of EAPs, 45–57. See also
Models of EAPs
Development of EAPs, 5, 7–12; in
assessment/treatment model,
81–82; critical issues in, 11–12;
data collection in, 31–33,
265–266; documentation of,
261–263; implementation
strategies in, 31–41; marketing
techniques in, 24–30; motivation
for, 7–8, 31–32, 81–82; physicians
in, 120; planning for evaluation in,
245; policy statement in, 13–23;
responsibility for, ongoining, 406;
social workers in, 150–151
Disability claim monitoring, in early
intervention programs, 99
Disciplinary processes, 404–405;
supervisory orientation on, 186
Dissemination of EAPs, 395
Documentation of employee changes,
222–231; compared to
measurements, 224–225
Drug abuse, 8, 319–324. See also
Dependency, chemical

Economic aspects. See Financial
aspects
Education and training, 16, 181–199;
effectiveness of, 405–406; of
employees; in assessment/
treatment model, 85, 87; on
chemical dependencies, 319–324;
effectiveness of, 405; nurses in,
166; prior to relocation, 286–287,
288–289; in union-based

programs, 100; evaluation of, 252; health-related. *See* Health education and promotion programs integrated with other company programs, 34–35; of management and supervisors, 34–35, 38–39, 181, 183–188; in assessment/ treatment model, 84, 87; on chemical dependencies, 320–321, 322; on disciplinary process, 186; effectiveness of, 406; on mental health, 137; on performance appraisal, 184–186; on problem-solving skills, 187; psychiatrists in, 137; seminars for, 186–188; skill preparation for, 356; in union-based programs, 100; of program staff, 4, 181–182, 189–199; on alcoholism, 370, 375–378, 379; in assessment/referral model, 73–74; in assessment/treatment model, 89–92; on attitudes, 195; on communication skills, 193, 197–198; competence standards in, 355–356; on confrontation strategies, 198; effectiveness of, 406; elements of program for, 196; on follow-up procedures, 194–195; on human behavior, 190–191; knowledge component of, 190–192; on personal and work-related problems, 191–192; for physicians, 116–117, 119; on referral process, 192, 193–194; on roles, 190; in service center model, 62–63; on situation analysis, 192–193; skills component of, 192–195; for social workers, 145, 149, 153, 377; variations in, 50; on work organization, 191; psychologists' role in, 158–159

Effectiveness of EAPs, 222–231, 395; alcoholism industry affecting, 397–398; barriers to, 331, 393–408; in behavior health model, 405; in broad-based services, 403; compared to costs.

See Cost-effectiveness of EAPs; disciplinary system affecting, 404–405; documentation of, 226–230; educational programs affecting, 405–406; employer support affecting, 398–399, 401–403, 404; integrated with workplace, 403–404; mental health services affecting, 385–386; program staff affecting, 399–400; supervisor participation affecting, 401–403; treatment resources affecting, 400–401, 404; unions affecting, 399

Employee(s); assessment of. *See* Assessment, of employee(s); awareness of EAPs, 251; questionnaire in assessment of, 267–268; changes in, 210, 223–224; attribution of cause of, 210; documentation of, 226–230; in health promotion programs, 294–295; job performance measurements in assessment of, 226–227; concern with changes affecting; in computerization of workplace, 419; in international relocations, 281–290; of psychiatrists, 134–135; of social workers, 152–153; education and training of. *See* Education and training, of employees; evaluation of EAP by, 251; identification of problems in. *See* Case finding; needs of; assessment of, 37–38; conflicting with interests of employer, 350–353; program responsibilities of, 17–18; psychiatrists as, 139; psychologists as, 160–161; as variable in EAP evaluation, 249–250

Employee Advisory Resource Program, of Control Data Corporation, 320–324

Employee Referral and Follow-up Form, 267

Employee and Supervisor Awareness Questionnaires, 267–268

Employing organization; analysis of, 260–261; Company Profile and Analysis Form in, 261; in assessment/treatment model, 81–82; attitudes towards EAPs; adversarial, ethical issues in, 348–350, 352; and effectiveness of programs, 398–399, 401–403, 404; contributing to employee problems, 304–305, 340, 351–353, 386–388; health policies of; nurses' concern with, 166–167; risk profile for, 296–297; interests of, conflicting with employee needs, 350–353; management and supervisors of. See Management and supervisors; meetings with key people of, in implementation stage, 35–37, 82–83; networking in, in marketing of EAPs, 28–29; norms of; in evaluation of EAPs, 248, 253–254; program staff conforming to, 139, 160, 206; in peer intervention model, 107; quality of work life in, 333, 409–417; in service center model, 58, 60–61; stressors in, 304–305, 351–353, 386–388; training of referral agents on, 191; values and ethics of, 356–357; variations in size and structure of, 54–55

Ethical issues, 332, 342–359; in advancing client's cause, 351–353; in adversarial environment, 348–350; in assessment/treatment model, 90; in auspice and sponsorship decisions, 345–347; in competence of EAP practitioners, 355–356; in conflicts between employee and employer interests, 350–353; historical aspects of, 343–344; in labor-management conflicts, 349–350; in mental health services, 389; in occupational social work, 153; in roles and missions of EAPs, 347–348; in social policy decisions, 357–358; in treatment decisions, 353–354; in welfare capitalism, 344–345, 349

Evaluation. See Assessment
Executives. See Management and supervisors
External marketing of EAPs, 25
External programs; broad-based, utilization of, 234, 236, 239; in service center model, 58–68; variations in, 49, 50
Exxon Corporation programs, 278

Families; of alcoholics, 378; of executives, in stressful relocations, 281–290
Fee structure, in service center model, 63
Feedback on EAPs, for program control, 266–267
Financial aspects; of alcoholism, 371–373, 378; of EAPs; in cost-effectiveness analysis. See Cost-effectiveness of EAPs; ethical issues in, 346, 354; in management support, 173; in psychiatric treatment, 133; in service center model, 63; social policy issues in, 338–339; in third-party payments, 52; in welfare capitalism concept, 344–345
Fitness programs, 295
Flexibility of programs, in assessment/treatment model, 82
Follow-up procedures, 72; evaluation of, 251; training of referral agents on, 194–195
Foreign countries, stress of relocations to, 281–290
Full-service programs, 11
Funding. See Financial aspects
Future of EAPs, 418–421

General Motors employee assistance program, 172–173

Generalists on EAP staff, 68; in service center model, 62

Geographic influences on design of EAPs, 51, 55

Goals of EAPs; in assessment/ treatment model, 83; compared to goals of quality of work life programs, 409–410, 411; policy statement on, 15–16, 83; statement and measurement of, in evaluation procedures, 246, 255, 263–264; variations in, 53–55

Health education and promotion programs, 17, 271–272, 275–280, 291–303; in assessment/treatment model, 85, 87; coordinated with EAPs, 278–279, 291, 296–301; cost-benefit analysis of, 295–296; high risk population in, 298; interdependence of changes from, 294–295; lifestyle concerns in, 277–278; low risk or healthy population in, 297; moderate risk groups in, 297–298; nurses in, 163–170; physicians in, 115–128; program planning for, 279; recent trends in, 276–278; stress management in, 279, 295–296; traditional patterns of, 276; in union-based services, 98; and utilization of EAPs, 278

Historical aspects of employee benefits and services, 80–81, 343–344, 393–394

Hospital-based EAPs, 9

Humanistic-existential therapy, 94

Humanization of workplace, 409

Humor, in stress management, 313

Hypertension control programs, 295

Identification of employee problems. See Case finding

Impact of EAPs. See Effectiveness of EAPs

Implementation of programs, 5–6, 31–41; in assessment/treatment model, 82–85; data collection for, 31–33, 265–266; distribution of literature in, 38; documentation of, 261–263; and integration with other company systems, 34–35; key personnel in, 36–37; management in, 36, 176, 265; needs assessment in, 37–38; order of activities in, 39–40; physicians in, 124; planning stage in, 31–33; rate of, 395; specific activities in, 35–39; training of supervisors and managers in, 38–39

Independent programs. See External programs

Inducements to seek assistance, 46–48; in peer intervention model, 103; supervisor support in, 402

Information and referral programs, 11

Information system. See Data collection and management

Injuries, work-related, nurses' role in treatment of, 165–166

Insurance claims; for EAP services, social poligy issues in, 338–339; monitoring of, in early intervention programs, 99

Intake procedures, 48, 49; in assessment/treatment model, 86; variations in, 48, 49, 51

Integrity of EAP services, in adversarial environment, 348–350

Internal marketing of EAPs, 28

Internal programs, 9–10; assessment/ treatment model of, 80–94

International relocations, stress of, 281–290

Interviews; with employees; in assessment/referral model, 70–71; prior to international relocation, 282–283, 288; training of referral agents on, 193, 197–198; in selection of EAP staff, 174–175

Job performance reviews. *See* Work performance reviews

Knowledge component of referral agent training, 190–192

Labor organizations. *See* Union(s)
Life events, stress value of, 305; in international relocations, 283
Lifestyle concerns; in health education and promotion programs, 277–278; in preventive programs, 339; in quality of work life programs, 333, 340, 409–417
Limited utilization programs, 11
Location of EAP office; accessibility of, 81, 234, 237, 348; in assessment/treatment model, 81, 88; managerial support in, 175; and utilization of program, 234, 236, 237, 239

Maintenance of programs, in service center model, 65
Management information systems (MIS), 207–208, 209
Management and supervisors; alcoholism in, TOPEX study on, 332–333, 360–369; awareness of EAPs, questionnaire on, 267–268; education and training of. *See* Education and training, of management and supervisors; evaluation of EAP by, 251; information needs of, prior to implementation of EAP, 265; physicians in, 126–127; psychologists in, 160–161; relationship with unions; in management-sponsored programs, 178, 179; role of EAPs in, 349–350; in union-based programs, 97–98, 100, 101; reporting results of EAP evaluation to, 257; role in EAPs, 17, 113, 171–180; and

effectiveness of programs, 398–399, 401–403, 404; ethical issues in, 346; historical aspects of, 344; in identification of problem employees, 401–403; in implementation process, 36, 176, 265; in motivation of employees to accept treatment, 402; in referral process, 176–178, 251, 331, 402–403; and utilization of services, 234, 236, 238, 240; stress of, 305; and alcohol-related problems, 365–366; in international relocations, 281–290; using EAPs, 40; values and ethics of, 356; welfare capitalism practice of, 344–345, 349
Mandatory referral procedures, 19–22
Marketing of EAPs, 5, 6, 24–30; access to decision makers of organization in, 26; analysis of target population in, 25–26; and closing of sale, 26–27; consultants in, 29; external, 25; internal, 28; and mental health services, 382–383; organizational networking in, 28–29; physicians in, 123–124; plan for, 24–25; program promotion in, 28; in service centermodel, 64; traditional techniques in, 24–25
Matching concept, in assessment/referral model, 75–78
Medical model of EAPs, role of occupational physicians in, 115–128
Meetings, in implementation of EAPs, 35–37, 82–83
Mental health services, 331–332, 381–392; accountability of, 385–386; control and value issues in, 389; effectiveness of, 385–386; future directions of, 419; identification of work environment contributing to employee problems in, 340, 386–388; integrated with other services, 388; matching of

clients and appropriate programs in, 384–385; obstacles to, 388–389; preventive programs in, 383–384; promotion and marketing of, 382–383; of psychiatrists, 129–143; of psychologists, 155–162

Mission-oriented EAPs, 347

Mobility, geographical, and stress, 304; in international relocations, 281–290

Models of EAPs, 4, 11, 43–109; assessment/referral programs, 43–44, 69–79; assessment/treatment programs, 44, 80–94; geographic influences on, 51, 55; peer referral programs, 44, 102–109; service center programs, 43, 58–68; union-based programs, 44, 95–101; variations in, 43, 45–57

Monitoring development and operation of EAPs, 260–269

Motivation; for achievement, in alcoholism, 363; for establishing EAPs, 7–8; assessment of, 31–32; in assessment/treatment model, 81–82; variations in, 53–54; for help-seeking, 47–48; in peer intervention model, 103; supervisor support in, 402

Needs of employees; assessment of, 37–38; conflicting with interests of employer, 350–353

Networking, organizational, in marketing of EAPs, 28–29

Neuropsychology, 94

Non-directive counseling, 94

Norms of work organization; in elevation of EAPs, 248, 253–254; program staff conforming to, 139, 160, 206

Nurses, occupational, roles and responsibilities of, 17, 112–113, 163–170; in counseling, 166; in environmental health, 166–167; in health education, 166; in human relations, 167, 170; in preventive programs, 164–165, 160; in recognition and treatment of illness and injury, 165–166; in rehabilitation, 167, 169; in screening programs, 164; in stress management, 169

Objective(s) of EAPs. See Goals of EAPs

Objective model of EAP evaluation, 263–264

Office space; accessibility of, 81, 234, 237, 348; in assessment/treatment model, 81, 88; managerial support in, 175; utilization of, 234, 236, 237, 239

Orientation meetings, in implementation of EAPs, 37; with employees, 37, 84; with supervisors and managements, 38–39, 183–188

Outcome evaluation, 247, 253

Out-of-house EAPs, 10

Parent organization. See Employing organization

Participative management, 409

Passive behavior, in stress, 311

Peer encouragement of drinking behavior, 365

Peer intervention model, 44, 102–109, 298; in airline industry, 103, 105, 106; compared to supervisory model, 103, 106–108; concern with work organization in, 107; principles of, 103–104; recovery models in, 107–108; safeness of accepting help in, 106, 108; selection of peer committee in, 105–106; self-referrals in, 104–105

Perceptions, faulty, and development of stress, 309–311; correction of, 314–315

Performance, work-related, See Work performance reviews

Philosophy of program, statement of, 13–14

Physical fitness programs, 295

Physicians, occupational, 115–128; biases and prejudices of, 116, 117–119, 376; education of, 116–117, 119; roles and responsibilities of, 17, 112, 115–128; in development phase, 120; extent of, 122–123; in implementation stage, 124; as liaison, 126; as manager, 126–127; in promotion of programs, 123–124; in record handling and confidentiality issues, 121–122

Policy and Program Development Form, 262

Policy statement, 5, 12, 13–23; in assessment/treatment model, 83; on data collection, 22–23; documentation on development of, 261–263; integrated with other company policies, 34–35; on objectives of program, 15–16; on philosophy of program, 13–14; on referral procedures, 18–22; on roles and responsibilities within program, 16–18; in union-based programs, 97

Preventive programs, 4, 271–330; for chemical dependencies, 272, 319–324; health education and promotion in, 271–272, 275–280, 291–303; high risk population in, 298; low risk or healthy population in, 297; mental health services in, 383–384; moderate risk groups in, 297–298; nurses in, 164–165, 169; psychiatrists in, 132; rational-emotive approach to, 272, 325–330; for relocations, 279, 281–290; social policy issues in, 339–340; for stress management, 272, 304–318; in relocations, 279, 281–290

Problem-solving skills, in supervisory orientation, 187

Procedures in EAPs, 5; evaluation of, 246–247, 250–252; in policy statement of assessment/treatment model, 83

Productivity of workers, as concern of occupational psychiatry, 134–135

Professionalism; in assessment/referral model, 74–75; in assessment/treatment model, 89–92

Promotion of programs, methods for, 28

Promotions, and occupational stress, 304

Psychiatry, occupational, 112, 129–143, 405; in case management, 135–136; guidelines for, 138–140; historical background on, 130–132; in stress management, 140–141

Psychologists, occupational, 112, 155–162; as clinicians, 159–160; as corporate employees and managers, 160–161; as educators, 158–159; as researchers, 155–157; as testers, 157–158

Psychotherapy, 9; analytically-oriented, 94; in assessment/treatment model, 86, 89–90; matching of clients with appropriate type of, 384

Public agencies, EAPs based in, 9

Publicity on programs; in assessment/treatment model, 84, 85; evaluation of, 251, 252; questionnaire for, 267–268; in implementation stage, 38; inducing employees to seek assistance, 47, 48; in quality of work life programs, 413

Quality of work life programs, 333, 340, 409–417; compared to EAPs, 410–417; union opposition to, 349

Questionnaires; on awareness of EAPs, 267–267; on employee needs, 37–38

Rational-emotive approach, 272, 325–330; in assessment/treatment model, 86; concept of acceptance in, 325–329

Recidivism; in assessment/treatment model, 86; definition of, 94

Record-keeping. See Data collection and management

Recovery models; in alcoholism, TOPEX study on, 360–369; in assessment/referral model, 73–74; in peer intervention program, 107–108

Re-entry process, 45, 48; after international relocations, 288; management support in, 178–179

Referrals, 45, 48, 49; alcohol-related, 292–293; in broad-based programs, 202, 232–242; in assessment/referral model, 69–79; in assessment/treatment model, 84; compared to population at risk for problems, 292–294; evaluation of, 251, 396, 397; Employee Referral and Follow-up Form in, 267; by management and supervisors, 176–178, 251, 331, 402–403; mandatory, 19–22; by peers, 44, 102–109, 298; policy statement on, 18–22; suggested, 19, 233, 236, 238–239; training of referral agents on, 189–199; in union-based programs, 9–100; variations in, 48, 49, 50, 51; voluntary, 18–19, 104–105, 233, 236, 238–239, 251

Rehabilitation, nurses in, 167, 169

Relaxation techniques, in stress management, 311–312

Reliability of measurements, 225

Relocations, international, 281–290; and adjustment to repatriation, 287–288, 289; assessment and selection of candidates for, 282–283, 288; cost of, 281–282, 289–290; in life change units, 283; culture shock in, 283–285;

education prior to, 286–287, 288–289; stress of, preventive approach to, 272–273, 279, 281–290; successful, problems in, 285–287

Reorganization of workplace, in quality of work life programs, 409–417

Research on EAPs, 4, 215–217; compared to evaluation studies, 215–216; data management affecting, 203–221; dissemination of findings in, 216–217, 229, 257; future areas for, 222; in implementation process, 31–33, 265–266; practitioner consultation with researchers about, 216–217; program staff in, 228–229; psychologists in, 155–157

Responsibilities in programs; for evaluation, 218; for ongoing development, 406; policy statement on, 16–18

Restructuring of belief system, in stress management, 312–314

Retrospective analysis of EAPs, 247–248

Role(s); of employee(s), ambiguity or conflicts in, 304–305; in employee assistance programs, 111–180, 405; ethical issues in, 347–348; of management and supervisors, 113, 171–180, 401–403; of nurses, 112–113, 163–170; of physicians, 112, 115–128; policy statement on, 16–18; of psychiatrists, 112, 129–143; of psychologists, 112, 155–162; referral agent training on, 190; of social workers, 112, 144–154

Role-playing techniques, in supervisory orientation seminars, 186–187

School-based EAPs, 10

Screening programs, nurses' role in, 164

Self-acceptance, in rational-emotive approach, 328–329

Self-assertion, in stress management. 315–316
Self-awareness exercises, in referral agent training, 195

Self-help methods, future directions of, 420
Self-referrals, 18–19; to broad-based programs, 233, 236, 238–239; evaluation of, 251; in peer intervention model, 104–105

Seminars; on chemical dependence, 321–324; for supervisory orientation, 186–188
Service center model, 43, 58–68; administrative issues in, 62–64; advantages and disadvantages of, 66–67; company services in, 60–61; compared to EAP consortium, 60; consultation services in, 61; counseling services in, 61; definition of, 68; delivery approaches in, 64–65; funding source in, 63; information system in, 63–64; marketing strategies in, 64; pragmatic issues in, 64–65; program maintenance in, 65; quality and quantity of programs in, 64; staffing of, 62–63; structure of, 59–60
Situation analysis, in referral agent training, 192–193
Skills component of referral agent training, 192–195
Smoking-cessation programs, 295
Social policy issues, 332, 335–341; ethical decisions in, 357–358
Social relationships in workplace, in quality of work life programs, 411–412
Social workers, occupational, 112, 144–154; education of, 145, 149, 153; on alcoholism, 377; reform-oriented, 347, 348, 352
Specialists on EAP staff, 68; in service center model, 62

Sponsorship of programs, 406; ethical issues in, 345–347
Staff of programs, 50–51; advocacy role of, 337; in assessment/referral model, 73–74; in assessment/treatment model, 89–92; competence of, 355–356; conforming to norms of work organization, 139, 160, 206; education and training of. See Education and training, of program staff; and effectiveness of programs, 399–400; generalists and specialists on, 62, 68; managerial support of, 171–180; nurses on, 163–170; physicians on, 115–128; program evaluation by, 218, 244; psychiatrists on, 129–143; psychologists on, 155–162; in quality of work life programs, 412; requirements for, 174; in research, 228–229; selection of, 173–175; in service center model, 62–63; social workers on, 144–154; stress and frustration of, 78; turnover of, 207
Steering Committee, roles and responsibilities of, 16
Stress, 304–318; behavior in, ineffective, 310–311; modification of, 315–316; belief system in, 307–309; restructuring of, 312–314; definition of, 306; of executives, and alcohol-related problems of, 365–366; extra-organizational factors in, 305; health promotion programs on, 295–296; life event units as measurement of, 283, 305; mediating variables in, 306; in medical model, 126; mental health services for, 386–388; nurses' concern with, 169; perceptions in, 309–311; correction of, 314–315; preventive approach to, 272, 304–318; psychiatrists' concern with, 135, 137, 140–141;

relaxation techniques in, 311–312; in relocations, 279, 281–290; social workers' concern with, 152; work environment contributing to, 304–305, 351–352, 386–388

Suggested referrals, 19

Supervisors. See Management and supervisors

System A activities, 45; variations in, 46–48

System B activities, 45; variations in, 48–51

System C activities, 45; variations in, 51–52

Systems approach; to employee assistance programs, 1–4; to evaluation of EAPs, 264–265; of occupational social workers, 145, 153

Tak team approach to EAPs, 416–417

Time assessment in data collection, 23

TOPEX study, 332–333, 360–369

Training. See Education and training

Treatment programs, 45; for alcoholism. See Alcohol use and alcoholism, treatment programs for; in assessment/treatment model, 44, 80–94; community resources in, 51; and effectiveness of EAPs, 400–401, 404; ethical issues in, 353–354; evaluation of, 72, 76, 251; funding of, 52, 63, 354; goals of, 76–77; in-house, 52; matching concept in, 75–78, 384; social policy decisions in, 336, 339; variations in, 51–52

Unemployed workers, EAP services for, 346–347, 350

Union(s); evaluation of EAPs by, 251; in implementation of EAPs, 35–36; information requirements of, 265–266; in opposition to EAPs, 349–350; relationship with management; in management-sponsored programs, 178, 179;

role of EAPs in, 349–350; in union-based programs, 97–98, 100, 101; roles and responsibilities of, 17; in support of EAPs, 95–101. See also Union-based programs

Union-based programs, 4, 10, 95–101; early intervention strategies in, 98–99; educational activities in, 100; effectiveness of, 399; evaluation of, 100–101; historical aspects of, 344; policy statement in, 97; referrals to, 99–100; psychiatrists in, 131; utilization of, 234, 236, 238, 240

United Airlines employee assistance program, 172, 173

Utilization of programs, 94; assessment of, 251, 396; in assessment/ treatment model, 86–87; in broad-based services, 233, 234; in health education, 278; in joint union-management services, 234, 236, 240; in mental health services, 382; office location affecting, 234, 236, 237, 239; in peer intervention model, 103

Validity of measurements, 225–226

Visibility of services, 82

Voluntary referrals, 18–19, 104–105, 233, 236, 238–239, 251

Welfare capitalism, 344–345

Wellness programs, 276

Work organization. See Employing organization

Work performance reviews; in alcoholism, 320–321, 363–364, 374–375; in case finding, 47, 48; in chemical dependency, 320–321; in evaluation of EAPs, 211–212, 226–227; suervisory orientation on, 184–186; in TOPEX study, 363–364; in union-based programs, 97–98

About the Authors

Kim Ankers, MA, holds an MA in Psychology from Carlton University. She has been with the Addiction Research Foundation as Research Assistant in the Operations Research Unit and from 1979–1982 as Senior Research Assistant in the Employee Assistance Program Center. Currently Ms. Ankers is Senior Research Assistant in the Foundation's Sociobehavioral Treatment Services. She has authored and co-authored papers on EAPs.

Terry C. Blum, PhD., is Assistant Professor of Sociology at Tulane University, where she has been a member of the faculty since 1982, having previously served at SUNY–Albany and Brooklyn College. Her Ph.D. is from Columbia University, and her publications have focused on macro-social structure and research measurement issues. She is presently co-director of the Tulane Research Study, focused of EAP structure and process.

Bernard Boyle, MSW, obtained a Masters degree in Social Work from Carlton University in Ottawa, Canada, and is presently employed as the Divisional EAP Coordinator for the Addiction Research Foundation of Ontario. He has worked in the addiction field and the EAP field for the past 10 years. He was seconded for three years to the Canadian Labour Congress. There he assisted in the development and implementation of guidelines for the involvement of Canadian unions in Employee Recovery/Assistance Programs.

Katharine Hooper Briar,DSW, is an Assistant Professor of Social Work at the University of Washington and teaches courses addressing social policy, the world of work, and unemployment. She has given a number of addresses on occupational social work and on unemployment and is the author of several publications on unemployement. Actively involved with the National Association of Social Workers, (NASW) she has chaired a statewide effort to promote demonstation projects in labor and industry and serves as a member of the NASW Occupational Social Work Task Force.

William R. Byers, CAC, MSW, ACSW, has worked in the EAP field for 10 years, formerly directing the EAP for Kelsey Hayes, a subsidiary of the Fruehauf Corporation. He has specialized education and experience in providing services to alcoholics and their families as a certified alcoholism counselor and also is an experienced therapist providing treatment for people and families with a variety of mental health problems. He is currently the Assistant Director of the New York State Division of Alcoholism managing the Occupational/Industrial Bureau, having responsibility for policy development, funding, planning, developing, and implementng EAPs throughout New York State.

Jean B. Case, MD, is an Assistant Medical Director of the Medicine and Environmental Health Department of Exxon Corporation. Prior to joining Exxon in 1978, she was in private practice as an internist and rheumatologist. For the past five years she has been actively involved in preventive medicine and the development and implementation of a health education and health promotion program for Exxon employees.

Mark Cohen, MPH, MSW, DSW, has 13 years of professional experience in the treatment of alcoholic and chemically dependent persons in addition to his many years of experience as a psychotherapist. He has authored a number of articles on alcoholism, drug abuse and other public health concerns which have appeared in professional journals and developed a hospital-based EAP before assuming his current positions at American Express Company.

D. W. Corneil, is the National Advisor to the Government of Canada's Employee Assistance Program. He is also an expert advisor to the joint World Health Organization–International Labour Organization project on "Alcohol in Employment Settings."

William G. Durkin, Ph.D., initiated Atlantic Richfield's EAP in 1974, where he continues to work as its manager. He is a native of New York City where he received his BBA and MBA in Industrial Psychology from the City University of New York. He also received a Ph.D. in Counseling Psychology from Lawrence University in Santa Barbara, California.

Albert Ellis, Ph.D., is the Executive Director of the Institute for Rational-Emotive Therapy, New York City. He is the author of more than 500 articles and of 46 books and monographs, including *How to Live With a "Neurotic," Reason and Emotion in Psychotherapy, Humanistic Psychotherapy, A New Guide to Rational Living,* and *Handbook of Rational-Emotive Therapy.*

John C. Erfurt, is an Associate Research Scientist at the University of Michigan's Institute of Labor and Industrial Relations, and co-directs the Institute's Worker Health Program. He has conducted research on the physical and mental health consequences of different supervisory styles and work shifts, and of unemployment. Since 1973, he has studied the worksite as a location for identification and control of various types of chronic diseases, including hypertension and alcoholism and has written several manuals as well as other publications detailing this work. He is a consultant to numerous industrial organizations regarding the implementation and evaluation of worksite health programs.

Jennifer L. Farmer, MA, is currently Director of Employee Assistance Programs, Inc., Vice President of Employee Assistance Research Institute, and National Treasurer of the Association of Labor-Management Administrators and Consultants on Alcoholism (ALMACA). She was formerly Program Director for the Association of Flight Attendants-Employee Assistance Program; served on the faculty of Colorado Summer

School for Alcohol Studies, Texas EAP Symposiums II and IV, Psychotherapy Institute on Alcohol Studies, and National Occupational Programming Training Institute (NOPTI); and was a counseling psychologist in private practice.

Louis A. Ferman, Ph.D., received his Ph.D. in Sociology and Industrial Relations at Cornell University. His research and publications focus on employee problems in the workplace and job displacement. Currently, he is Professor of Social Work and Research Director of the Institute of Labor and Industrial Relations at The University of Michigan.

Andrea Foote, Ph.D., is an Associate Research Scientist at the University of Michigan's Institute of Labor and Industrial Relations, and co-directs the Institute's Worker Health Program. She is also an Adjunct Associate Professor in the Department of Sociology at the University of Michigan. She is interested in the sociology of health care delivery particularly within industrial and labor settings and has conducted research on the process and outcomes of various health care delivery models. She is also interested in the preventive aspects of worksite programs, and consults with numerous organizations regarding their health-related programs.

James L. Francek, MSW, is a family man, fisherman, occupational social worker, and resident of Connecticut. He is a graduate of the University of Michigan's School of Social Work. He is the manager of the Employee Health Advisory Program for the Exxon Corporation in New York and Chairperson of Occupational Social Work Task Force for the National Association of Social Workers. He is a past president of ALMACA and formerly directed and developed similar EAPs at both the Ford Motor and Kelsey Hayes Companies. He is a national and internationally recognized figure, lecturer and consultant in the field of EAPs.

Thomas D. Francek, MA, is the Director of Occupational Services, Oxford Institute; former Industrial Services Coordinator for Eastwood Clinics; author, and speaker; and has an MA in counseling from Wayne State University. He has over 10 years experience in alcoholism treatment and is a recognized lecturer and consultants on EAPs.

Patricia A. French, RN., is a consultant with the Employee Assistance Programs Center at The Alcoholism and Drug Addiction Research Foundation of Ontario. Her background experience of twenty years with the Foundation includes a variety of clinical and administrative postitions. Since 1977 she has been involved in the design and implementation of the ARF/EAP Monitoring System and has co-authored a number of reports resulting from the use of the systems. To date, this system has been implemented in a number of organizations in the metro Toronto area. Permission has also been given for use of the system to organizations in Australia, Alberta, Newfoundland, New Brunswick, and Ontario.

Brad Googins, PhD., is an assistant professor and Director of the Human

Service in the Workplace Program at Boston University. He is also the chairperson of the Research Committee for ALMACA (Association of Labor-Management Administrators on Consultants on Alcoholism).

Susan Isenberg, MA, is the Assistant Manager of Employee Counseling, Hughes Aircraft Company; former Executive Director of the Lincoln EAP, Inc,; consultant to the Australian Foundation on Alcoholism and Drug Dependence; member of past NIAAA and ALMACA National Committees.

Otto Jones, MSW, is the President and Chief Executive Officer of Human Affairs, Inc. He is a Clinical Professor at the University of Utah Clinical School of Social Work; ex-marine; owns and operates Cattle and Bison (buffalo ranch); and is also actively involved in youth communities athletic programs.

Samuel H. Klarreich, Ph.D., is the Employee Assistance Program Director at Imperial Oil Limited, and received his BA, MA, and Ph.D. degrees from the University of Toronto. Previously, he was Chief Psychologist at a major Toronto hospital for six years. He has advanced training in hypnosis, biofeedback, and a variety of psychotherapies including rational-emotive therapy. He has conducted more than 100 workshops on such topics as stress management, designing and justifying EAPs, and evaluation and cost-benefit analysis of EAPs. He is a member of more than a dozen professional associations. He has written articles on a variety of health-related topics and has recently been selected to appear in the *Who's Who of Frontier Science and Technology*.

Edward J. Larkin, Ph.D., received a Ph.D. in Clinical Psychology from York University in 1972. In addition to several years as a therapist at the Addiction Research Foundation of Ontario, he directed the Foundation's Operations Research Unit for several years. During this period, computer-assisted monitoring systems for community development and outpatient treatment programs were developed and implemented. Dr. Larkin directed the EAP Center in Metro Toronto from 1979–1982 and is currently the Head of the Addiction Research Foundation Assessment and Follow-Up Unit. He has authored a book on the treatment of alcoholism and papers on program evaluation.

Janis L. Levine, MSW, spent two years at Boston University before obtaining her BA and BSW at McGill University. She obtained an MSW at the University of Toronto and is the past Program Manager and counselor of the Employee Advisory Resouce Program at Control Data Canada Ltd. She currently is the manager of the Employee Advisory Program for Esso Resources in Calgery, Alberta. Ms. Levine is a member of the Kidney Foundation of Canada, Ontario branch. She has published some health-related articles and was a field instructor at the University of Toronto, Faculty of Social Work.

Ian Lipsitch, MD, is a consulting psychiatrist for Southern Bell and IBM; faculty member at Emory University School of Medicine; co-author of a book on crisis intervention; and recieved his medical training at the University of Rochester and Yale University.

James J. Manuso, Ph.D., is a Corporate Consultant; former Assistant Vice-President and Director of Planning for Health Systems at Equitable Life Assurance Society; past President New York Biofeedback Society; co-founder of American Institute of Stress; editor of *Occupational Clinical Psychology* (Praeger Publishers); Ph.D. in Psychology, New School of Social Research; MBA from Columbia, and Certificate in Management from Harvard; and a widely published and recognized speaker.

John B. Maynard, Ph.D., is currentlly Executive Director of Employee Assistance Programs Inc. and President of Employee Assistance Reseach Institute in Colorado. He was formerly Program Coordinator for The University of Colorado's Employee Assistance Project, outpatient therapist for Boulder Drug Abuse Services Project, instructor in the Counseling Department of the University of Colorado at Denver, and private practitioner of psychotherapy.

Lockie Jayne McGehee, Ph.D., is Director of Corporate Services at the Institute for Rational-Emotive Therapy; Assistant Professor in Psychology at Rutgers University; has a Ph.D. in a Clinical Psychology from Duke University; is a consultant to Exxon Corporation; and a speaker and writer.

Alan McLean, M.D., is the Area Medical Director for IBM Corporation; Clinical Associate Professor of Psychiatry, Cornell University Medical College; and his most recent book is *Work Stress*.

Daniel Molloy, MSW, has been associated with the National Maritime Union Pension and Welfare Plan Personal Service Unit since September, 1976. He has done graduate work at both Iona College and the Hunter College School of Social Work, where he is presently pursuing doctoral studies. Mr. Molloy is active in the New York City chapter of NASW, ALMACA, and is coordinator of the New York State Assembly Occupational Alcoholism Task Force.

C. Eugene Moore, MD, is an Assistant Medical Director of Exxon Corporation and physician contact for the Employee Health Advisory Program and medical aspects of company operations in the Middle East and Africa. He is certified in Occupational Medicine and Internal Medicine.

Leonard Moss, MD, is a consulting psychiatrist for Mobil; certified in psychoanalytical medicine; assistant Clinical Professor in Psychiatry at Cornell University; graduate of the College of Physicians and Surgeons at Columbia University; and the author of a book entitled *Management Stress*.

Lewis F. Presnall, is an Industrial Relations Consultant; former Director of

Behavioral-Medical Programs at Kemper Insurance Group and National Council on Alcoholism; and a well known author, consultant, and lecturer.

John C. Quinn, BA, MS, MHSc., is a community health educator and EAP consultant. He was Director of the New York State Employee Assistance Program which provided assessment, referral, and training sevices for 250,000 workers. He is currently serving as Employee Assistance Labor consultant at the New York State Division of Alcoholism and Alcohol Abuse.

A. J. Riediger, Ph.D., has combined clinical, academic, and administrative interests in his involvement in employee assistance programming. His background in hospital and community mental health provided the basis for development of a behavioral health program for the Alberta Public Service in 1976. Dr. Riediger administered this program for five years and completed his doctoral dissertation on the role of the supervisor in EAP. He received his Ph.D. in Counseling Psychology from the University of Alberta. He is presently employed as supervisor of Therapy Programs at Forensic Assessment and Community Services at Alberta Hospital, Edmonton.

Paul M. Roman, Ph.D., is Favrot Professor of Human Relations, professor of Sociology and professor of Epidemiology at Tulane University, where he has been on the faculty since 1969. He is author or co-author of many publications on EAPs, including *Spirits and Demons at Work*. His current research concerns the structure and diversity of EAPs across work settings.

Jack Santa-Barbara, Ph.D., C. Psych., is a Principal of Corporate Health Consultant in Mississauga, Ontario, Canada, and Director of EAP Services. Dr. Santa-Barbara has a degree in Social Psychology from McMaster University and a background in human service program development and evaluation. He has been involved in the review and development of several innovative programs across Canada, and was the founding president of the Canadian Evaluation Society. Dr. Santa-Barbara has also published widely in the area of psychotherapy research and family assessement procedures, in addition to operating broad-brush EAPs Dr. Santa-Barbara has an interest in applying social marketing techniques to mental health and lifestyle issues.

Martin Shain, M.A., is a Senior Scientist and Head of the Occupational Programs Research Section at the Addiction Research Foundation of Ontario. He has been involved in evaluation and program development in both public and private organizations. He is the first author of a book on EAP and has written numerous articles in the field. Currently, he is engaged in a program of research designed to investigate the usefulness of incorporating health promotion concepts into EAPs.

Charles E. Shirley, MSW, has been the director of Industrial Programs for the Alcoholism Council of Greater New York since 1976, heading a team of industrial consultants whoses efforts have resulted in the installation of over

50 EAPs in New York City. He is an adjunct professor at the Fordham Graduate School of Social Service, teaching courses on occupational social work. With his wife, Kay, he founded and now directs FACT, an agency specializing for over ten years in the treatment of families of alcoholics in the New York City area.

Sherri Resin Torjman, MSW, obtained a Masters in Social Work from McGill University in 1976. She worked for several years as a community mental health worker for the Canadian Mental Health Association. She has written a Training Program for EAP Referral Agents for Health and Welfare Canada. This course is being used throughout Canada as the major training program in the EAP field. She has had numerous speaking engagements on the subject of "Mental Health in the Workplace" and has published material in this area. Ms. Torjman is presently on contract to Health and Welfare Canada developing a training program on the prevention of drug-related problems.

Madeleine L. Tramm, Ph.D., is the Director of the Amalgamated Health Assistance Program, Amalgamated Life Insurance Company, in an innovative effort to systematically provide EAP services to all group policyholders of a medium-sized insurance company. Dr. Tramm has worked in the field of alcoholism since 1977 when she became involved in developing educational programs for women afflicted by the disease, and created a nation-wide occupational program for the 400,000 member Textile Workers Union. Dr. Tramm received her Ph.D. in Anthropology with distinction from Columbia University.

Sandra Turner, MSW, entered the realm of employee assistance programming from the field of alcoholism treatment in 1977. She has worked various functions in employee assistance programming: marketing, initiating, administering programs in government and the private sector, as well as providing assessment, referral, counseling, and training services for those programs. Sandra is active within ALMACA and NASW to promote the expansion and enhancement of occupational programs.

Michele Vinet, MSW, completed her Master's Degree in Social Work at Boston University in 1980. She has worked on research in occupational social work with the Washington State chapter of the National Association of Social Workers (NASW). Her doctoral studies concentrate on the needs of workers and their families.

James T. Wrich, is a noted consultant, lecturer, and author in the EAP field. He has helped develop over fifty programs, including the nationally recognized system at United Airlines, of which he is the director. He taught a course in EAP Development at the University of Minnesota, and is the author of several publications, including *The Employee Assistance Program,* which is regarded as one of the standard texts of the industry.

David A. Wright, MSW, has directed the Employee Assistance Division of

Family Service Association of Toronto since its inception in 1978. These programs currently cover a population of 100,000 employees and dependents from twelve Toronto firms. Mr. Wright holds an MSW and has specialized in project planning and development in both the family services and child welfare fields.